Living is Forever

Living is Forever

A NOVEL BY
J. Edwin Carter

HR HAMPTON ROADS
PUBLISHING COMPANY, INC.

PRINTING HISTORY
Hardcover edition, 1990.
Trade paper edition, 1992.

Hampton Roads Publishing Company, Inc.
891 Norfolk Square
Norfolk, VA 23502
Or call: (804)459-2453
  (FAX: (804)455-8907

If you are unable to order this book from your local bookseller, you may order directly from the publisher. Call 1-800-766-8009, toll-free.

ISBN 1-878901-40-0

10 9 8 7 6 5 4 3 2

Cover rendering of "The Seven Symbols" by Anna Szok

Printed in the United States of America

Prologue:

I didn't want to write this book

This prologue is a factual statement of the events and experiences which mandated the writing of this book. The book deals, for the most part, with events that lie in the future. As man perceives time and space, events cannot be factual until they occur in physical form and are observable by man. Therefore, by definition, the story of *Living Is Forever* is fiction.

* * *

Saturday, June 23, 1984, was a lovely day, a good day for a swim we thought, and while Meredith, my spouse, prepared a light lunch, I went down to see that the pool was in proper shape. I had finished my chores, including backwashing the filter, and had just restarted the circulating pump when it happened. I don't know why I fell. I remember straightening up and moving back half a step in the small equipment room; then I seemed to rise up in the air and fall, rump first, onto the concrete floor. It was more a feeling of being dropped than of falling backward, and I hit the only open area of concrete in that part of the building. This caused a clean break in the bone between the right hip ball joint and the leg bone. There was a large bruise on my right rear bumper, but there was no evidence of striking any of the equipment in the crowded space, and there were no cuts or scratches to suggest that I used my hands or arms in an effort to break the fall.

In the emergency room at the hospital the surgeon showed me the X-ray and said, "At your age, we do not depend on the bones knitting. We have much better luck if we install an artificial metal part. Since the socket is not damaged, we only need to put in the ball portion of the joint plus the necessary configuration to fasten it to the leg bone. With this procedure the odds are about twenty to one you will be back on your feet before the summer is over."

"Sounds good to me," I said. "Let's get on with it."

"There is a problem," he replied. "We know what is wrong, and we know how to fix it, but we don't have the parts. The supplier does not work on weekends, but I will call him Monday and give him the exact dimensions. He will grind the part to size and ship it by air. I suggest we assume it will arrive on Tuesday, and that we schedule the operation for Wednesday."

While waiting for the spare part to arrive, I had time to think, but for all my thinking I could not understand what made me fall. I told those who asked that I must have tripped over my own shoelaces, but I knew that was not the cause. Then one night I relived the accident in a dream.

The dream was clear, crisp, and to the point. I was in the dimly lit equipment room. I was straightening up after having restarted the circulating pump. A hand and wrist appeared out of the shadow and moved toward me, the index finger extended. The finger touched me in the center of my chest, lifted me easily into the air, turned me face up to the ceiling, and slammed me down on that one small uncluttered patch of concrete. The picture faded. I recall nothing more except that the hand and arm were delicate and slender and devoid of hair or blemishes. They could have belonged to a teen-age girl or a ten-to-fourteen-year-old boy.

Now I had an answer to why I fell, but it was hard to believe, and I dared not tell it for fear the men in the white coats would come and carry me away.

A few nights later I had another dream. It was sharp, well organized, and in sparkling color. This time my wife, our son Joe, and I were driving through the countryside. It was a sunny spring day. The road ahead was not familiar to us and when we came to a fork, we could not decide whether to take the right branch or the left branch. The only building in sight was a gift shop. It appeared to be open, and Meredith suggested we stop, see what they had for sale, and ask about the two roads.

A man and a woman were busy getting the shop ready for the tourist season. He explained they were not really open yet, but since we were there, it was OK to look around. I saw a cup I thought unusual, but when I tried to put my finger in the handle to lift it up, the finger passed right through it and the cup did not move. The woman hurried over and asked if I needed help. I said I would like to buy the cup but was unable to pick it up. "I understand the problem," she said. "I will wrap it for you."

I do not know who paid for the cup, but the woman handed me the change which promptly slipped through my fingers or passed through the palm of my hand and fell on the counter. This caused me some alarm, and the man rushed over to say they were really not open for business yet and we shouldn't be there. "Please go," he said.

After leaving the hospital, I told my wife about the two dreams. We both felt they were related and contained some sort of message, but we had no idea what the message might be. The immediate priority was to get back on my feet, and the dreams were pushed into the background.

I made good progress and before long was able to exchange my crutches for a cane. Soon I was able to walk without the cane. I also began to wake up at night or in the morning with a strange feeling that I should write something. This made no sense to me, so I ignored it. Then I had a relapse that sent me back to my cane and almost to the crutches. I assumed I must have done something wrong and returned to my exercises with renewed dedication, and in about three weeks I regained the ability to walk without the cane. The odd feeling that I should be writing something was back again (stronger this time), and I tried to get a clue to what I should write and why, but there were no clues, so again I pushed the feelings aside. Then I had another relapse. This one did put me back on crutches. It also sent me back to the doctor.

His examination, complete with new X-rays, failed to show any reason for my problem. He did note, however, that my left leg was shorter than my right (a condition existing all my life) and recommended that I wear a lift on my left shoe to better distribute my weight. He thought this might help. Perhaps the lift did help, but it did not solve the problem of the relapses. Neither did the strange urges go away.

It was Meredith's suggestion that we call Alex Tanous in Portland, Maine. Alex is well known as a talented psychic, and he might have a useful interpretation of the dreams and the unexplained feeling that I should be writing something.

We had met Alex some ten years earlier in New York City, and in the course of that first evening's discussion, I told him my mother had several dreams during her life that she identified as visions. All contained accurate information and most foretold an imminent death of a relative. I related the one that had the most dramatic impact on our family.

In this vision my mother was told she would lose one of her three children, and was asked to decide which one it would be. "Not Edwin," she had responded, "He is my baby, and not Louise, she is my only girl. Not Charles, he is my first born. No! I can't choose; I can't let any of them go." She woke up crying. Two weeks later my thirteen-year-old brother Charles was dead, a victim of the terrible flu epidemic of 1918-19. I was three years old at the time.

Obviously Alex has an excellent memory. He asked some detailed questions. "Exactly where did the finger touch you?" I showed him. "It was directly over your heart," he noted. "It was an act of love."

Then without hesitation Alex continued, "It was your brother who pushed you. For whatever reason, he was chosen to die instead of you or your sister, thus cutting him off from all the exciting things he planned to do with his life on earth. You may feel you have accomplished your goals, but he wants you to make the most of your remaining years. Clearly there is something specific he wants you to do. Other means of getting the message to you have failed, so this shock treatment was used to get your attention."

Alex said the second dream indicated I was at a point of major decision. I was at a fork in the road. There was no way I could go back, so only two options remained, and my decision would determine the course of the rest of my life.

"What should I do?" I asked. The question was heartfelt, because I remembered that in the dream I was unable to pick up or hold solid objects. I had a suspicion that one of those forks in the road was a dead end.

"Listen to those urges you have," Alex replied, "and the next time you feel you should do something, try it whether it makes sense to you or not. If it is to write something, sit down at your desk with paper and pen and see what happens."

I did as Alex suggested, and this book is what happened. By some means I was supplied with key thoughts and concepts. At other times it was more like a mental picture, but it was up to me to weave it all into some kind of story. Often I would be half through a chapter before I knew its purpose, and my greatest frustration was not knowing until I started the last chapter how and when the story would end. This resulted in a very unusual sequence of chapters. It was so unusual that, once the full story was known, my human advisers persuaded me to rewrite the whole thing in a more commonly accepted form.

When I wrote the first version of this Prologue, four years had passed since I fell (was pushed) and broke my hip. During that time I came to feel I was working under the direction of a kind of Editorial Board and that my brother Charles was involved in some capacity. They would toss me a bone to gnaw on and then review the results. If they didn't like it, I just had to keep trying until they did. How did I know something was rejected? I would immediately run into a stone wall in my efforts to continue with the story. If I refused to continue trying, nothing else would work for me. If I continued with this attitude, my hip would collapse, and I'd be hobbling about on a cane again.

At least half a dozen times I deliberately tested the resolve of my Editorial Board, and my wife is my witness that they never wavered. Finally it became clear that if I wanted to play golf now and then, or enjoy any other activity, I had to adhere to a schedule which equated to an average of about 20 hours a week of work on the book. "Hallucinations," you say. "A victim of your own imagination," you say. Perhaps so, but that does not lessen the pain or frustration of the relapses that occurred when I failed to report for work or the relief experienced when I returned to my task. After twenty or thirty of these cycles, even the most stubborn person learns which is the most attractive option.

Now, after still another revision, it is finished, this time with professional advice and assistance from the publisher. Throughout all of the reorganization and rewriting, however, the Editorial Board has never allowed changes in those passages deemed to represent the real essence of the book. From my own experience I came to know which subjects were in the "no change" category. During the final phases of preparing the book for publication there were many debates and discussions about other portions of the manuscript, but little or none about those subjects so dear to the hearts of the "guys upstairs". This has amazed me, as has the sequence of unlikely events leading up to an unusual contract with the publisher. It causes me to suspect that other persons involved in this project were pushed or nudged or otherwise persuaded to play their respective roles. This is only speculation, of course. I only know what happened to me.

By the time the publication date rolls around, some six years will have passed since I took pen in hand and sat down to see what would happen. There is much I have come to understand in the process, and I trust there is at least one person somewhere who will read the book, will understand it, and be glad that it was written.

I cannot say with certainty who wrote the book, but I feel more like some kind of surrogate than I do an author. Perhaps the real authors should be listed as Charles Carter and The Editorial Board. To date, however, I have been unable to determine the legal status of such an arrangement, and the "guys upstairs" do not offer advice on what they consider to be trivial details.

One thing I do know. I would never have arrived at this point without a lot of help. In addition to professional advice, there was great moral support from family and friends. "Go for it," was their attitude. Beyond support there was my wife's incredible patience with me and with the disruptions to her life. There was pressure on her during those six years, she can tell you, pressure to support and assist but to never offer advice.

Then there was that special man behind the scenes, Dr. Karlis Osis, Emeritus Chester F. Carlson Research Fellow with the American Association for Psychical Research. It was Karlis who introduced us to Alex Tanous, the Alex who advised me to sit quietly with pen in hand and wait to see what would happen. It was Karlis, in his quiet way, who **insisted** that I complete the book. It was Karlis who repeatedly reminded me that the book **must** be published and who introduced me to Eleanor Friede of Eleanor Friede Books, Inc., the Eleanor who sent the manuscript to exactly the right publisher at exactly the right time. What a remarkable series of coincidences. Or were they? When you have finished the book, you decide.

Foreword

by Dr. Karlis Osis,
Emeritus Chester F. Carlson Research Fellow,
American Society for Psychical Research

This novel brings to life basic truths of enormous significance. While the setting is in the future, there is full awareness of the cutting edge of our developments. The age-old roots of our Western civilization and the values and wisdom that made it strong, human and creative unfold vividly in unforgettable characters placed in extraordinary situations. As they struggle through shattering catastrophes and rebuild the new earth, we experience the deeper essentials, the eternal verities almost lost in the hustle and bustle of modern life — the very core which makes us fully human and fulfilled.

This does not leave us with rosy romanticism. Equally strong are portraits of the destructive negative forces in individuals and societies — as ruthlessly destructive as the worst natural catastrophes ever known. Unlike Hollywood's good guys and bad guys, the portrayal of these qualities is profound.

The very seeing eyes of the author discern the realities behind the fashionable, be it "new age" or "return to family values," ruthless individualism or utopian socialism, religious doctrines or anti-religious stances. Freedom and pluralism are highly respected, but not lost in extremes of individualism. A deeper order of things emerges like the "forgotten truth" of the famous philosopher Houston Smith. Behind the ever-flowing trivia of political rhetoric and the theoretical and philosophical squabbles of our academe, something stable emerges, which stays put. It is here called cosmic laws of action and reaction, which, in the long run, determine why some individuals, like some families and some cultures, flourish while others descend and decay.

I heard one writer say that a good novel or play tells what life is *all* about. Indeed, that is true, except that "all" is often slighted, leaving out the healthy, the altruistic, the spiritual parts of it, which expand our lives toward the mysterious depth of the inexpressible. This novel tackles the inexpressible, and in my judgment does it well. The forgotten truth comes alive in flesh and bones, and in modern clothing, too. The very edges of scientific findings and imagination are breathing life there. We can expand our awareness and grow with it.

The backdrop of the novel is a catastrophe which shakes not only the earth but our institutions as well. All our life-supports are interwoven in them. This novel wakes us up to the immense consequences that must follow such a catastrophe if we are unprepared, as now. It is clearly portrayed what a difference preparedness would make, if it is efficient and wise.

The prologue tells us how the author, who was not a writer but a very successful businessman, was compelled to write the book in unplanned, spontaneously emerging spurts of insight, like revelations coming red-hot as if from another source. I fully accept that it came that way, with the author never knowing how the next chapter would be or how it all would end. With some frustration and discomfort, the author seems to accept the explanation of a psychic insight by Alex Tanous.

For many years before his recent illness and death, I conducted experiments and case studies with Alex. He contributed the best results in laboratory experiments and also excelled in field work — an exceptionally talented man. I can accept the author's statement to me that but for Alex's insight and common-sense advice, this novel might never have been started, much less finished. For this he deserves full credit.

Nonetheless, my research in parapsychology and creativity suggests another explanation, for which the Greeks created the symbol of the Muses. Artistic creations as well as scientific ones sometimes do emerge from a highly gifted unconscious as spontaneously as a volcanic eruption. Creations of Friedrich Nietzsche, Johannes Brahms and Aldous Huxley, to name a few, at times came that way, as did Kekule's basic insight in organic chemistry — the structure of the benzene ring. This is the interpretation I personally prefer, but I would not rule out others.

Most remarkable to me is the extreme force the Muse had to use to liberate the imprisoned splendor of the born writer — even resorting to breaking bones. And we have here the strong will of the highly intelligent man who was able to lead an international business empire through difficult times, but who in his youth wanted to be a writer.

Thanks to the Muse for this very uplifting book, so needed in our time!

CONTENTS

I. Dissension

1. The Grand Lady
Wednesday, October 17, Z 96

The Grand Lady sat in her wheelchair in a patch of October sunshine and did not hear the little gravity car land in the clearing beside her house.

She was enjoying her view of the valley and its surrounding hills. In the Year Zero, when the ground shook like a wet dog, great landslides had roared down the mountains, blocking streams and creating many new lakes such as the one in view, that covered most of what had been the valley floor. But the forces that had destroyed so much of the Old Earth had struck these peaceful hills and valleys only a glancing blow. Except for the lake, the view from her hillside was not much changed from days long gone. The New Earth was largely healed.

This year, as every year, the hills blazed with every shade of yellow and red (birches, maples and oaks), punctuated by the patches of dark green that were stands of evergreens. And all of it was mirrored in the lake below, along with the clear blue of the autumn sky. Spectacular. She loved the valley in the fall.

But then, she loved the valley in the winter too, when the snow fashioned its own kind of fairyland. And in the summer, when its rich green forests and cool streams were bursting with life and activity.

Really, spring was perhaps the most beautiful and exciting season of all. She shut her eyes to better remember the pale greens of the first foliage and the bustle of birds and countless other creatures as they set about providing for each new generation. The plants were busy then, too. She imagined being Maria von Trapp, racing through fields of wild flowers and singing the lovely songs of the Old Earth movie *The Sound of Music*. The Baron von Trapp had built his American home on this same Vermont mountainside, only a short half mile from where she sat in front of her own comfortable cottage.

Except for a few students of the old art forms, only the dwindling number of survivors of Year Zero would even have heard of *The Sound of Music*, but it was one of her earliest and most pleasant memories of the Old Earth. She reflected — as she had done many times before — that if all the peoples of the Old Earth had observed the values of the von Trapps, the terrible events of Year Zero need not have occurred.

She heard footsteps in the dry leaves, and she turned to see a young man approaching from the landing pad.

"A thousand pardons, Grand Councilor-at-large, if I am early and have disturbed your rest," he said politely.

"You are not early, Ralph," she said, "and I was not sleeping, only daydreaming of things long past. At my age, one has so many things to remember."

"You are old in years," Woodbine said, "but if I may be permitted to say so, time has bestowed a grace upon you that can be felt as well as seen."

"A very graceful compliment, Ralph," she said lightly. "I'll wager you do very well with your female colleagues."

He colored slightly. "The compliment was most sincere, my lady. The qualities that enabled you to survive Year Zero and overcome the challenges that followed are still much in evidence."

She smiled at him. "I am aware that the compliment was sincere, and I thank you for it. I was merely teasing you. That is one pleasure of the young not forbidden to the old for reasons of health. Come, sit down and tell me what is on your mind. This is not an official meeting, so we need not bother with formalities."

"Thank you, Grand Lady, I will try to come directly to the point." A pause while he organized his thoughts, and then he took his first step into deep waters.

"You know my feeling about our history. It should be taught to all the people of the New Earth. If current generations are to preserve and improve our new world for those yet to be, they must know the whats, wheres, and whys of their own history. Everyone agrees that before we decide where we are going, we should know where we have been and where we are now."

He frowned, concentrating on saying it right.

"We need a comprehensive written history — accurate and complete, without gaps and deletions and twisting of facts. Written records of the early years are very sparse, and documentation has been weak in all periods. We should be filling in the gaps and checking the facts while we still have people alive who were there when the history was made. Indeed many of those who helped make that history — people such as yourself, Grand Lady — still live. I want to write that history, as you know."

He took a breath. "And to insure that my history is as good as it can be, I want an unrestricted mandate from the World Council."

The Grand Lady had been fond of this young man almost since birth. His grandparents had been friends of hers, and he often reminded her of them.

"I have heard this speech many times," she said, smiling. "Each time the content remains the same, but the arguments become more forceful and complete. You know that you and I are in agreement on the merits of your case. But we agreed that you should have five to ten years of outstanding performance before approaching the World Council with such a sweeping request."

"My biography of Judge Mark Enslow has received favorable notice," he said.

"To be more accurate, it won wide acclaim, and deserved to."

"*General Scott's Wars with the Lowland Pirates* is doing well, also."

She smiled again. "Granted. And it is certainly the best account of that period that has been written."

"Many of my short historical sketches are now appearing in textbooks used in our public schools."

"Yes, yes. All this is to the good. Still, you have been a qualified professional historian for a little less than two years. You are anywhere from three to eight years ahead of schedule."

The Lady stopped and looked closely at the young man. "Six months ago, when we met to discuss material you were preparing for my biography, you didn't have this in mind. What has happened since? You are upset."

Woodbine smiled, a little wanly. "Why should I talk, when you can read my mind?" He rubbed his hands together as if washing them, a nervous mannerism she had all but teased him out of.

"I must admit, I am becoming frightened. A harmless little wart I described to you ten years ago has suddenly begun growing like a cancer."

The Lady smiled. "Remind me of the wart," she said. "Sometimes a frightened mind is clouded and hard to read."

"Ten years ago, I told you how some of my fellow undergraduates insisted on seeing sinister meanings and selfish motives in everything our leaders did. I told you then that I believed that their cynicism was fueled at least in part by the fact that what we knew of Year Zero and the early years of the New Earth was such a jumble of fact and fiction. You know the crazy stories people tell."

"Remind me," the Grand Lady said quietly.

The young man looked uncomfortable. "There were many rumors, often self-contradictory. Some said that some of you — some of the leaders — relied upon powerful psychic abilities. Some said that in desperate moments, you have called for assistance from powers who were not of this world."

"Supernatural powers?"

"That depends on who is talking. Some said supernatural, others said — well, alien. Some claim that many of our essential scientific advances — most notably the gravity car, the core of the government's power — were actually gifts from beings of another planet.

Worst of all — as I imagine you remember — some charged that you and other leaders sold your souls to those alien beings for this one secret."

He held up a hand to forestall a protest the Lady had no intention of making. "It's all nonsense, I know. That should be obvious to anybody with common sense. But even common sense is often turned against the government — there are those who say that these stories, these myths, were fabricated by the government to keep the people in submission."

He paused, but she made no reply. "Such assertions always annoyed me, but they seemed like typical undergraduate student activities, posing no particular threat to anyone. They never seemed to be particularly important."

"I quite concur in that opinion, as you know."

"Yes, but now, my lady, events force me to change my opinion."

"Why?"

"Because of what I think I see." He paused, again, to marshall his arguments.

"Until recently the complaints were a confusing puzzle to me. Although the carping seemed to be more or less what I have heard since college, yet somehow something was different. I would have been hard-pressed to explain why; it was an intuition. So, as a good academic, I set out to search for a meaningful pattern. I began to make notes about the differences in the old and new approaches."

She watched him pull a folded sheet of paper from his shirt pocket. "You've made yourself a crib sheet."

"Of course, my lady," he said, matching her smile. "I was a student long before I became a professor." He consulted his list. "The current handouts accuse the World Council of hiding behind a wall of classified information. They say that if there is any need for so much information to be classified, the people should be told what it is.

"They demand that the government admit that its leaders have no supernatural powers and are not allied with powerful alien forces.

"They say the government should no longer be allowed to hold the people in bondage by claiming we would lose the essential gravity car technology if its secrets are revealed.

"In short, the handouts say, we are being governed by a group of power brokers who would deny the people their rights to a richer life in order to maintain their control."

"This is much what the malcontents have always said."

"Yes, my lady — except for the emphasis on declassification and on the gravity car. But that difference is highly significant."

"Why?"

Woodbine's expression was that of the cat who ate the canary, only to find that it didn't much like the taste.

"My lady, at least eighty percent of the written material was directed at the secrecy surrounding the gravity car. I found this significant, and this led me to check on what was happening at World University and the other three regional universities." He paused, as if reluctant to give his conclusions added vitality by bringing them to the light of day.

"The same handouts and little booklets were appearing everywhere. Oh, there were cosmetic differences to make them seem to be of local origin, but the content was the same. I have a collection of dated handouts I can show you."

She waved the offer aside.

"Moreover, as far as we can pinpoint it, each new argument or tactic appeared first in Region One — New America South — and one to two weeks later at the other universities."

Hedi's face was a mask. "Were you able to identify any of the individuals originating the written material?"

"I made the attempt, of course, but I failed completely. I am sorry. I must tell you, though, that the key sympathizers and supporters of such arguments seemed not to be students but young instructors and administrative people in the educational system.

"I should add one more thing, perhaps the most significant — contributions are never requested, yet there is no shortage of funds to support this campaign. These are the facts, Grand Councilor-at-large. What would you conclude?"

The Grand Lady accepted the challenge without hesitation. "It is a highly organized effort, worldwide, directed from New America South. There is plenty of money, its leaders are skilled in the art of covering their tracks, and it has a very important objective — to force the World Council to declassify all information on the gravity car."

Her right fist, resting on her lap, was clenched. "Now let me ask you, Assistant Professor Ralph Woodbine: What persons or organization could want so badly to see the secret of the gravity car revealed, while wanting equally badly to keep their own identity concealed?"

"Do I dare say it, Grand Lady, when it appears impossible?"

"Do we dare ignore it?"

For a minute or so they sat in silence.

"How would your request to the World Council for an unrestricted mandate to write an honest and complete world history bear on the problem?" she asked.

"The underground group we suspect would consider me as an unsuspecting ally ... a cat's paw extraordinary. We would need only observe the sources of my support. Of course, there must be some help in high places to follow up the leads."

The Grand Councilor-at-large looked thoughtful. "You know that by making your request prematurely, and suggesting you will need classified information, you invite rejection of the thing you want so much."

"I know that," he replied. "But under the circumstances the risk seems justified." She could not doubt his sincerity.

"I have heard you," the Lady said. "I understand what you have said. This is Wednesday. Come back at ten Friday morning, and we will discuss the matter further."

The young man stood up and bowed ever so slightly to show his deference; then he departed in silence.

2. Martha

The sun dropped below the hilltops, adding the reds and golds of the sunset to the canopy of colors displayed by the autumn leaves. The chill in the air spoke of frost by morning. Still the Grand Lady sat, looking over the valley with unseeing eyes, her thoughts many miles and years away.

"You will catch your death of cold," Martha said, using an Old Earth saying. "Here, put this shawl around you, and I will take you back to the house. You should have called me sooner." She started pushing her sister's wheelchair toward the warmth of the cottage.

"Thank you, little sister," the Lady responded with a smile, "I don't know what I would do without you."

"I fancy you would do quite well," Martha said. "The Grand Councilor-at-large is loved by all, and anyone in the world would be honored to take care of her. Of course I only do it because you are my elder sister, and Mother always said the young should be respectful of the old; but if you don't start behaving yourself and calling me when you need to be brought in out of the cold, I may just turn you over to the people."

The Lady smiled absently, but said nothing until the two women had entered the house and Martha had settled her sister in front of the fire that had just been lit in the living room fireplace. Then she spoke, a trifle sadly. "You wouldn't believe all the world loves me if you'd heard what Ralph Woodbine had to say."

"Ralph? He wasn't rude to you, surely? It seemed that the two of you were having quite a conversation."

"No, of course he wasn't rude. He's quite a polite young man. But he told me that we have a serious problem, Martha. I must call the president tonight."

"Now, please don't tell me you are about to get involved in another big project, Hedi! You need to rest for a few months! You are — supposedly — at least semi-retired, you know. You have no obligation to respond to everybody who wants a favor."

"Martha, you know I love you dearly, and I feel very fortunate to have you with me while Sam Wun is gone and I'm confined to this tiresome wheelchair. Nor do I blame you for being exasperated with me. But this is serious."

She proceeded to recount, in precise detail, her discussion with Ralph Woodbine. Martha did not interrupt, and sat silently for several minutes after she had finished. Then she stood up. "I'll fix us a light supper we can eat by the fire, and then we can talk about what must be done," she said. She went off to the kitchen. The Lady knew that Martha wanted time to think.

"I told you he was smart before you talked with him the first time, all those many years ago," Martha said when she re-entered the room with their supper tray. She placed the tray within her sister's easy reach and sat down beside her. "Do you believe he was being honest with you?"

"Quite honest, and deadly serious."

"I don't doubt it," Martha said. "He takes after his parents, and his grandparents. He has all the right genes in all the right places. And if I were nineteen again, I might add that he fills his jeans in all the right places, too. He's a very attractive young man."

"But heredity ...."

"...isn't everything. I know. But I also know, and so do you, and now even the experts admit, that people are not created equal."

"They have..."

"They have an equal right to develop the talents they have, but they don't start equal. Remember Mother on the parable about the talents?"

Hedi did, very well. One advantage to age was that early memories seemed to become clearer, sharper, more alive, each year. Martha proceeded to tell her anyway.

"Mother used to say that Jesus was telling us that we were not all endowed with the same equipment, and that the important thing was to do the best we could with what we had. As I say, young Woodbine has been given a lot of equipment."

"Yes," the Lady said. "And if he continues the way he's started out, he'll establish a track record that will convince everybody in sight. The trouble is, he doesn't have that record yet. He's made an excellent start, but he doesn't yet have it."

"Since when are you so interested in other people's judgments?"

"In this case, I'm *very* interested. I have no choice. The more credible Ralph's credentials, the more credible his conclusions."

Martha smiled wryly. "Would you feel more confident in his conclusions if he had better credentials?" She laughed at her sister's expression. "I know, I know. But that's the point. Hedi Carlton Johnson is convinced. Who's going to second-guess her?"

"Surely you're not serious. People have been second-guessing me for many, many years. As a matter of fact, when it comes to the Second-Guess Hedi club, you were a charter member."

"Founder, I believe. But you know as well as I that nobody in authority is going to take lightly anything you say is a serious challenge. Which means — as you already know — that it lies with you. If you dismiss young Woodbine's concerns, he'll get nowhere pursuing them, and will damage his career, perhaps irreparably. On the other hand, if you go to the president, he'll pay attention."

That was like Martha. She was always a person of action. She made decisions quickly, using good common sense, an active intuition, and a broad command of facts lodged in her excellent memory.

"I did some thinking while I was in the kitchen," Martha said bluntly. "I know you won't want to belabor the president with my convictions on heredity, but still I think you will find it useful to point out to him that Ralph Woodbine comes with some rather impressive credentials. Or should I say connections? After all, the president may be a statesman, but he is also a politician. Hugh Scott was already dead by the time Ralph was born, but the president will remember him."

"I should think so," Hedi said shortly.

"And he'll know Mary Scott, if only as a scholar of great merit in philosophy, history, and languages. She was Dean of History and Languages, first at the Regional University and then at the World Institute for Advanced Studies. Not to mention her work on the technical library."

"She served as interpreter and special advisor to four presidents. He'll remember her. He was at her funeral five years ago."

"So he was. I had forgotten. Mary was never as famous as Ralph's other grandparents."

"Fame isn't everything. She made her contribution."

"Oh, yes, no question about it. But Steven Woodbine is almost as famous as General Scott."

"In time, probably he'll be even more so, I imagine. You can believe Carlos'll know who Dr. Steven Woodbine is — and not just as the retired Director of Medical Research at Retech." Retech was the only privately endowed research laboratory in the region.

"That leaves Maria Woodbine. The politician in the family. The president will remember her, too. She was elected regional governor twice."

"Yes," the Lady said, tight-lipped. "She was serving her first term on the World Council when that accident damaged her spine and caused her to retire."

"And if all those distinguished grandparents weren't enough, Hedi, consider young Ralph's parents. They have received more awards and commendations for the performance of their farms and their accomplishments in applied agricultural research than anyone can keep in mind."

"Lovely people, those. I've always marvelled at how things work out — how the children of such famous parents became farmers."

"Why, Hedi, it's perfectly natural. They represent the moral and ethical values of their parents. In fact, I think their parents' fame was one reason why they devoted themselves to agriculture."

"Another reason was that they knew how desperately the world needed food in the early years," the Lady said simply.

"In any case, it is an impressive heredity," her sister said. Martha stood up and picked up the tray. "I shall leave you in privacy to make your phone call."

"Better push me into my office, Martha, if you don't mind. I'm going to want to use a secure line."

3. The President

Sorry to disturb you, Mr. President."

Carlos Fernandez was always gracious. "A call from the Grand Councilor-at-large is an honor, not a disturbance," he said. She could hear the smile in his voice.

"Surely you needn't always refer to me by title," she said. "You make me feel old."

"My lady, first impressions are most lasting. I can never forget the excitement in my school when you visited. Hedi Johnson, Chief Executive of the District of New England and governor-elect of Region Three! One of the architects of the World Code of Survival. And, not least, the heroine of the battle of the dam.

"Ah, and your message! You urged us to work to strengthen the society that had survived from the Old Earth; to lead it, step by step, back toward the democratic freedom some nations of the Old Earth had once enjoyed. I, being perhaps overly impressionable, resolved to do just that. So you see, your visit shaped my life. Do you wonder if I remain a bit formal in our dealings?"

He laughed. "To me you will always be that exalted personage, and in your presence I often feel very like a schoolboy again."

"I fear, Carlos, that your outrageous flattery, however well intended, merely underlines the disparity in our ages. I do hope I haven't called you away from something important."

"Whether it is important is not for me to say, but I will tell you what I was doing. I told Robert, my personal secretary, that I did not wish to be disturbed, and I retired to my study to engage in some unhurried thinking about.... Well, can you guess what I wanted to think about?"

"The elections."

"Correct, naturally. I know better than to attempt to keep secrets from one of your abilities. Yes, that's precisely what I was thinking about. Here I am, about to begin the fifth year of my term, a time when my biggest concern should be the question of what I will do after my term ends at the end of next year. Instead, I find myself up to my neck in urgent political questions. My supporters tell me that the upcoming district elections may well cost us our majority in the World Council."

The Constitution limited presidents to a maximum of two non-consecutive six-year terms. But district elections — elections to the world government's legislative body — were held every four years.

"Because of the uproar over secrecy?"

"Apparently. I must say, Grand Lady, that I don't understand it. Given our track record, I would have thought we would be secure in the people's affections. But for some reason, the people seem to be losing their trust in their government's intentions."

Hedi thought of Ralph's conclusions. "You don't think this is normal inter-party bickering, then?"

"My lady, I don't. The tenor of the criticism we hear is not dissatisfaction with our performance — it is entirely rooted in distrust."

"Your Presidency offers no reason for distrust, Carlos."

"Thank you, my lady. Neither, in my opinion, does that of my predecessors. As matters stand now, an impartial history should report that my Presidency has been one of solid progress. Nothing spectacular, though."

Carlos had consulted her frequently during his term. He had told her frankly that he would have liked to launch some great project to add some spice to his record and make it worthwhile to stay in the political arena, but every proposal he had examined was either of debatable value or was not timely.

"I trust you are not apologizing for your administration, Carlos. Those who understand appreciate your contribution."

He sighed. "You are very kind. And, indeed, I am not so disappointed with the results of my term. But what I really want is to continue working for the cause closest to my heart — promoting the orderly pursuit of democratic freedom. You realize, with phase one of the World Code of Progress enacted into law, the political stage is now set." Carefully, he added: "Thanks to my predecessor."

"He initiated it, Carlos, but as chairman of the Executive Committee of the World Council, you had something to do with it too. Your support played a key role in getting the proposal adopted. You should be proud of your part in the matter."

"I am, I am. But now I have been thinking about the next steps. I begin to think that the greatest threat to progress is impatience on the part of those who wanted to move faster. I remember my own youth. How impatient I was! I wanted everything for everybody, and right now!"

"Impatience is a prerogative of the young, Carlos."

"To be sure. But one day a professor of political philosophy, observing the impatience and intemperance of my answers in his class, told me something I have always remembered. He said creating freedom was much like creating a child. First, freedom must be conceived as something much to be desired, something worth working for and, if need be, fighting for. And then, once conceived, freedom must progress through a natural growth sequence. Forcing an early birth might well kill the baby."

Hedi could see the president's earnest expression.

"I am worried. In the thought centers of the world, is sound political philosophy being taught? There are too few professors who understand the fundamentals, and too many students taking only the political courses that will teach them how to get elected. Perhaps I could contribute to correcting this situation."

"How?"

"When my term ends, perhaps I could become a college professor, and begin to preach what I have tried to practice."

"In other words, you are daydreaming about giving up the world of politics for that of academia," Hedi said lightly.

Meeting her tone, he said: "Unmasked! Except that I prefer 'planning' to 'daydreaming,' yes." He sobered. "But I am talking too much. You bring bad news."

"Now how can you know that, Carlos? Psychic abilities?"

"Logic. You called on the yellow phone, which is of course a prerogative, to use your word, of your present and former positions. Since I know better than to suspect you of misusing the yellow or red phones, your choice of lines implies that your message involves government business, has a high priority, and might contain classified information. In short, it is unlikely to be good news."

Hedi got down to business. "Carlos, you're right. We have a problem. In fact, I suspect it's the same problem you're already worried about. Only I'm afraid the stakes are higher than you suspect."

"Is it?"

"Yes, only worse. I think you're right — control of the Council may well be at stake. But if my suspicions are right, we're talking not about party politics but about a threat to our very democracy."

"I am listening, I assure you."

"A young man named Ralph Woodbine came to see me this

afternoon. He's a brilliant young man, and I've been a friend of his family for many years."

"I remember Ralph Woodbine quite well," Carlos answered. "He was working on his biography of Mark Enslow while studying at the World University, and since I had known the judge quite well, he came to me twice for information and advice. He did an excellent job, in my opinion. Presently I lack only one chapter of finishing his recently released work on General Scott."

"His grandfather, Carlos."

"So I understand. Very well. Please continue."

The Lady gave him a condensed account of her meeting and her subsequent discussion with Martha.

"You will remember that on a number of occasions we discussed the need for a complete and factually accurate history of the New Earth and the events that preceded Year Zero. And we agreed that even if the World Council could be persuaded to endorse such a project, they would almost certainly insist that many sections be classified and withheld from publication."

"You would like to see that decision reversed?"

"Carlos, perhaps the time has come. We may lose the elections if we don't. And if our suspicions about the sources of the discontent are correct, we will have handed them a chance to seize control of our government. Of our world."

There was a pause. "What do you intend to say to the young man Friday morning, and what do you want from me?"

"I would like to offer him my support and assistance, but I need to know that you agree and would lend a hand here and there. I also want to know if you will join me again in attacking the security problem. While we're at it, I'd like your ideas on who you think is currently stirring the witches brew."

The president hesitated. "Give me an hour to think about it, and I will call you back."

The security officer was very careful. He asked to check the Lady's identity on the video tube and also by voice pattern. He asked her to check the room to be certain doors and windows were closed and locked and then to turn on the special scanner that searched the area for electronic bugs. Only then did he switch the line to the president.

The president's voice seemed wearier than before. He sighed. "With all due respect, my lady, my world was far more peaceful and orderly prior to your call. Now I must rethink everything."

"I'm sorry to have to burden you, Carlos. I wouldn't have, if I had been able to see an alternative."

"I am quite sure of that, and I know it is no less of a burden on you. You mustn't mind an old man's repining against fate."

Hedi smiled at that, as he had intended her to. Not yet 85, he was, according to the current thinking of medical experts, about at the middle of his expected life span, and was enjoying an exceptionally vigorous middle age.

"When I hung up the phone after your call, I called Robert and asked him to bring me the files on the Woodbines from our private index of Who's Who in Region Three. And I looked at the file on General Scott, too. I wanted to see if we had any information on the lives of his children."

"Interesting reading?"

"It didn't take long to piece together the relationships. If Ralph Woodbine has access to the knowledge of his grandparents — added to what you could tell him — he has two-thirds of the history he's seeking, before he begins. And so I must decide what could be done to help or hinder him. And what should be done."

"No easy problem."

"No. I knew I must either encourage you or try to persuade you to forget the whole affair. I could find no middle course that made sense."

"Well, which is it?"

"My lady, you know my style. I don't turn private conversations into political speeches. I am not going to wave the flag. But it seems to me that my duty is clear. I must decide on the basis of what is best in the long run for all of our people. Our people, who have endured so much. I am too young to have lived through the time immediately following Year Zero, but among my early memories are accounts of the final battles with the Lowland Pirates. In my school years I heard many firsthand accounts of the deeds and tragedies of that time. I am very mindful of my responsibility to the living and the dead who sacrificed for us."

"I have always believed in your sincerity, Mr. President."

"Thank you. Unfortunately, sincerity does not automatically guide us toward correct decisions. Life would be much simpler if it did."

"You are about to say that nonetheless we must do our best; which means you have decided. Come, Carlos, what are we to do?"

He chose to answer her indirectly.

"While I was waiting for the documents I had requested, I began reading the last chapter of *General Scott's Wars with the Lowland Pirates*, the chapter titled 'Unanswered Questions.' At first I tried scanning it, but I quickly saw that I would have to read it carefully. When Robert returned with the files, I told him to alert the security officer on duty to the fact that I would want to place a call on the red line to Hedi Johnson at about ten thirty." He paused, a form of verbal underlining. "That was when I told him to make a line check for security before and after the call."

"I understand," the lady said. "You found something."

"Well, I read the chapter on 'Unanswered Questions' and I read through the files on Mary Scott and Lucy Woodbine, and I began to sort out possible courses of action. You do, I am confident, realize the stakes involved. A wrong move could ensure failure, and certain key questions beg for answers. To a frightening extent, we will be blundering about in the dark."

Another pause. "Nonetheless, there is little doubt in my mind. If the Grand Lady is prepared to ride forth once more to do battle, I want to be with her. So I agree that you should promise support to Mr. Woodbine — provided he meets certain strict conditions.

"First, of course, he must understand that if any remnant of the Lowland Pirate organization survived, it must have done so by enabling its members to assume false identities. You must be certain he understands the implications of this."

"Namely the fact that they're likely to respond violently to any activity that threatens to expose them."

"More than that: He must fully realize that our garden grass may contain many snakes, including, for all we know, some of our most apparently reputable and even perhaps our most esteemed citizens. For all we know, this group may include some of those we most trust.

"Therefore, I impose a condition he may not like, but this is an absolute. Under no circumstances must he take any action on his own without first checking with you. You may not sense every pit beneath his feet, but you will do better than he would."

"Carlos, I accept your conditions. Rest assured I will spell them out plainly, along with my whole-hearted agreement."

"Thank you. I trust he will have sense enough to listen carefully."

The president rubbed his eyes. "There are so many things we do not know. I, at least, do not. This young Mr. Woodbine, so well connected. Can that be an accident? Or could he be the one we have hoped for? How much does he already know? Have his grandparents passed along their considerable first-hand knowledge to their children? And if so, how much did those children — this young man's parents — tell him?"

He paused, started to speak, paused again. "It is even possible they might have told him things that did not appear in the published portion of General Scott's personal diary."

"Meaning that you think he has had access to classified information."

She could see him shrug on his end of the line.

"I merely pose it as one of many questions to which we have no answer. The Security Committee of the World Council thought that its copy of that diary — the copy it classified and published excerpts from — was complete. Perhaps it was — but where is the original?"

"I had always assumed that Mary had it."

"So did we all. But when she died, it was not found among her effects."

Hedi thought about that. "It could have been destroyed by natural causes. In those days, there were enough of them, God knows."

"Yes, that's certainly so. But there would be some who would hope it never came to light. Some with strong motivation to see that it didn't."

"Which means that the danger to us from this project could come from either of two directions, or from both."

"Yes. From those who want nothing held back, and those who want certain facts buried."

"I understand, Mr. President. For what it's worth, I think you've made a wise decision."

"I hope so." Again he sighed. "Usually I sleep well and awake refreshed, but I suspect that this will be one of those nights. I'll toss and turn, seemingly for hours, and then I'll get up, put on my robe and slippers, and make my way to my easy chair near the picture window in the living room.

"You know the view from there on a moonlit night, my lady. The sky is clear tonight; the full moon will light the city, and in the distance, beyond the plateau upon which we perch, I will see it reflected on the Atlantic, dark and restless.

"We have created a good city on this new land, my lady, a good world capital. The population is not large, and our public buildings are not massive, but the city is new, and clean, and beautiful, and I have always thought it appropriate that this new island, thrust up from the ocean by the gigantic pressures generated in the turmoil of Year Zero, was chosen as the site of our beautiful capital city."

"Well, that was just common sense. The fact that it is not a volcanic island made it relatively safe, and the fact that none of the regions could lay claim to it made it politically neutral."

"Yes. Most appropriate in every way. And very beautiful at night. Sometimes, too, seemingly very fragile."

"You are a poet, Mr. President. The world community is fortunate to have you in your position. I hope it will have you there again, a few years hence."

"Well, I'll not be burning any bridges, particularly in light of the snakes you've just stirred up. Mixed metaphor. Good night, my lady."

4. Ralph
Friday, October 19, Z 96

Martha was not up when Hedi awoke Friday morning, although it was broad daylight. In Sam's absence, Hedi had to wheel herself into the kitchen to start the coffee brewing. Before much time passed, Martha arrived in the kitchen, following the aroma trail of fresh coffee.

"Why are you doing that?" she asked. "As long as Sam is off in Region Four, making breakfast is my job."

"It's wonderful that he discovered living relatives over there after all this time," Hedi said, letting her take over, "but his absence certainly underlines the fact that his help is the only thing that makes it possible for me to maintain this cottage."

"Great consequences stemming from a simple gesture of kindness," Martha said. "Who would have thought that the lost little boy in that first week after Day Zero would one day wind up running your household?"

After Hedi had helped four-year-old Sam Wun obtain care after Day Zero had left him orphaned, their lives had diverged. A full 30 years had passed, and then one day Sam Wun had showed up at her door, having figured out that the famous Hedi Johnson had to be the lady who had (he was convinced) saved his life. He had wangled a position as her bodyguard, and had remained ever more firmly a part of her household ever since.

"I don't know what I'd do without him — when you're not here, of course." Switching gears, she proceeded to outline her approach for the meeting with Ralph.

"I completely agree with your logic," Martha said, "but you may have trouble avoiding involvement with his personal problems. He will likely have many before he is through. I hope you will not forget that your first priority is to recover from surgery."

"I think that by now I have learned to control my emotional impulses reasonably well," Hedi responded, with a touch of annoyance. When Martha said nothing, Hedi silently conceded that her sister was right. Ralph Woodbine had always been special to her. Was it merely because he was Hugh's grandson?

Hedi waited for her visitor in the study. To emphasize the bus-inesslike nature of the meeting, she sat behind her desk. No notes or papers were in sight — she had the complete agenda for the discussion neatly organized in her head.

Ralph arrived on time. She saw him approach the house from the direction of the landing pad on the south lawn. She heard the door chimes and Martha's cheerful voice inviting him in. She heard him politely decline the offer of a cup of coffee. Moments later Martha ushered him into the study and departed.

"Please sit down," she said, indicating the chair across the desk, "and we will get right down to business. I think it would be best if we took no notes, but there are a number of points that you should engrave firmly in your memory."

"Thank you, Grand Lady," the young man responded as he took his seat. "My future will depend on your advice, so I will listen with great care."

The Grand Councilor-at-large ticked off item one on her mental agenda and leaned forward to emphasize the point she was about to make. Her eyes met his steady gaze, and she realized that to an uncomfortable extent his future *was* in her hands. No wonder that while his ears listened for her words, his eyes sought to fathom her thoughts. To her great consternation her carefully planned words would not come. Instead she heard herself blurt out, "Did you know I once had a son named Ralph?"

There was a long moment while she watched Ralph Woodbine regarding her soberly, trying to understand the meaning of this unexpected question. Then he answered carefully, and she could see that he sensed that this great lady had unintentionally exposed a very raw nerve.

"I have heard the story from my grandfather about your losing a son named Ralph one night and finding another named Peter the next morning. It is a remarkable story from a period in our history when tragic and dramatic events were the order of the day. I must talk with you soon about its treatment in your historical biography."

"We can discuss that problem later. At the moment let me use this personal matter to illustrate a point," she said. She *would* regain control of herself and the conversation! "You come to me as one with proven talent and a potential for genius. You propose a mission for yourself that I know to be difficult and dangerous. It is also important, and it must be undertaken by someone sooner or later. You argue that the time grows late for such an undertaking, and I agree. It is logical, therefore, that I support you."

She found that she was having to struggle to keep her breathing even and calm. "However, my son Ralph died because I accepted conventional logic. You have been like a godson to me, and I don't want to lose another Ralph by failing to question a proposal that sounds logical, but which may have hidden flaws. You understand?"

"Yes, Lady," he said. Clearly, he did not understand at all. Let it go.

"With that understood, let's move on to the conversation I had with the president last night."

"So you really did talk with the World President about me?"

"I talked with him about mutual problems. It is necessary that I know if I can count on his support. I have that assurance provided certain conditions are met, but before we get into the conditions, let me tell you our analysis of the problem.

"The president and I think that the unrest you reported to me on Wednesday may be nothing more than a natural expansion into the adult population of the student discontent you described ten years ago. It could be, also, that charges of deception and needless classification of information are being developed as a means of winning power at the polls for this new political party that is being organized."

She watched him closely, and knew he was aware of it. "The third possibility is that a remnant of the Red Prince's organization of Lowland Pirates still exists — or, more likely, has been succeeded by another organization with the same goals and beliefs.

"Before we show our own hand we need to know all that can be learned about these three possibilities."

"Are these, then, the only possibilities?"

"Of course we may learn there is some other force at work," she conceded. "The point is, we need information. To go blundering about in the dark invites failure."

"Do you believe that the Red Prince or any of his immediate family are still alive?"

"You know as well as I that their deaths have all been well documented —." She paused, and noted that he had the wit to remain silent, waiting for the other shoe, as they used to say. "— except that of the eleven top leaders reported dead, only one body was ever produced as evidence. You also know that the Red Prince had an obsession about the gravity car. He saw it as the scepter with which he could rule the world."

"Does it seem probable to you then, Lady, that the Red Prince still lives?"

"I have suffered too much at his hands to think objectively about him, but your analysis of the verbal attacks being mounted against the government seemed to me to contain that same obsession about the gravity car. What's your opinion?"

The young historian considered the question carefully. "Of one thing I am convinced: we do not know the full story of the Red Prince and his Lowland Pirates. The facts available to me when I wrote *General Scott's Wars with the Lowland Pirates* came primarily from General Scott's records or from government sources in this region. Most of the records kept by the Lowland Pirates were either lost, destroyed, or hidden away. They have never been found.

"Many believe General Scott's diary is incomplete. Three copies are in existence, but no one seems to know the whereabouts of the original, and it is difficult to tell if pages were torn out. I suspect they were removed by someone, and that they reflected what Scott knew or suspected about the Red Prince. My grandmother Mary never speculated on these matters publicly, but she told my mother that at the time of his death her husband believed the Red Prince and many of his key supporters to be in hiding in Region One."

"New America South. Where he'd just been fighting them," Hedi said thoughtfully.

"Of course that was many years ago," Woodbine said, equally thoughtfully. "By now they are likely dead, or they have assumed other identities and begun new lives, losing themselves in the general population. That is a long answer to a short question and I don't suppose it means much to you."

"It means that you think the Red Prince — or the heir to his throne — still lives and aspires to rule the world, but that you aren't about to say so. True?"

"It is true, but only a hunch. I don't know how you read minds like that."

"I was trained by a magician named Sam Theos," she replied. "Don't worry, I won't quote you. Suppose we just agree that, along with the other possibilities, any chance that the Lowland Pirate organization still lives must be thoroughly checked out."

"Agreed," Woodbine said.

Hedi drew herself up straight in her wheelchair, and found herself thinking of Hugh Scott.

"Now for the president's conditions.

"First, he insists he will not launch any kind of operation involving me until I am fully recovered. This could take as long as six months.

"Second, he will begin at once to mobilize intelligence gathering forces available to him, and put them to work tracing the sources and uncovering the purposes of the propaganda being directed against the governments of the New Earth. During this period, I am not to discuss the matter with anyone else except Martha, and you are not to discuss it with anyone else except your parents. We should continue to observe and analyze as best we can, but there could be real danger involved, and we should keep our heads down until the information gathering phase is complete and we have agreed on a plan of action. There must be no premature disclosure regarding our suspicions. Do you agree?"

"I agree, and I am pleased to be able to talk with my parents, but I may not be able to persuade them that personal danger is a real threat."

"It may be a lot easier than you think. Actually the president and I both think your parents might have some useful knowledge. Of course, they may try to discourage you from becoming involved in a potentially dangerous project. As a parent, I would not blame them for that."

"What of my request for a World Council mandate to write an unabridged history of the New Earth? Was that discussed?"

"Yes it was, but you know quite well an unabridged version of our history cannot be published as long as so many key facts remain classified. How we proceed depends on what we learn about the present attacks on the World Government. If we conclude there is a bandit organization at work, we will consider the idea of using your petition to help identify the people behind it. If we conclude there is no such organization, Carlos has promised to join me in another try to get World Council approval for declassifying all government documents. If this effort is successful, it becomes much easier for you to secure your mandate, and we will support your petition."

"I am delighted," Ralph said, "but the historian in me makes me ask one more question. Why is there so much opposition to declassification when all threats of external attack have vanished?"

"Have they?"

He stopped for a second. "That is the general belief."

"So I'm told," she said drily. "Well, for your information, there are two reasons. One is classified, and I cannot reveal it to you. You know the other reason, but have chosen not to state it."

"I'm afraid I don't understand," he said.

She smiled thinly and took a book from the center drawer of her desk. "Then let me read you a passage from your recently published history of our wars with the Lowland Pirates." She turned to a page she had marked. "'After the devastating defeats suffered by the armies of the Red Prince in the Battle of Henniker in Z 29 and in his all-out campaign in Z 31 to drive a wedge along old route I-90 to the Inland Sea,'" she read, "'the rate of desertions from his fighting forces and from the general population under his control increased sharply. Later, when the Red Prince was reported missing and presumed dead, highly placed persons in his organization began to throw themselves on the mercy of the newly organized government of Region Three. Some of these managed to bring considerable wealth with them, and they were allowed to keep it, if they could show it was honestly acquired. If it had been stolen or plundered, however, it was confiscated and used to help bear the cost of caring for the large number of deserters and refugees who were destitute.

"'This policy tended to drive those with great fortunes in ill-gotten gains to forge new identities for and attempt to lose themselves in the population of Region Three or escape to other regions. Some of these were caught, but it is safe to assume that many were not and have become respected and law abiding citizens. If they were able to smuggle in their wealth, they may now be in positions of considerable economic and political influence.'" She looked up at him. "You could have added one more sentence, and I suspect you thought of it," she said.

"Yes," he conceded, "I could have noted that they would likely go to great lengths to avoid exposure. But this seemed self- evident."

"Then it should be equally self-evident that they would regard the opening of all government records to public scrutiny as leading to possible exposure, and would oppose such a move. I am convinced this has been a factor in defeating declassification efforts in the past, and that some would kill in order to escape exposure."

She put the book down. "Now I must ask if you accept the conditions I have outlined."

"I accept the conditions, and from the bottom of my heart, I thank you."

"Then we have a deal. I will call the president this evening."

"And I will call my parents."

5. The Missing Clues
Monday, October 22, Z 96

"Sam," Hedi said, "you know that Martha and I are delighted you've found living relatives in New Asia. But something tells me there's more to your story than relatives."

Sam hesitated. "I would not wish to cause needless alarm."

"Give," Martha demanded. "The suspense is killing me."

They could see him make up his mind. "Very well. Among the relatives I met in Region Four was a cousin who is a senior intelligence officer in the Regional Government. When he learned I was in the personal service of the Grand Councilor-at-large, he expressed concern about the level of protection being provided senior officials. He said he had recommended to the governor that security be tightened in Region Four, and that the World Government be warned that evidence of subversive activity existed."

"What kind of evidence?"

"He said he had lost two good agents, investigating. He seemed to think that was pretty convincing evidence." Sam paused. "He specifically recommended that I be alert in protecting the Grand Lady from harm."

Martha looked thoughtful. "I presume the president has been informed?"

"I have no way of knowing," Sam said.

"May I suggest that you see that the word is passed to him? It's better to be safe than sorry."

"I quite agree, Miss Carlton. I shall do that now." He left.

"Sam may have stumbled onto something," Martha said.

"Maybe," Hedi said restlessly. "All we can do is wait and see. Martha, suppose you wheel me out to the patio. It's time we had a little chat."

They were struck by the early afternoon warmth. "It must be Indian Summer," Martha said.

"Yes. My bones will enjoy soaking up this warm sunshine."

There was a quiet moment while Martha settled herself in a chair and they sat absorbing the day's smells and sounds.

"Well, now you have your Great Wun back."

"Yes, I do. And that means that you, if you run true to form, are ready to be moving on. I know that." Hedi shifted in her wheelchair. "But it seems to me I've been detecting what Mother would have called a bee in your bonnet. Have I not?"

Martha smiled wryly. "I sometimes think life would have been much less complicated if you'd spent less time around Sam Theos. Yes, Madam Mind Reader, I do. I think I've found a way to kill two birds with one stone."

Hedi waited.

"You know how I feel about genealogy and heredity. And you know how long I have unsuccessfully advocated a worldwide project to trace the history of as many families as possible back to their old earth origins."

"I do."

"You know why I think it's important — the New Earth needs every talent and all the abilities it can find among its people. That means we have a real interest in finding latent talents among our schoolchildren as soon as possible, to assure that those talents do not go undeveloped. Tracing family lines offers valuable clues to inherited abilities and tendencies. Of course, the public won't necessarily see the importance of it."

"People are always interested in their own family history," Hedi said. "At least, they are when they're not overwhelmed by the necessities of the moment."

"I think one could argue that time has arrived. We have survived and we have begun to reconstruct our society. The Period of Stability is over: Phase One of the World Code of Progress has been enacted. We have time and leisure now, for projects like this. That's the carrot. The stick is this — we are running out of time to accomplish it. I am as anxious to do this before the survivors of Year Zero die off as Ralph is to get his histories written. Are you with me so far?"

Hedi smiled. "Yes I am — just as I was all the other times I've heard this, these last few years."

"All right. Well, while Ralph is beating the bushes to develop the history of our national heroes, I would like to see everyone's family history completed back as far as possible, at least with respect to births and deaths."

"I thought the Department of Records of the World Government had already accomplished that."

"It has complete data on births and deaths beginning with year Z 33, and some of the regions can go back a little further than that. But no reliable public records cover the early years of the Period of Survival, much less the years before Year Zero. And every year, valuable information is being lost as we senior citizens die out, taking our memories with us."

Hedi nodded. "Still with you."

"All right, now look at this. More than once, Region Three and Region Four have asked me to head a task force to do this kind of work."

"And you've always refused."

"Because they wanted it done on a regional basis, and I have insisted that it cannot be done properly except on a world basis."

"Which didn't happen because the World Government declined to act until all four regions agreed on what they wanted. And they never could come to agreement."

"That's right. Except that over the past few weeks, with the help of a little quiet persuasion from the president, the governors of the four regions have had a meeting of minds. They submitted a joint request to the World Council on the day you had surgery, and the Council approved the request the next day."

"The next day?!"

Martha smiled quietly. "Well, it was so obviously a good idea, it met little resistance."

"No behind-the-scenes pressure applied, I suppose," Hedi said skeptically. "This bears all the earmarks of a certain former pupil of Len Adams."

"Anyway, by the time you were interested in the news again, my project was no longer a news item."

"And the idea of bringing it to my attention slipped your mind until just now, of course."

Martha coughed discreetly. "In any case, after consulting with the Council's Executive Committee, the president called me and asked if I would accept an appointment to head the task force."

"Quite a considerable task force, I should think."

"Yes indeed. I would be Special Deputy Director of The Department of Records of the World Government. The department director is a friend of mine — she proposed that I be appointed until such time as I considered the project complete. Carlos is willing to set it up that way, if I say I will do the job. I haven't yet said I will."

"Why not?"

"I've been waiting to talk to you. It's a ten-year project at least. At my age, I cannot rely on having the good health and energy needed. But Carlos was insistent that I reconsider my answer, and inferred it would be difficult to find anyone else that everyone could agree on. I asked him to give me a couple of weeks to think about it. He agreed on ten days."

Martha stopped, expecting some comment from Hedi, but Hedi was silent.

"You see the tie-in. This might very well uncover some Lowland Pirates who have hidden behind false identities."

"Oh, I see it. And maybe somebody will try to sabotage your program..."

"In which case, we will have flushed them out of cover."

"And you believe in the project anyway."

"Of course. It is a good idea on its own."

"My guess is you have pretty well decided what you should do. Even though you're still a youngster, I'd say you've earned the right to make your own decisions. I'll help any way that I can."

"Thanks, Hedi. I guess I knew you would give me that kind of response. I won't play games with you. I've decided that if you are willing to die with your boots on, Martha is not going to be out of step. Unless you feel it is a mistake, I will call Carlos tomorrow and tell him I'll undertake the organizational phase and all the pilot projects. This will require about three years. Then I will want to turn the project over to someone else."

"Go to it, little sister," Hedi said. "I must say your project and mine may turn out to be related in some interesting ways."

"I would be willing to bet on it, big sister."

They sat in comfortable silence for some time, each pondering how she might best proceed.

"I called the surgeon and made an appointment for Thursday afternoon," Hedi said. "He offers hope I can exchange this ton of plaster for a light walking cast. That means a schedule of exercises, and probably regular visits to the physical therapy center. So, obviously I'll have to work from my base here for some time. But I should have a better idea of what I can do and when I can do it after I see the doctor."

November 10

Ralph Woodbine closed his notebook and removed the tape from his pocket recorder.

"It takes a lot longer to re-hash all this history than it did to live through it," Hedi said.

"I trust you still think it worth doing," he said. "My list of questions continues to grow along with my knowledge of the era."

"Oh, I'm willing to go on as long as you are. In truth, I rather enjoy thinking of the old days. Your questions sometimes bring back things I haven't remembered in 50 years."

"I am glad that you enjoy the sessions," he said, smiling, "because if I have my way, there will be many more."

"That's fine." She watched him neatly stack his materials beside him. "And how are your parents?"

"Well, thanks. I brought a tape of the conversation I had with them last month after my visit to you."

"Oh?"

"Yes, it's very interesting."

He paused to arrange his sentences. "When I left you last, I was, as always, surprised by the speed with which the Grand Councilor at large moved, once she decided action was needed. It is a characteristic of yours that I must feature in your historical biography."

"Skip the flattery and proceed," Hedi said drily.

He smiled, knowing that she knew his sincerity. "When I got back to the university Friday night, I called my parents and asked if it would be convenient for me to come home for the weekend. I spoke to my mother, and actually I gathered it wasn't all that great a weekend to visit — my parents had planned to spend Saturday reviewing the status of their forest products business, and my father had a meeting Sunday afternoon. But Mother must have heard something in my voice — she said I should come."

"Lucy inherited her father's ability to establish priorities quickly," Hedi said. "Hugh Scott could always make the appropriate decision. And she is a mother, of course, with a mother's intuition. So you went."

"I did. I was still using the personal-use gravity car my parents won with their World Council Prize for Excellence."

"Luckily for you."

"I am well aware of it. If I couldn't borrow it, I could never shuttle back and forth between the world capital and Region Three the way I have been doing lately." He returned to his theme in a way that reminded Hedi of Hugh Scott. "I started with the report I gave you ten years ago on college campus unrest, and told my parents what we suspect today. After a while, my mother said, 'I suspect that President Fernandez thinks I may have information passed along by my parents that has not been otherwise divulged. Hedi Johnson probably encouraged him in this view.'

"I said, 'Then I should disabuse her of that idea at once.'

"'Better not,' Mother cautioned. 'To some extent it happens to be true.'

"I told her I wanted a record, and she said she didn't mind, as long as I was careful who I played it to."

He put a tape in the recorder, and he and Hedi sat in the quiet study listening to the voice of Lucy Scott Woodbine.

"When your grandfather Scott was killed in Z 38, I was only fifteen years old. My mother had shielded me from knowledge of the constant danger my father faced. She was very close to him, and together with her good friend Hedi, knew more about what the general was doing and thinking than anyone else.

"As you know, after your grandfather had wiped out the last organized resistance of the Lowland Pirates, he responded to a plea from Region One to help them defeat a similar group which had infested what used to be the upper reaches of the Amazon River and still controlled it after thirty years of fighting. By Z 38, he and his army of volunteers had assisted our friends in destroying this last pocket of criminals on the New Earth.

"But in the midst of the victory parade there, he was shot in the back at long range by an unknown assassin. They flew him back to the base military hospital here by gravity liner, but he died a month later. The last person to see him was his personal intelligence officer, Major Thomas Rogers. Major Rogers was never seen again after leaving the hospital that night, and some believe that my father died at his hands, not from the assassin's bullets. All of this is history that you know quite well. Now let me tell you some things you do not know."

Hedi could feel Ralph's eyes on her as she sat looking at the pocket recorder, listening to his mother's voice.

"Mother did have the original copy of Hugh Scott's much- sought-after diary," Lucy's voice continued, "and there was evidence that several pages had been torn out. Three years after father's death, my mother's home was broken into and ransacked and the diary disappeared. She found a note saying that much grief would befall her grandchild — you — if we reported the diary missing. She heeded that warning, and so have we."

Ralph's voice came into the room from the little machine. "You know that I feel obligated to report all of this to the Grand Lady, who will pass it on to the president."

"That's OK," Paul Woodbine's voice said. "Just as Hedi told you, you are in a potentially dangerous game. We wish you were out of it, but you must do what you believe must be done, and we want to help as much as we can."

"There is more," Lucy said. "You have made use of my mother's diary. You will notice that when father died she discontinued the diary. She said she held in her heart all the memories she wanted to preserve. There may have been other reasons, but that was the only one she would admit."

The words called forth a strong sense of quiet, loyal, dependable Mary Scott, as clear as if she were in the room.

"During the rest of her life," Lucy's voice continued, "she wrote to me every week, but the letters were always confined to family chitchat." There was a slight pause. "In addition, there were the special letters she never mailed. Instead she would wait until she saw Paul in the regional capital. She would hand the letter to him to bring home to me. As she requested, we would read the letter and then place it in the security vault that contains our tax records."

Hedi listened with painful concentration.

"There were perhaps seven or eight letters, and they dealt entirely with things she had come to believe but could not prove. I have not read them in many years and am not prepared to quote from them now."

Ralph snapped off the machine. "That's about all," he said.

Hedi looked to see if he had heard what she had heard.

"Ralph, did you hear what your mother was *not* saying?"

"Why, that those letters probably contain information my grandmother thought might be important."

"She's saying a lot more than that. Come, Ralph, as a historian you were trained to read between the lines of historical documents — treat your mother's statement as such a document."

She watched him work it out, and saw when it came to him.

"Mother knows exactly what's in those letters!"

"Of course. She wouldn't have forgotten her mother's secret legacy to her. And she's afraid to have you see them."

"Which means they must have the evidence we're looking for."

"Not necessarily. In fact, almost certainly not. I can't envision Lucy concealing that sort of evidence. Nor her mother before her."

He looked confused. "What can it be, then?"

"Clues," she said shortly. "Mary must have left her daughter some clues, and Lucy is afraid you're going to follow them up."

"Yes, I suppose so," Ralph said. "And she's right. I am."

"Well, first you'll have to persuade your mother to help you. Has she said she'll show you the letters?"

"Well — sort of. I wasn't able to pin her down on when she intended to get them from the vault."

"No. I'm not surprised. Clearly, your mother isn't anxious to see you start on this 'what-if' game."

6. Cause For Concern
December 10, Z 96

Sam Wun came out to them. "President Fernandez' secretary would like to speak to the Grand Councilor-at-large and, if convenient, to

Martha Carlton," he announced in his most formal manner. "Visual identification was requested and, if agreeable, I will place a Visophone call from your study in ten minutes."

"Please do," Hedi replied. "Will you join me, Martha?"

"How could I refuse?"

Sam bowed and left. Martha said, "He's pretty formal, isn't he? What do you suppose is going on?"

"I think Sam is greatly excited about something. This is his way of covering it up. Come, let's go in and find out."

Sam placed the call, and remained in attendance until the identification procedure was complete.

"President Fernandez is aware that your sister is visiting you," the secretary said. "He would like to know if you could spare Sam Wun for three days. The Chief of Central Security would like to offer him an appointment as a security agent assigned to the Grand Councilor-at-large, and give him some special training and instructions. We will send another agent to be with you while Mr. Wun is away. If this will interfere with your physical recovery in any way, please say so, but if you have other questions, the president asks that you please trust him."

Hedi looked at Martha, who nodded her assent. "We can spare Sam," she said, "and you can tell Carlos he can trust me to have some questions for him at my earliest opportunity."

"He will be pleased at your response," the presidential secretary said, "and I expect he will be prepared for your questions. Now if you could put Sam Wun on this circuit, I will transfer him to the security chief."

Hedi called Sam, and then she and Martha returned to the sun porch. "I suppose this has something to do with the investigation Carlos has launched," she said, "but I've no idea what it could be. When Sam has finished talking with security, perhaps he can give us a clue."

When Sam returned, he no longer tried to conceal his excitement, but there was also an element of alarm in his voice.

"The chief said the president has ordered a general review of security services provided to key world officials, with the view of ensuring the consistency and adequacy of these services. He reminded me that, on the record, I am still on leave of absence from the Armed Forces on special assignment as bodyguard to Hedi Johnson. He wishes to terminate the old arrangement, and instead appoint me as a security officer assigned to insure the safety of the Grand Lady."

"All right. And?"

"He said I would need two full days in the capital to learn certain communication procedures and the general rules of the Department. He is sending a senior agent with a gravity car tomorrow. I will use the gravity car to travel to the capital and return on the third day. The senior agent will remain here while I am gone, and for a few days after I return, to give me additional instruction. I trust this meets with your approval."

"It does," the Lady replied.

December 11

The government gravity car bringing Sam Wun's temporary replacement arrived the next day. Hedi and Martha watched from the window as Sam greeted a man of similar features and build. A moment later he appeared to introduce his replacement. "This is a great and pleasant surprise to me," he said proudly. "This is the cousin I told you about meeting when visiting Region Four. This is Colonel Tu Wun of Region Four Security Forces. He is the senior officer sent to be with you while I am gone."

"It is my honor to meet two such distinguished persons," Tu Wun said with a slight bow, "and I envy my cousin's privilege of serving the Grand Lady all these years."

"We are pleased to have you here, and hope you will be comfortable. But if you are with Region Four security, how do you happen to come to us from the World Government?" Hedi asked.

"I am on temporary assignment with the World President's security unit. The only statement I am authorized to make is that President Fernandez wishes to provide better and more uniform protection for senior officials of the government and requested assistance from the governor of Region Four."

"Meaning that you aren't going to tell us what is going on," Martha said. "OK, I have another question. My hobby is the study of inherited family characteristics. Do the Wuns always come up with such short snappy first names as Sam and Tu, and if so, what do you do for nicknames?"

"Sam has one of the longer Wun names," Tu Wun replied with a straight face. "As for nicknames, my associates in the world capital call me Countdown."

"I should have known better than to ask. Hedi, I think I had better go with these two Wuns, and make certain the colonel's accommodations are adequate. I will also advise him of our daily schedules and routines. Sam is so excited, he has probably forgotten."

December 14

When Sam returned from the world capital three days later, Tu Wun met him on the landing pad. The two talked for more than half an hour before Sam reported to the Grand Lady. When he did enter her study, he was surprisingly calm and unusually serious.

"I have much to tell you, but only one thing is really important," he said. "The president wants you to call him at six tonight. After that perhaps we can talk more freely."

Promptly at six, Hedi asked Sam to place the call. He put it through on the red security line and requested visual identification. Carlos Fernandez appeared on the screen a few moments later, and she stated her recognition. She heard Carlos go through the same procedure; then the picture faded and Carlos was speaking.

"I appreciate your patience and your trust," he said. "I have been visiting with the governor of Region Four, and since my return I have been busy hearing reports from my security chief.

"In brief, these experts are convinced a well-organized effort is being directed from Region One to arouse such a public outcry that the government will be forced to reveal all that it knows about the gravity car. We have not been able to learn exactly who is directing this effort or what cause it is supposed to serve.

"Tu Wun became aware some time ago that his security organization was under surveillance by someone anxious to know if the regional or world governments were suspicious of anything. He now knows they will kill to protect their identity. He and your own Sam Wun are free to tell you the details. Do you have any questions for me regarding our training and redesignation of Sam Wun for your better protection?"

"No further questions on that score, Carlos", she replied, "but I know you must have something more. Agent Tu Wun showed up here with two cases of special equipment, and spent two days searching for 'bugs' and installing devices that would show if the secure channels to the capital were being monitored."

"That is the main reason we sent him there," Carlos replied. "What did he find?"

"He found three devices that have been implanted over the past 50 years."

Hedi had never seen Carlos so tense. "Operative?" he asked.

"Not recently, he says. One malfunctioned, and the batteries ran down on the other two. But, Carlos, who are the spies, and for what purpose? We have had half a century of peace. Do we fear civil war? Tu Wun reminds me that the possibilities include commercial and political spying, as well as subversive activity."

"Yes," Carlos said perfunctorily, "we must remember to consider all possibilities, mustn't we? But I think the time has come to discuss our suspicions and actions and plans with your son, Peter Smith Johnson."

"Why Peter?"

"Because he is in charge of the gravity car program, and he is our prime contact with those who loaned us these marvelous machines.

I need to discuss with him what we should tell them about our current activities and plans."

"I lean toward being fully forthcoming with them. I'd not be surprised to find that they know more about it than we do," Hedi said. "And perhaps it is time we also talked to Grand Councilor Ho Sun about our thinking. He is the fourth person on their active list of contacts, and we would need his help if we try for declassification."

II. Preparation

7. The Beach
April, Year Z-Minus-12

She had been led to this beach by a dream. At least, she hoped this was the beach.

In those days, she was a lovely blonde who attracted male attention without effort. On this particular day, she had acquired a follower, but she paid him no attention. She had no eyes for undergraduates this day. She was walking the sands in hopes of finding an older man, a man she had not yet met, but hoped to recognize.

The temperature was nearing a delightful eighty degrees. Directly in front of her, as she walked, was the flat, wide, white sand flecked with black. To her right she could see the ocean, all glittering jewels of spray and tumbleweeds of foam, reflecting the sky's deep blue out beyond the breakers. To her left, the beach ended in dunes that abruptly climbed 10 or 15 feet and gave way to a row of twisted, gnarly trees, whose tangle of limbs were totally devoid of leaves for two-thirds of their length. Quite a difference from Ohio. And quite a difference from all the other beaches she'd searched these past few months.

She kept alert as she walked, glancing methodically from one side of the beach to the other, looking for *him*.

Suddenly she left the water's edge and went running across the beach. She bounded up the wooden steps onto the dune with the easy vitality of youth and came to a stop directly in front of an elderly gentleman who was sitting on a concrete bench looking out over the beach scene.

"I know you," she said. "I have seen you in my dreams and I have been looking for you for months and months, from Key West to Virginia Beach."

He regarded her soberly, then courteously rose from the bench. "And why would such a pretty girl be looking for an old man like me?"

At first she had been positive. Now her deep blue eyes regarded him uncertainly. "Probably you'll think I'm crazy, but I *do* think you're the one. You look like him."

"Do I?"

"Yes, and you've *got* to be him, or none of it would make any sense."

"Things always make sense when viewed from the proper angle," he said. "Perhaps I can help you do that. It would be my pleasure to try." He sat down again, seemingly making himself comfortable for a long stay. By a gesture of his hand, he invited her to join him, but she remained standing.

She was forthright. "I'm hoping you can tell me what my dreams mean. If you can't, you can't be the right one."

"Well, let us assume that I *am* the right one, Miss —"

She flushed. "I'm sorry, I'm Hedi Carlton, I'm finishing my junior year at the University of Virginia. I'm 19 — 20, soon — and I need advice in the very worst way. I don't even know your name."

"Well, Miss Carlton, perhaps it would be better for you not to know my name just yet. Why don't you call me J? That's not my name, just the letter 'J,' one of my initials."

She looked dubious. "Just 'J'? If you don't mind, I'll feel more comfortable calling you Mr. J."

"'Mr. J' will be fine."

"Do you live here?"

"No," he said thoughtfully. "No, I cannot say that I do."

"You're in one of the motels, then?"

"No," he answered again. "I am here only for the one day." He said it, she thought, almost wistfully, as if referring to a vacation almost too short to be enjoyed. "Now, tell me why you were looking for a stranger."

"It's because of the dreams. You are the only one who can tell me what they mean."

"And how do you know that?"

"The dream said so. Don't you know *any* of this?"

"Sit down, please, be comfortable. Now suppose you start from the beginning, and we shall see if I can help."

Hedi took a deep breath. "The first dream happened the second night after I returned to school last September," she began. "It was not like any dream I had ever had before. Everything was in brilliant color, and I heard the sounds and even smelled the smells." She paused.

"Please go on," he urged.

"It was like I was drifting through space. Everything looked just like the pictures the astronauts take. There was the earth, the most beautiful thing I ever saw with its pure white clouds and blue waters. I was looking at the Pacific Ocean: I could make out the outlines of Japan and Indonesia. To the east there were several dots that must have been the Hawaiian Islands. It was all so beautiful until the explosions began."

"What kind of explosions, my dear?"

"Volcanoes. Entire mountains were blowing up, sending clouds of dust high into the air. Sending red-hot rivers of lava over the surrounding countryside. I could hear the sounds and smell the sulfur fumes. I saw the ocean begin to boil above the Pacific trenches, sending vast clouds of steam and columns of water to join the volcanic dust.

"Then clouds of smoke blotted out the earth, and I couldn't see anything. But I could feel the heat from the steam, and I found myself choking on the dust. Worst of all, I could hear millions of people screaming in fear and pain. Then I woke up crying." She tried to smile, embarrassed at the tears in her eyes. "Pretty crazy, huh?"

"No," he said. He said it gently, but firmly. "You were given a very meaningful message. It would be quite proper to call it a vision. What did you do about it?"

"I didn't know what *to* do. I had the same dream four nights running, until I almost didn't dare to try to go to sleep. Finally my psychology professor asked if I were okay, and I told him about it."

"And was he helpful?"

Hedi made a face. "He said I should remember that dreams were symbolic and rarely, if ever, contained a literal message."

"So you were on your own?"

"Boy, was I!" She smiled, a more natural smile than the one she had produced a moment before. "First I told myself to stop the foolishness before it started interfering with my schoolwork. That didn't do any good. Then I tried praying. My family is Methodist, and I figured if the dream had anything serious to say, God ought to be able to help me figure it out."

"Certainly that seems wise. Did prayer help?"

"Well, to tell the truth, not much. Or at least, not right away. The first night, a Friday, I did get a little sleep, but only a little. Saturday night wasn't any better, but when I did fall asleep, I woke up Sunday morning with a strong compulsion to go to church. Alone."

"That would be unusual for you?"

"Going alone would be. Most Sundays I go to church with two of my friends, but one of them had left the campus for the weekend, and the other decided to sleep late, so I didn't have to invent an excuse.

"I arrived late purposely, so I wouldn't get involved in conversations. I slipped into a rear pew just as the minister began his sermon. He was talking about God putting us here for a purpose. He said we should seek to know that purpose and, with God's help, try to carry it out."

"Do you believe that, Hedi?"

"I guess so. I mean, it takes just as much faith to believe that we *aren't* here for a purpose, doesn't it? And what's the point?"

He nodded, amused.

"Anyway, when the minister began his final prayer, I closed my eyes just for a second, and almost at once his voice faded away. I seemed to be floating above the congregation. Then it was a warm cloudless day, and I was walking beside the ocean. There were hundreds of others around, but suddenly one face came into focus. Your face, I think. Somebody said, 'Find him!'"

"And then?"

"And then I opened my eyes and they were singing the closing hymn and I could see the usher smiling at me as if to say 'Well, you stayed out too late last night, but at least you made it to church.'"

"Your dream doesn't seem to have said where to look to find me. How did you handle that?"

"It wasn't easy," she said frankly. "I had to decide which beaches to explore, and find the time to do it, and then come up with an explanation for my parents. I figured if I tried to tell them the whole story, I'd wind up on a psychiatrist's couch.

"Fortunately I'd traveled a lot with my parents, and we'd been to a lot of beaches. They don't all look alike, you know. I was pretty sure I'd seen you on an Atlantic beach, somewhere between Virginia Beach and Key West.

"I won't go into the traveling I did, or the excuses I invented. But I used up Thanksgiving and Christmas visiting friends I'd gotten to invite me for the holidays, searching out the beaches and coming up empty. I tried the big ones first, and kept on looking. I got pretty discouraged."

"But you didn't quit."

"I was tempted to. But I decided to try it once more during spring break, if I could get approval from my parents to hit the beaches with the gang. I thought this time I'd drive myself around the smaller, quieter beaches on the barrier islands. And in mid-February I had another vision." She closed her eyes and shook her head as if to shake it off.

"A pretty bad one?"

"It started out much like the one before," Hedi said, "except that the earth was obscured by a dark haze: volcanic dust suspended in the upper atmosphere, it seemed to me. Then I could see the outlines of the land and oceans. The whole planet seemed to be suffering violent storms."

"Thunderstorms?"

"All kinds of storms, everywhere: in the air, and underground, and in the depths of the seas."

Her mouth tightened. "It was horrible. I saw islands disappear and continents break into fragments. I saw enormous walls of water rising up from the oceans, destroying whole cities when they struck land. On many low-lying coasts, waves of unbelievable height swept inland for miles, destroying everything in their path.

"I saw the ground split from the Gulf of Mexico north through the Mississippi and Ohio river valleys. It widened into a great canyon that swallowed the rivers and the valleys and everything, including my own home town in Ohio. As I watched, huge cracks spread north from Pittsburgh to Lake Ontario, and then along the St. Lawrence river to its mouth. At the same time, the waters of the Gulf of Mexico came pouring into the great rift and flowing northward, cutting the country in two from the Atlantic to the Gulf."

She paused, but he made no move to interrupt.

"It looked as if the mountain ranges and high plateaus of the earth were sinking and the level of the oceans rising, so that millions of square miles were covered with water. And the sounds were terrible."

Very gently, he asked, "And then?"

"And then gradually the picture faded, and I was looking at an expanse of peaceful ocean. And then a mist began to rise from the water, and I could see a filmy picture of a sandy beach, with people on it. And there was your face again, and I heard the words 'Find him.' Through the mist, I could see that the water covered the land as far as the eye could see. Then I woke up." Meeting his eye squarely, she said, "Now I'm hoping you'll tell me what's going on."

"Very well," he said. "Your persistence and receptiveness have earned you a straight answer."

"So you *are* the one."

"I am the one."

"And you knew I was looking for you?"

"I did."

"Why didn't you signal to me or something? I might have missed you."

"It doesn't work that way. I knew you were looking for me. What I did *not* know was whether you would persevere until you found me. If you would not, it was not my role to actively help you. But you did persevere, and I congratulate you on that. I congratulate you, also, on your ability to receive these unusual communications. Now I understand why you were chosen."

"I don't know what you are talking about," she said, frowning a little. "You make it sound like I don't have any say in this thing, whatever it is."

"I'm sorry to have given that impression. The truth is that your decision will control, and none of us can overrule you."

The old man seemed to recede into a world of his own, and for the first time Hedi looked at him closely. His build was slight, yet not frail. He gave no impression of weakness. Clearly he was very old, and yet in a sense he seemed ageless. It was as though at some point he had ceased to age in a physical way, yet had continued to acquire experience and wisdom — and for a very long time, indeed.

"Obviously, the dreams convey a message about a catastrophe that may befall the earth. I must say it will most likely come to pass, and in the not too distant future as things are measured here."

"Here?"

"On this planet."

She watched him closely, warily, searching for signs of quiet mockery in the lined face.

"It is still possible that disaster may be averted," he said evenly, as if unaware of her scrutiny, "but the chance of the world escaping a painful reaction becomes less with each passing day."

"I've always heard that that kind of thing is predetermined somehow," she said carefully. "I mean, the things I saw in my dreams were caused by the laws of nature. My parents would say that God can spare us if it's His will, but either way, I can't see that there's much we poor humans can do."

The old man smiled. "In an absolute sense, I suppose the Creator can do whatever He likes. However, as a practical matter, you have the whole thing backwards."

"Backwards how?"

"The event you have been pre-viewing was not ordered or created by God. Humanity has been busy creating it for a very long time."

"Who has? How?"

"I can tell you that every act of violence one person undertakes against another, and every inhumanity one nation invokes against another, increases the likelihood that such an event will materialize. You have glimpsed the one currently most likely. Mind you, that scenario is not the only one possible. There are others, even worse, waiting to happen."

"Well, I hope not," she said absently.

There was something fantastic, something surreal, about actually discussing the material of her dreams. In these past few months, she had often stood among others, seeming to listen to their chatter (and saying enough to seem to participate) while trying to ignore mental films of catastrophes that hadn't happened and maybe never would happen. The presence of her friends had done nothing to diminish the power of the events showing in the theater of her mind. The dreams had seemed no less important, no less true, than when she awoke and lay awake in the darkness, staring at the ceiling.

But it was harder to believe in future catastrophes with the sun's warmth caressing her bare shoulders, and the sun's reflection on the water dazzling her eyes. She couldn't quite believe that the old man was taking the dreams — was taking her — as seriously as he seemed to be. Why should he? Why should anybody?

"In any case," the old man said softly (completing her thought rather than breaking into it) "what does this have to do with you?"

"Well — yes. Now that you mention it, what *does* it have to do with me?"

The old man hesitated. "I do hope you will not suspect me of fencing with you, my dear, if instead of attempting to provide you with a direct answer I ask you to find it."

"But I don't *know* what!"

Kindly, but urgently: "Try. Reach inside and see what you come up with."

She spread her hands in a gesture of helplessness. "I don't know what it is that you want me to do."

"For this moment only, I am asking you to relax your death-grip on logic and thought, and observe what happens when your conscious mind relaxes." He smiled at her to take the sting out of his words. "Quite obviously, you are a very bright, intelligent young lady. You have been blessed with a fine mind, and, as people used to say, you have improved your advantages. But there is more to awareness than consciousness. Perhaps these dreams have been provided you, in part, to help you realize this." Another smile. "When that very active mind relaxes, Hedi, what comes knocking on the door to tell you why you are having these dreams?"

She closed her eyes, very aware of the sun — and his gaze — on her face. What did it mean? And how were you supposed to think without thinking?

"Don't try to think," the old man's voice said, as if answering her. "Keep the question in mind, but try to keep your mind blank."

She couldn't imagine how to do that. She decided, as a compromise, to concentrate on the feel of the sun on her skin, and the faint, far-off sound of the surf. A beautiful day. Hard to believe in the reality of disasters on such a beautiful day. But presumably even after disasters, there would be beautiful days again.

Her eyes popped open. "Oh!" Then she hesitated.

"Yes?"

"Well, it's embarrassing. I mean, it sounds so —. But you did tell me to look for whatever popped into my head...."

"No need to apologize, my dear. What was the message?"

"It wasn't a *message*, exactly. I just thought, maybe it's a warning." Her face colored. "Well, obviously it's a warning — what I'm trying to say is, suddenly I got the feeling that maybe it's a warning for *me*." She peered at him intensely. "You understand? It's crazy, but just for the moment I had the feeling that something — or Someone — had a special interest in seeing me survive." She laughed. "You get the idea — Hedi Carlton, the indispensable. Pretty dumb, huh?"

He continued to watch her, calmly, not joining in her laugh. "Is it?"

"Well, sure. I mean, who am I that anybody should care whether I survive or not? There's an awful lot of more important people in the world."

"Are there? How can you know that?"

She smiled at him. "Oh, come on! That's very nice of you, but...."

"My dear, I'm not being particularly nice at all. I merely state facts. You are a most important individual, far more than you can imagine. More, perhaps, than you *dare* imagine."

Incredulously: "Me?"

Firmly: "You."

"Bu-, I mean -, I'm confused," she said. "This is very flattering, but I can't imagine why anybody would think so."

"We have our reasons. Good reasons."

She echoed him. "'We?'! Who are you? CIA?" She said it with another smile, but she could feel her pulse accelerate.

He met her smile. "Not CIA," he said. "Not FBI, either. Nor do the names matter, particularly. The only thing that matters, at the moment, is persuading one Hedi Carlton that she is a most important individual indeed."

She shook her head helplessly. "I can't believe any of this," she said. "The dreams were bad enough, but this is worse, almost. I mean, you expect that sometimes you'll have crazy dreams, but I never expected to be having this kind of conversation right on a public beach. I keep thinking you're talking to the wrong person. You really want someone else."

"You, my dear. Not someone else."

"But *why*? Why *me*? There's nothing all that special about me!"

"To the contrary, my dear, there is much that is special about you." He looked away from her, staring out at the ocean, and then, precisely as though he were reading a file, he began to recite the facts of Hedi's life.

"Hedi Carlton. Eldest child of Glen and Nora Carlton of Marlee, Ohio. One sibling, Martha, three years younger." He met her eye. "To understand someone's character, always look at their family." He went back to gazing at the sea.

"There would have been more siblings for Hedi, but after two miscarriages in the interim between live births, Nora Carlton was advised to limit her family."

Hedi stared at him. He ignored her stare.

"A happy family, not wealthy, but by no means poor, and enjoying the respect of the community."

He smiled at her. "The parents were compatible, even though the mother had a college education and the father did not. The daughters were healthy and intelligent — not to mention extremely attractive. In fact, Hedi grew up to be a beautiful blonde and Martha was stunningly dark-haired, after her father."

"Flattery," Hedi said — but she smiled.

"Not flattery at all," he replied. "Simple truth."

He looked out again at the water. "They experienced problems and sorrows, of course, but no major tragedies. Nothing, in short, destroyed the pattern of the wholesome down-to-earth life the parents had created. And so Hedi and Martha grew up in this benign atmosphere." He glanced at her fondly. "Conducive to trust," he said.

"You've been checking into my background," she said in disbelief. "Why have you been doing that?"

He held up a hand. "One thing at a time, my dear. I am attempting to demonstrate that we have solid grounding for our belief in you. And I remind you, you found me.

"Your parents, for instance. We know they are both from solid Ohio stock. Your mother grew up on a farm, in fact, if we are not mistaken."

"Grandpa Cook's," she said automatically.

"And we know that your father is a schoolteacher's son who grew up in a pleasant town on the banks of the mighty Ohio River. We know that after high school, he worked for three years on the river boats that pushed the heavily laden barges between Pittsburgh and New Orleans. We know that he made good pay, saved all that he could, and, with the help of his family and a friendly banker, was able to buy the business of a local merchant when the man decided to sell out and retire.

"A good man, Glen Carlton. A happy man, too. From the start he was a successful merchant, well-liked and trusted by his neighbors and customers. And after he married the pretty farmer's daughter he had known since high school, he was even happier. He would have liked to have had a son, but Glen loved his daughters and his wife and considered himself the most fortunate man on earth. Still does."

Again he smiled fondly at her. "The whole family has been favored by fortune, it seems to me. Have you ever thought how very fortunate you have been in your family, Hedi? I may call you Hedi?"

She smiled wryly. "Sure. It sounds like you know me well enough."

"I made it my business to know you," he said simply.

"Why?"

"Because of all the good that you might do. Could there be a better reason?"

"This is all so confusing."

He smiled. "Confusing? Forgive me for contradicting you again,

Hedi, but I know you find this frustrating, and a bit threatening, perhaps, but not confusing, I think.

"I was saying, you have been quite fortunate. Your parents were careful not to spoil either of you — that is why you always had chores to do around the house, and why if you wished to earn extra money, you had to earn it by doing odd jobs at the store."

"Oh, well, the store was kind of fun, especially since Mother was there a lot anyway, helping."

"Yes, but you see, not every child would think that was fun. Not every child is raised to think that way. That upbringing is part of your good fortune."

"To be honest, I never liked it as much as Martha did."

"You turned to other activities when you entered your teens. Martha spent so much of her spare time in the store largely because of her keen interest in people."

Hedi frowned. "I'm interested in people."

"Of course you are, but not in the same way. You are very different people. The very fact that you are so different in many respects is a factor that has made it easier for the two of you to get along so well."

"We're different, that's for sure. I guess you wouldn't have had to do much investigating to find that out, whatever your methods were."

He didn't take the bait. "Your sister is less intellectual than you. Or perhaps I should say she is less interested in the abstract. She prefers the practical to the theoretical."

Hedi frowned again. "You make her sound like a Philistine. She isn't like that."

"No, of course not," he said. Again he seemed amused.

"What's so funny?"

He hesitated, then grinned, a surprisingly boyish grin, Hedi thought. "Forgive me; it was the logic behind your reaction. I said she prefers practice to theory — you took that to be an insult. But the world does need practical people, you know. They do make a real contribution."

"Are you saying I'm not practical?"

"No, no, quite the contrary. But practicality comes in many varieties.

"In school, you and your sister were both good students, but your different temperaments and interests led you down different paths. You were attracted to philosophy and history, and to the application of theory and logic. And so it seemed perfectly practical to you to study the major religions of the world.

"But Martha is more interested in application than theory. She likes to observe people's actions and reactions, and her communication skills are becoming increasingly evident by the day. She pictures herself as someday being sought after by governments and all kinds of other organizations because of this expertise."

His glance was perhaps a bit sardonic. "She makes it clear that for her, career comes before marriage, does she not? And you, on the other hand, want to develop a skill that will enable you to be independent and earn your own living, but have no ambition to be a professional career woman. Correct so far?"

"I don't see how you can know all this, but yes, everything you're saying is absolutely right."

"Excellent. I am happy to hear that we have not been misinformed." He peered at her more closely.

"You are different in other ways, too. I cannot imagine Martha studying parapsychology."

Hedi smiled and shook her head. "No, I can't either. I suppose you know that's why I chose UVA."

"I do — you wanted to be where Dr. Stevenson did his pioneering work in exploring parapsychology and reincarnation. I have no doubt that some of your contemporaries think your interests strange, but it seems your minister does not think so."

"Oh, you know about that, too? I can't believe the things you know about me. I often stay to talk to him after youth meetings at church. I have so many questions."

"I take it that he does not fault you for that, or for your interest in other religions?"

"He says that if Christianity can't stand up to scrutiny and comparison, then I should be seeking something that can. He's said that on several occasions."

"I am sure you have raised deep, often unanswerable questions — and I am equally certain that he has enjoyed discussing them. No doubt he, too, would like to know for sure if the miracles described in religious history actually took place or if they were only symbolic."

He seemed to digress. "Think of the questions, Hedi! The miracles. Were they real? Were they clever magic tricks? Or were they outright fabrications?

"What about the stories of faith healing? Do they relate to what doctors call the patient's 'will to live'? Or are all the stories about faith healing frauds? Did Jesus actually teach his disciples how to perform miracles, and does everyone have the latent ability to learn?

"What is heaven really like? Could a spirit revisit the earth, and if so, could it walk through walls? Could such a spirit be heard or seen by the living? These are important questions, Hedi, particularly to a man of God — if he truly is a man of God."

"I do wonder, sometimes, what he thinks of our discussions."

"I fancy I can tell you. He sees a very attractive young woman, very bright, a little younger than most of her classmates, but obviously mature beyond her years. I do believe he senses for you a special destiny, and in this he is not wrong. I think you would be surprised to know how often he has prayed that something he has said, or will say, will help you meet whatever challenges lie before you."

Hedi laughed uneasily. "Oh, that's too much."

"I assure you, it is the absolute truth. There are challenges beyond your imagining awaiting you — if you agree to accept them."

"You mean I have a choice?"

"Life is choice. You are the only one who can decide what you will do."

"Challenges," she said.

"Important challenges, Hedi. Tasks that perhaps no one else on the face of the earth can accomplish. Tasks, indeed, that may prove to be beyond your strength, though I trust not."

She said nothing, but her eyes did not leave his.

"You have the potential to help millions survive the aftermath of the great dislocation. Even more important, you can help the survivors preserve values that have evolved from the creative efforts of so many good people over thousands of years. You can have great impact in this area."

"But, the responsibility! What if I couldn't do it?"

"It is true, you may fail, even though there are many chances of success. But you are the only one who can decide to try."

"Well, of course I'd want to try," she said, hesitating, "if I can bring myself to really believe what you're saying."

"The only thing I can say is that belief is a form of choice."

"And the choice is mine."

"Precisely."

"But there's so much I don't understand, and so much more I don't know. I wouldn't know what to do first."

"We are here to help you with that. But first you need to think carefully about the commitment you will be making. You will face hard choices, and hard work. You will find yourself giving up many good times that an intelligent and beautiful young woman could be having." His eyes twinkled. "On the other hand, I can promise you it will never be dull, and I feel certain that you can count on your family and friends for the support you will need."

"I don't know," she said. "I'd need to think."

"Of course. Why don't we meet again tomorrow morning?"

"I thought you were staying only the one day."

He smiled broadly. "You pick things up. That's good. Allow me to correct myself. If you wish us to meet again, I will make it my business to be here." He stood up. "Tomorrow, then?"

"Yes, sure," Hedi said quickly, "but where will we meet?"

"This place will do. I will be right here. You can depend on that." With this assurance, he walked away toward the parking lot, and quickly disappeared from her sight.

8. Action and Reaction

Sure enough, when Hedi arrived at their meeting place the next morning, Mr. J was there, sitting on his bench and looking thoughtfully out to sea.

"I've been awake half the night," she said immediately. "I'm bursting with questions."

The old man smiled at her. "So I see," he said. "I can see the question marks sticking out all over you. Fire away." He gazed at her fondly. "And don't be afraid of wounding my feelings. Say what you really think."

That hit close to home, and at the same time made it easier for Hedi to do just that.

"Well, the first thing is that people are always predicting the end of the world. I've studied the major world religions, you know. I read a lot of old books, particularly old novels, and it seems to me that every so often, a sense of upcoming doom starts spreading around, and everybody predicts the end of the world, but it never happens. I guess I worry about getting caught up in that kind of delusion."

"It is true," he said judiciously, "that the end of the world has been often predicted. If we had time for a strictly intellectual discussion, I might argue that those predictions have often come true metaphorically. Take the widespread uneasiness that spread through Europe at the end of the 19th century. Artists, particularly, had a sense that an era was soon to end. You may be familiar with Yeats and his dreams of 'unknown perishing armies,' or Jung's visions of Europe drowned in a sea of blood. Were those visions in error?"

"The world didn't end."

"Metaphorically it did. A new civilization was born — is still being born — descended from Europe, but not Europe."

He shifted gears. "However, as I say, this is but an intellectual discussion. Fascinating, but not the most pressing item on our agenda.

"In answer to your objection, I can only say this. Do not allow yourself to be trapped by the deception that the earth is only physical matter, any more than a great university is made up merely of buildings and grounds. Without students and teachers, that great center of learning is destroyed, even though the buildings still stand. Take away the desire to teach and learn, and you have ended an era of progress — you have reversed thousands of years of constructive evolution. There are many ways in which the earth can come to an end as a valuable element in the Creator's master-plan for the universe.

"I didn't mean to infer that some disaster would make this ball of physical matter disappear from the heavens (although that *could* happen, mind you). And I'll bet that if you go back and look carefully at the predictions of the religious prophets, or at periods when intuitive groups or individuals sensed impending disaster, you will find they were not so much thinking of the physical death of the earth as of a drastic change in their lifestyle, or the likely loss of their own physical lives.

"You want to know if you may believe predictions that the world as we know it will soon come to a violent end. My suggestion is that you judge the probability by the nature of those who believe in it. If you find only the eccentric and the unbalanced, perhaps you may safely disregard the warnings. But if you respect those who believe in the possibility — the probability — of disaster, then you must look at the matter more closely.

"For instance, you might be surprised to know how many organized survival training projects are making specific plans and preparing people to survive different kinds of catastrophes. In the past such groups were small, poorly financed, and looked upon as insane — you would say, a bunch of nuts. Now the large number of people frightened over nuclear war or ecological catastrophe has made survival training respectable and much better financed."

"Larger numbers doesn't necessarily mean more credible," Hedi objected.

He nodded. "Quite true. But these are people who are successful in their own professions and in their own lives, not kooks or misfits. What is needed is for you to judge the individuals yourself. Would you like to do that?"

"That isn't a rhetorical question."

"Not at all. I have a good friend who directs such an effort. His group seeks to prepare the mind and spirit for a major disaster. They operate all year, but a primary activity is a summer camp held in Maine. There you can find instructors of great wisdom who can address all of your questions. Interested?"

She hesitated. "If I could afford it, I suppose. Is it expensive?"

"Those who can afford to are asked to pay their way. Those who cannot are provided a means for earning their keep. I can ensure your admission this summer, if you are interested."

"I might be. I still do not understand how we humans could create the kind of disaster we are talking about."

Mr. J fell silent for a minute. "Perhaps it would help," he said at last, "if you fully understood that in making mankind in His own image, God made us co-creators with Him and gave us great latitude in deciding how to use these creative powers. Thoughts are the tools we use to create. Anything that you fashion in the factory of your mind becomes a real thing and is permanently recorded on the fabric of time for all to see."

"'Mind is the builder,'" Hedi said promptly. "Edgar Cayce."

"Precisely. Now, these are creations of pure energy. Thought forms and spirit images have shape and character, purpose and beauty, and many other characteristics found in physical things. They do not obstruct either vision or movement, however, and so one cannot use them as barriers or touch them or see them in the usual physical way. Earth scientists have learned that energy and matter are the same thing. Thus you or any other physical object can be regarded simply as a lump of frozen energy. The thing to remember is that no matter how they wind up, thoughts are things."

"Well, can these mental creations be materialized as physical things?"

"The answer is yes, and it is possible to do so immediately — as soon as the thought-form is created — but I am afraid a good explanation requires concepts and words not yet known to mankind. The best I can do is attempt a kind of parable. Shall I go on, or am I confusing you further?"

"Please go on," the girl said quietly.

"I know you took lessons in making pottery," he said. "Think back to how you made something — a vase, perhaps. You created it in your mind first. You may have made a drawing of it, but it lived first as a creation of your mind. Then you took the clay and used your hands and some simple tools to transform it to a physical likeness of your thought creation. You froze the image by firing the clay in an oven, and the materialization was completed. You see?

"It is this easy creation of beautiful and pleasurable physical things that makes life on earth such an attraction and such a challenging test of one's character and understanding. On the other side of the veil, you can easily create vases of unsurpassed beauty, but to materialize one of them into a physical object requires a thought form of much greater intensity, and the application of more energy than you as an individual may wish to commit. As a member of a large group with the same objectives, it becomes much easier. Still, because it does take so much energy, you will rarely find it worth doing."

"So things are only created here on earth?"

"Here in matter. It can be done there, as here, if you have the will."

"The faith that moves mountains."

"None other. If enough of us have the same vision, and hold it with sufficient conviction, anything is possible. Thus the mountain can be moved, or destroyed, or replaced."

"How did you know I took a course in pottery and made a simple vase? You tell me things that are true, but how do you know about them? You talk of life after death as though you know it exists. Are you speculating, or do you really know all this?"

"I know. There is life after death — and life before birth, for that matter."

Almost in fear, she asked, "Who are you anyway?"

"I can only tell you that I have had a great deal of experience in the art and science of survival. In fact, I have become a kind of consultant on the subject; that is why I am working on this project."

"In other words, you aren't going to give me a straight answer."

"In other words, the only answers I could give would only mislead. We haven't sufficient time to fill in the background that would enable you to understand my answer. We have more important questions to answer, you and I. More pertinent questions, such as, 'What is this all about?' Shall we return to that?"

"Yes," she said. "But I'm still curious."

"Everything in due time, my dear girl. For now, let's concentrate on why the earth is in such danger. It's a matter of law: specifically, the law of cause and effect — which I prefer to call the laws of action and reaction."

"What laws are those?" Hedi asked. "I remember studying Kepler's three laws of motion — equal and opposite reactions, and all that — but I assume you are talking about something entirely different."

"Not so different as you may think. It had not been my intention to get so deeply into such matters, but I was advised you do have a need to know, so, if you wish to get into deep water, I will give it a try."

"Go ahead," Hedi answered. "My father always said that once the water is over your head it doesn't matter how much deeper it gets."

"Bold man, your father. Very well."

The old man seemed to marshall his forces. "I must ask you to accept two sweeping assertions. You can find supporting evidence and logic if you look for them, but it is not my role to provide proof.

"First, the Creator did not finish the job of creation. Not in a single stroke, and not even yet." He smiled another of his beautiful, playful smiles. "I often imagine He thought, 'What would be the fun in creating something once and for all?' At any rate, only the framework was provided. He seems to expect us to participate."

"We're supposed to put in the finishing touches, you mean?"

"That's how it seems. We work to institute variations and improvements. Some are worthwhile, some aren't. It is an evolutionary process of refining and improving. Some changes lead to improved strength, greater beauty, increased wisdom, or more harmony — these survive and grow. Those having an opposite effect become weaker and wither away."

"That would certainly help explain why there's so much wrong with creation," she said.

"Yes. And *since* that creation is not complete, it follows that the only constant is change, gradual or explosive. This is true of things of the spirit, no less than things of the flesh.

"Earth scientists deduced the principles of physical evolution, with its sophisticated techniques for selecting and adapting life forms to cope with changing physical environment. That was a significant breakthrough."

"A great breakthrough that turned millions of scientists into atheists," Hedi said wryly.

"Ah, that was part of the great tragedy. The mortal combat between scientists and proponents of traditional religious theory was not inevitable. They might have concentrated on seeing what they could learn from one another."

"It certainly *seems* inevitable."

"Only because both sides concurred in the same great mistake. A stupid mistake," he said with great emphasis. It was the first time Hedi had seen him so close to being angry. He seemed to glow with fire. "Why did they choose to assume that the technique selected to create the physical life form we call man has anything at all to do with the Creator's ability, or His decision, to imbue that form with a spirit of eternal life?"

He stopped, aware of the intensity of her gaze. "I get carried away," he said. "Anyway, that is my first sweeping assertion — that creation is not yet finished. The second is that this is an orderly universe in which all components have meaning and purpose."

Hedi smiled. "I don't have any trouble with that one."

"Not as stated, perhaps. But have you thought through the ramifications?"

She smiled again, a little helplessly. "Oh, probably not. I don't seem to have thought anything through very well."

He raised an eyebrow. "Fishing for compliments? I see nothing wrong with your thinking; some of us have been at work longer than you, that is all. New worm, please."

She couldn't help laughing.

"But at this point you should be objecting to the implications of what I told you earlier. I said all of us are free to dash about creating whatever pleases our fancy, and everything is undergoing constant change. Does this not suggest chaos, with all outcomes being a matter of pure chance? Yet at the same time I told you that the systems of evolution, spiritual and physical, inevitably suppress discord and ugliness, building harmony and beauty. Does this not suggest a contradiction?"

"It does," she said slowly. "I hadn't thought about it, but it really does. It's the old question about predestination versus free will. How can we be free agents, if the end is predetermined?"

"Or in other words, how can we be sure the guys in the white hats win? And, if we are sure, how can we be sure that the guys in the white hats aren't just puppets?"

She giggled. "That's about it, but that's a funny way to put it."

"Any ideas on the subject?"

"None whatever," she said placidly. "Your move."

"The answer lies in the laws of action and reaction. They provide needed control, and yet leave us with a remarkable degree of free will. These are universal laws. They are not broken because they cannot be broken. They ensure that evolution works."

"I'm not sure I get it."

"There are no words to explain the perfection of their functioning. I can only try to give you some useful examples. I don't suppose you know anything about electronics? Acoustics?"

She shook her head, smiling. "Sorry."

"Well, it isn't important, but if you did, I might explain the action and reaction in terms of a regenerative electronic circuit or a harmonic sound effect."

"Better stick to simple stuff," she said. "I'm a psychology major, not a science major."

He smiled, mulled his next move.

"The basis of the law is simple, really, but perhaps not so simple to explain. First, let us consider individual actions.

"Whatever you do or think or feel is registered on the fabric of time, and causes a reaction. Constructive thoughts and emotions generate a reaction that is in harmony with them — it strengthens them and increases your energy. Unhealthy thoughts — hatred, anger, greed, fear — are also received by time. Again the reaction generates energy in proportion to the strength of your emotion, but destructive emotions subtract from, rather than add to, your energy resources."

"Virtue is its own reward," Hedi said brightly.

"Well, yes, except that you must understand that nothing and nobody is making judgments about good and bad. Destructive emotions are destructive of your spirit not because someone is punishing you, but because their very nature is opposed to the energy that is your spirit."

"It sounds about the same to me."

"Perhaps I can make it clearer. I emphasize thought and emotion rather than physical deeds and events — spirit is more important than flesh. However, the laws work the same way in the physical realm, and perhaps the distinction is easier to comprehend.

"If you hold your hand on a hot stove you get burned; you feel pain. There is no judgment of good or bad, but a simple reaction to an unhealthy action. Because the reaction is immediate and unpleasant, we learn early in life that it is better for us if we do not place our hands on hot stoves."

"The hot-stove example I understand. But in real life, cases of poetic justice don't seem so widespread. 'There's no justice,' people say."

"They say that because in physical life, unfortunately, few examples are as clear-cut as in analogy. The law is unbreakable, but rarely instantaneous. Many times, the laws of action and reaction work so slowly as to be invisible. And when the inevitable reaction is substantially delayed, it becomes more difficult to relate to the action. Often the time span is greater than one lifetime.

"Also, during our life on earth, our ability to see the inevitable reactions resulting from our every thought and deed is obstructed by the limitations of our five senses and our lack of understanding of space/time.

"Nonetheless, that is the connection, the reconciling element, if you will, between predestination and free will. Your previous actions have inescapable consequences; they determine the circumstances in which you find yourself at any given moment. But your future circumstances depend upon your present actions, which are not determined. It is by controlling your thoughts and actions that you exercise your free will. Does it seem to you that we have wandered far from the subject of how humanity creates catastrophes?"

"It does, a little," she admitted.

"Perhaps we could walk along the beach while I try to tie things together."

They walked in silence for more than a mile along an almost deserted stretch of beach. They rounded the point of the island and came to a place where erosion had laid bare the roots of many trees, toppling many. Dead roots and branches extended from trunks half-buried in the sand, making many places to sit or lean without getting damp or sandy. On one such derelict Hedi and Mr. J stopped to sit.

Without preamble, he began again.

"What I said about individual actions and reactions is true, but we do not live alone. We live in groups, and the heterogeneous actions of a group of people and the resulting reactions can become very complex.

"Think of it as voting. In countries such as yours, voters determine the composition and actions of the government by individually voting for or against a given name or proposition that appears on the ballot. Evolution is determined in somewhat the same way. The evolutionary changes that will affect earth and its inhabitants stem from actions comparable to on-going, non- stop elections.

"Everyone votes, whether they know it or not, and they vote more or less continuously. In fact, the voting on matters of great moment may include many generations and extend over hundreds or even thousands of years before the final reaction is created.

"An individual votes with his thoughts, emotions, physical actions, and spiritual creations. The principle of one man, one vote, has no place here, however, and some votes weigh much more heavily than others. It depends on the strength with which a conviction is held, and the character of a creation or action; that is, how constructive or how destructive it is, how harmonious or how discordant, how ugly or how beautiful. If you wish, imagine a giant supercomputer integrating many billions of these individual actions, weighing each for strength and quality, determining one or more reactions which constitute a correct response. The decision and the attendant reaction may result in either the destruction or the survival of the entire group. In either case, the decision is entirely objective and impersonal.

"The evolution of the immortal 'you' as an individual is entirely a consequence of your own decisions. But in the case of groups, the sun shines and the rains fall on the just and the unjust alike. That is what your religion tells you, and that is the way it works."

Hedi immediately picked up the implication. "In other words, you're saying that personal morality offers no guarantee of safety in catastrophes."

"And is this not in accordance with common sense and experience? This fact lies behind many an apparent injustice."

"I see. I really do. It makes sense."

"Does it? I am delighted. This brings us to the catastrophes themselves."

Hedi grimaced. "I can't wait," she said.

"It is an unpleasant subject," the old man conceded. "Still, it is what we have to work with.

"From time to time, the actions of the human race have caused purges of various magnitudes. Or perhaps a better word might be 'rebirth,' since this is the usual method of effecting a new start when things are going badly. Often such a rebirth on a world scale causes major changes in the physical environment. Some have almost wiped out the planet's human population. In such cases there have been too few left to preserve a highly organized society, and man started over as scattered bands of hunters and fishermen. Each time, mankind then had to struggle back to a more enjoyable and more constructive level of society."

The image filled Hedi with nausea. "How can you talk so casually about people being wiped out like ants in a flooded ant hill?"

"Forgive me," the man responded. "I must sound very callous. But the truth is that while individual life should be treated as a sacred trust, it is also true that earthly death doesn't eradicate anyone."

"Oh, come on! That's entirely too convenient. Hitler kills six million Jews, Stalin kills 20 million kulaks, but it doesn't matter, it's all illusion."

"It certainly does matter. Everything, as I said, breeds its own consequences. But death simply moves a being from one level of consciousness to another. And sometimes the actions of large groups make it necessary to move most of the 'chickens' to another home so the hen house can be cleaned. I apologize for the crude analogy."

Hedi smiled. "I think I finally understand what you are saying," she said. "Perhaps it took something a bit crude to get through to me. But why does the need keep happening?"

"The trouble is that, as a group, humans have not yet learned to deal with their own success. As individuals, humans tend to be very smart, but too few combine intelligence with wisdom. Great potential for constructive change carries with it great potential for destructive change, and in the end man has given the majority vote to destruction. In this current cycle much has been accomplished that is constructive, and we hope to preserve the more positive changes even if a negative vote again brings on a catastrophic reaction. That is why I am here, and that is why I am seeking your aid."

Suddenly they were at the nub of the matter, and Hedi felt her stomach constrict. "I feel like I'm going to be sick," she said.

"Butterflies, my dear. Perfectly natural. Pay no attention to them. They are telling you it is time to leave the heavy philosophy and get down to the nuts and bolts." He stood up. "I think we can start walking back now, and talk as we go."

She stretched her long legs, throwing her shoulders back and her chin up. "Isn't it another gorgeous morning, Mr. J? I can't believe we've had two such lovely days and spent them talking about how it's all going to end."

"I assure you, our discussion may have been theoretical, at times, but it has not been academic. The time is coming, my dear, when your help will be desperately needed."

"You keep saying that. But what can I do in the face of something so gigantic?"

"More than you think."

"Can I help avert it?"

He paused, as if considering. "I'm afraid matters are far too advanced for that."

"Even if I got a group of us together? Praying that the earth be spared?"

Again he hesitated. "No one can say what will turn the course of events, but I must say the odds against success are staggeringly high."

"Why?"

"You must understand the fabric of forces we are enmeshed in. First, of course, are the usual negative effects of hate, anger, greed, and false pride. Then there is man's cruelty to man. Fed by a lust for power, this can cause massive damage — as has been demonstrated many times in the earth's history."

"But this isn't anything new."

"No, but the percentage of violent acts perpetuated in the name of the Creator has become very high. Look at the religious war in Northern Ireland, with clergymen on both sides suggesting that since their cause is good, murder is somehow acceptable."

"Some of them, not all of them."

"No, not all of them. Perhaps not even a majority. Still, it has its effect. And it's the same in poor destroyed Lebanon, Christians, Muslims and Jews all calling on God to strike down their enemies. Believe me, blaming one's own inhumanities on the Creator adds a great deal of weight to these destructive actions."

"But people have always done that! That's not unique to our time."

"No, not at all. But the cumulative effect is great. And there is another factor making for another purge: the misuse of science. In particular, the danger of nuclear war, which could wipe out essentially all life on earth, making it impossible to salvage the truly great advances of this present cycle. The danger of this is so high that many hope a different and less complete purge will occur first."

"But who would start a nuclear war?" Hedi asked. "I don't believe the Russians want one any more than we do."

"No one in his right mind would start such a war; you are correct. Only a madman such as Hitler. But you have had such people before; you have them now, though not in seats of great power, and you will have them again."

They walked, and Hedi thought. "You said 'the truly great advances of the present cycle.' Do you mean the constructive side of our technology?"

"Not at all. I refer to government by consent of the governed.

What you call democracy. It was a tremendous breakthrough in evolutionary history."

Hedi was puzzled. "It was?"

"It was indeed. Only in this cycle has the idea of individual rights and freedoms effectively surfaced. Those freedoms have been repeatedly asserted and then crushed by the rulers of the day. Each time they have returned stronger than before. It has come in a variety of styles and colors and sometimes it has failed. But now people seem to have come to understand that they, themselves, must nurture and protect their liberty. It is working in very different environments, among very different peoples. Believe me, it is a major advance."

"Doesn't the giant cosmic supercomputer give us a lot of positive votes for this development?" Hedi asked.

"Indeed it does. And there are other constructive things, too. More people than ever before are showing real compassion for their fellow man — concern that he have good food, good air, pure water, good medical attention, and good shelter. That concern even extends to allowing people to die with dignity and with as little suffering as possible. Much research is being done to extend both the length and quality of human life.

"Many undertake such work for unselfish reasons, wanting to leave the world in better shape than they found it. I could give many examples of the same sort of unselfish endeavor, and all of them generate votes for the guys in the white hats."

"But not enough."

"Such people are still in a minority, after all. Still, their actions have resulted in a substantial delay in the next purge. We are anxious to preserve these good things in the event of a catastrophe, so that humans have a head start for the next cycle."

Mr. J paused. "Now it is time to ask you to think on these things and tell me what you wish to do."

Before answering, Hedi asked Mr. J to describe again how the survival training camps worked. Then she fell silent, and Mr. J waited patiently.

"Suppose I agreed to try," she said. "How would I go about it? What would I do first?"

"If you were to say yes, all you would have to do is return to school. Within 24 hours, you would receive a note and an application form from my friend, Sam Theos, the director of the survival training group in Maine. You would fill it in, send it, and then concentrate on your school work for the balance of the spring term."

"I'd definitely be accepted?"

He smiled. "Guaranteed."

She pondered. "But suppose none of the things we have been talking about happen? I still have a life to lead. I would like to get something out of that life, and I'd hope to leave this world just a tiny bit better from my having lived in it. And I feel I should develop some skill that will enable me to earn my own living. After all, as you say, I have to be practical."

She smiled shyly. "And then there's the question of finding the right man, getting married, and having a family. I wouldn't want anything to interfere with that. I can't see just forgetting about all that and concentrating on learning how to survive a catastrophe that may never occur. Even if it does, I might be better off dead than living in the kind of world that would follow."

"I would advise you to stick with your objectives. They sound right for you, and they do not rule out the kind of exposure and training I suggested. You might have some difficult choices to make later on, though. How difficult depends upon the attitude of your family," Mr. J said. "Would they support you?"

"I think they would," Hedi replied.

"Then the decision rests with you. Obviously you want your life to count for something. That is why the laws of action and reaction led you to have those dreams, and why you worked so hard to learn what they meant. I can tell you it is possible the world will become a much better place because you lived in it, but it is your choice. Again, I cannot promise you success."

Hedi took a deep breath. "All right," she said. "I'm still not real sure what I'm getting myself into, but I'll do it."

Mr. J's expression was compounded of many elements: elation, satisfaction, affection, concern, relief. "You will have help from many sources, more than I could ever give you."

"And when will I see you again?"

He chewed on his lower lip, evidently knowing she would not like the answer. "I don't know that you will need to see me again."

"Wait a minute," she said with a trace of anger. "That isn't good enough. I'm going to need a lot of help. I'll need reassurance, I'll need advice. You can't just leave me on my own."

"You may be certain that if I am truly needed, I will be nearby."

"That's not much help!"

"More than you think, perhaps. And I promise you this — if you ever need to act out the role you just volunteered for, I will give you a clue as to who I am. When you receive the clue, take it as a sign that the catastrophe for which you have prepared is very close at hand - probably no more than five days away. Certainly less than a week. And please believe me. We will meet again some day, and we can sit by the sea and talk for as long as you like about anything that pleases you."

Her anger had evaporated. "I suppose I have no other choice. I will be frightened, but I will do the best I can. I do hope you are a real person."

"Give me your hand and close your eyes," he answered. Then he squeezed her hand very tightly. "Now tell me, do I feel like a ghost?"

His handclasp was firm and warm. It felt very real. She opened her eyes to tell him so, but he was gone.

9. The Chief
July, Z-Minus-12

Hedi returned to Ohio for the final few days of spring break, and promptly started campaigning.

"*Somebody* should be making plans and training people to survive disasters," she said. "Suppose there's a nuclear war? The war itself would be a tragedy, but think how much more of a tragedy it will be if we lose all the knowledge we've worked to acquire over the past ten thousand years." Mindful of Mr. J's emphasis on thoughts and emotions, she added: "And it's just as important to preserve our highest values. I don't think that's going to happen automatically. Somebody has to think about it ahead of time, and be ready if something happens."

Her mother listened carefully and then said, "It's a tall order, but a noble thought. I'm pleased to see that you are concerned about such things."

Her father was less positive. "It is a good thought," he conceded, "but kind of on the impractical side."

Hedi was happy enough with these responses. She had planted the seed. The day after she returned to school, the mail brought a large business envelope stuffed with application forms for the six-week survival session beginning July 15th.

The note was signed by Samuel Theos, Director of Education, Survival Training Association. The return address was a post office box in Bangor, Maine. An enclosed pamphlet located the camp on a remote lake in west central Maine and contained general information about the activities and training available.

She spent the rest of the day and much of the evening answering the numerous detailed questions in the application form. The next day she crossed her fingers, dropped the application in the mail, and — following Mr. J's advice — threw herself into her school work. For the rest of the year, she sprinkled her letters home with articles on various disasters that might strike the earth: comets or giant meteorites striking, new ice ages, etc. Then she sent information on the camp, asking permission to enroll.

"Your mother and I can't understand how anybody can be taught to survive a nuclear war," her father said humorously, the day after receiving her letter, "but this bee seems to be pretty firmly fixed in your bonnet. If it's bothering you so much, we think maybe it's best that you see what can be learned on the subject. We won't pay for the whole thing, but we'll do this much — we'll put up three dollars for each dollar you earn toward defraying the cost of the camp." She said a silent little prayer of thanksgiving for being blessed with such understanding parents.

"But one more thing, Hedi," he cautioned. "You have good judgment. When you get to this camp, use it. Don't just accept everything anybody says to you. Weigh it. Don't go overboard."

"I won't," she promised.

July found her in Bangor, Maine, watching, along with a dozen other students, as the twin-engine Otter seaplane landed to bring them to Sam Theos' camp.

The Otter had been especially equipped for bush flying. It took off from a small lake near Bangor, Maine, and flew over a hundred miles of uninhabited timberlands before landing on the beautiful lake that served as the survival camp's front yard. The Otter taxied over to the loading dock, and there was the man Mr. J had called Sam — Sam Theos, known to one and all as the Chief.

He looked to be middle-aged, perhaps 45 to 50, built a little bigger than average. His broad forehead, with its thoughtful furrows, spoke of more than intelligence; it spoke of wisdom. His eyes were penetrating, but she noted the smile crinkles in the corners. He radiated kind understanding — but she did not miss the message of the large, square chin, which suggested patient determination.

Immediately, Hedi was warmed by his eyes and his hearty handshake. "Hedi Carlton, glad to see you," he said. "Our mutual friend recommended you highly. I was very glad to receive your application." Then he was turning to the next in line, greeting each as cordially as though they were old friends, apparently in all sincerity.

At five, the new arrivals met in the auditorium for orientation. The Chief was direct and simple.

"You are all adults, and you will be treated as such. The fact that we have separate women's quarters is not to be taken as a sign that we accept responsibility for policing your behavior. That is up to you.

Hedi knew her parents would be pleased at the fact that women's quarters were separate. Any different arrangement might have been hard for her to explain to them.

"I see the camp this way — you are here to work, and we are here to help you do so, even when you tire. You will put in five eight-hour work days, with an additional two hours of recommended reading each evening. On weekends, we will give you a little rest and a chance to make your own recreation. In our experience, informal bull sessions make up a good deal of this, and they are sometimes quite valuable in their own right.

"You may spend weekends as you please, but for your own safety you must remain within the boundaries of the camp. Certainly you will find them spacious enough."

He passed out copies of the first week's schedule.

"You see that the first two weeks are devoted to orientation and a brief look at five kinds of disasters. Each student will then tentatively select one of these categories for in-depth study. The next four weeks provide general instruction in the selected category.

"Those of you who return for either the fall camp or next year's summer camp can then begin specialized training in the chosen field, or can switch to general instruction in another category.

"In the material sent with your application forms, it was noted that this was not a physical training camp. There are thousands of places you can go for physical training, and we can give you a list of some good ones. Our task here is to prepare you mentally and emotionally for the stresses you are likely to face. Above all, we want to provide that which will strengthen your spirit. Those making decisions in the aftermath of the disaster may or may not need muscles of iron, but they will certainly require a wise and resolute spirit."

He paused to let that sink in. "Okay, that's it for tonight. Those of you who are going to work to help defray expenses, please stay on for a few minutes. The rest of you are free until 8 a.m. tomorrow."

The administrative manager produced a list of the types of weekend work available. Hedi chose waiting tables, thinking to learn more about her fellow students in that way. "I'm really here," she said to herself. "I'm really starting survival camp."

"It is typical that those seeking admission to this survival training camp are concerned about some major disaster to the earth and its inhabitants, and want to know what, if anything, can be done about it. I assume this group follows that pattern."

The Chief looked around the room at his new students, and met nods of agreement.

"That's fine. But I hope you are thinking not only of physical survival, but also of saving some of the social, moral, and spiritual values that have evolved over the last several thousand years." Hedi naturally thought of Mr. J.

"In my opinion, the degree to which advances in philosophy, science, and religion are preserved will determine the extent to which people survive catastrophe as advanced societies. There is overwhelming evidence that catastrophic events have occurred before. Each time, enough life has survived to repopulate the earth. But knowledge and social values have often fared poorly. I and most of the teaching staff are here because we believe another major catastrophe is likely, and because we wish to help ensure that something more than physical life survives. I assume most of you were drawn here by similar motivation."

Holding up the paper he had passed out, he said: "You will notice from the syllabus that we have divided possible disasters into five categories, as follows:

"Category One disasters are defined as those caused by the observable actions of mankind, disasters that therefore can be averted — could be averted — by ceasing or reversing such actions. Nuclear war, for instance, is always the single greatest concern, whatever the present political climate. There are others. Damage to the atmosphere from disturbing the carbon dioxide balance or the ozone layer, either of which could cause disastrous changes in the earth's ecology. Unknown problems arising from scientific research with lasers or germ warfare.

"Category Two is concerned with the long-range effect of acid rain, the use of chemical fertilizers, application of insecticides, and other uses of chemicals which could poison the land, the water, or the food supply. Many civilizations have already died because their misuse of technology destroyed their environment. The Sahara, for instance, was a granary before deforestation changed the climate. The Middle East seems to present many examples of cultures that died when their irrigation practices resulted in contaminating their farmland with evaporative salts. Our own technological ability is much greater than that of previous cultures — but unless we use it in a wise and far-sighted manner, our added power merely means greater ability to do damage.

"Category Three includes possible results springing from man's experimenting with genetic engineering, or from an accident of nature. Persons worrying about this category could point to new diseases that have appeared from time to time, causing much suffering and death before countermeasures could be developed. Man's tampering, added to nature's mutations, might produce a disease with the potential of wiping out all life on the planet earth. A few centuries ago the bubonic plague, known as the black death, attacked in a series of epidemics. There was no known cure. In one epidemic one hundred million people died; another wiped out three fourths of the population of France. AIDS is a more recent example of a new disease. Until brought under control, it has the potential for triggering a world scale disaster." He looked out at them grimly.

"What's worse, nobody knows what evils ruthless dictators might unleash with the new genetic technology.

"Category Four covers massive destruction by forces from outer space. This includes hits by comets, meteorites, black holes, chunks of antimatter, etc. It could also include attack by intelligent beings arriving from other worlds in the vastness of space. Don't laugh. I see no reason to assume we are the only planet in the universe with astronauts, and no reason to assume we are the most advanced.

"Category Five consists of catastrophic damage caused by forces on or within the earth. Such damage might include earthquakes, extensive volcanic activity, tidal waves, even the rising and sinking of extensive tracts of land. Such damage is often very difficult to predict, and is seemingly impossible to prevent. Yet in some ways, geologic catastrophes are easier to get a grip on; they offer more 'handles' to use for planning purposes.

"Okay," he said. "So much for doomsday. Let me see which of you are interested in which area of study. How about a show of hands?"

Hedi noticed that about half the students seemed primarily concerned with the problems of category one — problems stemming from human action. There were quite a few environmentalists, too, concerned with categories two and three. Fewer admitted to interest in category four. Category five corresponded to what she had seen in her visions, and this was the category she selected for special study.

The Chief discussed some of the material to be covered in various lectures, and drew their attention to hidden connections between various topics.

"Now, students returning for advanced studies will be arriving during the day, and they will begin to tell all kinds of incredible stories about members of the teaching staff and some of the special lecturers." Deadpan, he added, "They might even tell stories about Sam Theos. Be wary of what you believe on that subject."

He got the expected polite, almost nervous chuckles. "In all seriousness, I want to prepare you to meet some very unusual individuals. A number of these teachers represent philosophies, religions, and levels of consciousness that will be strange to you. This institution does not necessarily endorse everything its instructors think and do, any more than it does its students.

"In other words, who you believe, and what you believe, is up to you." Just what father said, Hedi thought with surprise — use your judgment.

"Instructors will try to answer questions about their experiences and their beliefs, but their objective — our objective — is not to convert you to their way of thinking. The objective, let me stress, is strictly to apply their special skills to one problem — how to assure the survival of the best values of the current world society in the aftermath of a devastating shock or series of shocks."

He paused, mentally shifting gears. "One thing more. Before the day is out, you may begin to hear stories that seem utterly absurd."

A hand raised. "Sir, what sort of things?"

The Chief looked at him expressionlessly. "Oh, mental telepathy. UFO's. That sort of thing."

The student made no comment.

"Faced with such rumors, some students will pack their bags and request immediate transportation out of here. Such requests will be refused."

He surveyed them with a long glance. "I understand the response, and have a certain sympathy with it. But in fairness to you, as well as to this institution, we insist that you wait until you have met and listened to these remarkable teachers. Hasty judgments are rarely good judgments."

"But, sir," objected the same student, "we signed up for practical instruction. Are you saying that if we don't want to spend our time listening to far-out topics, we have to, whether we want to or not?"

"Only once. After that, anyone who objects to certain topics will be placed in a separate group and, as far as practical, assigned instructors with similar philosophies."

Again he looked around, as if estimating their openness to new ideas. "Let me say, however, that insulation from distasteful new ideas is rarely useful in survival training."

New ideas, distasteful and otherwise, were not long in coming. Speaker followed speaker, at first keeping each to his specialty, then increasingly referring to things the students had heard from others. The students filled notebook after notebook with snatches of lectures. Required reading was followed by additional reading, and still more reading. And the speakers became more and more provocative, challenging the students to disagree, and thus discover what they themselves thought.

The topics at first seemed quite distinct.

Maintaining order:

"I was a policeman for over 20 years, and I've been a consultant for a lot of years since. I can tell you flatly, I would rather face anything on earth than a mob out of control. To keep control, or gain it, you must establish communication. To do that, you must get their attention. This is central to a great deal of police work.

"There are many ways of getting the attention of an individual, but a mob is another matter. Mob action is often deliberately provoked by an individual or a small group, who then find they cannot stop what they've started."

Captain Benedetti paused to study the serious faces of the students. "I hope none of you ever have to face a mob, but most of the kinds of major disasters you have been discussing here will generate riots. The results can be bloody, and it is essential that control of these mobs be established. We can catalogue certain things that cause mobs to dissipate. There is the heavy rainstorm, preferably cold. That's why riot-control experts often use water cannon. Another approach is to cause extreme discomfort to large numbers — for example, tear gas.

"There are other ways," he said tersely. "Explosions massive enough to shake the earth nearby, perhaps. And, of course, a mob will often disperse out of sheer exhaustion. Once dispersed or shocked into paying attention to reason, the mob might still re-form. That's why you must use the time you bought to reach leaders willing and able to prevent it.

"By all means, use modern riot control methods if you can, but remember that mob rule means the complete breakdown of all law and order. Nothing is more destructive. Mobs must be controlled whatever the cost, and to control them you must first get their attention by whatever means you have available. It can come down to deciding whether or not to shoot them down with tanks, or helicopter gunships."

He picked up a sheaf of papers. "This is your first assignment. I have outlined a situation in which you, as chief of security, must make such a decision. Some of the resources available to you, and some considerations, and some alternatives, are listed for you. But in this exercise, as in real life, your resourcefulness may make the difference between success and failure.

"You may make whatever assumptions you wish; however, you will have to defend those assumptions, as well as your reasoning and your ultimate decision, before the entire class." He smiled. "I will be a remorseless critic of everything proposed. I encourage each of you to do likewise. The object of these exercises is to encourage you to make your mistakes here and now, where the consequences are limited to momentary embarrassment, rather than later, where they may be measured in lives and resources. However, I will insist that criticism be constructive, rather than destructive, for a very fundamental reason. There is no surer, quicker way of drying up potentially helpful ideas than to pounce on ideas that aren't yet well thought out."

He handed out the papers. "Now, let's look at the situation I have outlined. . . ."

Wilderness survival:

"Perhaps you believe in life after death. I hope you're right, because most people are going to die in the kind of disasters you have been discussing. Perhaps you even believe in reincarnation. I hope you're right, because I like it here and would welcome another crack at living here.

"Maybe your goal is to help others survive. Very noble, I say, but you aren't going to help very many if you are dead. Let me be perfectly clear. I am talking about staying alive under very difficult circumstances, and the name of that game is the 'will to live,' physical survival.

"Unless you live, there is no tomorrow for you. Unless somebody lives, there is no tomorrow for society. If you can bring along automobiles and TV sets, that's fine. If you can bring along hospitals and churches and universities, that's even better."

He was Clint Norman, the Department of Interior's expert on Wilderness Areas, and there was no doubt that he knew how to keep their attention. He looked like what he was, a man who had spent most of his life in the great outdoors.

"Leaving aside the creeping type of disaster, it may be that wilderness areas offer the best chance for survival. Of course, this assumes that you have a strong will to live, and that you know how to survive in the wild without help from any source except Mother Nature herself. If law and order breaks down in the densely populated urban areas, you will see casualties resulting from riots, massive fires, epidemic disease, fighting over a rapidly diminishing food supply, and then, when that supply is exhausted, starvation. Those casualties will very likely exceed deaths chargeable directly to the immediate disaster. But in the early days few, if any, of the urban types are likely to penetrate the wilderness areas. There you may have a chance. Any questions so far?"

No questions. "All right, let's look at our first exercise.

"You are a member of a group of survivors, doing quite well in a wilderness area in Wyoming. But word of your success has spread. Desperate refugees from less fortunate places ask — demand — that you share your food, shelter, and medical supplies.

"You are humane individuals. You would like to help. But it is obvious that as their numbers increase, you will be overwhelmed. In fact, if something isn't done, you will be wiped out.

"I will divide the class into teams, each one representing the group's governing council. Each team will meet to decide what the council should do. Each team will elect a spokesman who will present its decision to the class as a whole. In addition, each individual will be required to tell the class his or her personal position and the reasoning behind it. Then we will discuss what results the council's action produced. I expect this exercise to require several class sessions."

Disaster planning:

"Two types of preparation must be considered in planning for a major emergency. First, the provision for physical needs: stores of food, water, medical supplies, and shelters to protect them. Depending on the nature of the anticipated emergency, shelters for people may be needed, or means of moving people to safe locations might be essential. The wide range of possible threats makes advanced planning difficult, but we should not throw up our hands in despair. Instead we should rank possible disasters in the order of the likelihood of their occurrence, and try to prepare for those at the top of the list. For example, earthquakes would rate priority attention in California and Alaska."

Dr. Matthew Winslow was a distinguished professor from a large western university, an expert on the effects of severe stress on large groups. He had written and lectured widely on the need for all levels of government to have disaster emergency plans.

"The second main requirement for an emergency plan is trained people. Technical proficiency is essential, but is only one essential. The other is that there be recognized leaders able and willing to organize and direct whatever action is required. In some situations, the willingness to act may be the biggest problem of all.

"A third thing that would be required regardless of the type of disaster is a system of communication and the people to operate it. Those who know what happened must be able to reach those who need to know, and if the person who knows what should be done cannot contact those who must do it, then all of the other planning will be useless. And I must stress to you, the enemy of communication is chaos — mass hysteria can do far more damage than that caused directly by a natural disaster. There is nothing we can do to prevent a large meteorite from striking the earth, but there are things that can be done to minimize damage from the after-effects."

Hedi, with the rest of the class, was scribbling to list the major points.

"We will discuss these points extensively in the coming sessions, but we will do it in the context of a project. You will select the two disasters most likely to strike the State of Maine in the next 200 years, and will outline disaster plans for coping with them.

"You will assume that some elements of the present state government survive, but — " he smiled, "— you will also assume that due to death or disability, the posts of governor, director of information and planning, and director of internal security all need to be filled on essentially no notice. You will draw up a list of qualifications for each post, keeping in mind any particular requirements caused by the nature of the crisis you have created, and explain how you intend to search for individuals capable of filling the bill."

By the end of the first day's classes, Hedi had begun to see how the various topics related to each other. The other students began to file from the room. She remained in her seat, thinking: mobs must be brought under control at any cost; for physical survival the name of the game is the will to live; unless leaders were willing to act, all other preparations might be for naught.

"It all comes down to guts," she told herself with the assumed toughness of the very young. "Good old intestinal fortitude. What makes Mr. J think I have the guts for this?"

"I can't remember when he was ever wrong about a thing like that," remarked a voice behind her, and she turned to see the Chief smiling at her.

"Do you always go about reading peoples minds?" she asked, somewhat crossly.

"No," he replied, a twinkle in his eyes. "Usually it makes pretty dull reading."

Before Hedi could think of a good response, Samuel Theos turned and left the room.

10. What Is Man?
July, Z-Minus-12

"What is man that God is mindful of him? Did the Creator spin the earth to end the day; then light a billion stars to guide man through the night? If so, why make ten billion more that man will never see?

"What are the cosmic laws, and what punishment is meted out to those who break them? Is there a heaven and a hell?

"Does anything exist beyond the grave? — or does the woman birth her child to work and play, love and hate, suffer and die, and thus complete some random cycle only to fertilize the soil?

"Does man return to earth to live again, as some believe? If so, where does he live before his birth?

"Is immortality only for the few, or does it, in various ways, belong to all?

"What are the boundaries of the universe, and, when we find them, what mystery lies on yonder side?

"If there be no God, does some computer run the cosmos with decisions made at random, or is there a logic to command it? Either way, who wrote the program?

"What does man know except that he exists? Does not the chipmunk know as much, and perhaps the oak tree too?"

The speaker's name was Cheng Tu. The summary sheet on him gave his age as about 130 years. Hedi couldn't decide if she believed that or not. Supposedly he had spent some sixty years studying under masters of increasing knowledge and understanding, until finally his understanding was of such a high order that his peers urged him to go forth into the world and serve the people, since there was nothing more he could learn in the solitude of the monastery.

He was known for trying to resolve differences between religious groups, and for speaking out against those factors that weakened the moral stamina of society. Still he was best known in the academic world of scholars and teachers. Clearly the Chief regarded him as a highly prized member of his staff.

"We like to ask questions such as the ones I have just recited. They are important questions, and it is important that they be asked. But all too often, when the answers are not forthcoming or do not please our fancy, we invent those that better suit our convenience or enhance our ego. I cannot answer all the questions I have posed, but let me make one fundamental point. The Chief invited me here, not to teach religious doctrine, but to discuss the influence of the universal laws on the nature and timing of the natural catastrophes you are here to learn to survive."

He paused and looked from student to student.

"In the cosmos of my Creator, a law is not a law if it can be broken. Instruction or advice can be disregarded, but not laws. The universal laws are laws of action and reaction, and they cannot be broken. It is not a matter of rewarding good or punishing evil — the reactions to your actions are inescapable. Unless you understand this point, there is no merit in pursuing other questions."

Hedi was brought up short. "The universal laws cannot be broken," Mr. J had said. At that moment, the speaker paused again. His dark, brown eyes looked into hers, and a faint smile formed on his lips. She knew that he knew what had passed through her mind.

A young man held up his hand. "Yes. You are—?"

"Hugh Scott, sir."

"Lieutenant Scott, is it not?"

"Yessir. Sir, you make creation sound cut and dried. Are you saying God cannot forgive? Do we have to suffer the consequences, no matter what? What happened to salvation by the Grace of God? Christ taught that forgiveness was the only way."

"Ah, but Lieutenant Scott, at the moment I am dealing only with the universal laws, and you also ask questions about salvation. Your tape recorder will remind you that I said it is not a matter of good or evil. The reactions to your actions are inescapable, regardless of whether you see them as rewards or punishments. If God does not condemn you for your unwise action, for what do you ask his forgiveness?"

The young man flushed with embarrassment, realizing his question had not been well put. Hedi felt sorry for him and tried to rescue the situation with a question of her own.

"But it seems to me," she said, "that you are saying that the Creator had the power to make these universal laws, but lacks the power to change them or suspend a specific law in a specific instance. Is this true or have I misunderstood you?" Scott turned in his seat to see who had come riding to the rescue.

Dr. Tu turned the question over carefully in his mind. "The power of a God who can create this marvelous cosmos cannot be limited in that power by the likes of me, so the answer to your question has to be that he who made the law can change it.

"Still, my understanding is that the universal laws are so perfect in design and scope that there is no need to change them or make exceptions. In none of the levels of consciousness or states of understanding I have experienced have any such changes been called for. The laws ensure God's perfect justice, which is justice without malice. The Creator provides answers to our prayers and displays his love and mercy by giving us understanding of His purposes, and the wisdom and courage to apply that understanding.

"But we are straying into deep theology, which is off our chosen topic. Let us take a ten-minute break and then return to continue our discussion."

"Thanks for getting me off the hook with Doctor Tu."

Hedi instinctively liked Hugh Scott's looks. He was undeniably military. He held himself effortlessly ramrod- straight, and positively radiated responsibility, self-confidence and self-discipline. Yet none of this made him unapproachable — quite the contrary. And he was young — probably only a couple of years older than she. She was woman enough, too, to give weight to the undeniable fact that this slim young man with his dark hair and brown eyes and military air was handsome. ("Dashing," she decided.) "I'll bet he has a thousand girlfriends," she thought.

She smiled at him. "Well, I thought your point was perfectly valid, and I didn't see any reason why he should get off easy, just because he was able to come up with a snappy answer."

They laughed, partly because they instinctively liked each other, partly because they were young. It was the beginning of what would be a life-long friendship.

"How old are you?" she asked, surprising herself.

He didn't seem to find the question remarkable. "Twenty- four," he said.

"I'm 20, and it's clear to me that you and I are the babies of the class."

"I guess we will have to stick together in self-defense, then," he said.

Acting on impulse, before she could reason herself out of it, she asked, "What are you doing here?"

When he gave her what her father would have called a funny look, she hastened to explain. "Dr. Tu knew who you are. He knew you are a lieutenant. Army? Air Force?"

"Army."

"I'll bet he doesn't know everybody's name and rank."

"I'll bet not everybody here even *has* a rank."

He laughed, and she giggled, and she liked him even more. "That military shell isn't the whole story," she told herself. "I'll bet he's a lot of fun when he's at ease."

She said: "No, but really. Did the Army send you here?"

"Oh, yes and no. They assigned me, but I had to do some pretty strong lobbying first to get them to do it."

"What are you supposed to be doing here? For the Army, I mean."

"About the same thing you're probably doing here, only for their information rather than strictly for my own. You might say I'm scouting out this survival school, looking for material that might be useful to the Army. There's nothing like being prepared, you know." A shadow passed behind his eyes. "I think the time will come when we need these survival skills. What I'm afraid of is that the people with the knowledge won't have the authority, and the ones with authority won't have the knowledge."

Hedi became aware that inside this self-confident professional was a thoughtful, intelligent individual, painfully aware of the damage that could be done by wrong decisions, or by indecision, or by malice or ignorance. She liked him even more. Yet somehow she knew there was more, so she said nothing.

He hesitated, lowered his voice, and said: "I suppose it isn't a secret. I'm also supposed to report back on the political orientation of the school and the kind of philosophies being taught."

She didn't much like the sound of that. "That sounds like spying," she said in a voice that — try as she would — she couldn't keep quite as friendly as before.

But he didn't seem to notice, or was determined not to notice. He winked at her. "Think of it as avid curiosity," he said. "You know how nosy men can be."

She couldn't help smiling. He did seem awfully nice.

He certainly didn't waste any time returning to the fray. No sooner had the class reassembled than he challenged Dr. Tu. Politely, but firmly.

"Sir, could you explain how what you describe as the universal laws of action and reaction could result in the kind of catastrophe that we fear? It seems to me you are mixing things. Morality is one thing, physical existence another."

"Indeed they are not," Dr. Tu replied, equally politely, equally firmly. "They are two aspects of the same reality."

"I'm afraid I don't understand."

"Yes, this concept is foreign to many in the West, and it may require a bit of effort to comprehend. But the effort is well worthwhile, I assure you, for effective action rests upon right understanding, and right understanding depends upon clear sight. Allow me to attempt to clarify my view."

"If it will take us too far afield, I don't mind shelving it for now," the young lieutenant said. Hedi got the impression he was a bit embarrassed.

"You fear that in answering your question, I will waste the time of class members," Dr. Tu said. "This is not so. Your question leads us to the heart of a most important question, and into territory new to almost everyone here." For a fleet second, Hedi had the impression that Dr. Tu let his eyes meet hers as a symbol of his secret recognition. Then she told herself she was crazy.

"And, I assure you, this discussion is most germane to the great goals being pursued here.

"You have heard of karma?"

A student somewhere behind Hedi made a sound of impatience. "Oh, not that California stuff!"

Dr. Tu didn't seem offended. "Karma was understood long before there was a California," he said, amused. "Who can tell me what they think it means?"

An intense, black-haired young man in the front row half-raised his hand. "Isn't that the idea that whatever bad happens to you is because of something bad you did sometime in the past? It's tied in with all the stuff about reincarnation."

"Yes, it is, particularly in the popular culture. Almost more so in America today than in my native India, where unfortunately it has been used to justify a pernicious system of hereditary castes." He permitted himself a slight smile. "I trust that as Americans come to understand the doctrine of reincarnation, they will not feel compelled to adopt the distortions that have been grafted onto it over the years.

"However, we are not here primarily to discuss reincarnation. The topic of life after death is not particularly germane to the question of avoiding that death in the first place."

He smiled and they laughed. Classrooms, Hedi thought, never change.

"Lest you begin to wonder when I shall begin to read palms, let us hasten to the question of how the laws of action and reaction connect to the topic of how to survive so-called natural disasters.

"To begin, the reactions to individual actions are relatively easy to explain. Actions directed at another person might be of constructive or destructive intent. Regardless of intent, the other person might be helped or hindered, or unaffected, or even unaware, of the existence of the act or the intent. The one certainty is that the person initiating a destructive action will be the one most damaged by it, and the one taking constructive action will derive a greater benefit than the person he is trying to help. In one way or another this point is stressed in all of the great religions of the world. And this is not mere wishful thinking. It is the expression of a scientific truth."

Cheng Tu paused to let the significance of his assertions sink in. "When they do not lie very close together on the same time line, the relation of action to reaction may be difficult to discern. This is because there are gaps in your memory as you move from one level of consciousness to another.

"Once the mists that obscure your vision are cleared away, however, it becomes crystal clear that the only way you can help yourself is to lend a hand to someone else. It follows that the bad guys in the black hats lose, not because the good guys in the white hats are instructed by the Almighty to ride forth and destroy them, but because the bad guys have created the seeds of their own destruction."

"Maybe so," Professor David, a man in his 50s, objected, "but the process sure takes a long time. Look at Hitler. For that matter, look at Stalin. Maybe they're going to pay for their sins in another life, but that's not much consolation for the millions of people who died in concentration camps."

"Or the millions who died in the war they caused," another man put in.

Hedi thought she knew the answer to that, and sure enough, Cheng Tu's explanation followed Mr. J's.

"What you say is so, and yet is not so. When groups are involved, the principle is the same, but justice follows a more complex course. In a group of many persons, such as a society, a weighted average of all individual actions determines the net reaction.

"Reactions involving societies, or nations — or planets — are not determined hastily. Enormous amounts of energy are involved."

"Sir, what energy are you speaking of?"

"The energy generated by the creative actions of all of the persons involved. It accumulates in constructive or destructive form, as the case may be, until a decisive imbalance is reached, which fuels the appropriate reaction.

"If the vote is close, that is, if constructive and destructive actions tend to cancel each other out, many thousands of years may pass before a decision is developed and a major reaction event is triggered."

"Such as now," Lieutenant Scott said.

Dr. Tu nodded. "Many fear that we are approaching such a time, and that the reaction will be a destructive cataclysm of major proportions."

Hedi had had months to accustom herself to these ideas, and they now seemed plausible, even natural. But she could see that most of the class were where she had been in her conversation with Mr. J — somewhere between incredulity and perplexity.

After a moment of silence, a woman in her middle years raised her hand.

"Yes. Your name is —"

"Norma Hill. You make statements of a very profound nature. I think it only fair to ask the source of your knowledge and authority." The lady spoke in very crisp, definite sentences. Someone who likes to dot every 'i' and cross every 't', Hedi thought.

Again Dr. Tu paused before answering, Hedi noticed. Apparently he was not afraid of thinking before speaking; therefore, not afraid of appearing indecisive or uncertain.

"Yours is a fair question. My statements are based on a study of all religions, but I must admit that my beliefs are heavily affected by sixty years of study and meditation in a Buddhist monastery."

Norma Hill spoke again. "We have been told that you are considered to have become enlightened. Can you tell us what that means?"

"Very well. I do not know how many others would agree with my rather simplistic definition, but I will give you my own answer. You will recall what I told you earlier — we know that we exist, and that is all we know. All else is belief, however sincere; it is opinion, however rational, based on limited knowledge. Now I must modify that statement.

"To believe is necessary, but our ultimate goal must be to know. If by prayer, meditation, revelation, or any other means you can acquire any additional certain knowledge about God's creation and purposes, then I would say that you have been enlightened to that extent."

"So enlightenment is just a figure of speech?"

"Not at all. But obviously there are countless levels of enlightenment, and they can be seen in different contexts. I believe that being born again, being illuminated, being filled with the Holy Spirit, and similar religious terms can mean the same thing, if they are all genuine experiences."

Norma Hill was still dotting 'i's. "Could you tell us how such enlightenment occurs? Do you hear a voice? See a vision? In what language is the message expressed? How do you know that it is 'certain knowledge'?"

"I can speak with certainty only for myself. After many years of training I became sensitive to the thoughts of others, even at great distances. I understood the techniques of mind control over body functions. I knew the relationship between emotions and good health. At times I felt I had shared for a brief moment the knowledge and understanding of the Universal Mind."

"That still sounds pretty vague," she said uncompromisingly.

Dr. Tu smiled. "You remain unsatisfied. So did I. But then finally my senior teacher, an enlightened Master of great distinction, told me that I was seeking an understanding of things that could not be put into words, since the necessary words did not exist. He warned me that the goal could be attained, but not described."

Another smile. "I spent three years in a rigorous discipline of thinking and praying with wordless emotions, and listening for answers with a completely blank mind. For three years I talked with no one, indicating physical needs by signs when required. I remained isolated from all manmade sounds except music."

Another long pause. "Gradually I found myself knowing not only the thoughts of others, but the buried emotions that lay behind them. From this I learned that thoughts, like words, could practice deceit, while the deep emotions of the spirit could only speak the truth. Then it happened — a sustained enlightenment in which I shared with the Creator some small portion of His Cosmic Purpose. It was certain knowledge because it was His knowledge." Another smile, a beatific smile. "But I cannot describe it, for it cannot be described. Some years ago, someone said, rightly, that 'what cannot be said, cannot be said. And it cannot be whistled, either.' Typical Western irreverence; typical Western directness."

Cheng Tu fell silent, and an absolute quiet pervaded the room. Somehow even the sounds of nature, which normally could be heard in the background, had been excluded. And for the first time in her life Hedi saw an aura, a sheath of pulsing light the color of a sunbeam, that surrounded Cheng Tu and seemed to dispel every shadow cast by the overhead electric lights.

The mood was far different when the class met with Dr. Ludwig.

Richard Ludwig was a noted, but often controversial, Swiss physicist, mathematician and geographer. He did not waste words, nor did he mince them.

"The Chief has said the reason people come here is because they are afraid of something," he said bluntly. "Let me tell you what frightens me. I am afraid mankind will destroy itself before it has a chance to learn anything more about the cosmos. I'm talking about nuclear war. Mankind's last war, ladies and gentlemen."

He held up a hand. "I can see by your faces that you think I'm out of date. You think that both the Soviet Union and the United States realized the danger, and that both countries know better than to risk starting such a war. You may be interested to know that I agree with you — they won't.

"But that doesn't change my opinion one bit. Even in the 1950s, when I was a lot younger, and which now seems like ancient history, I never thought we'd come to war as a result of somebody's calculated, reasoned decision.

"The problem is that never in history has mankind's effort at disarmament prevented war. Sooner or later, if matters follow their normal course, someone will precipitate a nuclear war. And that will be the end. Either in the initial exchange, or as a result of radioactive fallout, life on this planet will cease to exist. Perhaps certain marine life will survive, but that is little consolation to us, surely." He noted a raised hand. "Yes?"

"Jim Freemark. Dr. Ludwig, if the Russians aren't going to start the war, and we aren't, who is?"

"I expect the war to be started by the leader of some minor country. Someone with delusions of grandeur. Someone with a messianic complex, willing to destroy the world in order that 'right' as he sees it, prevail."

"That's insane," Freemark objected. "How can anything prevail if the world is destroyed?"

"You are quite correct. It is insane. However, it has happened in the past that madmen have attained positions of power."

"Hitler," Freemark said.

"Among others. And the situation is more dangerous today. To initiate the destruction of the world, it is not necessary that the madman control a major power. His state need only be large enough to afford a few nuclear devices. And these, I scarcely need remind anyone here, unfortunately have become quite affordable."

Nobody in the classroom felt like arguing the point. Like the others, Hedi felt chilled.

Dr. Ludwig drilled on, relentlessly. "Nor is that the worst of the situation. We must also factor in the possibility of accident. A glitch in the computer programs controlling the launch sequence of our missiles, or the Russians'. A lethal mistake in identification that causes one side to think that the other has just launched a full-scale attack." He shrugged. "The possible scenarios are endless."

Freemark objected. "Some of those accidents have already occurred," he said. "Back in 1959, our system mistook the moon for
incoming Soviet missiles. But they didn't jump to the conclusion that
the computer was right. They just overrode the system."

"That's less persuasive as a example than it might be," Marion
Halpak said. "I am a staff interpreter with the United Nations. I
happen to remember accounts of that incident. The reason the
military didn't believe the radar was because the Soviet premier of
the time, Nikita Khrushchev, was visiting Washington. They didn't
think the Soviets would launch an attack that would destroy their
own leader. If it had happened a month earlier, a month later, who
knows?"

"My point precisely," Dr. Ludwig said. "Unless the fundamental
situation changes, sooner or later the missiles will be used. The only
hope I see is that man's ability and desire to wage a high-tech war is
first destroyed by some lesser catastrophe."

Lieutenant Scott jumped in on that. "Surely you don't mean that
literally?"

"I do. As long as the missiles and the atomic bombs exist, they are
a mortal threat to life on earth. And not just missiles and bombs — I
remind you that biological and chemical warfare is potentially quite
as lethal. The enemy of mankind is not atomic bombs, or guided
missiles, but the mentality that causes war. Unfortunately, I cannot
conceive of any disarmament campaign, however sincere or extensive, that could eliminate that mentality. Yet, intuitively, I cannot
believe we will see the end of the world. What I expect, instead, is
a category five disaster."

Hedi started. Category five again — destruction emanating from
the earth itself.

"You have a particular something in mind?"

"I do." Like Cheng Tu, he paused.

"All of you know that if a wheel on your car gets out of balance
— due to a bulge in the tire, perhaps — you feel a bump each time
the wheel goes around. This condition, if not corrected, can make
the car begin to vibrate badly. Eventually something will break, and
the car will go out of control.

"Everyone knows that the earth is covered with bulges, and we
have known for a long time that it wobbles a bit as it rotates. If it
were perfectly smooth there would be no wobble, but all of the land
would be covered with water, and the water would be about a mile
and a half deep.

"I am convinced that sooner or later the earth must eliminate
enough bulges to significantly reduce the imbalance. This need not
flood the entire land mass, and I believe enough might be left to
support a healthy remnant of the human race."

An elderly gentleman raised his hand. "Louis Enderman, Dr. Ludwig. Do you have any views on what might trigger a correction?"

Dr. Ludwig shrugged. "I can venture some educated guesses. I estimate that the earth's crust is under such great stress that it would take only a tiny push to precipitate a violent readjustment. We know that for some unexplained reason the earth's magnetic field has reversed many times during the past few million years. For all we know it could happen again tomorrow, and it just might generate enough physical shock to serve as a trigger.

"You want another possibility? A large meteorite striking the earth. Another? Some have wondered if an underground nuclear test might trigger it, although I myself think it would take more than that. There is no shortage of possibilities."

"Can you envision a mechanism that might cause the imbalance to be corrected?"

"I can visualize the earth's crust splitting open in the many places where it is relatively thin. This would disgorge huge amounts of lava.

"This discharge would be encouraged by the enormous weight of mountain ranges such as the Himalayas, and high plateaus such as the one in northern Arizona. Lava discharged into the sea would combine with the sinking of land masses to reduce the size of its bulges, bringing the earth into an acceptable balance. Perhaps half to three quarters of the land might be covered by the oceans in this process."

Inevitably, Hedi thought of her dreams.

Another student asked, "Is there anything mankind could do to prevent this disaster?"

"No."

"How about Divine intervention? Everyone could pray for that."

"You will have to ask someone else that question," Dr. Ludwig answered curtly. "I have seen no evidence of divine intervention, and have no knowledge of the existence of a divine being."

A young woman who appeared to be in her thirties asked, "Are you an atheist?"

"No," the scientist replied. "I am closer to being an agnostic. I simply do not wish to waste my time on matters that are not subject to proof, and in my view this applies to all religious beliefs and mystical addictions."

This pronouncement generated a moment of silence. Then Lieutenant Scott raised his hand. "Dr. Ludwig, I am somewhat familiar with your work in many fields. At West Point we studied some of your theories in physics, and I know you have made important contributions in mathematics. I read your paper on 'The Life Cycle of Planet Earth.'

"Earlier you expressed a personal fear that the human race would be destroyed. You must believe in something, or you would not work so hard or be so concerned about what happens. Would I be out of order in asking what motivates a person like yourself?"

"The question is well put. I believe in the power of the human mind to eventually discover the basic laws of nature.

"The increasing rate of progress in pushing back the boundaries of scientific knowledge is vastly exciting. Society can now support large numbers of research scientists in specialized fields. The fallout from this research increases the productivity and the living standards of those workers who produce such essentials as food, shelter, and clothing for the likes of me — which makes them willing and able to support even more scholars and scientists. I am afraid that too severe a disaster, or a disaster in the absence of effective leadership, will result in all of this being lost."

"Scientists aren't the only professions depending on someone else for the essentials of life," Scott said. "Think of doctors, merchants, policemen, teachers...."

"Of course, of course. But this only reinforces my point. Civilization depends on specialization. To that extent, it is fragile."

He concentrated on Scott. "You ask why this matters to me. Let me tell you that the odds favor the existence of other planets in the cosmos able to support intelligent life, but I doubt there are any so wonderful as planet earth.

"Here we can experience the pure elegance of mathematical logic, while on a more emotional level we can immerse ourselves in the exciting sounds of mathematics converted to music. Where else is there such wonderful color, such delightful smells, such a range of emotions, or the ability to touch and feel such exciting things? I treasure the sight of a full moon painting its shining path on a restless sea as much as I do the satisfaction of prying open another of nature's endless secrets.

"To me, life on this planet is sufficient reward. Though I have no hope for eternal life for myself, I can hope to live on through some small contribution I make to the joy of generations yet to come. You have asked your questions, and I have made my speech. My ambitions are not nearly so great as those of my friend Cheng Tu, but they are sufficient for me."

When the class met again with Tu, Norma Hill was ready with a question. "Dr. Ludwig described in some detail a category five disaster that he felt was certain to occur. He said that there is nothing mankind could do to avert it, and that there was no such thing as Divine intervention. He made no prediction about timing, but did say he hoped something of this sort would happen before man destroyed all life by precipitating a nuclear war. Would you give us your views of his opinions?"

"Dick Ludwig and I are very familiar with each other's views. On occasion I have accused him of being a rather poor agnostic, in that he practices what the world's major religions preach; what I myself preach. The only way to help yourself is to give a hand to someone else, and Dick Ludwig does exactly that.

"I do not agree that the disaster he describes is an absolute certainty, but my perception is that the odds are better than ten to one that it will occur. I agree with him that it would be preferable to an all-out nuclear war."

"What do you see as the mechanism of the disaster?" another student asked.

Cheng Tu paused to reflect on the direction of the questioning. "Perhaps I can save time," he said, "by reminding you that I am not a scientist. However, I am inclined to accept Dr. Ludwig's view on the earth's equilibrium problems and the event most likely to trigger a violent relaxation of the tension existing in the earth's crust."

"What strengths will we need to survive the disaster that has been described, or is an individual's survival purely a matter of luck?" Hedi asked.

"According to the Christian scriptures, the sun shines and the rain falls on the just and the unjust alike," Cheng Tu responded. "You will need courage, and you will need faith in the purpose of your God, but unless you are in the right place at the right time, there is not much you can do in advance to ensure living through the initial onslaught of the catastrophe.

"One thing I would urge. Many animals can sense a gathering storm before it can be seen or heard. All of you have sensitivities and perceptions that are largely undeveloped. It is possible you may sense an approaching disaster, and have a hunch as to what you should do about it. Pay attention to any such perceptions. Aside from these generalities, we must confine our survival training for category four and five catastrophes to surviving the aftermath."

11. Dear Hugh
June 3, Z-Minus-11

Dear Hugh,

Thanks for your letter, which demonstrated to my surprise that men can be discreet, as well as nosy! Just kidding, but I can see that you didn't tell me half of what happened when you reported back after survival camp. If your superiors were anything like my parents, you got a pretty thorough grilling.

I don't mean that my parents were unpleasant, of course. They weren't. But it was completely clear from the minute I got back that they intended to hear everything that had happened from first to last. Did you ever try to tell somebody everything that happened in six weeks? Particularly six crowded weeks? Well, of course, the answer to that rhetorical question is yes, isn't it? That's *exactly* what you had to do.

Anyway, I spent ten days at home before returning to school, and my parents were observing me closely the whole time. Wanted to see if I'd joined the lunatic fringe, I think.

Was I absolutely honest with them? Well, to tell the truth, not completely. I gave them a factual report that included all of the pertinent points, but I didn't reveal my own opinions on many of the more controversial issues. Which is pretty much what you did when you reported to your officers, I'll bet!

So, when my father asked me if I found the experience useful, I told him I wouldn't have missed it for the world, which was true. I told him I found it comforting — which I do — just to know that a lot of intelligent people are giving serious thought to questions of surviving major disasters. I told them that even though surviving the initial catastrophe might be a matter of luck, much can be done to survive the resulting hazards, and I told them I think everyone needs to know something about these things.

Naturally, this was the first shot in my campaign to come back this summer to take one of the advanced courses. And now we're a little less than a month away from starting!

My mother surprised me. She said that she thought that if we had a nuclear war, the fortunate ones would be those who died in the first blast. "I'm not sure I would want to survive," she said.

Of course, I said, "Don't say that, Mother. If you don't have the will to live there isn't much chance for survival," but she said the kind of battles I'd been talking about were for the young. "Old folks and weaklings had best be out of the way, otherwise no one will make it," she said, and she was dead serious. I'd never thought my mother had given much thought to these things.

Anyway, I gave the subject a rest for a while after that.

(Tuesday. Got interrupted, never got back to this.)
I talked to you about my sister Martha. Do you remember any of it, I wonder?

I told her a lot about what had happened, and she listened, but mostly she wanted to talk about her own plans. Natural enough: She was getting ready to begin her freshman year at Dartmouth.

I bring her up because she told me she wants to wind up in charge of public relations for a large organization or a prominent political figure. She has it all planned out: what she'll have to know, what experiences she'll have to have, etc., etc. That means debates, speeches, TV and radio experience, maybe work for newspapers and magazines. A lot of work!

She's so ambitious, and so organized. She doesn't think I'm truly being practical in pursuing this survival stuff. Do you ever find yourself wondering about it? Remind me, we have to talk about it. Hopefully you can talk me out of any doubts!

Of course, Martha and I are very different. She doesn't seem to care a thing about love and marriage, and children and grand-children.

(Thursday. More interruptions. If this keeps up, I'll be able to hand this to you in person, instead of mailing it. But I'm determined to finish this today.)

My parents have agreed to pick up the tab for one more year of schooling, so that I can get my Master's. My grades were good again this year — I had a lot of psychology courses, and worked one in on parapsychology — and they didn't seem to mind. I was happy about that, but even happier when they said I could also take the advanced survival course this summer!

Well, on to my big news. I was pretty well decided on grad school, but not very decided about a career. Then my mother came up with the bright idea of consulting Uncle Jake — that's her older brother, who's a doctor specializing in diseases of the kidney. Nowadays he spends most of his time as a special consultant. He is widely known in the medical community in Cleveland and has contacts all over the state. Mother figured he'd be happy to advise me and open some doors.

So we went to Cleveland to see him, and he wanted to know my ambitions. I told him I'd like a career just like Mother's. He was surprised, but I told him my mother has been happier in that role than any woman I know. So then he wanted to know right away if I was ready to get married! I told him that before I get married, I want to develop a skill so that I can support myself.

We talked awhile. I told him I'd found the study of psychology very interesting and would like to be able to apply it to people who need help. I asked him about getting an Ohio license as a Medical Assistant in Psychiatry. Immediately he called the State Medical Examiner's office and got me the requirements for obtaining a Medical Assistant's license in Psychiatry or Applied Psychology. Then he called a friend in Columbus who is Dean of the Graduate School of Applied Psychology and got a list of academic courses I'd need to —

Well, you don't want all this detail. The upshot is this: I'm going to try to get both a Master's and Medical Assistant's certificate. By working part-time under the supervision of a qualified doctor while I study, I'll get credit for half of the hours of work experience needed. Uncle Jake thinks I can have both my Master's degree and a state license in fifteen to eighteen months, then, after another two years of actual experience, I can apply for a rating as a Senior Medical Assistant.

It helps to have somebody in your corner who knows the ropes!

Uncle Jake said if I plan to live and work in Ohio, it would help to do my academic work and gain my 'hands on' experience here. That's fine with me. I'd always thought in terms of Ohio anyway.

Almost as an afterthought, I asked him if he thought psychiatry was a good choice of field. He laughed and said if I have the stomach for it, nothing could be better than psychiatry. "It's the fastest growing business in the country," he said. "Millions of people need the psychiatrist and know it. Millions more are off their rocker and *don't* know it. I wouldn't be surprised if some day we discover that normal people are in the minority." He said he personally prefers kidneys. He said at least when a kidney jumps up and dashes out of the room, you have a pretty good idea where it is going and why.

Then he came up with yet another friend, a psychiatrist who is donating half of his time to a Columbus clinic for disturbed children. He said I'd get a lot of satisfaction and excellent training there, and assured me that he was confident I'd be hard-working and reliable. Quite a responsibility!

Well, I obtained an appointment to talk with Dean Curry in Columbus. (This letter is going on forever, isn't it? But I'm so impressed with my good luck, I just feel like writing it all out, and you're the unlucky person on the other end.) He quizzed me on the depth of my interest and knowledge in psychology. To my surprise, he even touched on the never-never-land of parapsychology, and the possibility that the mind contains powers as yet unknown or un-proven. I was discreet! At least, I tried to be. I thought of all our great sessions last summer, but I certainly didn't mention them!

I must have done okay, because the dean said I could apply for admission as a candidate for a Master's Degree in Psychology. He told me my chances of being accepted were very good!

So then, since I was in Columbus anyway, I went to see Dr. Philip Exter at the Children's Clinic.

Hugh, I absolutely fell in love with that man! He let me observe as he worked with six of his little patients at the clinic. Ranging from six months to twelve years in age, they exhibited a wide range of severe mental problems. He was SO good with them!

And he knows so much, yet he knows he has to consult with others in other fields. For example, he showed me a 12-year-old boy who cannot, or will not, talk. The boy had taken the family car without his parents' knowledge, taking his ten-year-old brother with him. He was trying to impress his friends with his daring and skill. One ditch and one oak tree later, the car was wrecked, he had suffered a blow to the head — a modest concussion — and his brother had lost both legs.

Tests failed to reveal any brain damage that would explain his inability to talk or understand messages conveyed to him by others, so people concluded that he had an emotional problem growing out of a severe feeling of guilt.

Dr. Exter told me he believes the trouble is physical. Something has destroyed the boy's ability to process language in either direction — he thinks the section of the brain that deals with language has been damaged. He arranged for a brain surgeon at the clinic in Cleveland to have another look. I don't know what happened.

There was a six-year-old girl who sits and stares blankly at the wall. Has done it from birth. He believes it to be a genetic defect, and is getting some experts from Harvard to try to help him find out.

He had a nine-year-old boy who has twice tried to commit suicide. Found that there had been an experience of abuse and rejection inflicted on him as a small baby. He said, "This we know how to treat, now that the root cause has been discovered. Even so, the help of an understanding minister may be needed. This is often true of older patients with religious backgrounds."

Yes, a doctor relying on religion! He noted my surprise. "If you are to be truly concerned about the health of another human being," he said, "you must be concerned with the whole person. The whole person consists of Body, Mind, and Spirit. The worst cases of all are those where the spirit is sick."

I stayed there two more hours. He told me to get in touch with him this fall when I go back to school (assuming I do, but it looks pretty good) and he'd get me a trainee job. He said, "The pay will be nominal, but the rewards are great."

The way I feel at the moment, I'd work for him for nothing!

So now you know all my news, and when we see each other we won't have anything to say to each other! See you soon.

Sincerely your friend,
Hedi

12. Strange Encounter
July, Z-Minus-11

The float plane made a wide sweep across the lake; then, turning into the wind, it settled smoothly onto the water and taxied to the landing dock.

"There's the reception party," Jim Freemark said. "I don't see the Chief there, though."

Sam Theos was not waiting for them on the dock, but Hugh Scott was. Hedi gave him a hug.

"Hoped you'd be on this flight," he said. "Jim, how are you? Tony, Helen."

He finished shaking hands and picked up Hedi's canvas-sided carryall bag. "This all your luggage? You travel pretty light for a woman."

She stuck out her tongue at him. He grinned. "Come on. I'll fill you in on what I was too discreet to put into my letter."

They walked up toward the women's quarters.

"It feels so great to be back here!"

"Yeah, I feel that way myself. I got in last night and it took me hours to go to sleep. I wound up wandering around down here by the water."

"So give," Hedi said. "What happened?"

He shook his head sorrowfully. "Just like a woman. All curiosity, no patience."

"Just like a man. All self-control, no consideration."

They grinned at each other. Hedi was very glad to be with him again, listening to his teasing, watching him effortlessly toting the bag that had made her walk lopsided in Bangor between the baggage claim area and the counter where she had signed onto the Otter's flight. Plus, it was another beautiful day and classes would start soon.

"You were so right about my not telling you half of what went on," he said. "Very perceptive of you. But let me tell you, that discretion that amazed you so" — they again exchanged light-hearted grins — "couldn't have been any more necessary. If they'd found out that I sent somebody a letter repeating a conversation with my superiors, I wouldn't be in trouble — I'd be history. No more survival training, no more good recommendations. No more Lieutenant Scott, in fact. You'd be addressing your letters to *Mister* Scott. And maybe sending them to Leavenworth, for all I know."

"Are you serious?"

"Well, I don't know how far they'd want to carry it, but they take a very dim view of security breaches."

"Does that mean you're liable to get into trouble talking to me?"

"Always," he said light-heartedly. "But no more so in this case than usual."

It took her a moment to catch the good-natured insult. "You will be in more trouble than usual, if you keep that up. Seriously, Hugh, what happened? If you can tell me, I mean."

"Okay, Hedi, here's the story. You remember I told you last

summer that probably the only way they'd let me return would be to study the aftermath of a category one disaster."

"A nuclear war."

"Right. And when I received my orders, they instructed me to report here for six weeks of advanced training in disaster survival, so I figured I was right.

"But a few days after I get my orders, I'm summoned by Colonel — well, by my commanding officer. I enter his office and I find a major-general there, somebody I've never seen before.

"Turns out he's Chief of Intelligence for the U.S. Army, and why do you suppose he's visiting?"

"To see you," Hedi said matter-of-factly.

Scott looked a bit deflated. "You know, Hedi, sometimes you take all the fun out of life. Do you realize how ridiculous an idea that is? That a two-star comes all the way to — well, never mind where — the point is, generals don't usually come to see lieutenants; lieutenants go to see generals. And they do it on the double, practicing saying 'yessir, sir.'"

"But this time was different."

"It certainly was. It turns out that the general was interested in only one thing — telling one Lieutenant Hugh Scott to enroll for category four training. Isn't that wild?"

"Makes perfect sense to me." Hedi said it calmly enough, but she shivered. She thought of Mr. J.

"What do you mean?"

"Sounds to me like you're being groomed. Evidently he thinks you show unusual promise."

"I'll tell you this — something weird is going on. The two-star talks to me about what I'd learned in last summer's camp. Believe me, I was framing my replies carefully — I didn't want them changing my orders because something I said sounded too weird. I didn't want them starting to have doubts about my balance, or my judgment."

"A lot like me and my parents."

"Yep. But in my case, it didn't come out the same way. The two-star tells me that when I get back this time, I'm to deliver a verbal report to him and certain of his colleagues. I am to do this prior to submitting a formal report. He said the meeting has already been scheduled for the day of my return."

"Wow!"

"'Wow' is right. But there was a bigger wow. Just before he dismissed me, he remarked that I was not to delete anything in the verbal report just because it sounded a bit far out."

"He knew that's what you'd done after last summer."

"It sure looks that way."

"Which implies that he has a pretty good idea what you're hearing up here."

"It implies a heck of a lot more than that — it as much as tells me that this two-star has a direct line to the Chief. And it wouldn't surprise me if he has been up here for some courses himself."

After a moment, Hedi said, "Hugh, how did you happen to find out about this camp? I know you did your best to wangle a spot up here last summer, but whose idea was it originally?"

"Mine." He paused, thought about it. "At least, the general idea was mine. Scout around, see what's being taught, see if there are any ideas the service could use. I bucked the idea up the line and they went for it."

"But when they went for it, they had their own ideas on where to send you? Or did you pick this place yourself?"

"Well, in due time when the reply came on down the line, they included a list of possible places. I liked this place and a couple of others. I didn't much care which one I wound up at."

"They came back with a list of places. Pretty efficient of them. Hugh, your suggestion — would that be a pretty unusual suggestion, do you know? Or is it the kind of idea that's in the air?"

He shrugged, his eyes not leaving hers. "I don't know anybody else, particularly, who's worrying about the subject."

"But they already had a list of places."

They had stopped walking. Scott set down her bag and stood looking at her.

"Somebody was already thinking along those lines," he said, "you're right. I should have figured that out."

"And then a bright young lieutenant comes up with the same idea, all on his own. And that lieutenant gets his idea approved, he gets to spend the six weeks at a camp on their list, and when he comes back, he finds out that a general is extremely interested in what he has learned. But I'll bet you a doughnut that the general already knew everything you'd seen and heard up here."

Scott was very still. For that matter, so was Hedi herself.

"It must take a lot of money to keep a place like this running," he said thoughtfully.

She looked at him. "What are you thinking?"

"Now you have me wondering if it gets any DOD funding."

"Wouldn't that be a matter of public record?"

"Not necessarily. There are discretionary funds, I'm told. Whatever this camp costs would be petty cash. It would just be a question of whether the Army thought it was worth supporting."

After a minute, he met her eyes again. "Do you know something about all this that I don't know?"

"I just think somebody has his eye on you, Hugh. Didn't you get a sense of that?"

"Well —"

Their eyes met.

After a moment, she said, "I'm not going to ask you the kind of question that I couldn't answer if you asked me, Hugh. So let me just say that for reasons of my own, I get the sense that your future might be of interest to more people than just you."

"But I'd like to know why they want me to concentrate on category four. Disasters with their origin in outer space. Comets? Meteorites?"

"The thing that comes to mind is UFOs," Hedi said. "Do you suppose it's that?"

"Beats me. I've been over all the possibilities, including being bumped by the moon. I just have no idea, and the general did not invite this lieutenant to ask questions."

"Well, I'm in category five, so I suppose I won't be seeing a lot of you on weekdays. Promise me you'll tell me what's going on as soon as you find out?"

"Sure, if I can."

"Oh, that's right. It might be wrapped up in so much secrecy that you can't tell me about it."

He grinned, deliberately breaking their mood. "I just hope it isn't so secret that they won't tell me!"

Hedi and her group spent two weeks examining the implications of category five disasters, working hard on detailed problem solving. The instructor would pose a problem; the class would try to pick it apart, examining its structure, trying to ferret out all the hidden possibilities — good and bad — contained in the scenario.

After some preliminary examination of problems and possibilities, the class would split into teams. Each team worked separately, then the class reassembled and examined what each team had come up with. Then the instructor would change the terms of the problem and they would go through the process again. Time and time and time again. Scenario after scenario, permutation after permutation. From time to time Hedi thought about seeing Hugh, but there was never time. This year, even weekends were filled with work, as though somebody's timetable had accelerated, leaving them hanging on for the ride.

At about 7 p.m. on her second Friday night at the camp, the pattern of her days — and her life — changed. Permanently.

She was walking back to the women's quarters after dinner. The Chief came up from behind her.

"Always working, even on a beautiful evening like this," he said.

She smiled at him. "Working?"

"Weren't you thinking about the reading you still hope to get through tonight?"

"Still reading people's minds. You must save a fortune on telephone calls and postage stamps."

He gave out a low laugh. "Only receiving, I'm afraid. Transmitting I still have to do the old-fashioned way. That's what I am doing right now, in fact. I wanted to say a word to you privately, and I had to pick my moment. You are a very popular young lady."

He held up a hand. "Now, don't argue with what we both know is the truth. What I have to say will take only a moment.

"Tomorrow morning I intend to take a few people out on the launch. I would like you to be among them. There are some people I want you to meet. Can I count on you?"

"To go out on the lake on a beautiful day? Sure."

He smiled. "Don't get your hopes up too far, Hedi. I hope you will find the outing pleasant, but we won't be waterskiing, exactly."

She tried to read his expression. "Well, I'll be happy to go," she said. "I suppose we're having a sea-going seminar?"

"Be on the dock at eleven, Hedi. But don't talk about it, please." He turned off the path, and she continued on her way, wondering.

To her delight, there on the dock at ten of eleven was Hugh Scott.

"Hi, there, Hedi," he said cheerfully. "Working hard?"

"You bet. They're running us ragged in category five. I certainly hope they're doing the same to you space cadets."

He grinned. "I'll tell you, our instructors have come up with every sort of problem you could think of, and then some."

"Not much like a vacation, is it?"

"Not till I got my invitation for a trip on the launch. That's starting to look more like the real thing."

"Speaking of that," she said, looking around, "where is the launch?"

"No idea. Maybe the Chief lined up more than one luxury cruise. You have any idea how many people are coming?"

"Nope. Did the Chief give you the impression we're in for a floating seminar?"

"He didn't give me a clue, but if he's involved in it, you know darn well we're going to wind up working, some way or another." They grinned at each other. "And speak of the devil, here he comes now."

The launch came in smoothly. The Chief was standing in the stern. "Hop in," he said. "No point tying up."

Hugh held Hedi's hand while she stepped over into the stern, and she found herself wishing there was more occasion for him to hand her into boats. The camp discouraged physical contact between students.

Scott jumped in after her, and immediately the skipper began backing the launch out onto the lake again.

Impulsively, Hedi asked, "Aren't we going to wait for the others?"

The Chief shook his head. "Nobody else was invited. Just you two and me, and two to crew the boat, and a friend I'd like you to meet. Please come into the cabin."

"Oh," she said weakly as they followed him. "I knew the launch could seat twenty; I just assumed we'd be in a big crowd."

"We have who we need," the Chief said. "Hedi Johnson, Lieutenant Howard Scott, I would like you to meet my very good friend Max."

Max seemed to be a middle-aged man of some substance. Solid. Impressive, in fact. He radiated ease and quiet self-assurance. Clearly, he was someone who got things done, someone accustomed to being around those others who get things done.

They shook hands all around, and the Chief motioned for them to sit down at a small table near the rear of the cabin.

"Max," the Chief said, "I trust that you have no objections to my speaking for you, for the moment."

"I believe I know what you are about to say. Please proceed."

"Thank you. I'd like to convey to you youngsters the full scope of the honor being done you by my friend here. Max represents a certain government. He has broad powers and commands vast knowledge — he has at his fingertips the largest collection of facts available on earth. On more than one occasion, he has rendered invaluable assistance to me and to the survival camp by sharing his vast store of information.

"I have discussed the two of you with him, and he in return has asked to talk to both of you — that is the honor I spoke of. That's all I have to say. Now this meeting is up to the three of you."

"Mr. Ambassador," Scott asked promptly, "will you tell us what government you represent?"

"Yes, Lieutenant, but first let me explain that I am not an ambassador. I have been honored with the title of Special Envoy to Planet Earth."

Suddenly, very vividly, Hedi saw a sandy beach and an elderly man. "...as time is measured here." "Here?" "On this planet."

Hedi could feel the vibration of the craft as it moved through the water. It's like the day on the beach, she thought. There's something unreal about still feeling the material world around you while you're talking about something that can't be true.

Quite obviously, Scott was unsure how to take the statement.

Logically, it should be a joke; but nothing about the situation had the feel of a joke. "H- how long have you held this position, sir?"

"Since my last major renovation, which according to your calendar occurred in 1942."

Hedi said, "Renovation?!" But Hugh persisted. "And before that, your excellency?"

"Before that I served on earth for 4,897 years as a Senior Representative of the Chief Councilor. In both capacities I have represented The Union of Five Central Planets."

Scott's face mirrored the emotions she herself was feeling: doubt, bewilderment, caution, an uncontrolled if grudging interest.

"My instructions come from the Central Council of the UFCP through whatever channels the Council designates." Max smiled. "As for titles, I prefer that you call me Max."

"Max can be described as a diplomat because he represents a government and speaks on its behalf," the Chief said. "You will notice I never said he represented an earthly government. He represents the people of these five planets. In English, we could call them The Elustreons."

"Whew," Scott said frankly. "This is a lot to swallow all at once."

"You are wondering if this could be some kind of a practical joke," the Chief said matter-of-factly, "or perhaps a test the Army has cooked up to see if you have your feet on the ground. The answer to both questions is — no."

The Chief's eyes went from Scott to Hedi and back again. "I agree — it's a lot to swallow. Perhaps it will facilitate matters if I tell you right now that it is neither. Not a hoax. Not a test. You have my word of honor on that."

Well, as far as Hedi was concerned, that was the end of that. If she couldn't trust the Chief's word, there was no point to anything she had been doing these past 14 months — including her conversations with Mr. J; including her dreams.

She felt a wild impulse to ask Max what the weather was like at home. She swallowed that, and asked, instead, "Sir, how did you get here, and where do you live when on this planet?"

"I was sent here originally on what you would describe as a remote-controlled UFO. My government would describe it as a magnetic field propulsion carrier with auxiliary gravity control. I have no residence on this planet. We have several maintenance and refuge stations in your solar system, the nearest being on the reverse side of your moon. When not working here, I am usually at the moon station waiting orders or reorganizing my constantly expanding library of facts."

Hugh's face furrowed as he tried to absorb what he was being told. "You spend all your time reorganizing facts? That sounds more like work for a librarian than for a diplomat."

"Then I can only say that in this instance appearances deceive. The information I acquire and process is vital to my work."

"Come, Hugh, surely you are aware of the value of accurate, timely information in planning action."

Scott looked at the Chief. "'Action,'" he echoed. "Sir –, I mean, Max, what is your mission on the earth? Are you at liberty to inform us?"

"I certainly am. In fact, to inform you is a definite and not trivial part of my assignment.

"To respond to your very pertinent question: Within the limits imposed by the cosmic laws, the intent of my government is to assist earth's inhabitants to survive the aftermath of the next catastrophic purging, which is likely to occur in the near future."

"It had to be something like that," Hedi murmured. "So you're going to save us from ourselves."

Max turned to her. "No, not as you think. My government has learned from experience over many, many thousands of years, that great care is required when intervening in an evolutionary process. We will not function as your guardian angels. You must listen to the angels provided you."

Analogy? Flat statement? Hedi was about to pursue it, but Scott stepped in.

"So you won't step in to stop us from bringing on a disaster, but you'll help us mop up after it? Is that it?"

"Again, you do not yet have the right idea. Everything depends on what happens, why it happens and how it happens. If the disaster is nuclear war or any other cataclysm within the control of the present generation of earth people, we will not intercede. I am sorry if this seems harsh.

"Neither will we intercede to help those who are not doing all they can to help themselves. This is why we do endorse programs designed to assist in physical survival, even though they may be of limited effectiveness.

"Neither, again, will we intercede if the only result would be survival of physical life. The opportunity must exist for survival of body, mind, and spirit. If survivors are too few in number, they will spend all their energy in the battle for physical existence, and gains made in the realms of mind and spirit will be lost. In such case, we would consider the situation beyond retrieval."

Hugh Scott was ready with another question. "Max, can you tell us what part of your mission refers to the United States?"

Max seemed to be picking his words with care. "My government's mission in the United States is the same as in all other nations, but we do find working here a bit safer and more productive than in most other places. This perception springs from the giant step forward your country took in 1945."

"That can only refer to the atomic bomb," Hugh said, frowning again. "But how does that represent a giant step forward?"

"I refer to your decision not to use the bomb after World War Two ended," Max replied. "In the name of insuring peace, your country could have imposed its will on the entire world. No one else had the atom bomb; no one could have resisted. It was the first time in the history of the earth that any nation passed up anything approaching such a sure bet to rule the world.

"There have been other constructive developments of mind and spirit in many parts of the world that strengthen my government's desire to help, but this was the most telling. Besides, we owe you something for the mistakes our ancestors made and the resulting harm done in the distant beginnings of your evolutionary history."

Hugh pounced on that. "What mistakes?"

But the Chief intervened. "Hugh, if Max says it, you can put it in the bank, but I'm not sure this is the time to go into all that."

"No," Max said. "It isn't. We don't have time."

Hedi had been observing Max closely. Two things were beginning to penetrate her mind.

"Max," she said, "you speak a perfect American version of English. It's a little too perfect. How many languages do you speak? And do you speak them all without an accent?"

"I recognize and speak 17 different tongues that are in active use today," Max said, watching her with interest. "My vocabulary in each language includes a large number of slang expressions, and I speak each without accent."

"I see. I have a second question I hope you won't think too personal. You claim to be nearly 5,000 years old. Is this claim a spoof of some kind, or are you serious?"

"Quite serious, I assure you."

"Well, how does someone your age keep his skin so healthy and free of wrinkles? Your skin has a youthful, healthy tone. It's completely devoid of blemishes. For a man claiming to be 5,000 years old, this seems, uh, rather remarkable."

His serious expression faded into a mischievous smile.

"You asked, but will you believe? The truth is this — my skin is cleaned and treated with special preservatives every fifty years or so by highly skilled attendants at one of our maintenance stations. Once or twice every thousand years it is completely replaced. The workmanship is really quite good. With regard to languages, in this department I truly represent the latest in high technology."

"You talk as though you were a computer," a startled Hugh blurted.

Max smiled at him. "My full name is Maximum Fact Banker," he said. "I am a fully computerized diplomatic robot."

13. The Elustreons
July, Z-Minus-11

"Robot!" For once Hedi's and Hugh's reactions were identical. As she put it later, they sat there trying to remember how to close their mouths again.

Max sat back, clearly enjoying their reaction. The Chief, too, was laughing.

"You two are back to wondering if this is some elaborate joke." He laughed again. "It isn't, although I admit I love the look on your faces right now.

"What I told you earlier is quite true. Max is a true ambassador. Indeed, perhaps a perfect ambassador. He is known only to those he elects to meet. He never expresses his own opinions and thus always states precisely the views of his government. And he is immune to disease of either mind or body. All these are desirable qualities in an envoy, surely?"

But Hedi wasn't listening. She was trying to absorb the reality of what she had been told. She was talking to a robot!

But he still didn't look like a robot. Didn't sound like one. Didn't seem to think like one. He looked just like everybody else.

"Max," Hugh said, "why do the Elustreons send robots to talk with us? Why don't your superiors send living envoys to represent their interests? No offense intended."

Max's smile certainly seemed human. "No offense taken, Lieutenant. Robots do not get their feelings hurt easily."

Hedi wondered if Max was saying that he did have feelings that could be hurt. But she couldn't find a way to pursue the question, nor did it seem the time and the place.

"Your question, Lieutenant, requires some background information if you are to understand the answer.

"The Five Central Planets do not provide a carbon-oxygen system to support the kind of life you have here. There, essentially all oxygen is combined in solid compounds, and carbon is much too scarce.

"Instead, the life-support system of the Elustreons evolved within a silicon-hydrogen system. You might call it the 'silicon/ammonia system', since ammonia is the source of hydrogen. The halides (fluorine, chlorine, and bromine) are also important elements in the

life support process. All plant and animal life depend on this system."
Max paused. "Am I being too technical for you?" he asked.

"You're losing me," Hedi said, "but we hear you. We can figure
out what you're saying later."

"Very well. Other differences need mentioning. For instance, the
temperatures on the surface of the Five Planets are higher than here,
and the normal body temperature of an Elustreon is a steaming 182
degrees Fahrenheit. A friendly embrace from one of their sultry 182
degree maidens would have you on the way to the nearest trauma
center.

"The difference in chemistry also makes living matter look different. There is a tendency toward a translucent appearance, and
the eyes of people sparkle like cut and polished quartz. We think it
is all very beautiful, but you might think it strange to see a shadowy
heart beating through a translucent chest, and one penetrating look
from the brilliant quartz eyes might blind you."

Scott had asked the question, but Max was directing his attention
to Hedi equally.

"You begin to understand the difficulties involved? Living Elustreons would find it unsafe to come here, nor would it serve their
interests to do so."

"That explains why you conceal your activity?"

"It does in part. But there are other reasons. For one thing, it is
the view of my government that we cannot obtain a valid study of
you if you are busy trying to study us. Thus, it is best that most of
you be unaware of our presence. In the distant past the Elustreons
came in person, but now the function is handled better and with
greater safety by the Diplomatic Robot. Much of our study can be
conducted by remote observation or by unmanned vehicles, but
some things require someone who can move among you as though
he were an earth person, someone who can establish trusted contacts.

"Believe me, this policy of robot intermediaries was carefully
considered before adoption. My superiors, after considering the
difficulties involved, found no good alternative.

"Suppose, for example, that the Elustreons were to equip themselves with life support equipment and walk on the earth. Certainly
they could do it, just as you equipped your astronauts to walk on
your moon.

"But can you imagine the attention they would attract on the
streets of your cities? And if the strange-looking creatures inside the
protective apparel could be seen, there would be outright consternation. First would come fear — the authorities would be called upon
to capture or destroy them."

"But presumably the authorities could be alerted in advance," Hugh said. Hedi nodded. Hugh was using his head, as usual.

"But then what? A few might understand, but think of the reactions of the rest. In the interest of science, some would wish to cage them for observation and study. Others would justify dissecting them like laboratory rats to learn what made them tick. Power-hungry dictators would be more than willing to torture them for their advanced technical knowledge. Turned loose among the people, they would face the hazard of having their life-support equipment torn to bits by souvenir hunters. Do not tell me they could secure protection and freedom of movement from a friendly power like your government. You cannot protect your own Presidents from assassins."

"They'd be like civilized people among savages," Hedi said. "But surely they'd be able to assure their own physical safety."

"Of course, the Elustreons are quite able to protect themselves, but they do not wish to hurt anyone if it can be avoided. And, let me repeat, it would work against your own interests and their objectives."

"I guess I don't quite have a full understanding of what those objectives are," Hedi said. "I can't believe they're interested only in helping us get through our troubles."

"You are quite correct, although I would caution you not to undervalue the strength of the altruistic impulse."

"After all, Hedi," the Chief put in, "that's why you're here at camp. Why I am too, for that matter. Altruism is a very underrated motivator."

"The primary reason the Elustreons are in your solar system is to study how beneficial evolution of mind, body and spirit occurs in your world of carbon and oxygen.

"This is all very well," Hugh injected, "but why do you need to study us and our evolutionary processes?"

"It is for a very good cause, but to explain it fully requires the review of many thousands of years of history, and we haven't time to do that. We have a more urgent, a less theoretical task before us."

Max turned to the Chief. "If you don't mind, I would like to communicate with my superiors."

"Sure," the Chief said. "Right here?"

"I think somewhere up in the bow would be better. I shouldn't be long." Max left the cabin, and Hedi and Hugh looked to the Chief.

"As I understand it, Max's superiors monitor everything that transpires while he is in contact with people on planet earth, and, if need be, can provide instructions on a second-by-second-basis."

Hugh said, "How?"

The Chief smiled and shrugged. "Ask him."

Hedi said, "I don't yet see the purpose of this meeting. Was it just that Hugh and I could get to meet Max?"

The Chief cleared his throat. "You should understand that I have told Max certain things that I have otherwise held confidential. Hedi, he knows all about your meeting with Mr. J. Hugh, he knows of your contact with the general."

"Knows more about it than I do, I'll bet," Hugh said wryly.

"Yes. Well, he should — the general is his principal contact in this country."

Hedi and Hugh sat absorbing the implications of that statement.

Max re-entered the cabin. "I am to be picked up at 2:30 p.m. at the north end of the lake," he said. "There will be some fog. Please give your captain the necessary instructions."

The Chief nodded and left. Max immediately began to speak.

"As you see, I have only a limited amount of time. It is time to explain today's meeting.

"My superiors judge that a disaster of magnitude four will soon strike the planet earth. They further judge that the two of you, if you survive, are most likely to play leadership roles in the critical aftermath. The odds on your surviving, you will be interested to know, are rated at almost two chances in three."

"What about the Chief?" Hedi said immediately. "Wouldn't he naturally play a leading role?"

"What about the general?" Hugh said.

"We do not commonly discuss the probable future of a given individual with any other individual. We are making something of an exception in discussing your joint future with the two of you, but that exception cannot be extended to include the discussion of the possible fate of others. Let me put it this way — in the aftermath of a magnitude four disaster, the difficulty will lie not in deciding who is to be leader, but in finding enough competent people to assume the necessary responsibilities."

The Chief re-entered the cabin. "Okay," he said.

Max nodded and continued. "My purpose, Hedi and Hugh, is to satisfy each of you that I am the thing I claim to be, and that I represent an association of planets who will be able to help the earth people in limited but important ways. Should it become appropriate, the UFCP wishes to provide this help through designated contacts acceptable to us and to earth's leaders. Each of you qualify as either a contact or a leader. Please ask me such questions as are needed to satisfy you that I am what I claim to be."

Hugh was ready. "The Chief said you can communicate with your superiors on a second-by-second basis. This suggests that your superiors must be near by."

"Does it?"

"Well, otherwise, even a message travelling at the speed of light would suffer a noticeable delay."

"I am able to communicate with my superiors by means of 'simulated thought transfer.' The people of the Five Central Planets learned to communicate by thought transfer thousands of years ago. Now and then an earth person will learn something of this science. Cheng Tu, for example. However, to the best of our knowledge, I was the first robot in the galaxy to have such capability."

"Are you suggesting that thoughts travel faster than light?" Hugh asked.

"Of course," Max replied. "Everything does, if it is completely free of physical components. In fact, it does not 'travel' at all. What is not located in space may be considered to be everywhere at once."

While Hugh was absorbing that, Hedi stepped in with a question. "You say you are a robot, but I can see your chest rise and fall. Are you breathing? Do you also have a pulse?"

Max held out his right arm, inviting Hedi to feel his pulse. She checked it at the usual wrist location and felt the regular beat of a healthy heart.

"You would also feel it at the other normal check points," Max said. "You see I am most often engaged in presenting myself as a person. The breathing is partly window dressing, but I do use a type of fuel cell as an emergency energy source, and this requires a supply of oxygen. The air introduced into my body by the breathing process is carefully filtered so dust and moisture will not damage my working parts."

"You must be a marvel of mechanical design to move about in such a normal human way," Hugh said. "Is there any way I could have a look inside?"

"Sorry," Max replied, "my mechanism wouldn't like that any better than yours would, and for the same reason — it is busy sustaining itself. My physical structure is an exact replica of a healthy human skeleton."

"You are flesh and blood, then?"

"The material is synthetic, of course, and is stronger than human bones, but otherwise it is an exact copy. Our scientists then synthesized a material with the same characteristics as human muscles. It responds to electrical and chemical signals in the same way as do your muscles, and is attached to the skeleton in the same way and at the same locations as in an earth person."

As an aside, he added, "I am told this was the easy part. The breakthrough came when the scientists finally learned what signals to send to obtain a desired response, and how to time the arrival of multiple signals to several different muscles to obtain a smooth, coordinated movement."

"I can imagine," Hedi said. "If the Elustreons are as different from us as you say, they must have found it quite difficult to synthesize a creature in our image."

"Indeed. Until the idea of the diplomatic robot was conceived, there was no need for such refinements, and robots were designed as specialized mechanical devices, each type efficiently performing certain kinds of tasks. I was the first of the diplomatic robots, and my programmers have allowed me the vanity of expressing a certain amount of pride in this fact."

Hedi repressed a smile, and thought she saw an answering twinkle in his eye. "I have a technical question," she said. "Earlier you told Hugh our law that nothing moves faster than the speed of light does not hold for things having no physical components. You appear to be a very solid physical object; it must have taken a very long time for you to get here."

"It did take a long while, but not nearly so long as you think. You measure time by the ticking of a clock, a device of your own invention. Clock time is useful to you in limited ways, but has no cosmic validity."

She looked at him in bewilderment. "Time is time, no matter how you measure it."

He shook his head, a very human gesture. "Time does not pass; consciousness passes. Physical objects and events are positioned along time lines." Evidently he could see he was losing them. "You measure space as though it were an object having dimensions, but in truth, space is always just large enough to hold the physical events and objects that exist, but no larger. Without those objects and events it is nothing. Thus, you take two false concepts and calculate a rate of motion that is an illusion."

"I don't follow that," Hedi said, baffled.

"One of your problems — by 'you' I mean earth people — is that you travel in a one-dimensioned time that lies like a huge wad of string between you and the object or event you wish to reach. Not only must you travel along miles of string to reach something only a few inches away, but the light you are using to navigate what you believe to be a straight line is also following the same devious path. It is as though the time line also served as an optical fiber. This persuades you that your illusion is not an illusion, but reality.

"Perhaps one day you will learn to navigate in multidimensional time, skipping not only from thread to thread, but also from fold to fold in the fabric of time. Then you can travel directly to the object you wish to reach. Then you can travel with the Elustreons to explore the marvels of cosmic creation."

"I'm sorry," Hedi said, "but I'm lost."

"Me too," Scott said.

"No matter. We are not here to discuss physics."

"In any case, we're out of time," the Chief said, "unless you can stay longer than you'd said."

"No, I'm afraid the time has come for me to leave."

"Are we going to see you again?"

"I do not know. Be assured of this, however. If disaster comes, and if it is appropriate to offer help, an envoy of the Elustreons will be in touch with you. Should this come to pass, please remember me and greet the envoy as a friend. Now stay back with Sam Theos, who will explain to you the manner of my departure."

Max made his way to the small after-deck. A patch of heavy fog swirled about the boat. There was a flicker of light followed by a distinct hum coming from the cloud, a hum more felt than heard. Then the fog lifted and Max was gone.

As the boat turned and started back toward the camp dock, the Chief sat staring at the spot where Max had stood.

"It's amazing," he said to no one in particular.

"It sure is," Hugh said fervently. "I'd love to know how he did that!"

The Chief seemed to come back to the present. "Oh, I wasn't talking about that. I suppose that's amazing, too, the first few times you see it. I was thinking that it's amazing how attached one can become to that machine. You'd think it was alive. It can't express emotions, but it is so polite and considerate, you just have to like it. Max's programmers and his superiors must be pretty nice people."

"Do you think we will ever see him again?" Hugh asked. "Now that he is gone, I have a thousand questions. At least I know why the general wanted me to study category four disasters, but I am afraid I failed to ask Max many of the questions the general would have wanted me to ask."

"Don't worry," the Chief replied, "your general probably only wants to be able to talk to someone."

"I thought you were going to explain the manner of Max's departure," Hedi said to the Chief.

"One of Max's little jokes," the Chief responded. "He knows I can't explain it. I can tell you that the fog is generated so that you cannot see what happens, but I have seen him depart without it."

"What happens?"

"A small vehicle he likes to call his space cab descends silently from above and hovers at a height of about ten feet. A hatch opens in the bottom of the craft, and a cone of dim bluish light projects downward. Unless he is already standing there, Max steps into the center of the cone of light and then seems to float up into the vehicle. Then the hatch closes, and the craft takes off."

"Does it make any noise?"

"Hardly any. You feel a slight hum, maybe."

"It goes straight up?"

"Usually it takes off very quickly in a vertical direction, yes. But it can fly in any direction and has a great range of speeds."

"How big?"

"Not very large, holding perhaps four to eight persons. They come in either a cigar shape or in a squashed spherical shape. I am told that these vehicles are operated by an engineering robot that can also perform a number of maintenance functions."

"And this is what lets them range all over the universe?"

"I am informed that they are built primarily for operation within our solar system, and can attain speeds of up to 45% the speed of light. A few are pressurized and can accommodate a variety of life forms, but I am told that the majority do not carry living creatures and have no need for controlled atmospheres."

"So they can operate anywhere."

"All are very corrosion resistant, apparently, and can operate in temperatures from near absolute zero to over 1200 degrees F. I tell you all of this on Max's authority and with his permission."

Seeing that Hugh was making notes of this technical information, Hedi asked another question. "Do you believe the Five Central Planets exist, and that they are peopled with living creatures like the Elustreons Max described?"

"Yes, I do," Sam Theos responded.

"Have you seen any of the Elustreons?" Hugh asked.

The Chief hesitated. "Apparently they do not appear on earth in physical form since they developed the diplomatic robot some five thousand years ago. Consequently, I have not seen them here."

Chief's careful answer and Hedi's study of parapsychology mandated the next question. "Chief, do they come here in an out of body form?" she asked.

"I am not at liberty to tell you anything more on this subject," the Chief replied.

"Have you ever been there in that form?"

"I am not at liberty to tell you anything on that subject, either," he said.

"Can you tell us the location of the Five Central Planets?" Hugh asked.

"The earth is located well out on one of the great spiral arms of our galaxy," Sam replied. "The Five Central Planets are near the center of this same arm. Perhaps some day you will meet Max again, and he will tell you the ancient history he mentioned; then you may hear about the three inner planets and the space wars waged by their ruthless inhabitants."

"Something to look forward to," Hugh murmured.

"One thing more," the Chief added. "You were not sworn to secrecy by either Max or me, but I would recommend the use of discretion in discussing your experiences of today."

The boat arrived at the dock. "Chief," Hugh said haltingly, "I don't know how to thank you for including me in this expedition."

"Yes, that goes for me too," Hedi said quickly.

"I didn't have anything to do with it. It was Max's request. Naturally, I'm always very pleased when he asks to meet any of my students."

"Does that happen very often?"

The Chief grinned. "Never mind. All you need to know is that when Max asks to meet you, it's because he and the Elustreons see you as having very unusual qualities."

14. Call Me Roy
August, Z-Minus-11

Another Friday, another dinner time. But this time, it was the last Friday of the session, and this time she was still at dinner, and this time it was not the Chief, but Hugh Scott. He came to her table and plopped himself down opposite her, his eyes sparkling with excitement.

"What gives?" she asked. "You look as though you had been invited for a ride in a space cab."

He laughed out of sheer high spirits. "Better ride than that," he said. "Lasts longer, has more ups and downs, extensively time-tested — you can't beat it!"

"Hugh, what in the world are you talking about?"

"I want you to meet somebody tomorrow."

She lowered her voice from instinctive caution. "Somebody out of this world? Somebody we've met before?"

He laughed again. "Out of this world, yes. But you haven't met her. Her name is Mary Aldrich, and she's going to take me for the ride I was talking about; in other words, she's going to marry me."

"Oh," Hedi said. She told herself swiftly that there had never been the slightest romantic tinge to her relationship with Hugh. "Oh, how wonderful for you. She must be somebody special." She hoped she was hitting the right tone. She couldn't be sure.

Perhaps she was. Yes, her best judgment told her that he was taking her reaction at face value. "She is going to make a lot of people jealous, you know."

Hugh seemed to glow, and Hedi thought again how much she

liked him as a friend. Friendship, she told herself sternly, was better in some ways than romance — more dependable, less turbulent. The little twinge she was feeling wasn't possessiveness, she said to herself; she was just concerned that Hugh find someone worthy of him.

"We haven't had much time for talk," she said. "But it's Friday night and the course is almost over, and we're not going to do one bit of studying tonight. So you don't have one thing to do that's more important than telling me the whole story. How long has this been going on?"

Hugh had never been a bit less than proper with Hedi; he had never led her on in any way. Yet now he seemed almost embarrassed. Hedi wondered how much of her complicated reaction he was picking up.

"Since my senior year at West Point," Hugh answered, "but she did not want to get married until she had completed her graduate work at the university. She has surprised me by working hard and cutting the time down by one full semester, so we have set a date in January for the wedding. You must come."

"If the bride invites me, I'll be there," Hedi answered, "but if I were she, I would guard you very carefully."

And so on the last Saturday of the session, Hedi met Hugh Scott's bride-to-be, and that evening had dinner with the radiant young couple. She found herself, unexpectedly, prepared to be quite critical, yet Mary quickly won her over. Mary was physically attractive but not beautiful. Somehow that helped. And, although she had made a record as a brilliant scholar of philosophy and languages, she had a pleasant, outgoing personality, and positively radiated friendly interest in Hedi. In fact, Hedi had to admit, Mary's eyes reflected an inner beauty of mature wisdom not often seen in one of their age.

"I'm not jealous," Hedi told herself. "I just would have hated to see Hugh wind up with anything but the best. And it looks like he has made an excellent match."

Odd, though. Hedi was sincerely happy for them; she liked Hugh and she decided she liked Mary; she had the feeling that marriage was less likely to remove Hugh as a friend than to add Mary as another. Odd that these excellent and quite accurate reflections didn't do a thing to ease the cramped sensation in her chest, the sudden sense of emptiness, of something missing.

Perhaps this had something to do with the way in which, upon her return to Ohio, she threw herself into her work. Her classes, under the expert direction of Dean Curry, were too interesting to be regarded as work, and if the schoolwork was interesting, her experiences as a trainee at the Children's Clinic were nothing short of fascinating.

Here, for the first time in her life, Hedi knew the joy of helping those completely unable to help themselves. She also knew the sorrow of seeing the best efforts of everyone end in failure. She threw herself into her work, and the months flew by.

January, Z-Minus-10

"Is this Hedi?"

"Yes?"

"This is Sam Theos."

"Oh! Chief, this is quite a surprise. Is something wrong?"

"Not a bit of it. I got your letter and this is my way of answering you."

"You didn't have to do that!"

"Has it occurred to you that I might be lazy, and this is easier than writing? Also, I don't mind hearing your voice again after all these months."

She couldn't resist teasing him. "I can see that you must be anxious, or you wouldn't bother with the telephone."

He laughed. "I see you haven't been changed by life in what they call 'the real world.' And from your letter, I gather that you are head-over-heels in love with work and school alike. No time for social activities."

"You saw me at Hugh Scott's wedding."

"Oh, sure, but how much fun have you had lately?"

"Why, Chief, don't you want me to do well at my profession?"

"Of course I do, Hedi. But speaking for the moment as an honorary Dutch uncle, I'll remind you that all work and no play makes Jack a dull boy, and probably doesn't do Jill much good either."

"Well — I hear what you're saying, but I don't think I'm working too hard and anyway I don't see what I can skip. I'm just sorry I haven't been able to make more time for other things. As it is, I don't see my parents except on holidays, and a weekend every now and then. And I'm really sorry I haven't been able to make time for any of your seminars."

"So your letter said. That's one of the reasons I'm calling, to tell you not to worry about it. The training you are receiving where you are is likely to be quite as useful as anything you could learn at my camp."

She was delighted. "Are you sure?"

"I certainly am. After you complete the work for your Master's degree, and for your license as a medical assistant, then we can talk about what comes next."

Feb. 23

Dear Hugh and Mary,

Big day for me! I got the word yesterday that I passed the state exam, and so now am licensed to practice as a Medical Assistant in Psychiatry. (Thus endeth four years of college, nine months of graduate school and six months of practice. Clearly this is the end of my education: Surely I have now learned everything that can be reasonably expected.)

Then today Dr. Exter invited me to lunch. Between a bunch of compliments that I am much too modest to repeat (but will remember syllable by syllable!) he told me that my basic training is over. 'Most of what you will learn in the future will come from experience,' he said, and I think he's right. When it comes to teaching you something, nothing matches real life.

Anyway, he said he'd talked to the Clinic's director and to the Chairman of the Board of Directors, and they'd agreed to his offering me a permanent job!

Do you know what he said was important? What he called my 'genuine concern for the patient's welfare.' He said such concern comes through to the patient, and sometimes is more valuable than all other treatments in effecting a cure. Well, I can certainly see how that would be true, but wouldn't you think that every trainee would have that concern? I certainly assumed so, but maybe not.

Really, it was all very flattering. He apologized for the fact that, being a charitable agency, the clinic couldn't offer as much money as I could get elsewhere! As if I could find another place where I could learn as much and gain so much satisfaction!

He told me to take my time and think about it, but I'd already discussed the question of where to work with Uncle Jake. Naturally, with his connections, he'd been able to find me the range of pay and working conditions in Columbus, Cleveland and Cincinnati. Whenever I asked him what I should do, though, he always refused to answer. "It's your life, kid, and you have to make the decision," he says. "You will find people everywhere who need your help. Some will have more money than others, but they will all need help."

The only definite suggestion he ever makes is that I consider whether or not to go for the Senior Medical Assistant rating and, if so, which doctor I'd want as supervisor during advanced training. Not much help, huh? Or maybe it was. I decided to take the clinic job and go for the Senior Medical Assistant rating, with Dr. Exter supervising. I admire him so much! Sometimes I marvel at my luck in getting to work with this brilliant diagnostician working at the frontier of applied psychiatry.

So that settles that. But as soon as one thing gets settled, something else seems to pop up to take its place. As soon as I got back home, I started having that same dream again, the one I told you about long ago Hugh, the time I told you about Mr. J. Mary, I don't know if you remember, but Hugh will, and can tell you.

I don't know if there's anything psychic about it, but I feel a growing need to re-establish contact with the remarkable people we met at the Chief's survival training school. I guess my first official act at the clinic is going to be to ask for time off — without pay, I suppose, if necessary — and then ask the Chief if I can revisit a certain camp in the Maine woods.

My sister Martha had some pretty important career news, too. She has been accepted by the University of Texas graduate school. Not only that: She has landed a job this summer, starting just three days after she graduates Dartmouth, as a junior reporter for a Houston newspaper.

You will remember, Hugh, that Martha chose Dartmouth University because she loves New England and also, maybe mainly, because her friend Jane Adams was going there and wanted her to do so too. She and Jane had met at a church camp when they were sixteen, and had stayed friends. They visited each other at every opportunity.

That friendship has worked out very well for Martha. Jane's father is a power in Vermont politics, and I gather he also exerts considerable influence in neighboring states and even across the border in Canada. He's quite well off, so he can do pretty much as he pleases. He apparently prefers being king-maker to running for office himself. Martha tells me he is very close to the Governor of Vermont and his staff.

Well, since Jane often spent weekends and holidays at home, and Martha frequently went home with her (Ohio being a little too far for weekend jaunts!) Martha has gotten to meet many of the region's political figures in the past few years, and it is clear that Mr. Adams has become very impressed with her. He can see her intelligence and beauty, her ambition and determination. She's someone who knows what she wants and has a plan for getting it, and he admired that. (I trust she never sees this letter, or there'll be no living with her!)

He helped her get interesting summer jobs to help her relate her studies to the real world. The summer after her freshman year, she worked in the city editor's office of a medium-sized newspaper. Then a letter of introduction from Mr. Adams helped her land work as a sidewalk reporter with a TV station news team. Last summer, following her junior year, she got to work as a temporary assistant to the Vermont governor's Executive Assistant for Public Affairs. Since this gentleman was in the process of switching to his election-year role as the governor's campaign manager, Martha was exposed to the art of communicating ideas and images — quite a different world, she says, from the simple reporting of facts. And now this summer she's to work for a big paper and then start grad school.

She'll be home in August for a few days before school starts, and I expect I'll see her then. Hopefully I'll be just back from the Maine woods.

Hope all is well with you two. Somebody write and tell me the news.

Sincerely,
Hedi

August, Z-Minus-10

In early August of Hedi's first year as a licensed medical assistant, the winds of change began to blow.

She had spent busy months working with seriously disturbed children. To her the work was an exciting challenge, and nothing fascinated her more than listening to Dr. Exter lead her deeper and deeper into the marvels of the brain and the mysteries of the human mind. Bearing in mind the Chief's admonition about all work and no play, she had made more time for recreation and social affairs, and so her circle of friends grew wider. She was invited to parties, and gave parties in return. She went to concerts, movies, lectures, the theater, and amusement parks with men and women of her own age.

Often they went in groups, and many of the couples were married. At other times she went out with one of her female friends, but just as often it was with some young man who invited her.

There was never a shortage of admiring young men, some interested in the quick mind and sparkling personality, some in the beautiful body. Most of these young men were entirely acceptable males according to the standards of the day, but there was no one she felt she could talk with about her experiences of the last four years.

Many young men eagerly took her home in the evening and reluctantly told her good night in the foyer of her apartment house, but there was no one she really wanted to ask up for a cup of coffee. As she considered the activities and priorities of most other young women she knew, Hedi began to wonder if there was something wrong with her.

But Sam Theos had responded to her letter with a wonderful offer.

"I am arranging for a panel of medical experts to lead a one-week seminar on health problems that would arise in the aftermath of a major catastrophe," he had said. "Would you like to serve as my assistant in organizing and conducting the meetings?" He included an invitation to stay another week and participate in his annual series of open discussion sessions with members of his teaching staff and a few selected advanced students.

Hedi had immediately called her supervisor at her home and asked to take vacation beginning with the last full week in August. Permission granted. She had then called Sam long distance to accept his offer. She figured that the rest of the month would be a matter of waiting out the time until she could leave for the camp.

But one Friday morning (she noticed, later, that many important things happened to her on Fridays, for some reason) Dr. Exter called her at work to announce that he had been delayed by an emergency request from the police.

"There is one thing I would appreciate your doing, if you have time," the doctor said. "I have an appointment to meet a Doctor Johnson at the Clinic at 11 a.m. He is interested in seeing what we do, and afterward he is taking me to lunch and giving me his pitch for a very interesting project he has been promoting in Cleveland. If you would apologize for me and show him around the Clinic, I would appreciate it. Tell him I should be there in time to have lunch with him."

"I'll be delighted to do it," Hedi replied. How delighted, she had no way to know.

Doctor Johnson arrived on time. He was much younger than she had expected — about thirty, she guessed. He exuded energy and purpose, and she put him down as the action type rather than the philosopher. Not bad looking either.

Hedi's supervisor served him coffee along with her usual concise description of the Clinic's history, purpose, professional and volunteer staff, and financing. When she had finished and had dealt with the young doctor's questions, she turned him back over to Hedi. "Our very competent medical assistant in Psychiatry will show you around," she said. "You might persuade her to let you meet some of the children Dr. Exter and she are treating."

As they walked about the Clinic, Hedi introduced him to whatever staff members they chanced to encounter and to some of the mentally disturbed children. In each case she outlined in advance the child's history and the current medical assessment of the problem. She had decided not to risk upsetting little Sammy by confronting him with a stranger. Sammy understood more than most of the staff gave him credit for, and Hedi knew he would be expecting Dr. Exter. He was not likely to accept a substitution. Suddenly she changed her mind. The visiting doctor seemed interested in the work she was doing and knowledgeable about problems of the mind.

"There is one more patient I would like you to meet, Doctor Johnson. Currently he is my very special patient."

"Then by all means take me to him, but first a question," he replied. "Do you prefer that I call you Ms. Carlton?"

"Most people just call me Hedi," she answered, wondering why her face felt so flushed.

"Most people call me Roy," he replied.

Hedi turned away from him and began describing the tragic case of little Sammy. He would think she was blushing like a high school girl, she fumed silently, and of course that was ridiculous. Aloud she heard herself describing how Sammy was involved in an auto accident one dark rainy night.

"His mother and father both died before rescue teams could pry open the smashed car and get them out. Shielded by his mother's body, Sammy suffered severe cuts and bruises, but he survived.

"That is, he survived physically. At the time, he was one year old and beginning to talk in sentences. Now he's two, and he hasn't uttered one word since that terrible night when he was rescued from a pool of his mother's blood." Her voice broke.

Dr. Johnson was following her closely. "Does he ever cry?"

"Very rarely. And he never talks or laughs. Only his eyes show expression. Recently I've thought those eyes have smiled at me, but probably not."

"He knows you care," Dr. Johnson said.

Hedi started. "That's what Dr. Exter says." She hurried on. "But most of the time his eyes and his little bruised mind are reliving that night when his parents had left him all alone. Over and over again, the sounds, the sights, and the pain of it all. I'm sure of it." She could feel a tear filling her eyelid. She willed it not to spill over onto her cheek. "Let's go in and meet Sammy."

Sammy's eyes were on the door when they walked in. He followed their every move as they approached his playpen. "Dr. Exter couldn't come today, Sammy, but he has promised to see you tomorrow," Hedi explained. She hugged the child and set him back down. "I have brought another nice doctor to see you today," she continued. "His name is Dr. Johnson.... Dr. Roy Johnson."

"I see someone's eyes smiling," Dr. Johnson said gravely.

Sammy grasped the side of the playpen and pulled himself to a standing position. His eyes regarded them solemnly; then they smiled again, and this time the smile spread ever so faintly across his entire face.

"I saw that," said a voice behind them. Dr. Exter came in and shook hands with his younger colleague. "Hedi and I have been working for six months to get a reaction like that."

"Just lucky," Dr. Johnson said. "I happened to be nearby when he caught sight of your assistant, that's all. Right, Sammy?"

They visited with the little boy for about 20 minutes. Hedi had never seen him so responsive.

"Your visit seems to have done him good," Dr. Exter said.

"Then I will be back often," Roy Johnson promised.

"Sorry I was late," Dr. Exter said. "If you've seen the Clinic, I suppose we should go to lunch. Do you mind if Hedi comes with us? She has been busy all morning doing my work, and we can all celebrate Sammy's accomplishment."

"Thank you," Hedi interrupted, "but there is work here that I must do. Maybe some other time."

Next morning, Hedi waited for Dr. Exter's arrival with more than normal eagerness. She was in her tiny office updating medical records when he appeared at the door. "Don't get up," he said. "I am going to scrounge a cup of coffee from Eunice and come back for a word with you before we make the rounds."

She hastily put away her files, and was once more reviewing the questions she wanted to ask, when Dr. Exter returned with two cups of coffee. "Eunice had just finished brewing a fresh pot," he said, pulling up the only extra chair in her office.

"I need the coffee," he continued. "That young eager beaver not only bent my ear for an hour over lunch, he also talked me into another two-hour session last night. Let me thank you again for your help. He was very much impressed with the work of the Clinic; he was even more impressed with its staff."

"What did he say?" Hedi asked, trying hard to sound calm. Dr. Exter, she thought, was looking at her with a touch of suspicion.

"You will have to ask him," he said. "I can tell you one thing. Your decision to have him see little Sammy was an act of providence. He said your description of the case, the way you treated the boy, and the way Sammy reacted to you almost reduced him to tears."

"It seemed like an act of providence to see Sammy smile," Hedi replied. "Why do you think that happened on the occasion of Roy's... I mean Dr. Johnson's visit?"

"Maybe Sammy sensed a special bond."

"What do you mean?"

"Roy Johnson lost both of his parents in an automobile accident when he was in college. They were returning home after taking him to school at the start of his sophomore year. It happened fifteen miles from the nearest hospital. There was a delay in locating an available ambulance, and they didn't arrive at the hospital for more than an hour. Both were DOA."

"Oh, how horrible for him!"

"He is convinced their lives would have been saved if they had received expert care thirty minutes sooner. He is determined to build a state-of-the-art emergency medical system. Probably that accident has a lot to do with his determination."

Apparently Dr. Johnson — Roy — was having trouble nailing down support in Cleveland.

"That community has already invested a great deal of money in health facilities of all kinds, including the modern emergency clinic where he serves as medical director and general surgeon. He has been able to sell his ideas, but the consensus opinion is that the project will have to wait a few years.

"He has already secured support for most of the needed capital from three charitable foundations, and they would accept any one of several cities as a suitable location. But they do demand strong operating support from local governments, plus enthusiastic participation from the medical community. Dr. Johnson is busy trying to find out if Columbus would provide the needed support."

"Why would he come first to seek support and advice from a psychiatrist?" she inquired.

"I suppose he figured a psychiatrist would have a pretty young medical assistant," Dr. Exter laughed.

"I'd like to hear more about his plan," Hedi said.

"I wouldn't be surprised if he tells you some day," the wise old doctor replied.

And so Hedi spent an aimless Sunday. She went to church, she called her parents as a substitute for the weekend visit she had promised earlier, but for some reason she seemed unable to concentrate on anything. She felt she was just waiting for something to happen.

At seven Monday morning, the phone rang and the venerable doorman announced that he had a message for her. Would Miss Carlton pick it up, or should he send it up when the eight o'clock shift came on duty? Miss Carlton opted to pick it up. Hoping she would not meet anyone on the way, she grabbed her best dressing gown and headed for the elevator.

She tore open the message on her way up on the elevator. The message was brief.

> Miss Hedi Carlton:
> Will be back in Columbus this Friday. Am inviting you and Dr. Exter to dinner at seven o'clock at the Hilton. Dr. Exter indicates his willingness to decline unless you require him as chaperon. Please advise. . . please.
> Roy

Hedi had a lot of trouble fitting the key into the lock of her apartment door, and wondered why. She sat down to write her response:

"Dr. Exter must make his own decisions, but Hedi Carlton accepts."

15. Friday Night Date
August, Z-Minus-10

Roy picked up Hedi at 6:45 Friday evening. When they arrived at the Hilton, Dr. Exter was waiting in the lobby.

"As I promised," he said to Roy, "I will have a drink with you, and then be off. Your company would be a pleasure for an old man, but you have no need of me, and I do have other things to do. I hear that your project is receiving quite a bit of support in the Columbus community."

Hedi could feel a pleasant little shiver run up her spine. It would be nice to have this fascinating young doctor stationed permanently in Columbus.

Dr. Exter looked at her. "Why don't you ask him the question you asked me?" But he gave her no chance to speak. "She wanted to know why you came first to see a psychiatrist. I told her you could tell her better than I could. Mainly because I'm not sure I know myself."

Roy did not hesitate. "Every minute of every day people require emergency treatment for all sorts of life-threatening conditions. To provide this treatment, we not only have regular hospital facilities, but also many well-equipped emergency clinics. But that leaves two deficiencies in the system."

He was directing his attention at them, yet he almost seemed to have left them, so intent was he on his vision. "First, too many people die before they reach the emergency treatment facility. Second, virtually all of the medical attention is centered on physical injuries.

"In cases like little Sammy, the really serious injury has been mental or emotional damage. We need trained persons on the scene who can spot this kind of injury and administer first aid. Then we need the expert psychiatrist or psychologist on call to follow up and provide full professional care when indicated."

He warmed to his subject even more. "If there is physical damage to the brain, we call on skilled brain surgeons, and that's all to the good. But equally serious emotional damage often goes unnoticed and untreated. Take the driver who perceives himself to be at fault in a fatal auto accident. He may not have a scratch on him, and yet have such severe guilt feelings that they destroy him. These feelings may go untreated until one day he is found hanging from a rafter, dead by his own hand. I think some of that could be prevented. It's all a matter of paying attention to what needs to be done."

True to his word, Dr. Exter had a drink with them and chatted for awhile, then told them to go claim their table and went on his way.

"A great man," Roy said of him after he left.

"He certainly is. And he's a great person to work for, too. He's brilliant. And he's so dedicated, he makes everybody around him work twice as hard, just trying to match half of the energy he's putting out."

They discussed the menu and placed their orders and made small talk. Roy seemed totally focused on anything she said. It occurred to her that such total attention from other young men she had dated would have made for an uncomfortable evening. But for some reason, she felt totally relaxed, even a bit euphoric.

"You have no idea how happy I am that you came tonight," he said abruptly. "I want you to tell me everything about yourself, from the very beginning, from the time your parents first met."

"You first", she said. "I'm the old-fashioned type. When danger lurks, I think the male should lead the way."

He was amused. "What danger?"

"From the day I was born, my mother has warned me that when the male invites the female to talk first, and about herself, danger lies just around the corner."

"You are spoofing me," Roy laughed, "but have it your way. Now what is it you want to know?"

"Please believe I really do have a genuine interest in your crusade for a state-of-the-art emergency health care system. The little I have heard is exciting. I would like to hear the rest."

"Hmm. Smart, as well as lovely. You know I love to talk about my work, and you also know it is a safe subject. Hedi Carlton, could it be you are afraid of your own emotions?"

She opened her mouth to protest, but he cut her off. "No, don't answer that. You have asked me to talk about one of my two greatest interests, and you are going to have to listen to a lot of talk."

Indeed there was a lot of talk. Between courses, even between bites, Hedi listened to an enthusiastic man talk about the dreams he wanted to make happen. He drew word pictures of his visions for her inspection:

* Modern physical facilities equipped to perform all of the usual and many of the unusual emergency medical procedures.

* A group of participating area and regional hospitals, picking up where the emergency treatment center left off.

* Full-time administrators, general surgeons, physicians, medical

assistants, nurses, and other technicians, including some versed in psychology and psychiatry.

    * Highly skilled professional specialists on call, for the really tough problems.

    * A fleet of emergency vehicles designed to reduce to a minimum those dreaded Dead On Arrival reports.

    "You know, the conventional well-equipped ambulance will do for problems that aren't immediately life threatening — these I'd designate as Class A vehicles. But we ought to have other kinds of vehicles, too, at least twice the size of the regular ambulance. They'd carry special equipment to rescue victims trapped in wrecked cars, or vehicles that had fallen into deep water." (Hedi thought of what she'd heard about the accident that had killed Roy's parents.) "I think of these as Class AA vehicles. They'd be able to deal with a variety of rescue and life support problems. Their drivers could communicate with police, fire, and military organizations. If necessary they could call in rescue helicopter teams."

    The waiter appeared with their coffee. Roy scarcely paused. "Back at the Emergency Center, each shift dispatcher would be on assignment from either the city or state police traffic control group, and he would be given special paramedic training so that he could better understand the reports and requests coming to him from the field.

    "Finally, I'd set up what I call the Class AAA mobile field unit. It would be a small hospital on wheels, about the size of a large inter-city bus. It could take off on short notice to the scene of a major accident and remain there for hours or days, if need be."

    "How would you staff it? You wouldn't want to assign a medical team to the triple-A unit full-time, would you? You waste a lot of their time when nothing was happening."

    "Absolutely right. No. What I thought we could do is fly medical personnel to the scene by chopper, or take them by car with a police escort. Then, if you had a major disaster like a train wreck, several of these mobile hospitals could be sent to the scene and the medical staff could catch up with them as soon as possible. By taking the treatment to the patient, we can often cut the critical delay time in half."

    He looked at her so earnestly that she wondered if he fully remembered who he was talking to.

    These were the main features, and all through dinner he went on to clothe them with the details his experience had shown to be of such critical importance when the chips were down and a life hung on the tick of a clock. The more he spoke, the more her admiration grew.

    Suddenly he stopped. He leaned forward and spoke softly. "Don't look now, Miss Carlton, but we are almost the only folks left. Do you think that might have something to do with the unusual attention we're getting from the waiter?"

Hedi laughed. "I suppose he wants to go home. Let's oblige him."

In the cab en route to Hedi's apartment, Roy apologized for monopolizing the conversation. "But it's your fault," he said teasingly. "I gave you the chance to talk about yourself, and you didn't take it."

"No regrets," she said, equally lightly. The back seat of a taxicab led to much greater proximity than the opposite side of a table in a restaurant, and made her aware that she would have to make a decision soon. "I was fascinated."

"I actually believe you," he said. "But that was only one of my two major interests in life. I wonder if you would have been equally fascinated with the other?"

"I'm sure I would. What is it?"

For what seemed a full minute, he said nothing. Then he said, "The other one is you, Hedi Carlton, and it is only fair that you know I intend to marry you."

She felt a kind of throbbing in her temples and wondered why it was so hard to breathe. She was unable to say anything intelligent. The cab driver's ears were swiveled backward a full 180 degrees. Fortunately they had arrived at the entrance to her apartment building.

"Can I stick around long enough to see how this comes out?" the driver asked.

"Not with the meter running," Roy answered as he paid the fare.

Great line, Hedi thought. Very clever under stressful circumstances. But then, that's what should be expected of a doctor, surely.

She could think of nothing to say. They entered the foyer, and she sat down in the small lobby near the elevators to collect her thoughts. He stood by silently, waiting for her to speak.

"First dates can be full of surprises," she ventured, "and I've had a variety of suggestions from a number of different men, but I've never had marriage proposed so early in the game. I must say it tends to flatter and disarm a girl. I don't know what to say."

"I haven't asked you to marry me... not yet. I only said I intended to. Before I ask you if you will marry me, I want you to know me and like me. I hope to earn your respect, and then I hope that you will discover that you love me. Then I'll ask you."

He smiled. "You see, I don't want to ask a lot of questions prematurely and get you in the habit of saying no."

"Either you are feeding me the best line I ever heard, or you are the most unusual man I know," she said. "It is hard to believe you are serious."

"Never more serious in my life," he replied. "I have thought of little else since I toured the Clinic with you a week ago."

"You had better come up and let me fix you a cup of coffee," Hedi heard herself saying. "We have a lot more talking to do."

As they got on the elevator, he took her hand and squeezed it tightly, but nothing was said until she opened the door to her three-room apartment. "I assume I can trust you to behave," she said.

"You can trust me to have the best intentions of behaving," Roy replied, "but don't trust those intentions too far. You are a most desirable woman."

Again she felt strange, as if she might be turning to putty. She fled for the safety of the kitchen. "Sit down and make yourself comfortable while I fix the coffee," she said over her shoulder.

Martha got home before Hedi, and as soon as she opened the door, she wanted to know what had happened. "I can see that something has happened."

"Oh, Martha," Hedi cried, "I do believe I have found him. I should say he has found me, but it doesn't matter. But I'm so afraid I'm going to lose him."

"You just met him. Why should you right away think you're going to lose him?"

"Because I'll be going to camp at the end of next week, and, when I return, I've promised to tell him what the survival training camps are all about and why I attend them. And when he hears the whole story, he's going to think I'm weird, and then I'll lose him for sure."

"Well," said the ever-practical Martha, "sooner or later he'll have to know, and whenever that is, he'll have to decide for himself, won't he? Unless you want to just give up the survival school stuff."

"Martha, I can't."

"Then what choice do you have? You're just going to have to take your chances on him understanding."

"That's a lot of help."

Martha shrugged. "It's the truth. I'll tell you what, though — if I were you, I'd worry more about going away and leaving him in limbo for two long weeks. There must be a gaggle of pretty nurses flitting about him all of the time."

Hedi hadn't thought of that. She looked at Martha in dismay.

"Perhaps I should go up and sit on him until you get back," Martha said innocently. "You know, just to protect your interests."

"Perhaps you should keep your cotton-picking fingers off him, little sister of mine. I would likely get back and find both of you gone."

"Who is going to be gone?" Nora Carlton said. "Hi, honey." She gave Hedi a hug.

"Hedi has found her perfect man," Martha told her mother, "and she won't let me near him while she is away at camp."

"Hedi is a smart girl," her mother said. "Tell me more."

That night, after their parents had gone to bed, Hedi and Martha sat up and talked until far into the night. Consequently, on Sunday morning Hedi fell asleep in church for the first time since she was a junior in college.

Again she was having a vision, but this time it wasn't an old man on an Atlantic beach that she saw. It was a handsome young knight in a doctor's white coat and a surgeon's mask, sitting astride a snorting ambulance and charging through heaps of wrecked automobiles. He was just about to sweep the pretty blonde damsel off the railroad crossing in the very nick of time....

Martha's elbow poked her in the ribs. "If you must talk in your sleep," she whispered, "please speak up. Some of the congregation can't hear you."

16. Who is Sam Theos?
August, Z-Minus-10

"**S**o glad to see you. It has been a long time," the Chief said, putting an arm around Hedi's shoulders and giving her a big squeeze. "Tell me what has happened to you since last you were here. What's the name of the fortunate young man?"

Hedi blushed. "How do you know there is any young man?"

"From the stars in your eyes."

"You don't see any stars, it's just that you're always reading my mind. His name is Roy. Dr. Roy Johnson."

The Chief's smile broadened. "Now tell me, which is more difficult, seeing stars or reading minds? I knew the stars were there, and I'll tell you *how* I knew.

"Last night I went for a walk down by the lake, as usual. At around midnight, I looked toward the clearing and saw this beautiful angel standing in the starlight, her face lifted up to the heavens. Then I saw two stars fall from the sky: one into each of her eyes.

"Since she was an angel, I didn't think it was all that unusual, but then when I saw you this morning I knew the angel was Hedi Carlton. I looked in your eyes, and sure enough, there were the stars."

"What a beautiful romantic white lie," Hedi exclaimed. "You

should write love stories. Perhaps I should check for stars in your eyes, too."

The Chief smiled. "I confess to a love mate," he said, "but not present on the earth. Seeing you under the stars last night reminded me how wonderful the time will be when I can be with her again."

"You leave me speechless," Hedi said.

"I doubt it," he said drily.

"You sound like Hugh," she said.

"Intentionally. Hugh Scott is a pretty sensible sort, wouldn't you say? Feet on the ground? Knows what's what?"

"Sure."

"Well? *He's* convinced."

"You're reading my mind again," she said. "Last night when I got here, I unpacked my bag and got ready for bed, and then, even though it was late, I wrapped a robe around myself and went out on that nice old- fashioned veranda, because you can see the lake from there. It was such a lovely clear, moonless night. I could see so many stars! When you live in the city, you forget how many stars there are when you're away from skyglow.

"I settled into one of your nice cane-bottomed rockers, and for the first time I felt like I had time to think. An awful lot has happened to me recently."

"Some excitement has entered your life."

She smiled. "I already had plenty of excitement. When you start getting visions of the earth coming apart, and then you meet somebody like Mr. J, you aren't exactly starving for excitement."

"But this is different."

"It sure is! This is absolutely spine-tingling. But it's as much worry as happiness, I think."

"Happiness because —?"

"Because I found Roy, of course. As you know full well."

"And worry because —?"

"Because suppose when he finds out about all this he thinks I'm weird?"

The Chief's expression was uncharacteristically somber. "As far as you know, right at this moment he is very interested in you?"

"He called me every night before I left Columbus."

"And I presume he knows where you were going."

She nodded.

"Well, did you talk to him about the camp?"

"He knows it is a survival training camp, and he knows it will last two weeks. But that's all he knows. In fact — "

"In fact?"

"He agreed not to call me, but he did ask me to get permission for him to fly up on the final Saturday, after the conference is over. He wants to see the place and he wants to meet you." She smiled shyly. "He's heard a lot about Sam Theos."

"So he is willing to investigate, but you are a little bit afraid that he won't understand, or won't approve."

"Well, yes. I mean, I hope he understands, and I hope —"

The Chief motioned her to silence. "I know. But you are at a point of decision, Hedi. It had to come sooner or later. It has come now.

"When we believe something not widely recognized by society at large, we can, for greater or lesser periods of time, keep our beliefs to ourself and appear to conform to what is seen as normal. We can compromise, in short.

"But if society remains unpersuaded, at some point we may be forced to choose between dying to our beliefs or dying to at least a portion of society. This is rarely an easy moment. Well, if he wants to come here at the end of the second week, I look forward to meeting him. Permission granted."

"But—"

"You are afraid of what he will think. I know. It has to be faced sooner or later."

She hesitated, searching.

"There isn't any doubt in my mind that Roy is going to ask me to marry him. He can make important decisions quickly — that's why he is so very good at his job. Patients don't die in his clinic while he tries to make up his mind what to do."

"But —"

"Well, I know that it's important that I don't hold anything back that might cause trouble between us in the future."

"Absolutely right."

"Well, that's what was on my mind last night. I felt like I needed help, so I did what I always do when I need help. I prayed. I asked God to guide me and give me courage."

"And that's when you walked out into the clearing in front of the building and looked up at the North Star."

"I wasn't particularly meaning to. My eyes just seemed to find it on their own. I was wondering how many persons it had guided to their destination. And as I watched, it winked at me. At least, that's what it looked like. I mean, I know stars are supposed to wink at everyone all of the time, but this time — well, it was like it was winking just for me. Then I was able to go inside and go to sleep."

"And did you sleep well?"

She smiled, a reflection of her relief the previous night. "Nothing but pleasant dreams."

The Chief asked her to meet him and Madge, his secretary, for breakfast the following morning. There he introduced her to a young man — perhaps a year or so older than Hugh Scott — named Ho Sun. He gave off an air of quiet confidence. Hedi was to find that Ho Sun did not talk a lot, but could be eloquent when he did have something to say.

"He is one of my brighter young advanced students," the Chief said proudly. "First one I've ever had from China." Officially a graduate student in geology, Ho Sun was actually in America as a representative of his government, which was very interested in the training camp.

"Ho Sun will handle the questions and requests of the panel members and guests relating to their physical requirements," he said. "Hedi Carlton will serve as secretary to the meeting. She will see that the necessary written material is distributed, and she will edit the minutes and the transcript of the meeting from draft material prepared by the regular office staff." He poured himself some coffee, and looked over at Hedi. "As a practical matter, this means you will be working hand in glove with Madge. My private secretary," he explained to Ho Sun. "Madge, coffee? Hedi? Ho Sun?"

Hedi was glad to hear that she would be working with Madge. Maybe now she could get some inside information about Sam Theos. Madge was rumored to know more about him than anyone else in camp. Unfortunately, she was also said to be the soul of discretion.

"All right, let's review the program." He buttered some toast, took a forkful of scrambled eggs and washed down the eggs with coffee.

"This first week's panel is for advanced students. Next week, after the students have left, we'll run the panel's findings up against a few people more. Few, but important beyond their numbers.

"We've lined up six technical experts for the panel. Two are public health officers experienced in dealing with epidemic-scale disease problems around the world. One is an expert in the field of medical equipment development. One specializes in tracking the latest advances in surgical procedures."

He took another sip of coffee. "The remaining two are in fields potentially even more important than the others. They have been conducting research in immunology, with special emphasis on the human immune system.

"I have asked them to assume that a series of natural disasters wipe out 60 percent of the earth's population in three weeks. Half of those remaining die before the end of the first year: starvation, exposure, disease, mob violence...." He let his voice trail off.

"The potential is high for much vicious fighting for possession of things needed for survival or for power."

"It is indeed, Ho Sun. Of course, in some areas, order will be quickly re-established. But in others, chaos and anarchy will reign."

"Followed quickly by dictatorial leadership established by brute force."

"Unfortunately true. In time, I think necessity will require local governments to unite under national banners, or even under a world government." He looked around him to stress what he was about to say. "The nature of the new world that rises from the rubble of the old will depend on the priorities established by these governments. That's part of the panel's job: to establish priorities within the medical domain for the preservation and application of existing resources."

Madge said, "Besides the six experts, how many students are we expecting for this panel?"

"Seventy-five. Mostly advanced students, with a few other interested persons I've invited. Hedi, your notes will have to be very detailed — you'll need them to produce a complete transcript of the proceedings."

Hedi swallowed at the thought of the responsibility she would bear, and she wondered about the identity of those "other interested persons." Wondered, but didn't wonder very long. "I thought we were going to tape the proceedings," she said in dismay.

"We will, and of course you'll have access to them to check your notes. But I think you'll find that a running outline of the discussions helps you immeasurably when it comes time to summarize a long session. If you don't do it as it happens, you wind up having to do it later anyway, getting it from the tape. Inefficient, and you are unlikely to do as good a job."

He finished his coffee. "While you're playing with those tapes, by the way, you might pick out a couple of the better ones and send copies to your young man. He might begin to get a feel for this place that way before he comes out."

"Thank you for the idea," she said happily. "I will. You are the second nicest man I ever met."

"Self interest, my dear. In the back of my mind is the hope that I can get him interested in this place, if I can show him something of what goes on here."

What went on there was chiefly work. Hedi spent evenings working with Madge on transcripts, and over the first weekend she and Madge worked on transcript and minutes both. When they paused for lunch on Saturday, she asked Madge if she ever did anything but work.

"Not when Sam is around," Madge answered, "but I don't mind. I never imagined that one man could be involved in so many exciting things. Believe me, Sam Theos is magic."

This was the chance Hedi had hoped for. "I know it. He's only the second magical man I've met in my life. Three, if you count Roy, but that's different. Tell me about him?"

Madge hesitated. "You know I don't talk about him even to my best friends, much less to someone I met so recently. But I will tell you his story, and I will tell you *why* I will tell you his story. I happen to know that he has great admiration for you. He has told me, more than once, that it could be that Hedi Carlton is one of the people of destiny."

Hedi was thrilled, but didn't dare move, for fear of tilting the decision against herself. Later she would let herself think about what she had just heard.

After a long pause, Madge asked, "Do you believe a person has a spirit as well as a body?"

"Yes"

"Do you believe that it is possible for the spirit to leave the body and travel to other places, while the body still lives but remains behind?"

"Yes, I have to. It may have happened to me. But then, maybe what I experienced were visions. Anyway, yes, I do."

"Now for the sixty-four dollar question: Do you believe a spirit can depart a living body, leaving it for another spirit to inhabit?"

It was Hedi's turn to pause. When she spoke, she was thinking aloud. "I don't know. I know that many people believe it happens. The Bible talks about possession by evil spirits, and I don't know why possession should be the exclusive domain of evil spirits. In fact, the Bible is full of talk about being possessed by the Holy Spirit. What you ask sounds pretty far out, but I do believe that, with God, all things are possible."

"I guess I can tell you my story on the basis of those answers, but I tell it in confidence and because I need desperately to tell it to someone. I trust I can rely on your discretion?"

"I won't breathe a word— That is—"

Madge laughed. "It's okay to tell Roy, as long as he won't want to tell just one other person, too."

Hedi looked smug, and Madge laughed again, reading her mind. She took a deep breath and continued.

"I'll tell it like a story. Once there was a man named Sam. He worked hard to finish a two-year junior-college-level course in electronics, and then landed a job with a major airline as a radar technician. He was happy with his job, and the airline was happy with him.

"He met a pretty seventeen-year-old high school girl who was earning a little extra money as a weekend waitress at a restaurant where he sometimes ate. She was delighted by the attention from this older man who had lots of spending money in his pocket. Five months later she dropped out of school and married him. Five months after that they had a baby girl.

"It was not the best of marriages from the start, but Sam worshipped his pretty wife, and she basked in his attention. Besides, he was a good provider compared with most of the husbands she knew.

"Twenty years passed. One evening, a pilot for the airline that employed Sam came by to see them. He had a proposition that would make them rich. A group of entrepreneurs had raised some money to start a small air-freight company. They would put up the funds, handle the administration and sales, and would own sixty percent of the company. He was to be in charge of operations and also be the chief pilot. The original employees would receive only nominal salaries, but would be given a generous share of stock in the company. Two second-hand jets had been purchased, and were being modified for freight service. He was looking for suitable operating personnel and wanted Sam for his chief of instrument maintenance. Sam's wife would be the receptionist for the operations group.

"Sam's daughter was now a young woman of twenty and a qualified secretary. She advised against it. The wife thought otherwise, and hounded Sam night and day until he accepted the offer, quitting his job after twenty-three years of service. 'When we're rich, you will be glad,' the pretty wife insisted.

"To make a long story short, less than a year had passed when one of the planes returning from a trip to South America was boarded by federal agents in Florida. They seized the plane with its cargo of illegal drugs and arrested the crew. Someone was able to warn the chief pilot back at the California headquarters, however, and when the agents arrived there virtually everyone was gone. Only Sam and a few low-level employees remained.

"Sam was cleared of having any involvement with drug smuggling, but that was small comfort. His pretty wife was gone, and after several months passed, he began to accept a connection between the flight of the chief pilot and her disappearance.

"When he did accept it, he was crushed. The joy of living drained out of him. He wanted to die, and why not? He was no longer needed. His daughter was able to take care of herself. His wife had run off with the worst sort of criminal. She had finally written a little note with no return address. Too bad, the note had said, that he was not smart enough to have grabbed some of the money and gotten away. He wondered what price she was paying for being rich.

"He prayed for some fatal accident to befall him. Somehow he felt overt suicide was wrong and would be an added burden to his daughter. So he crossed streets without looking and hoped that some incurable disease would strike him down. The doctor called it severe depression.

"In due time his mind created the result he sought. He caught the flu. The flu turned into pneumonia, and he developed an allergic reaction to the drugs that otherwise would have cured him. With his remaining strength he willed himself to die. The hospital called his daughter. The doctor said he was sorry, but there was nothing more he could do. They said her father was not likely to live through the night. When she came to his bedside and took his hand, he opened his eyes and pulled her down through the maze of life support equipment. 'I'm sorry,' he whispered weakly. 'You are a good daughter. I love you.' Then he slipped away into a deep sleep.

"Much later a nurse came and led her to a special waiting room, insisting she get some rest and promising to call her if there was any change.

"At three in the morning they did call. This time Sam's eyes were wide open. He was weak but alert. He smiled at her and asked that she get him out of the hospital as soon as possible. He said he had much work to do. Within a week he had a lawyer working to obtain a legal separation from his absent wife. Then he had his name changed to Sam Theos.

"Everyone said it was a miracle that he lived, but his daughter knew better. She knew that by some miracle Sam Theos lived, but she also knew that her father, Sam Woodrow, was dead. That is the story, and I have never told it before. Only you, I, and the two Sams know the truth." Two tears trickled unnoticed down Madge Woodrow's cheeks. "Do you believe me?"

"I believe you," Hedi replied.

* * *

They had come to the second week. Sam Theos looked about the room, making certain everyone was accounted for. There were 15 people in the room, identified by plastic badges showing first names only.

"Some of you prefer to keep your true identity to yourselves, so I will not make introductions, but leave it to you to become acquainted. To one and all, welcome to the second half.

"The purpose of this meeting is to stimulate our thinking through an uninhibited exchange of views. I ask that you not take notes or make recordings.

"Last week we listened to a panel of medical experts discuss an imagined situation so severe that full recovery might take half a century — or ten thousand years — depending on how resources are used. The disaster we pictured will create very severe shortages. Deciding who gets what under such circumstances becomes a

heartless-sounding business, but it must be done. Otherwise problems will be resolved by the law of the jungle.

"As our panel of doctors discovered, the questions are brutally
stark. There will not be enough doctors or medicines to go around:
Who dies for lack of care? There will not be enough food to go
around: Who starves? There will only be enough shelter for half the
population: Who freezes when the blizzard arrives?

"Food, shelter, health care....

"In last week's discussion, the medical experts concluded that,
under the conditions specified, life expectancy would drop dramati-
cally, the extent of the drop depending on the application of priorities and on whether a major scientific breakthrough occurred.

"They concluded that priority for medical care should go first to
those needed to provide food and shelter to society, to those needed
to protect society against attack from without and crime from
within, to those required to perpetuate the race, and to those
providing other essential services.

"The doctors then made a key policy decision. They decided that
no matter how severe the personnel shortage, a small percentage
(five to ten percent of the medical resources) should be assigned to
training new medics, and a similar percentage should be assigned to
research. Both of these groups should share the task of finding and
maintaining written information on the state of medical knowledge
at the time the catastrophe struck.

"The medical panel noted the progress being made in the fields
of genetic engineering and bio-feedback, and regretted the absence
on the panel of experts in those fields. It was felt that skilled medics
will always be the key to putting people back together when they
are broken up in accidents, but in other areas the need for professional medical attention can be greatly reduced by relying more on
the holistic approach to health.

"The group was united in the belief that the body's own immune
system is the weapon of weapons in the fight against disease.
Learning to fully understand, reinforce, and control this system will
be the greatest medical breakthrough in history. It should have first
priority for research.

"The panel felt it proper for the medical profession to make
recommendations, but the final determination, the application, and
the enforcement of priorities must be the responsibility of political
leaders. The panel refused to take a position on whether a democratic government could cope with the kind of problems it would
have to face. I suggest priorities as the main theme for our discussions," the Chief concluded. "Does anyone have a better idea?"

"Your choice is good, but I doubt we can get half way to first base
before running into the twin subjects of decision-making and leader-

ship." The speaker was a trim, middle-aged man with a distinguished frosting of gray in his neatly cut hair. Hedi had not yet been introduced to him.

"I agree, Jim," the Chief said, "but please elaborate for the benefit of the rest of the group."

"Priorities may be generated by scholarly study of high-minded people seeking only the best for everyone. Or they may result from emotional binges or demands intended to promote personal gain and power.

"If you are operating as an individual isolated from society, you can consider all of your options, decide on your priorities, and implement your decision. The moment you involve just one other person, however, the game changes. You must gain that person's agreement, or you must impose your decision by force, or you must abandon your goal. As more people become involved, the difficulty of reaching agreement multiplies. When the group becomes very large, leaders are necessary to the process of deciding on priorities. These leaders must have the ability to implement and enforce the priorities established."

"Thank you, Jim," the Chief said. "I agree entirely. The purpose of this training camp is to prepare potential leaders to face these kinds of problems. It is the only reason for my being here."

At the break, the man named Jim headed directly for Hedi. "You must be Hedi Carlton. I bring best wishes from Captain Hugh Scott, and his regrets that he was prevented from attending this meeting by a selfish officer of higher rank."

"Then you must be... "

"No names," Jim cautioned. "Just call me Jim."

"Can I call you by rank?"

"I think it would be better not to," Jim said.

"You certainly caused Hugh much puzzlement by sending him here. He's happy with the assignment, but he still wonders about your objective."

"He will know soon enough, but unfortunately he will not be free to tell you. When I return, I expect he will have been cleared to examine certain files that were classified many years ago by presidential order. Only the president can approve access, and he requires certain other endorsements. I can say Hugh is very complimentary of your intelligence and judgment, and I am delighted we have met. Now if you will excuse me, I must find one of your colleagues. His government is anxious that I meet him." He gave her a gallant little bow. Hedi watched him gravitate, as if casually, to Ho Sun.

For the rest of the week the twelve guest experts applied their unique talents to solutions for the overwhelming problems they saw in the aftermath of a world wide catastrophe. For Hedi it was an exciting experience, but one tempered with anxiety when, on Friday morning, the group split fifty-fifty on the question of whether a democratic government could cope with such problems.

"The argument over this question has grown uncharacteristically bitter," the Chief noted in ending the exercise. "Imagine how bitter it would become in reality, when lives and the human future were riding on the result."

"Probably it would be a much shorter debate," Jim said grimly. "Shorter, and maybe more violent." On that disturbing note, the seminar ended.

17. Truth Rock
September, Z-Minus-10

It seemed to her that 4 p.m. would never arrive. She was standing on the dock half an hour early, searching for any sign of the airplane from Bangor. As the minutes dragged by, conference participants began to join her. The plane would take them to Portland. She had to remain calm and friendly — she regarded herself as one of the hostesses — and make casual conversation and try to remain interested in these dozen individuals she had known only a few days, while inwardly waiting for *him*. Meanwhile the minutes ticked by. Five after. Seven after. Eleven minutes after the hour, when the plane was due on the dot. Surely nothing had happened. After all, 11 minutes was nothing. The Otter never attempted to maintain a split-second schedule. Certainly nothing was wrong, she told herself.

Nonetheless, it was a relief to see the little dot in the sky, to watch it grow bigger, to see the plane's pontoons finally ruffling the quiet waters of the lake again. Then she had second thoughts. What if he hadn't made the plane? What if some medical emergency had held him up? What if he'd decided at the last minute that the camp was all foolishness? What if —? She watched it turn and taxi to the landing dock.

The first person out of the aircraft was the only passenger, a young man who barely had time to steady himself before the usually reserved Hedi Carlton threw herself into his arms. She hadn't planned to do it, but somehow she was not surprised to find herself there. It seemed the most natural place in the world to be.

But then she remembered where she was, and had the somewhat embarrassing task of appearing cool as she introduced Roy.

The Chief, as he advanced to shake hands, smiled as if he were their father. "You have been lovers before, and you will be lovers

again. How wonderful the love that transcends time and space."
Instantly Hedi was filled with a new anxiety. How would Roy
respond to that? What if he thought the Chief was a lunatic?

Roy's marvelous friendly smile shined on the Chief. "I think you
are right about the past, and I hope you are right about the future,
Mr. Theos. You could expedite the process by putting in a good
word for me with Hedi — she pays a lot of attention to what you say."

"Oh, I don't think that will be necessary, Dr. Johnson. At the
moment, I am not even sure it would be possible. In the past, Hedi
seemed able to do several things at once, and do them all well. At
the moment, though, I get the feeling that the rest of us aren't even
here."

When Roy came down from stowing his bag in the room assigned
him, Hedi led him to her favorite path through the woods and along
the lake front. Hand in hand, they walked and talked and wished that
time would stand still.

When they came to Truth Rock, half in the lakebed and half on
the bank, she pulled Roy down beside her on its worn surface.

"This hunk of granite reputedly could tell many stories," she told
him.

"Oh?"

"When the white man came, friendly Indians warned him never
to take his lover there unless he was prepared to tell her the truth.
They said that those strange-looking formations on the lake bottom
over there are the bones of those who lied. The bones turned to
stone, and fell into the lake. That is why there are so many near the
Truth Rock."

"Then let me take the test first," Roy said. "I love you. I want you
to marry me. It doesn't matter what secrets you have yet to tell me.
Nothing could keep me from loving you. I don't understand it, for
we hardly know each other. It is still less than a month since we met.
I'm half inclined to believe that Mr. Theos is right about us."

"We don't call him Mr. Theos," she said absently. "We call him
the Chief."

"The Chief, then. In any case, I feel I've known you since time
began. It's as if I've been looking for you all of my life, without
knowing it."

She put her finger across his lips. "Please, don't tempt me so.
Before we join the Chief for dinner, I must tell you. I'm afraid to tell
you, because I don't know how you'll react. But I have to."

"Then tell me about it. And please don't let your bones turn to
stone."

"It's a strange story," she warned, but he merely nodded and
waited for her to tell it.

For over an hour Hedi talked. She started with her first dream, took him through her search for the old man on the beach, and then repeated in detail her experiences with Mr. J and in the years since. Roy listened intently, asking only a few questions to make sure he understood what she was saying.

She looked at him anxiously. "I don't want you to tell me you buy my story until you've heard it all. And [almost fiercely] I don't want you to say you love me no matter what. But if you think I'm lying, or I'm some kind of deluded fool, or a witch, I want to know it now."

He did not make the mistake of smiling. "Your bones haven't turned to stone", he answered, "and I don't think you are deluded. If you are a witch, then God should have made more of them."

Hedi was silent for a moment, her head still on his shoulder. "Thank you so much."

He scratched his head, an innocent gesture that for some reason made her want to kiss him. "So now you think it's a question of what I think of what you have told me," he said.

"Roy, I'm not sure what I think myself. I told you what I saw and heard, but I don't know how to expect you to believe all of it. I mean, I know what it sounds like. Hedi says she met a remarkably lifelike robot from another planet who came here five thousand years ago on a UFO. And she says after talking to her, he was picked up by another UFO flown by another robot. I know how crazy it sounds, and I'm not asking you to believe the explanations I've been given.

"But I do desperately need you to believe that I'm telling you the truth about what I saw and heard, whatever it means. It's the same as with the terrible visions of disaster I had. If you don't think I'm describing things as they really happened, you can only think I'm lying or I'm crazy. We couldn't brush that under the rug. Sooner or later it would gnaw through our love and destroy our marriage."

She waited through his long pause. Finally he said "Yes it would. You are both wonderful and wise. Now let me tell you a few things.

"In my work I have seen many people die. Some of these deathbed experiences have left me shaken by how little we know of the realities of creation. I do believe we save many lives by applying our modern medical skills, yet I have seen cases where the patient died because he did not wish to live. I have seen other cases where all of the skills of my very fine medical team were inadequate, and yet the patient lived for no apparent reason other than his determination not to die.

"I have observed the emotions of persons whose deaths seemed to be in harmony with both their physical condition and the expectations of their spirit. Their expression of joy over what they saw and felt at the time of death was so real I cannot ascribe it to mental aberrations. On only two instances have I seen a person show extreme fear of what he faced at the time of death. I fancy that much of my professional success is because I am somehow able to get inside my patients and know what they are feeling. I have no doubt that at the moment of death a person is not trying to fool anyone, and in many cases their minds are clearer and sharper than they have ever been."

He paused again. "In other words, I have no problem with your story. I have no doubt you saw and heard the things you describe. Some of them are beyond my comprehension, but not beyond my belief. I think we have no problem in agreeing that there are many truths we neither know about nor understand."

For a moment, Hedi was filled with relief, but then Roy continued.

"The problem is, I do have another worry which, until now, my own ego has obscured."

"You were making me so happy, and now I am frightened again," Hedi said. "Please tell me the problem and let me see if I can resolve it for you as well as you resolved mine for me."

Again Roy paused. "You made a commitment."

"I started down this road when I was only 19," she said at last. "I did, I made a voluntary commitment."

"You promised, and you are afraid to break your word."

"Not afraid, exactly. I don't think it's a matter of any physical harm. But if I broke my word to Mr. J, I know our love would soon burn down to ashes."

"You think he would punish you?"

"No, that's not what I mean. I mean it would change me, and that would change us."

He nodded. "Okay. I just wanted to be sure I understood. And you are afraid it's going to come to a choice between your commitment and me." She nodded, unable to speak.

"Well, I agree with you. That's a real danger. In the wrong situation, it could split us apart."

The unexpected pain was like a stab in her heart.

"Your story makes me look at things in a different light. It has always seemed to me I would have to be somewhat brazen to ask anyone to marry me — being a doctor's wife is no bed of roses. I suppose that's why I told you of my intentions so early — it gave you a chance to escape, and that way, if you didn't take the chance, it somehow salved my conscience.

"But now I realize you may have a destiny, a mission, transcending any purpose I could possibly have. So now the shoe is on the other foot, and I have to look at the possibility of playing second fiddle to your career. Do you see the problem this could cause?"

She nodded. "I think I do."

He smiled. "No you don't. The problem is that I am afraid that you, being the kind of person you are, will be tempted to put your loyalty to me ahead of the role you have pledged to accept. Believe me, if you should do such a thing I will know it, and we will have a terrible row about it."

Again relief. Hedi laughed. "We are being high-minded beyond belief. If we are truly in love, we can find a way to compromise the demands we place on each other. I will give a little, and you will give a little, and everything will work out."

She was willing to let matters rest at that, but he was not.

"In normal cases that is just the way things should work, but I am not talking about normal cases. Maybe I glimpse a vision of my own. What happens if you are faced with a mission requiring you to turn your back on husband, or children, or friends? Hedi, you will have to do it. Please promise me that you will do whatever it is you must do. Promise me that, and I will be content."

"It isn't easy," Hedi replied, "but if you feel that strongly, I promise, but I pray that it never happens."

"Me too. Now are you ready to answer my question?"

Before she thought, she said, "What question?" Then she laughed. "Oh, that question. Yes, Roy Johnson, Dr. Roy Johnson, I will marry you, if you haven't changed your mind."

"Good. When?"

"Whenever you say, as soon as you meet my parents."

"Okay. And when can I do that?"

"I can call them before we leave here in the morning."

"Good," he said briskly, spoofing his own usual decisiveness. "Then that's that. Now, isn't a proposal of marriage a contract, and shouldn't a contract be sealed with a kiss?"

Hedi sighed. "It certainly should, and the sooner the better, but I think we better wait until after dinner."

His face was a study. "After dinner?! Haven't I earned a kiss?"

"You have earned many kisses, but please wait. I'm really not very strong. We might never get to dinner."

"Madge is the best private secretary a person could have," the Chief said to Roy. "Hedi is one of the few people who know she is also my daughter."

Madge looked mildly surprised. "I didn't tell him, Hedi," she said. "As you know, he reads minds when he has nothing else to do."

"You may tell Roy the story later," Sam said to Hedi. "Now we should address our attention to the fish I caught while you were testing the legend of Truth Rock. Our very fine camp chef has just finished cleaning and grilling them, and fresher fish you are not likely to find."

During dinner Sam and Madge explained how the camp operated, the kinds of courses and seminars given, and talked about the remarkable people who comprised its volunteer teaching staff. At Roy's request, Sam summarized the medical panel discussions held during the prior week.

"Hedi sent me some of the material," Roy said. "I was impressed by the caliber of the people on the panel and even more impressed by what they had to say. Judging by the tape, you people got into it hot and heavy. That's good. I don't know a better way to find the hidden weaknesses of a plan than to lay it on the table and let everybody say what they think about it.

"Hedi has promised to tell me more about her experiences this evening. I am truly interested. After all, dealing with the results of small scale disasters is my life's work."

"Suppose you tell Madge and me about your ideas for emergency health care."

Roy needed no coaxing to talk about his favorite subject. Sam Theos listened carefully. When Roy had finished, the Chief said, "That is an excellent concept. Do you have a written description I could have? I'd like to incorporate it into one or more of our courses. Would you be willing to allow me to do that?"

"I would be more than willing. I'd be flattered. The answer is yes to both of your questions."

"Well, good. I appreciate it." The Chief cleared his throat and put his napkin on the table. "It was a pleasure to meet and talk with you. I know you came here in pursuit of one of my favorite people, and I thought it would be as well to size you up." He looked from Roy to Hedi. "I believe you deserve each other. Higher praise I could not give to either of you."

He stood up. "I will be gone by the time you two are up tomorrow. A friend is flying me out at dawn for a meeting with some of my colleagues. The camp's Twin Otter is scheduled to take some of the staff to Bangor at eleven, and I've told them to take you as well. Madge tells me you have made travel arrangements from Bangor."

He turned to Hedi and took both her hands in his.

"Don't worry about skipping next summer's six-week camp. You have won your spurs, and I am sure you will soon find your time filled with more pleasant demands. But I will call you from time to time to help me with one- or two-week special events."

He looked from one to the other. Hedi had never known him to be more fatherly.

"You have many choices to make, both of you. They are your choices — none of them are absolutely right or absolutely wrong. My hope for you is that you follow the highest truth you know, and select the most challenging future you can see in your dreams. Good-by, and God bless you."

III. Reality

18. No Time for Love

Little Ralph and Sally were in bed. Roy was at the hospital, working late as usual. Hedi and Martha were sharing late-night cookies and tea.

"So now your job with Congressman Godwin is finished," Hedi said. "What's next? Any chance of your staying around Columbus for a while?"

Martha sighed contentedly. "In a way, I wish there were. This visit is the first time in years that I have really been able to relax. It's made the visit a lot more fun. That, and my nephew and my new little niece."

"You're really very good with them. Ralph loves your visits."

Martha nodded skeptically. "And when am I going to start a family of my own?"

"I didn't say that. Didn't think it, either."

"Okay, sorry. Mother does, though."

"Well, you can't blame that on me."

"No, I don't. Really, I don't blame her, either. But I'm afraid she's going to have to rely on you for grandchildren."

"Not for more, I hope. Roy and I have done our duty in that line."

"You're going to stop at two?"

Hedi laughed. "Look who's talking? You've stopped at none!"

Martha grinned ruefully. "Touché." She helped herself to a cinnamon-raisin cookie. "Do you remember at your wedding how you threw the bridal bouquet in my direction and I didn't catch it?"

"Didn't try to catch it."

"It was like my arms just froze to my sides. I guess my arms knew I wasn't ready for marriage, and it wouldn't be fair to the other girls for me to grab the bouquet." She pushed the half-eaten cookie around on her plate. "Do you ever see the Scotts?"

"Phone calls, mostly. He's stationed in California at the moment."

Moodily: "Your wedding was kind of hard for me, I guess you know. I was delighted for you, and I loved Roy as soon as I met him, but there you were, and there the Scotts were, obviously very much in love still, and here was your sister, heading for perpetual maidenhood."

"A little young for that."

A wan smile. "Maybe."

"It's all in what you want, isn't it?"

"How do you know what I want?"

The last thing Hedi wanted was to anger Martha. She leaned

forward across the table. "Martha, seriously, I'm not trying to tell you what to do with your life. Different things are important to different people, I know that. What fits me wouldn't necessarily fit you. Your life is your own."

Martha nodded. "Thanks, big sister. I guess I knew you feel that way, but it does make things a little easier to hear it." Her lips thinned. "A little easier for you to say that than for me, though. Your life has everything."

Hedi didn't know what was safe to say. She poured herself some tea. "I know I've been extremely fortunate —"

"Oh, Hedi, I don't mean it in a catty way. You and Roy deserve everything you have. I know how hard you've worked. If I'm not mistaken, you got all of one week for a honeymoon."

Hedi smiled. "I'd used up my regular vacation, and the policy of the children's clinic was only one week off for a wedding. It didn't matter. Roy was so busy with planning his emergency treatment center, he probably wouldn't have wanted to take two weeks anyway."

Martha snorted in amusement. "That's romantic!"

"Well, he said it would be brief, but doubly sweet, and it was."

"And your life never slowed down. You kept working for the children's clinic, helping Roy on your days off. He talked EMC to everybody in sight until he made it happen."

"He didn't do it all by himself, Martha. If people like Dean Curry, Dr. Exter and Uncle Jake Cook hadn't supported him, he never could have gotten support from the state and city. And if they hadn't helped him get financing from nonprofit foundations, leaving him free to work on design and organization, the Columbus Regional Emergency Medical Center might still be only a daydream."

Hedi was in danger of getting lost in memories. "The ground-breaking was on the day after Thanksgiving, you know. On our first anniversary. I've always thought it was a fitting anniversary present. He did work so hard to bring that dream into being."

"Isn't that what I just said? And you passed your test and got your senior medical assistant license and worked as a volunteer at the children's clinic after you got too pregnant to keep working there. And you helped Roy with the EMC."

"And then in February little Ralph Johnson came into the world," Hedi agreed happily.

"And you signed up as a substitute medical assistant with Roy's EMC."

"Oh well, that worked out all right. That way they had somebody who could be called in on very short notice, when somebody called in sick, or when they had to accommodate for vacations. And whenever I came in to work, I was allowed to place the baby in the

EMC's daycare center. It worked so well with Ralph that I'm doing it again with Sally. My working there on that basis isn't any special accomplishment."

"Maybe you don't think so. It looks pretty impressive to mere mortal career women."

"Mere career woman? Martha, your career makes mine look absolutely pathetic!"

"Does it? Not to me, particularly. But I do finally feel like I am truly in charge of my life."

Hedi stared at her. "Finally? After everything you've done?" She used her fingers to tick off the steps in Martha's career.

"A master's degree from the University of Texas, graduate work at the University of California at Los Angeles, one summer job in L.A. working for a free-lance news gathering organization and an offer of a regular job if you'd wanted it."

"Which I didn't. I wanted to continue my studies."

"I know, but you'd made an option for yourself, if you'd wanted to take it. Then, let's see, you got far enough in your studies that you actually had your dissertation written, even though you never submitted it for approval."

"Most of my friends thought I was crazy, but I couldn't see that being Doctor Carlton was going to help me make the career I wanted. I figured I needed the experience more."

"I'd say you got it! You parlayed your ability to speak Spanish into a year's worth of work with Reuters, interviewing young college graduates on the hot topics of the moment. And talked them into your doing it on a one-year-only basis."

"They got their money's worth. I knew going into it that there would be a lot of work, long hours, on call seven days a week, with no vacation. They did all right."

"But they wanted you on those terms. They wouldn't have wanted just anybody. Then it was Washington and 'the Committee for the Re-election of Congressman Godwin', a Texas congressman with a tough election campaign coming up. He was another person who just happened to want one Martha Carlton."

"He needed somebody to help him build a better image in the eyes of the voters," Martha said dryly. "It turned out I was suggested by one of my old professors at the University of Texas."

"Well? That hardly disproves my point. You may not think you've been in charge of your career, but from the outside it certainly looks that way."

Martha poured herself more tea. "Far be it from me to disparage such success as I have had, Hedi. And this isn't false modesty speaking. But it has taken till now for me to find out what I really want to do. I want to sell ideas."

"That sounds like advertising," Hedi said. "That, or more politics."

"I suppose it does, but that isn't quite what I mean. Not mere partisan politics, anyway. I've seen what that does to people over time, and that isn't what I want. Life is too short."

"Well, surely you aren't talking about selling soapsuds."

"'Ideas,' I said. Good ideas. It doesn't matter whose, as long as I can agree that the idea is good. One thing I'm good at is marshalling arguments. That would be a big part of what's needed to sell ideas to those who can implement them."

"I suppose I see what you're driving at," Hedi said a bit dubiously. "But where do you expect to find this special kind of job? I wouldn't think they grow on trees."

"I am going to start in Washington. Washington revolves around power, and that's what ideas are — power, waiting to be released. It may take a little while to work it out, but maybe not as long as you might think."

"Well, maybe not. God knows the world could use some good new ideas. Or maybe I should say it ought to pay more attention to some good old ideas." She looked at her younger sister. What scene could be more peaceful than sitting in a comfortable kitchen late at night, two sisters sipping tea together?

"You know, Martha, I do feel that my own life is fulfilled. I never had big dreams, and the ones I had have already been realized. I have two beautiful children. I have a career. I have a wonderful husband who is as happy as I am. He loves his work and his home, and most of all he loves the children and me. The EMC system has gained him widespread recognition. He's in great demand for lectures and articles on similar projects. He has even been offered consulting work. We sound like an advertisement for happiness, right?

"But I can't keep what I saw in those visions out of my mind. A day may go by when I don't think of them. A few days, maybe. But they're there, like something waiting. And Roy told me the other night that he can't forget about them, either. He said, 'Sometimes I sense a chill wind blowing across the warm and loving landscape of my life.'"

Into the little silence, Martha said, "Very poetic." She said it seriously, not sarcastically.

"Yes, I suppose it is, at that. I hadn't looked at it as poetry, just as how he feels. Every night I pray that our happiness will last, and that somehow the world will be spared. I guess what I'm saying, Martha, is: If you can help somehow, by all means go to it."

* * *

Within a week of Martha's departure, Hedi got a late-night phone call from her.

"Did it!" Martha announced. "I leave for Spain tomorrow."

"My goodness! Well, you certainly did. What's going on?"

"I can't tell you everything. I had put in four days, circulating my very carefully prepared resume, getting in contact with people I knew, putting out the word that I was looking for a new assignment. Last night I got a call from Leonard Adams' Washington office." For some reason, Hedi found herself thinking there was significance in Martha's slight hesitation. "Mr. Adams had come up with a possible job for me."

"Well, Martha, go ahead! I'm listening, I assure you!"

"He wanted to know if I was available for a challenging assignment."

"I'd have thought he knew you better than that."

"He wanted to know if I was available, not if I was interested."

"Well, so what happened?"

"When I said I was, he told me he'd be in Washington in the morning and would meet me at the side entrance of my hotel and accompany me to the State Department."

"He just happened to be coming to Washington today?"

A pause. "You know he has old friends everywhere. One of them is a senior official in the State Department who was looking for a person for a very specific, very urgent task." Another pause. Hedi could hear the editing going on in Martha's mind. "He wanted somebody with a background in communications or public relations. Mr. Adams suggested me."

"Heavens, Martha, I'd think the government would have thousands of people like that. The State Department *alone* must have thousands!"

Another pause. "They wanted somebody who hadn't worked for the government. Somebody from outside."

"Somebody who could pretend she *still* didn't work for the government, you mean."

"Hedi, I can't go into it. They wanted an American citizen: somebody intelligent, unmarried, able to speak and write Spanish, and available for an immediate assignment. That narrowed the field, and I happened to fit it."

"I see. So what were they offering you?"

"Assistant communications officer in our embassy in Madrid."

Hedi found that for a long moment she could say nothing.

"Hedi?"

"I'm here. You said yes?"

"Of course."

"I see. Well, you've gotten your job. When do you leave for Madrid?"

"Tomorrow afternoon. That's one reason why I'm calling. I've been running around all day and I don't have time to call Mother and Dad. Will you tell them where I'm going and what I'll be doing?"

Now it was Hedi's turn to edit. "I'll tell them what you've told me," she said.

Another pause, and Hedi knew that Martha had caught the distinction. "I will cable them from Madrid when I arrive," she said. "Give Roy and the children a kiss for me."

"All right, I will."

A final pause in the conversation. "Hedi, I will tell you everything when I can."

"I know you will. I'll be anxious to hear it. Martha, take care."

"I intend to." There was a click, and Martha was gone.

"Oh God, Roy," Hedi said. "Martha's gotten involved in some kind of spy business."

"She what?"

"She says she's gone to work for the State Department and they have to have her immediately. They wanted somebody intelligent and unmarried, who didn't already work for the government. What else could it be?"

"Hedi, Martha is a very competent young woman. Scores of places must be dying to find people with her qualifications and energy and enthusiasm. She went to Washington to find a responsible job and it sounds like that's just what she has done." He stopped. "I'm not convincing you. I'm not even slowing you down. Why not?"

"Oh, Roy, it was the whole conversation. She wasn't telling me half of anything, and we both knew it. It was as if she thought the phone lines were bugged. It was the kind of conversation you have when you're talking to somebody you know very well, but you're on a bus or you're in an elevator, and there are all these strangers around."

"Hedi, you are building a lot out of a little. For all we know, the State Department gives a list of rules to its new hires: Here are the ways you will be discreet at home and around the world. Naturally anybody is going to carry that kind of thing to extremes when they're first exposed to it. First time she's home, she'll tell you all you want to know about it and more, bet you anything."

"Maybe you're right."

Roy laughed. "I know: 'Maybe you're right. But you aren't.'"

She smiled an unhappy little smile. "Now I've got to call my parents and pretend I believe that this is just a good career move on Martha's part, and nothing else. It feels like lying."

"Stick to what you know, and leave out all the suppositions," Roy said practically.

"Yes, I suppose I'll have to."

Martha did indeed cable her safe arrival, and she did write at regular intervals. She had very little to say about her work but quite a bit about a wonderful man she had met on the plane to Madrid. His name was Tim Flannery, and clearly he was the most exciting creature God ever made. He was 31 years old and had been married some ten years earlier. "Obviously the woman was stupid," Martha wrote, "because she divorced him a year later."

In her next letter Martha confided that she believed Tim was in love with her. "It would be so easy to fall madly in love with him," she wrote, "but we both have other priorities, and for now at least, there is no time for love."

Subsequent letters mentioned Tim often, but mostly in connection with his frequent absences. "My sister isn't telling me the whole truth," Hedi told Roy. "I feel it in my bones."

19. Mission

It was a night like every other, ending with the children asleep and a few minutes' relaxed chatting with Roy and then to bed together. She could feel his comforting presence beside her as she drifted off to sleep.

Then, without transition, she was on a beach somewhere, surrounded by the small night sounds beaches make: the slapping of water on boats, the hiss and murmur of the waves. There was no moon, no cloud. The sky was clear and filled with stars. Somewhere out to sea, a boat was sounding its horn.

She started walking, drawn in one direction by something she couldn't identify. Then she saw a lonely figure in slacks, sweater, and sneakers, standing by a lifeguard's tower. It was Martha, silently calling out for her, broadcasting a plea for help.

"Martha, I'm here."

Martha seemed astonished.

"Hedi! How did you find me?"

"You asked me to come. You're in trouble. Can I help you somehow?"

"I want to talk."

"Well, good. I want to listen."

A wan smile. "It's about Tim."

"That isn't any surprise. Tell me."

She seemed to stiffen, as though preparing to be struck. "Tim and I have been living together for four months. I didn't want to deceive you, Hedi, but I couldn't explain it in a letter. I love him so, and his life is in constant danger. I didn't know I could love a man so much that I would refuse to marry him. Can you believe that?"

"Maybe I can. Why don't you try me?"

"We knew right away we were in love, and we knew there were three options. We could leave the operation and get married; we could wait until the operation was over and then get married; or we could just live together whenever Tim was in town. Tim said he didn't want to do anything that would make me feel uncomfortable. He said he was willing to wait, and that it was my decision. I asked for time to think it through."

"Martha, you're going to have to give me some background on this.... You're losing me."

"All right. You remember I told you I was going to be working with the State Department?"

"I said to Roy right away you were getting involved in spying somehow."

"I should have known you'd read my mind. But let me tell you how it happened."

Len Adams had suggested Martha because they needed someone not only totally dependable, but also able, if need be, to face a certain amount of physical danger. Martha had to sign a temporary clearance document to receive certain classified documents and information; then Adams had accompanied her to the initial briefing. There were three others present: the senior state department official, a representative of the Defense Department, and a man from the CIA.

The CIA man had explained to her that her help was wanted in a covert operation, and had assured her that it had been approved by the president and reported to the special five-member congressional committee. "It is entirely legal," he had told her. "But tight security is essential to the operation's success and to the safety of many people. If you accept the assignment, you will be employed as Assistant Communications Officer in our Madrid Embassy, but your actual job will be to serve as the communication link for the American field unit. This also involves communicating with the French and British field units." The Soviet Union, she was told, was also working as an ally on the project, but was running an entirely separate show.

Hedi was very aware of the sound of surf nearby. "They gave me the basics of field operations: code names, cells, all that, so that if one of us is taken, we can't be made to reveal the identity of the others. Then they asked if I was still interested, and I was. I said didn't they need to know a lot more about me? They said they knew things about me that I had probably forgotten. So they described the nature of the problem and the high stakes for which we would be playing. I can't tell you what it was."

"It doesn't matter. Then what?"

"I signed on."

The next day, she was introduced to Tim Flannery, described to her as their field-team leader who "by a happy accident" would be traveling on the same plane to Madrid. "'You will get to know one another socially,' they told me. 'His papers will show he is working for the free-lance news organization that gave you temporary employment one summer. Good luck. We are glad to have you with us.' And then we were shaking hands and the meeting was over and Mr. Adams took me back to my hotel. I was thinking that although he had said nothing during the meeting, obviously he was no stranger to such matters. I told him 'You must have top-secret security clearance,' but he wasn't in the mood for conversation. 'I may have gotten you into a dangerous situation,' he said. 'Please believe that I thought it was necessary.'"

Hedi felt very much aware of the passage of time. "Martha, I think I understand what you got yourself into. I'm confident you did it for the best of motives. But what does this have to do with us? Why are we standing on a beach, wherever we are, an hour or so before dawn?"

"Tim left me three hours ago. More, now. Somewhere out there, in the tossing Mediterranean, he should have transferred from a motor launch to a small ship. By now he should be on his way to another rendezvous.

"I came to this Spanish resort hotel Friday night to meet him. He was returning from London, and he had no time to stop in Madrid. By meeting him here, I gained us another day and a half together. Hedi, it's a deadly game out there. He's playing for the highest stakes there are, stakes far beyond the value of any one person's life. I just had to have someone to talk to, someone I could trust, someone who would care."

"You have a decision to make?"

"It isn't that. The time for decisions is long past. I made my decision. I just had to be heard by someone who could understand."

"All right, Martha," Hedi said, unnaturally calm in reaction to her sister's agitation. "I'm here. Tell."

Seemingly alone in the early morning world, the sisters began to walk along the shoreline.

"I won't go into how I fell in love with Tim. I tried to give you an idea in my letters. But I had to leave so much out; so many things that would show you what kind of man he is."

"I know what it is to be in love," Hedi said quietly.

"Of course. Of course you do; it's hard to realize that other people have had the same experience. It's like saying that one person is the same as any other."

"Just the opposite. Everybody is special somehow. Maybe that's what love is — the finding of what's special in somebody."

Martha seemed struck by the thought. It seemed to Hedi that her agitation diminished slightly.

"I can't tell you a thing about the project we are involved in, Hedi, but it is important. To the U.S. To the world. I'm proud of what we're doing."

"But?"

"But it puts us in an impossible position. We can't desert our assignment. And we can't break the rule against marriage."

Hedi waited her out.

"I invited him to share my apartment. I wanted to share my life with him, as well as my bed. I didn't ask for a pledge of marriage."

She looked proudly at Hedi. "You understand? He is a free spirit, an old-fashioned soldier of fortune, willing, maybe eager, to risk his life if he believes the cause is good. I doubt he could live within the ties of marriage. To try to tie him to me would be to lose him forever."

"Are you sure?"

"He offered to marry me! I refused. He said he'd marry me as soon as the current assignment was completed, but I told him no."

Hedi waited.

"He was astonished, but he finally accepted my position. I think in his heart he knew I was right. We have had many hours of a kind of happiness I never knew existed."

"But it has its price."

"Oh, it does! Every time he leaves me, I feel a great fear, not knowing if I will ever see him again. And almost worse is the fact that I know that one day I must explain all this to Mother and Dad. To the law, Tim and I are two consenting adults, but I know that my church and my parents will think us guilty of adultery. Living in sin. Oh Hedi! Why has this happened to me? I don't know if I am being punished or rewarded."

The moment was too delicate for answers. The best she could do was feel her way toward her sister with careful questions. "Martha, did you want Tim so badly you could not wait? Are you feeling guilty?"

"No. I felt I could give Tim something with meaning, something he needed, and I knew he could do the same for me. I think marriage might work for me, and I could have waited, but I doubt it could ever work for him. If only I could tell you about this secret operation, it would be easier for you to understand."

"I'm not sure it would make any difference. Do you want to know what I think Mr. J would say? He would say your own thoughts and actions have created this result."

Hedi stopped walking, and waited till Martha had stopped and turned to face her. "You say marriage wouldn't work for Tim. Perhaps it wouldn't work for you either."

Martha started to protest, but Hedi continued.

"For years, all your actions have placed your career ahead of love and marriage, but all the while your thoughts have clung to the desire for them and recognized the need to experience a deep human love."

"So you think I am in sin," Martha said. There was an edge to her voice.

"No I don't, not necessarily. If you haven't wronged some third party, your actions haven't been destructive, and the reaction you are experiencing won't be destructive. But it may very well be painful — that's part of the learning. Mr. J would say it's not a matter of good or bad, but of actions and reactions. You create your own rewards and punishments. And Martha, I think I do understand, and I will support you when the time comes for you to level with Mother and Dad."

Back in Columbus, Ohio, Hedi Johnson awoke with a start, and sat upright in bed. "Oh," she said. "Was that a vision? An out- of-body experience? Or was it just a bad dream?" She ceased wondering when she received her next letter from Martha four days later. "I met you in a dream last night, and we had a wonderful chat. I wish I knew which of us was dreaming." Hedi knew that the answer was: neither.

* * *

Roy came home early. Hedi looked up happily from feeding the children. "Hi, honey, how come you're ..." She stopped at the look on his face. "Roy, what's the matter?"

His face was etched with lines she could not interpret.

"I don't want you to get too upset," he said. "Sometimes the papers get things wrong, you know."

"Oh God, something has happened to Martha!"

"No, no. That's not it. At least, not directly. It's..."

"Roy, don't beat around the bush," she said sharply. "Tell me."

He showed her a copy of the day's New York *Times*. There on page one was a blurred picture of a man blindfolded and standing with his back to a wall. A firing squad of four men appeared to be in the act of firing their rifles. The caption referred to the execution of an alleged CIA agent in Iran.

The accompanying story said that the photo had been released by a weekly paper of doubtful integrity, uncertain ownership, and radical philosophy, printed somewhere in Lebanon. A translation of the Arabic caption was included: "Another CIA spy was been caught, tried, and executed by our brothers from Iran. Though shooting is too good for such dogs he was accorded this dignity because he confessed to being a paid American agent and revealed useful information about the spy ring." The story in the *Times* noted that the original article "alleged this was yet another covert operation of the CIA that was kept secret from the American people." According to the *Times*, the Arabic article claimed that the executed spy carried papers showing him to be a freelance reporter named Cary Milton, but that Cary Milton was a known CIA agent named Timothy Flannery.

"Oh dear God," Hedi said.

"Keep reading. It gets worse."

She continued:

"According to the news story, which was unsigned, Milton, or Flannery, was apprehended in the Persian Gulf, caught planting mines designed to appear to be of Iranian origin.

"Neither the Central Intelligence Agency nor the State Department would speak for attribution, but a usually well-informed source confirmed that a Timothy Flannery is currently carried on the rolls of the State Department. This Flannery is currently on assignment to Madrid. Whether the two men are one and the same has yet to be determined. Repeated attempts Tuesday to contact embassy officials in Madrid were unsuccessful."

Hedi felt herself shaking. "Roy, what does all this mean?"

"I think it means we'll see Martha back on these shores in record time, if we're lucky. If she is lucky."

She could only look at him in dread. "Is she in danger, do you think?"

"No, I doubt it. You can bet that State is going to have her out of there pronto. If she and Flannery have been working together for 10 months, she'll be as hot as a two-dollar pistol, as far as State is concerned. They aren't going to risk leaving a trail like that for the media to pick up. She may very well be on a plane home right this minute."

She wondered at Roy's assurance: How much of it did he really feel, and how much was for her sake? Fortunately, the children needed her attention; she had something near to hand to take her concentration.

By the time Roy returned from the airport with Martha on Monday night, Ralph and Sally were asleep. Hedi held her close for a long moment, then held her off to look closely at her. "You look like you're exhausted. Let's get you to bed."

"I am dead on my feet," Martha said, "but if it's all the same to you, I would rather talk. Maybe then I can sleep."

After Martha had called to announce that she was back in the States and was on her way to Columbus, Roy had told Hedi that

Martha had sounded very tired. Hedi had disagreed. "It's worse than that. She's heartbroken and she feels all alone. That's why she's coming here before going to my parents'." If she had needed confirmation of her opinion, here it was. Martha's eyes were luster-less. She sat on their living-room couch and told them as much as she was allowed to tell. She spoke casually, flatly, as though reciting the end of a movie she'd seen.

"The photo in the news article was a fake, deliberately blurred before publication. I have seen a computer-enhanced copy of the original."

Roy asked, "How did you manage that?"

"Italian agents got it, and passed it on to the French."

Hedi said, "It wasn't Tim?"

"It wasn't a person at all. It was a dummy propped up against the wall."

"So Tim may be alive!"

"No. The dummy was dressed in Tim's slacks and jacket, and the papers they released were copies of the ones Tim was carrying. I am certain I recognized the jacket."

"He could still be alive," Roy said grimly.

She shook her head. "No. I know what you have in mind, but no. I knew from the start he wouldn't allow himself to be taken alive."

"The papers say he was executed after interrogation. We've been afraid they were telling the truth."

"That's what they want us to believe, and we are willing enough to pretend to believe it."

Hedi said, "But you are sure he was killed outright, and not captured?"

"We are sure."

Hedi breathed a sigh of relief.

Martha looked at her curiously. "Why the sigh, Hedi? He's dead either way."

"You know why the sigh. At least this way you don't have to think about him being tortured."

Martha gave a little shudder. "No," she said.

After a moment she continued.

"You must have read the president's statement yesterday, admit-ting that Tim was part of a covert operation."

"He said it was intended to recover weapons-grade nuclear ma-terial from a radical terrorist group," Roy said.

"That's right."

"He didn't admit that Tim Flannery was a spy, though. For that matter, he didn't admit that Cary Milton was Tim Flannery."

"No, and as far as you and Hedi know, he wasn't."

"All right," Roy said. "I take that to mean that nobody can prove it yet."

"I can't see why it makes a difference," Hedi said. "Why not simply tell the truth? Governments do too much covering up. It costs them support: People don't know what to believe."

Martha seemed disinclined to pursue the matter. "Everybody is going to use this as a political football," she said. "The White House and the Special Congressional Committee on Covert Operations is already besieged with demands for information. The left wing wants to prove the operation wasn't what the administration says it was. The right wing wants to find somebody to blame for the failure. That's why the president had to dissolve the operation and get exposed personnel back home as soon as possible."

"Don't you think the truth would relieve the political pressure?"

"Won't matter. Nobody's going to let this drop. They aren't after the truth. They're after political advantage."

After a moment, Roy asked Martha what had happened. "Tell us whatever you can."

"And tell us why it went wrong," Hedi added.

"All right." Still in a half-dead voice, she told them.

"Tim was leading a five-man team searching for the home-made atomic bombs. They found one in the hands of a certain terrorist group, and managed to 'liberate' it."

Hedi said, "Home-made?"

"Well, that's what we call it. Manufacture requires a few million dollars and facilities provided by some government, but next to conventional bomb production it's home-made.

"The idea was that the team would attach a sonic marker to the bomb, then deep-six it so the Navy could pick it up later from a submarine.

"Tim insisted on making the drop alone from a small boat, while his team waited about a mile away in a larger vessel.

He was dropping the bomb over the side when he was surprised by an Iranian gunboat."

Martha's voice still held no emotion. "He tried to run away in his little boat, to make it harder for them to find the exact spot he had dropped it. There wasn't any point in letting them retrieve it before the sub arrived.

"He didn't get far, of course, before they ran him down. Our team had their glasses on him — they saw him cut his engine, step into the glare of the spotlight and put his hands up. And they saw men from the gunboat take him in tow. They started stripping off his clothing before they were even under way. They wanted to see what he might have concealed on his person, you see."

"And there wasn't anything his team could do but watch," Roy said quietly.

"They were unarmed. The only thing they had to work with was a fast boat," she said. Something in her voice — a quiet pride, perhaps — told Hedi there was more to come.

"They very quietly closed to within half a mile of the gunboat and turned on their search light, challenging it to give chase, hoping to lure the commander into pursuing them. That would have led the gunboat a little further away from the spot where the mysterious object was thrown overboard, you see."

Roy nodded.

"The spotlight gave Tim his chance. He broke away and dived overboard."

Martha paused, a long pause.

"He swam as far as he could under water, but as soon as he came up they picked him up with a searchlight, and they cut him to pieces with a machine gun."

Hedi felt sick. "What a horrible thing," she said.

"Better than being taken alive," Martha said simply.

"What happened to the rest of his team?" Roy asked.

"The gunboat's first priority was marking the area of the encounter. The rest of Tim's unit made it out of sight and out of range. And the Navy picked up the bomb seventy-five minutes later and got safely away."

Roy said, "It is a remarkable story. Tim deserves the Medal of Honor."

"I would rather have him alive," Martha said. "Anyway, heroes rarely emerge from covert operations."

They sat for a short while in silence. "I have to get to bed," Martha said. "Maybe now I can get some sleep."

20. Joining Forces

Martha stayed a week in Columbus, then went to Vermont, to spend some time with Jane Adams. "I need some time to think," she told Hedi at the airport. "I thought I had my life lined up. Now everything is up in the air."

The gate area was deserted except for the airline desk officer. As long as they talked quietly, they could talk freely. "You've been through a lot, these past few months."

Martha stared at the carpet, biting her lip. "I thought I knew what was important in my life and what wasn't, but now I am not so sure."

Hedi thought of Martha's years of preparation and sacrifice, all aimed at a career other than wife and mother. She could think of nothing to say.

But Martha evidently sensed her thoughts. "Hedi, I respect your life; I envy it. But it isn't *my* life. I have to be doing something, and I want it to be something important."

"What you were doing sounds important to me."

"It was. But it's over. I couldn't go back to it now, and anyway, I would be too great a risk for them. They don't need the additional risk of exposure."

"Why? What's done is done. They can't change the fact that you worked for them."

"No, but if somebody stumbles on the fact that Tim and I were l— worked together, it will be a lot better for everybody if I am a former State Department employee. It won't get nearly the play it would if I were still on the payroll."

She stared out the window to the empty asphalt where her plane would sit when it arrived for boarding. "I have to have something important to do," she said. "I need some quiet time to think about it."

"When you find it," Hedi said, "we'll still be here. And no matter what you do, I'm sure you'll always find Mother and Dad just as supportive as ever."

Hedi had advised Martha to tell their parents the story of her life with Tim. As she had predicted, they were more understanding than Martha had dared hope.

"I just hope I will have something to tell them," Martha said restlessly.

Three weeks later, Hedi picked up the phone to find Martha on the other end. "Hedi, I'm starting to feel like the bad penny, always turning up again. Do you think you and Roy could stand having me as a houseguest again for another night?"

"Any time, and glad to have you. Something's up. What is it?"

"Rather tell you in person. Let me give you the flight information." And the next evening she was again sitting in their living room.

But this was a new Martha, or rather was more like the previous version. Her eyes had regained their sparkle of intelligence and enthusiasm, and she no longer moved in slow motion. Hedi knew that Martha would always carry the hurt of her loss along with the good memories — but they had been tucked back, now, out of sight. Martha was looking outward again.

"I guess I have come to ask if we can join forces," Martha said.

Hedi blinked. "You've got a new project and you want me to come in on it?"

"I have a new project, yes, but I wasn't thinking of asking you to come in on it. More the other way around."

Hedi noticed that Roy was wearing the expression she called waiting-to-hear-the-other-shoe-drop.

"I would like you to put me in touch with Sam Theos."

The project, predictably, had to do with Len Adams.

"Mr. Adams has come to believe that our marvelous systems of communication often tend to deceive the people rather than enlighten them."

"Can't argue with that," Roy said.

Hedi raised her eyebrows. "Conspiracy theory?"

"Some evil master-plan to mislead the public? No, something simpler than that. He thinks it happens because of the economic value of time. A minute of television time, or a page in the newspaper, can cost tens of thousands of dollars. Given the average person's short attention span, there's tremendous pressure on communicators to make stories short and dramatic, even at the cost of warping the stories by changing facts or omitting them entirely."

"There is such a thing as integrity," Roy said. "But I suppose integrity is always a scarce commodity."

"We think the problem goes deeper than that," Martha said. "Even with the best of intentions, how can anybody explain a complex subject in a one-minute news spot or a 10-inch newspaper story?"

Hedi noted the 'we': Martha had signed on to a team again. She said: "Well?"

"Mr. Adams wants to establish an organization to debunk the news."

Roy said, skeptically, "A new government agency?"

"Oh, no. A nonprofit organization. He thinks an independent organization could use advanced communication techniques to pressure our highly commercialized information systems to be more responsible."

"But where is the money going to come from? He who pays the piper calls the tune," Roy said.

"We are thinking that the organization might try any of several approaches to raise money by various means, but a charitable foundation would cover its operating deficits and would assure its financial independence."

"That only regresses the problem one step," Roy said logically. "Whoever controls the foundation still controls the organization."

"It would be Mr. Adams' money, first of all. He has important and wealthy friends in Canada, the United States and around the world who wish to be a part of the venture. He is confident the foundation can start with funding of at least three billion dollars. He has pledged a hundred million dollars of his personal fortune as seed money."

Roy whistled. "When people put up that kind of money, they are worried about something, and they are in a position to know that they have something to worry about. You can bet it's something more than correcting the flow of information about the causes of the latest airplane crash. What is it, I wonder?"

"The worst. We think there are about eight small nuclear bombs in the hands of radical groups taking instruction from Iran, Syria, Libya, Iraq, or one of the Moslem factions in Lebanon. Fortunately, they do not agree with each other, and fighting between them goes on almost constantly. But if anything should ever unite them, they could start a brushfire that could quickly get out of anyone's control. And if that hypothetical event also gained them the support of Moslem nations like Egypt, Saudi Arabia, and Pakistan, we could wind up with the whole world drawn into a nuclear holocaust."

Roy said, quietly, "And they have a particular scenario in mind, don't they?"

"They do. They think — and I agree with them — that the event needed to trigger this result is presently being fashioned in Israel."

Roy said only one word. "How?"

"As you know, the land provided to the Jews for a homeland after World War II did not include the site on which their ancient temple stood before it was destroyed by the Romans in 70 AD. Israel took this site in the 1967 war, when they occupied all of Jerusalem. It is the occupation of this land that offends the devout Moslem most, for on it stands one of his very holy places, 'The Dome of the Rock'.

"There is a large and powerful group of devout Jews, both in and out of Israel, who consider it their most sacred duty to rebuild the Temple. Until this is done, they feel they have not fully recovered their homeland, and have not kept faith with the prophets or with God.

"You may know more about this situation than I do, so correct me if I have some of my facts wrong. The important thing is that, until now, more cautious heads have prevailed in Israel, and the proponents of rebuilding the Temple have not had sufficient political strength to force the government to act. Preoccupied with other problems, we and our allies have not worried too much recently about the problem."

"I am not an expert," Roy said, "but I believe what you say is generally correct. It is a frightening prospect."

"There is convincing evidence that the more zealous Jews have been quietly gathering strength through a series of deals with other minority factions, and are now biding their time until the next major Arab terrorist act gives them the needed support from an enraged public. Then they will force the government to approve and implement the rebuilding of the Temple. This means destroying the Dome of the Rock — and that will unite the Moslem nations and trigger an explosion that could set the world on fire."

"If the picture is that grim, what does Adams' group expect to accomplish with an effort to debunk the news?" Hedi asked.

"He hopes that people in other nations can be shown there are two sides to the Moslem-Jewish debate, that both groups have legitimate problems," Martha answered. "Then he hopes these nations will be more cautious in pledging support to one side or the other. Deprived of assured outside support and feeling the pressure of world opinion, neither party will feel confident of winning by the use of force. It is precisely this kind of situation that takes opponents off the battlefield and brings them to the bargaining table."

Roy grimaces. "Pretty slim chance."

"It may be a real longshot, but who has a better idea?"

There was no answer to that.

Hedi asked, "You mean Mr. Adams would set up this group primarily to prevent a flare-up over the Dome of the Rock?"

"Oh no. There are many other situations, less dramatic situations, where exposing half truths and refuting half lies could resolve important questions."

"How do you fit into this scheme?" Roy asked.

"During its formative stages, Mr. Adams has invited me to be technical advisor to the group. I plan to accept his offer," Martha said.

"You said you want to talk to Sam Theos," Hedi said. "I don't see the connection."

"I would like to persuade Mr. Adams that major disasters other than nuclear war are equally probable, and deserve equal attention. After all this time, I think I am ready to have some involvement in your survival project, Hedi."

Hedi let out a long breath she hadn't realized she was holding.

"Welcome aboard, little sister."

"Another thing. If possible, I would like you to arrange for me to talk to your friend Captain Hugh Scott."

"Glad to do it," Hedi said. And so, five months later, Martha caught a plane to Bangor, Maine, where she met Hugh Scott, who was also waiting for the familiar Otter.

He told her he had been ordered back from a conference in London and instructed to proceed to the Chief's survival camp.

"Why?"

"I have no idea. They didn't offer explanations, only orders."

Hedi and Roy were already there, as — to Hugh Scott's vast surprise and delight — was Mary. They and the children had flown up a few days before in response to Sam Theos' invitation to come up "for a little vacation." Once they were there, he had told them why it had taken so long to arrange a meeting. "I wanted things just so," he said. "I like working out complicated arrangements in a way that pleases everyone — and I like to throw in a surprise every so often, too."

The surprise went off as Sam had planned it, when they met Martha and Hugh at the dock.

"As soon as you two recover from your surprise," Sam said, smiling broadly, "you need to get yourselves established in your quarters. In about half an hour, I will have a gentleman in my office who is very anxious to talk to all of you."

"I guess you aren't going to tell us who the gentleman is," Hugh said.

"You guess correctly."

Half an hour later, when Martha, Hugh, and Mary entered Sam's office, Hedi and Roy were already there. So was a handsome man a little beyond his middle years, with more than a touch of grey in his hair. He had a military bearing that belied his civilian clothes.

To Hedi's infinite amusement, Hugh was reduced to stuttering. "General, sir... I didn't expect... This is my wife, Mary, and this is Martha Carlton, Hedi Carlton's... I mean Hedi Johnson's sister. Martha this is Major General..."

"At ease, Captain," the general said. "Officially I'm not even here, so we can dispense with ceremony. Here I am known only as Jim." To Martha: "Perhaps Hedi has mentioned me to you?"

"Indeed she has. I am very pleased to meet you."

"The pleasure is mine," he said. "Now, if you don't mind, I would like to get our work done first; then we can engage in whatever activities Sam has planned for the evening."

His voice became all business.

"As most of the world now knows, the governments of Britain, France, and the United States became alarmed by persistent reports that certain unsavory characters had gotten their hands on a quantity of weapons-grade uranium and plutonium. Our friends in Europe suggested a joint operation to find and recover this dangerous material. What you do not know, Captain, is that Miss Carlton was a part of that operation."

Hedi watched Hugh's eyes go from Martha to her and back again. The general saw it too.

"Apparently Mrs. Johnson is not surprised to hear this, Captain, but she was not a part of the operation. Anything she knows about it came, ah, strictly through unofficial channels. I have made it a point not to inquire into the matter too strictly, and I would advise you to do the same."

He studied his fingertips for a moment. "That operation produced mixed results, some embarrassing, some tragic. But it is entirely within the realm of possibility that this meeting is not the least important thing to flow from it."

He paused. "I don't entirely follow you, sir," Hugh said.

"No, of course not. I don't see how you could. Miss Carlton's involvement in that affair brought her into circles dealing with extremely sensitive information, and also led to her having to sever official connections to such circles. But as my mother used to say, God never closes a door without opening a window. Miss Carlton, would you briefly describe Mr. Adams' debunking project for Captain Scott?"

In a few short sentences, Martha recounted what she had told Hedi and Roy some weeks before.

"Whether it will work or not remains to be seen," the General said," but either way, I love it. At least the man has the courage of his convictions and is willing to put his money where his mouth is."

Hugh said, "It sounds to me like you are liable to be like the man in the joke who walked down the middle of the road: He got hit from both sides."

"All sides," Martha said.

The general nodded. "Of course you are going to be attacked. They'll charge you with spreading your own lies and half truths. I can see the editorials and feature articles now: 'Debunking the Debunkers.' How will you defend yourself?"

"We have discussed that extensively. I recommended that we play hardball. The board approved."

"Have you worked out your policy?"

"We have. Our first step will be to demand that false allegations against us be publicly withdrawn."

"And if not?"

"If not, our lawyers will seek legal remedies; some of the best legal talent in the world has offered to represent us. Usually we will not be seeking money damages, but a court order for a retraction."

"That's wise. You want public support, not extra money."

"Exactly. We do not want our credibility damaged by appearing to seek financial gain."

"And what do you do when threatening to sue doesn't work?"

"Then we fight fire with fire. We dig into our attacker's motives. We look for skeletons in their closets. We look at the kind of friends they have and examine their past for possible activities contrary to the law."

"That sounds like blackmail," Hedi said.

"Not at all. We neither threaten nor do we make any deals requiring us to call off our dogs. Anything of real substance that we find will be made public knowledge, and no retraction they make will stop us. That isn't blackmail, but I do think it will have a lot of influence on the next person who considers attacking us falsely."

"It may not be blackmail, but it *is* hardball, there's no doubt about that," Sam Theos said.

"I'm with you all the way," the General stated. "Go get 'em, and if you catch a few military types in your net, I won't say a word. Now, with your permission, I would like to discuss some other matters."

There was the briefest of pauses.

"First, I have been authorized by the Joint Chiefs of Staff to ask Dr. Johnson to conduct a three-day seminar for senior medical officers. The subject for discussion would be the techniques he has developed for emergency treatment of the injured."

"I will be honored to do it," Roy replied.

"Splendid. Someone will be in touch with you to work out the details."

"Now let's talk a bit about our good friend, Hugh Scott. And let's hope he remains a good friend after it is all over."

To Mary, he said, "Sam had a brilliant idea when he invited you here. I am glad to meet you. More than that, I hope, by the time you leave here, that you will better understand why we do such oddball things and seem to be so inconsiderate of your husband — and of you."

Speaking again to the group at large, he said, "I've arranged that Captain Scott be transferred to my control on a confidential basis. On the record, he is an Army liaison officer working out of Boston, but behind the scenes, my office will decide his assignments and issue his instructions."

He turned to speak directly to Hugh. "I want you to be my representative in Vermont, New Hampshire, and Maine. I also want you to maintain close contact with Sam Theos. I trust that Miss Carlton will help you establish contact with the office of the governor of Vermont, and with the Adams group." Looking at Martha: "In return we may be able to give you some help from time to time."

"Can you give me an example?" Martha asked.

"For example, we stumble over quite a few skeletons in the course of our intelligence activities. If we find one useful to you, we just might tell you where to find it."

Martha smiled. "I am always happy to assist the Department of Defense."

The general had dispatches to read: He asked Hugh to come with him. Roy wanted to call the clinic to check for crises demanding his attention. Martha, Hedi and Mary remained to talk with Sam Theos.

"Martha knows in general what you are trying to do here, but she has a few questions to ask you," Hedi said.

"I certainly do," Martha said.

"Ask," the Chief said. "There's little that I know, but I have an opinion on everything."

"Your opinion, then," Martha said. "Do you think we are going to see a major catastrophe? If so, what kind? And when?"

Laughing, the Chief looked at Hedi. "Your sister knows how to get directly to the heart of a matter. I wish I could be that concise in my answers."

To Martha: "Taking your questions in order, I'd put the odds at 100 to 1 that a catastrophic event will occur. As to what it will be, I'd express it in percentages: I'd say we have a 45 percent chance that it will be a nuclear war, 45 percent that it will be a physical event emanating from within the earth, and perhaps a 10 percent chance of something else.

"Timing? I'd say there is a 50 percent chance within 7 years and a 90 percent chance within 30 years."

"Thank you. Final question: What can I do to help?"

He smiled at her. "There are many things you can do, including responding to the general's request and working with your sister. In general, I urge everyone to direct their creative energy toward preventing a nuclear war, for that is the worst of the likely disasters."

Mary said, "Do I understand you to say there is still one chance in a hundred there will be no disaster at all?"

"It is not an exact figure. I could just as well have said one chance in a thousand. There is a chance. A remote chance."

"But you don't think it is too late to head off a nuclear war?"

"Not in my opinion."

"Or an incident short of all-out war that nevertheless involves the explosion of nuclear devices?"

"Again, not in my opinion. I think I may say it is an informed opinion, but again, it is only an opinion."

Martha turned to Hedi. "Thanks for bringing me here. Now I am happy with the new goals I have chosen."

21. Ludwig's Story

Dr. Richard Ludwig was a man who lived by ideas, and he liked nothing better than to have an audience on whom to try them out. All the better when the group was as select as the few before him.

Hedi watched him look them over — the Scotts, the Johnsons, Jim, and the Chief, of course. She knew, intuitively, that like all showmen Dr. Ludwig was considering how best to win this particular audience.

"There is a region in our solar system where strange things are taking place," he began abruptly. "This region contains an enormous concentration of energy, energy which is constantly changing in intensity, character, and location."

He had their attention, and he knew it.

"Meteorites wandering into this energy storm explode and disappear in a flash of radiation. In addition, space in that area is distorted into a giant electromagnetic lens which is receiving focused beams of charged particles from the direction of the sun."

Ludwig looked over his glasses at them.

"Most of this enormous flow of energy passes through the magnetic lens and travels in an expanding beam into the more distant reaches of space. At times, however, some is reflected back toward the sun. This is of significance to us because the earth always lies directly in the path of any such reflected energy.

"Reflection seems to occur on an erratic basis and involves only a tiny fraction of the total energy flow. Some believe it causes such phenomena as the northern lights. No one knows what the consequences might be if a major portion of the energy were reflected back to earth in opposition to the earth's magnetic field, but some of us are rash enough to make guesses.

"I have been following the developing evidence for some years. This morning I want to take the bits of knowledge we have, add some theory, toss in a few hunches, and finally, use a little pure imagination to create a story relevant to the purpose of this survival training camp."

In the back of the room, someone applauded loudly. Hedi, like everyone else, turned to see that Dr. Cheng Tu had entered the room, and was sitting in the last row of seats. He smiled broadly. "Imagination! That is the closest to a statement of faith I have ever heard from my favorite agnostic physicist."

Dick Ludwig laughed. "Welcome, my friend," he said. "Seriously, I am getting into waters that are strange to me, but I have this picture, half theory and half fancy, that I feel may be of real significance. If you can throw any light on the subject, I will not even ask the source of your wisdom."

"Thank you," Cheng Tu answered. "I, in turn, hope to learn from yours."

"To protect my reputation in the scientific community, I am going to label this as informed science fiction. That way I am spared the burden of offering proof that I do not possess. Despite the fiction label, however, I firmly believe the events I will describe are within the realm of the possible, and the picture I will try to paint could be a scene from some future reality."

To Hedi's surprise, he asked those in his small audience to close their eyes to better see the huge, flaming, white-hot ball we call the sun, racing through space.

"Now I ask you to envision the small, cold spheres called planets, traveling in large, sweeping elliptical orbits around the sun. Concentrate on the planet called earth; notice how beautiful it is as it spins smoothly on its axis."

Hedi followed along in her mind as he suggested image after image, and soon it was as if she were watching a film.

"Look at earth's sunlit side, its ever-changing pattern of white clouds. The deep blue oceans. The land masses, marked by the shadows of their mountain ranges." She did, delighting in the spectacle.

"Move to the dark side of the planet. As your eyes grow accustomed to the darkness, notice that the shadow surrounding us travels with the earth as it moves in its annual trip around the sun, just as a man's shadow follows him when he walks along the street on a sunny afternoon." She did as he suggested. The shadow seemed to her, for the moment, almost a tangible thing.

"Take note," the storyteller urged, "that as long as you stay in the shadow, the earth is always between you and the sun. You should also know that the earth is blocking all manner of other unseen radiation being thrown off by the sun — among them, infra-red, ultra-violet, radio, X-ray, and radar-frequency radiations. If our eyes could detect these frequencies, we would see all kinds of shadows following our planet on the side away from the sun."

On instruction from the storyteller guide, she moved out to the edge of the earth's shadow. From there she could see the brilliant sunlight rushing past the earth, and could imagine the vast quantities of unseen radiation that traveled with the visible light.

"The great nuclear furnaces in the sun also spew out mighty streams of particles," he continued. "Many of these carry electrical charges, such as the electron with its negative charge, and the proton with its positive charge. Heavy particles like the proton are easily blocked by the earth's atmosphere, while others may bore into the earth's surface. This is true whether or not the particle is charged, but charged particles can be attracted or repelled by an electromagnetic field.

"The earth, as you all know, is surrounded by its own magnetic field. This field changes the course of those charged particles that miss the solid earth but pass through its magnetic field. There are many possible results of such deflections, but I want you to concentrate on one.

"Stand near the edge of the earth's shadow, keep your eyes tightly closed, and imagine you can see a beam of electrons rushing by in a straight line from the sun into outer space. You see them traveling in a straight line because I have pulled the switch on the earth's magnetic field. Now I close that switch — turn it on — and as the magnetic field builds up, watch the beam bend slightly and enter into the earth's shadow. Look across the shadow toward the opposite pole, and notice that beams of particles of positive charge are being bent into the earth's shadow from that direction. Try to imagine the energy concentrations that result when these beams meet at some common focal point.

"While you are still operating in the observer role, I want you to move in close to the earth," the storyteller said. "See if it really *is* round. See if it actually *is* spinning smoothly around its axis. Peer into the deep ocean trenches and observe the violence there."

Following these instructions, Hedi moved in close and saw (as she already knew) that the earth was not round, but flattened at the poles by centrifugal force and stretched at the equator. Moreover, it was not at all smooth. Its land masses were furrowed with mountain ranges in some regions and covered with low plains in others. There were massive high plateaus laced with deep canyons. The South Polar area contained a mountainous land mass capped with an astonishing thickness of ice, but the North Pole had very little land or ice above the level of the sea. Beneath the sea, she saw great valleys lying more than four miles below the ocean level.

No, the earth was not at all round and smooth. One would expect it to wobble as it turned, just as an out-of-balance auto tire wobbles when the car is in motion.

Following his lead, she backed away from the earth and observed it carefully from several angles. Indeed it did wobble as it turned, and listening very carefully to the ground noises she seemed to hear the solid crust groaning under the stress.

Looking next at the very bottom of the deep ocean trenches, she saw almost constant eruption of lava in many places. She was amazed at how thin the earth's crust was in the deep ocean. Very little additional stress would be needed to shatter it and allow vast amounts of lava to flow upward into the ocean.

"You have done well," Dr. Ludwig said. "You have observed half the story. Now it is my turn to do the work."

Ludwig put aside his storyteller role and resumed his accustomed role as scientific lecturer.

"Let me say right off that there is much ignorance about this matter. I want to acknowledge my own ignorance right at the start. It may be a very long time before we have the facts, but we know that something is going on out there.

"Frozen in the earth's rocks are innumerable little permanent magnets, which crystallized when magnetic compounds in molten rock cooled and became solid. They were magnetized by the earth's magnetic field; naturally they lined up with the magnetic poles, as good little compass needles should.

"For thousands of years these little magnets lay peacefully in place, happy in the knowledge that they stood in orderly ranks, all facing in the right direction. Then something happened. The earth's poles reversed their polarity, and suddenly countless little magnets were facing the wrong way. Try as they might, there was nothing they could do about it; they were frozen in place, condemned to be under constant stress.

"As more molten rock flowed from the earth and cooled, trillions of trillions of new magnets formed, and this new generation aligned themselves properly with the planet's new magnetic field. They too will lie peacefully until once more, for reasons not known to man, the magnetic poles change their location or their polarity.

"Changes in the magnetic field have occurred many times, and the record is frozen in the rock for geologists to read. We do not know why it happens, but obviously the earth has been able to survive the shock. We have no knowledge about the effect on plant and animal life, since recorded history does not go back to the last reversal of polarity. Whatever damage may have occurred, it is obvious that the species survived.

"We still don't know why the magnetic field changes, but new evidence does explain *how*. As you now know, streams of charged particles launched by nuclear reactions in the sun pass near enough to the earth to be deflected from their course. Depending on a variety of factors, some would be scattered in the vastness of space, but others would be focused somewhere far back in the shadow of the earth.

"Calculations show that this is not a focal point, but a focal area, a corridor extending roughly from 500 to 600 million miles behind the dark side of the earth. Awesome electromagnetic forces exist in this region of space and there is much more we would like to know about them. We do know that they form space into a magnetic lens or window which allows the focused streams of charged particles to pass through and proceed in an expanding beam on their journey into space.

"At least, this is normally true, but the small exceptions are important. They show that the window is not always perfectly transparent.

"Put another way, the magnetic lens can and does change its shape, with the result that some of the particles are reflected back to the earth, where they cause detectable magnetic aberrations in the polar regions.

"Nothing is constant in this entire sequence of events. To begin with, there is a large variation in the quantity and character of the particles thrown off by the sun. Some of these variations are amplified by subsequent events, and some are minimized.

"Fortunately, limits can be assigned to the extent of the changes, and the effect of the extreme conditions on the magnetic lens can be estimated. To make a very long story very short, over a period of a few hundred thousand years, the lens will assume changes in shape ranging from a perfect window to that of a perfect reflector. The flow of charged particles reflected back to earth is in opposition to the earth's magnetic field. When the reflected stream surpasses the critical strength, the earth's field will be overwhelmed, and its polarity will be reversed.

"What is all of this to you? Perhaps you don't really care about all the little magnets which are caught facing the wrong way. Let me remind you that there are trillions of trillions of these little fellows all trying to turn around at the same time. It must add up to a substantial amount of stress. Enough, in certain circumstances, to shatter the structural integrity of the rock."

He paused for emphasis, and took off his glasses in what seemed to be a moment of weariness. Hedi thought — he has a certain theatrical ability, and he knows it.

"Normally our planet can absorb this stress without catastrophic results, but when it is already in a state of imbalance demanding significant correction, the added shock of a polarity reversal is enough to change a series of minor disasters into a single overwhelming catastrophe. There is the imminent likelihood that the combination of events I have described will occur.

"That is my story. Are there any comments or questions?"

Naturally, there was a period of dead silence. Finally the General cleared his throat. "Assuming the accuracy of what you say, it sounds to me like magnetic reversal is a heck of a lot more probable candidate for our disaster than nuclear war, say."

"Certainly preferable," Roy added.

"Preferable, to be sure," Ludwig said. "As to whether it is more probable, that depends upon timing. As I said, I believe the change is imminent. That could mean an hour or a century."

"I have a technical question," Scott continued. "How can you be so sure the concentration of reflected energy will be sufficient to overpower the earth's magnetic field?"

"A good question," Ludwig replied. "I should have mentioned that the focal corridor, or area, accumulates energy for short periods, and then releases it in concentrated bursts. It appears that we have a situation comparable to a laser, wherein energy levels are multiplied many times."

Cheng Tu spoke, his voice soft but somehow assured. "Enlighten me, old friend —"

"Oops, here it comes," Ludwig said quickly. They all laughed.

"— but do you imply, in the scenario you so masterfully painted, that the coming events are in some way predestined?"

"You heard me say the timing is unpredictable."

"Yes, but I did not hear you say that the event may be determined, or affected, by human actions and emotions. I should not wish our friends to leave with the impression that this disaster may occur arbitrarily, for reasons having to do only with what people loosely call 'material conditions.'"

"I take your point." Addressing himself primarily to the others in the room: "You all know that Dr. Tu and I disagree on many things, central among them the question of whether we humans can know with scientific certainty whether or not the world is shaped by a divinity.

"I state flatly that I do not know, and cannot see how I could ever hope to know. But that position, as Dr. Tu well knows, is a far cry from asserting that there is neither God nor reason behind the world. To say no seems to me fully as dogmatic, and more unreasonable, than to say yes."

Hugh asked: "Why more unreasonable?"

"How can anyone prove a negative? Some have what they consider personal experience of God. I may not agree that their experience and feelings constitute any kind of proof binding on others, but their testimony remains. What personal experience can there be on the other side of the question? 'I know there is no God because I have never experienced Him'? That seems to me quite unscientific. One might as well dismiss the existence of a land of perpetual ice because one chose not to believe travellers' tales of Antarctica."

Mary put up her hand. "I don't see the relevance to Dr. Tu's question."

"Ah. Dr. Tu merely wanted me to point out — and I am happy to do so — that the lens in space changes shape and quality every so often for reasons we do not understand. For all we know, those reasons may have as much to do with human action and emotion as with what we regard as strictly 'material' causes."

Hedi thought of the visions of destruction that had started her down the path leading to this room.

22. Mr. J's Promise

Hedi picked up the phone to find Martha on the other end. She was at the Columbus airport and would stop over for the night if she wouldn't be a bother.

"I'll be there in half an hour, assuming I can get a cab right away," she said. "Tell Roy I'm going to take everybody out to dinner. That means the children, too. They're big enough now, and I get to see so little of them. Call Roy and tell him to come home early if at all possible." And within the hour Aunt Martha was helping Ralph and Sally build a castle from blocks, telling them about a handsome prince and a beautiful princess who once lived in just such a castle.

After they returned from dinner and got the children to bed, Martha, Roy, and Hedi sat down to talk.

"You have had a busy time of it," Roy said. "I think maybe you have made some progress, too."

"If you judge by how fast certain institutions are running for cover, we have. Some of them haven't had a fright like this for a generation."

"High time," Roy said.

"It sounds rather wearing to me," Hedi said. "Sacred cows being disturbed, legal battles raging, attack and counter-attack in the news media...."

"It is, a little," Martha conceded. "But it's fun, too. Mr. Adams is having the time of his life."

Roy chuckled. "I have to tell you, when I got home, I thought it was quite a sight: The director of communication for Debunkers, Inc. — Stingray Carlton, I believe she is termed in certain congressional circles — on our living room floor, playing blocks with my children. I wondered if they were quite safe."

They laughed at the incongruity.

"I don't suppose Hedi told you what your parents said to me last week."

Martha shook her head.

"Your mother said, 'I always knew we had two wonderful daughters, but I just don't know where they got so much talent.' He grinned. "Then your father said, 'Don't look at me, I still have mine.'" They laughed again. "Seriously, Martha, I don't expect they come right out and tell you, but they are immensely proud of both of you. When your mother said to me she hoped it isn't a sin to be so proud of you two, your father said, 'If it is, then I'm the biggest sinner in town.'"

"That's nice to hear," Martha said.

Hedi made a face. "They'd never say it to our faces. They'd be afraid we'd get a swelled head."

Martha laughed with her. "Yep. Your children are never too old for a little more character molding."

After a while, Martha came to the point of her visit.

"Hugh Scott called me last week. Said the general wanted to see both of us. Asked if I could meet him in Washington.

"Hugh was already there when I arrived at the general's office, and so was this handsome gentleman in civilian clothes. I was ready to back right out of there: He looked like he was just about to leave, and I thought maybe the receptionist had ushered me in too soon.

"However, the general greeted me cordially and told me the gentleman had been waiting to meet me." She glanced at Hedi. "He said, 'Max, this is Martha Carlton, Hedi Johnson's sister. Martha, this is Envoy Max Banker.'"

Hedi gasped.

"The Envoy took my hand and bowed gallantly. He said, 'I am honored to meet you. My government wishes to commend you on the work you are doing. We hope we can now count you as a member of the survival team.'

"I felt strangely excited, but on such short notice I did not connect him with your robot, Hedi. It was all I could do to say 'Thank you', and 'I am very pleased to meet you.'

"He said, 'Please give your sister our very best regards,' and then turned to the general and thanked him for arranging the meeting. 'Now I must be going,' he said, and the general escorted him out the door.

"About that time, I finally made the connection. I collapsed into a chair Hugh offered me.

"The general returned to his desk.

"I said, 'Was that the robot Max Fact Banker?'

"The same," he said. "Senior envoy of our space neighbors, the Elustreons. And that meeting was the entire reason for calling you down here.'

"I said, 'It was?'

"'It was indeed. By now Max's government has your picture, your fingerprints and a map of your mental processes.' He smiled at me. 'Also a scan of your emotional character.'"

"Oh Lord," Hedi said.

Martha laughed. "That was my reaction, too. I gasped. I said, 'Dear God, not that,' but he just laughed. 'It does shake one up, doesn't it?'"

"It sure does," Hedi said. "I never thought about it; I must be in their files too."

Martha said, "You will be happy to know that your friend just got a promotion. The general opened his center drawer and took out orders making Captain Hugh Scott Major Hugh Scott. Then he had me pin the oak leaves on, since Mary wasn't there."

"That's wonderful!" Hedi said.

"It surprised Hugh, that's for sure. It took him three or four seconds after the general extended his hand before Hugh was able to figure out that he was supposed to take it."

Hedi found that she was smiling; she could all but see Hugh's startled expression.

"Hugh said he wasn't certain he had earned the promotion. The general said, 'Oh, but you will, Major. Before this is all over, you will.'"

She could envision that statement, and that response, as well.

Martha took a breath. "I have rented a cottage in Vermont for the month of October and I want you to come up and use it for a couple of weeks. It's on a wooded hillside about thirty miles northwest of Hanover, New Hampshire. It's territory I know from college days; it's only thirty minutes from Jane Adams' home. And Vermont is so beautiful in October — the foliage is a panorama of breathtaking color. You know, this is where the real Baron and Maria von Trapp built their home after leaving Europe."

"The Trapps of 'The Sound of Music'?"

"The very same."

Roy smiled. "Point for you, Martha. You just got Hedi on the hook."

Martha gave Hedi a sidelong look. "And unless I miss my guess, Hedi, Mother and Dad will put in a strong bid to keep the children. You'll have two glorious weeks on your own."

Roy hesitated. "Two weeks is a long while to be away."

Hedi said nothing, knowing that something was in the wind.

"Don't say no until you have heard the rest of my story," Martha said. "There was more to the meeting than my getting to meet Max and Hugh getting promoted. After Max left, the general had a thing or two more to say to us.

"He said, 'Max tells me their latest analysis indicates we are winning in the effort to delay a nuclear war. Increasingly they endorse the Ludwig hypothesis — the reversal of the earth's magnetic field — as the most likely event.'

"Apparently it has become more likely as war has become less likely. The general said that the Elustreons had given him their own risk analysis of the best and worst places to be in North America if it happens.

"You know, he can be very ingratiating, but just this once he turned on his full authority. He looked from Hugh to me and said, 'I will give Major Scott a copy of the analysis for New England. I am required to treat the information as top secret, Miss Carlton, but on the other hand I am motivated to place key people well away from the seacoast.'"

Hedi noticed that Martha had ceased all movement, had become intensely still.

"He told me that Ohio is not a good choice, but that most of Vermont and the interior of New Hampshire would be. He was very definite about telling me that I should tell the two of you. 'But you are not at liberty to start a mass movement to northern New England,' he said."

Nobody rushed to fill the silence. Hedi thought of her parents and other relatives who would not get the word to leave Ohio.

"After he told us that, the general looked very tired and discouraged," Martha said quietly. "He said — almost as if he were talking to himself — 'If only people were not so cruel to each other.'

"Hugh and I didn't know what to say. Finally Hugh asked him where we should look for him in case of disaster. 'Probably drowned in this goddamned office,' he said, 'but if I'm lucky enough to get out, look for me either in the Catskills of New York or the Pocono Mountains of Pennsylvania.' Hugh said to me later it was the only time he'd ever heard the general swear."

Briskly: "In any case, you see the point of my offer. There's more involved than a little vacation. I'd want you to have a look at the area and meet the important people in the area."

Roy said, "Politicians?"

"Political leaders, yes, but other types of leaders too."

"Why?"

Hedi knew the answer to that. "Because political stability and the maintenance of order will be just as important as the stability of the ground we stand on."

"That's right. It is my hope — and the hope of others — that you will find yourselves a place of safety in New England. I feel sure that if you visit the area, you will fall in love with it. And surely you could afford to buy a place there."

"Could we, Roy?"

"Well — yes, we could."

"Maybe nothing will happen," Martha said, pressing her advantage. "If so, you will acquire a nice vacation place. But if what we all fear does take place, you will have a safe haven to go to. Relatively safe, anyway."

"Mr. J promised me advance warning," Hedi said slowly.

Martha said, bluntly: "Did he promise you safety, too?"

"No, you know he didn't."

"It's up to you to protect yourself. Isn't that what he said?"

"Not in so many words, but that's what it amounts to. I think protecting your own physical safety can be considered part of the test. If you don't pass that part, you don't have to worry about what comes afterward. If you do, you get new problems. Martha, did he say we couldn't bring Mother and Dad?"

Martha shook her head. "I told you everything he said. We are forbidden to broadcast a warning to one and all, but saving family is a different case. You can take them, if you can talk them into going."

Roy spoke, in a voice strange to Hedi. "Darling, what will you do if they won't come?"

Hedi knew in her heart that they wouldn't. "I— I don't know," she said, faltering.

Roy took her hand. "You made commitments long ago," he said. "To Mr. J. To Sam Theos. To me. To the children, too, if it comes to that: It's their future we are talking about. Their very lives. Hedi, you need to make up your mind to it. Will you promise to abandon your parents if they refuse to leave Ohio?"

She could see that he knew what he was asking. "I'll make you a promise in return," he said slowly. "If you will do what you know is the right thing to do, I promise that whenever you tell me that you have received Mr. J's signal, I'll drop everything and accompany you and the children to Vermont."

Hedi knew that for Roy to abandon the clinic would be like tearing his heart out. It drove home his point. "All right," she said, "I promise. I have no other choice. But let's pray we are never faced with it."

Roy looked at his wife for a long half minute. "We accept your kind offer," he said to Martha.

* * *

"No danger of a rock slide here," the state geologist said. "And of course we don't have mud slides like they do in California."

The two weeks had passed all too quickly, spent in meeting people and enjoying the countryside. Long winter evenings had found them talking more and more about finding a retreat near their favorite village of Stowe. And so, with the coming of spring, Hedi and the children had begun exploring Vermont, searching for a vacation hide-away and for a haven of safety should disaster strike. The children were good travelers, and she often took them for three or four days at a time. Roy had joined her when he could, but the search fell mostly to her.

By summer's end she had found it, a comfortable three- bedroom cottage of typical New England construction, sitting high on a hillside overlooking the lovely valley at Stowe. She had checked it out carefully, paying an architect to examine the building and assure her that she was not likely to find anything better in the area. She had even gotten the state geologist to examine the location and assure her that it stood on stable ground. In fact, a few years earlier people would have laughed when she asked about earthquakes, but in recent years there had been noticeable tremors. In any case the area was safe from rockslides, and, as he said, New Englanders didn't have to worry about mud slides.

She had shown it to Roy, who liked it immediately.

"Let's buy it," he said. "We can close on it by late September, probably."

"That won't give us time to furnish it properly before leaf season," Hedi said wistfully.

"There isn't any reason why that should stop us. We'll rent cots and other essentials and we'll sort of camp out for two weeks."

And so they did. But then, except for a brief visit at Thanksgiving and two brief skiing trips on which Roy took some friends, the house sat idle for most of the winter.

Hedi spent much of her spare time that winter making lists of the things they would need the following summer. She told herself she was merely looking forward to using their vacation home. She tried not to think about the unaccountable sense of urgency she felt about getting the Vermont place ready for use. Every week seemed to bring news of an earthquake or a volcanic eruption, or violent solar storms. Still — she told herself — she must not lose her equilibrium.

But starting early in the spring, Hedi began travelling to Vermont, getting the place ready for the summer. By mid-June, she declared it ready for use, and the summer found them there for every long weekend they could manage.

* * *

The Gideon Bible was lying open on the floor. She had seen it on the table before going to dinner. Now it was lying on the floor.

It was the end of September. Hedi had decided to take her parents up on their offer to keep the children while she ran up to the cottage to make certain that everything was in shape for their annual two-week October vacation. Sometimes she flew to Albany and rented a car, but this time she had driven all the way.

She had driven until she grew tired, late in the afternoon. She had stopped for the night at a small, clean-looking motel in northern Maryland. She had rested for a few minutes, washed her face and hands, tidied up her hair a bit, opened a window to let in a little fresh air, and walked across the parking lot to the restaurant for dinner.

And now, on returning to her room, she noticed that the Gideon Bible was lying open on the floor.

Her first thought was that someone had been in the room. Perhaps still was. She backed up and opened the door, ready to beat a hasty retreat if necessary. She noted with some comfort that there were people in the next room. After a moment, she summoned her courage and looked under the bed. She checked the little clothes closet and examined the bathroom. No one there.

She shut the door, closed the window and picked up the Bible. It had opened to the book of Revelations. She was looking at the 16th chapter, and her eyes came to rest on the 17th verse.

"And the seventh angel poured out his vial into the air; and

there came a great voice out of the temple of heaven, from the throne, saying, It is done.

"And there were voices, and thunders, and lightnings; and there was a great earthquake, such as was not since men were upon the earth, so mighty an earthquake, and so great."

The hair was standing up on the back of her neck, and she was trembling. Was this the warning? She had to talk with Roy. She picked up the phone and placed the call. No answer. Roy wasn't home yet.

Hedi sat down on the bed and closed her eyes, praying for guidance. She felt a strong breeze blowing in the room and heard the rustle of paper. She opened her eyes. The door was still shut and the window closed, but a breeze was turning the pages in the Gideon Bible. She sat as though frozen in place, watching the pages turn.

As suddenly as it had started, the breeze stopped. She reached for the Bible, torn between hope and dread. It was now open at the 41st chapter of Genesis, and her eyes seemed drawn to the 33rd verse.

"Now therefore let Pharaoh look out a man discreet and wise, and set him over the land of Egypt.

"Let Pharaoh do this, and let him appoint officers over the land, and take up a fifth part of the land of Egypt in the seven plenteous years.

"And let them gather all the food of those good years that come, and lay up corn under the hand of Pharaoh, and let them keep food in the cities.

"And that food shall be for store to the land against the seven years of famine, which shall be in the land of Egypt; that the land perish not through the famine."

She did not need to read any more. She knew the story well.

Joseph, the eleventh son of Jacob.

Joseph, the great survivor.

He survived the attempts of his jealous brothers to kill him. He survived their selling him into the land of Egypt as a slave. He survived the rage of his master's wife who tried to seduce him. He survived years of imprisonment resulting from her false charges against him.

Then he interpreted the Pharaoh's dreams and told him how the land of Egypt could survive the disaster that was about to befall it. It was Joseph that the Pharaoh chose to execute those plans. It was Joseph who enabled the Egyptians to survive and people from many other lands as well.

It was Mr. J who had interpreted her dreams, and told her there was a role for her in helping people survive a great disaster. It was Mr. J who seemed to appear and disappear at will, and who claimed to have had a lot of experience with survival. It was Mr. J who had promised to give her a sign if the disaster was about to occur, and at the same time give her a clue as to his identity.

Logically, all this proved nothing. But she no longer had any doubt. The catastrophe was about to strike. Perhaps in a few days, perhaps in a few hours. It was time to act. She had to find Roy. Again she reached for the phone.

23. It's Coming

Two rings. No answer. Three rings. Four. "Please, Roy," she said. "Please."

"Hello?"

"Oh, Roy, I'm so glad to hear your voice! We don't have any time to lose. Oh, Roy, it's coming, and I left the children with Mother and Dad."

"I just this moment walked in the door," Roy answered. "Slow down a little and tell me what happened. Where are you calling from?"

"I'm in a motel in Maryland. I had stopped for the night and —"

"Calm down, now."

Hedi took a deep breath, trying to regain her composure. "Remember, Mr. J promised me a clue if a catastrophe was imminent? I have that clue, just like he said. I don't know if we have the time to go into details."

There was a brief silence. "You are satisfied this is it?"

"Yes."

"What would you like me to do?"

Oh, she thought, thank God he isn't the type who only believes what he sees himself.

"I haven't had time to think, but shouldn't we carry out our emergency plan? I have to go back to get the children. It's after seven o'clock. It'll take me a little over five hours. It'll be after midnight — more like one — by the time I get to my parents' house. You can be half way to Stowe by the the time I start back."

"You think you can persuade them to come with you?"

"I'm going to try my best. Either way, win or lose, I'll be on my way back to Stowe in half an hour from the time I get to Mother's."

Even as she was speaking, her mind was beginning to race down a list of things to be done. "Roy, if you get to Stowe before I get back, try to alert Martha and anyone else you think might listen."

"No, wait," Roy said. "I will meet you at your folks' home, and we will go up together. Even after doing what I have to do here, I should get there before you do."

She would feel better with Roy. And probably it would be safer, too. "All right. I'll meet you there. Goodbye."

"Hedi!"

"Yes?"

"You have had a hard day. Please be careful driving back."

"Thank you, darling. I'll be careful," she said. "You too."

Moving automatically, scarcely thinking what she was doing, she locked the motel door behind her and pocketed the key. She was already on the interstate before she realized that she hadn't checked out. She shrugged, another automatic gesture in the empty car. If no catastrophe came, she'd have to straighten it out with the owner. Otherwise, it wouldn't matter.

She drove through the quiet night, finding it hard to keep her mind on the road. She told herself that a dead mother would be of little use to Ralph and Sally.

A little after 10, she got off the interstate and stopped at a gas-and-go place with a little eatery attached. She had them fill the tank and check the oil, then went inside to have a cup of coffee. At another time, she would have found the atmosphere quiet and restful. A young couple and their three children were indulging in milkshakes, perhaps a treat to make up for the day's long ride. Two truckers in a booth were eating steak and onions, and it smelled good. A tired businessman sat at the counter a couple of seats away from her, sipping coffee and looking at nothing.

The coffee tasted terrible, all acid and bitterness, but the warmth felt good. After a few minutes the caffeine begin to hit, and she felt, if anything, more tired than before, yet more alert.

The waitress was working her way down the counter, a half- filled pot in her hand. "More coffee, hon?"

Hedi let her fill the cup three-quarters full, then gestured for her to stop. She picked up the little metal pitcher and poured milk into the bitter black brew. This would have to be it. Too much, and she would begin to get the shakes. Besides, there was no time for more.

She found that she was engaged in a silent argument.

"Suppose this is all in your mind. Can you imagine how embarrassed you're going to be?"

"I don't care. This is one time I'd rather be embarrassed than be right."

"That's what you say now. But what happens when you start trying to explain to your parents that you think the world is coming to an end because the Bible fell open to a certain page?"

"They're going to think I've finally gone around the bend."

"You better believe they will. Your father is going to say he knew they never should have let you go to that survival camp."

"And Mother will say that people believe what they believe, and there isn't much anyone else can do about it."

"And the next time you come crying wolf, they will be just that much less willing to listen."

Crying wolf? Something within her turned, at that. (She pulled around an old man doing 50 in an ancient four-door Chrysler.) "I'm not crying wolf! Mr. J promised me a sign, and he gave it to me. It's up to me to heed it."

"And leave your parents, if they don't believe you?"

There it was again, the terrible unanswerable question.

"No! I can't. There are some things people can't do. Nobody can expect me to. They can't make me do it."

"And what about your promise to Sam Theos?"

"You can't always do everything you promise. I can't do it."

She drove the next few miles angrily, swerving the car with unnecessary violence when she moved out to pass other cars.

"Have to be careful. What's the use of getting killed on the way back to save the kids?"

But of course if she wasn't going to take them to Stowe, they were all going to die anyway.

Roy wouldn't like the way she was driving. And he had told her to be careful. She raised her right foot slightly. The car slowed to nearer the speed limit.

The thought of Roy gave her pause. He and she had made a pact. She had asked him to abandon his clinic, knowing that to do that would be to tear out his heart. He was coming to meet her. He would be there by the time she arrived, perhaps. He would have kept his promise.

"Roy keeps his promises," she said aloud. "So do I. And he isn't the only person I've promised."

She arrived at her parents' house to find Roy there.

"I got the kids up and dressed," he said, "and I got their clothes packed."

"Honey," Nora Carlton said to her, "it's the middle of the night. Can't you wait till morning?"

"No time," she said tensely. "It isn't safe here. We've got to get going."

"But they only just arrived. They will be so disappointed."

"Mother—" Hedi stopped. How could she get across to them? "Where are they?"

"They went right back to sleep in their clothes, the little lambs. They were so tired."

Well, that was a blessing. "Mother, where's Dad?"

"Right here."

"Mother, Dad, we have to go. I don't know how much time we

have, but there isn't much. The thing I've been dreading for a dozen years is on its way, and we don't have a lot of time to save ourselves."

She could see the look of patient diplomacy on his face. "Hedi, —"

"Oh, Dad, we don't have time to argue! I love you so much, I don't want to have to leave you here to die! PLEASE pack a few things and come on."

"You might look on it as a little vacation, sir," Roy said. "You were planning to have time with Ralph and Sally; why not have it up in Vermont? The place is plenty big enough, and you haven't even seen it yet."

Glen Carlton shook his head. "We can't just go off on ten minutes' notice. It takes longer than that to plan a vacation."

"Dad," Hedi said in anguish, "we don't have time. We've run out of time."

"People usually have more time than they take," her father said. "Surely you have enough time to tell us why you think this is it. Roy tried to explain, but I couldn't make heads nor tails of what he was saying."

"I was trying to think straight while I was dressing the children," Roy said. "I guess I didn't do a very good job of explaining."

Hedi looked at her watch. Eight minutes since she'd pulled in the driveway.

She took a deep breath. "You remember years ago, when I first started being interested in survival camps? I never told you why. At least, I never told you the whole story."

As quickly as she could, she sketched out the story of her visions, and Mr. J, and Mr. J's promise to her. She ended by telling them of her experience in the motel a few hours earlier.

"Divination by signs," Nora Carlton said dubiously.

"Not necessarily a sign of evil," her husband said. "But" — looking at Hedi meaningfully — "not necessarily infallible, either. It's a narrow line between intuition and superstition."

She looked at her watch. Twenty-one minutes. "Nothing is certain until it happens," she said, "but I don't dare ignore this warning."

She played her ace. "We can't stay here; Ohio isn't a safe place to be. Martha told me so."

"Martha?"

"Martha's debunking project has ties to the survival camp," she said. "You remember my friend Major Scott? He and Mary attended our wedding? He personally told Martha, and told her to tell me."

Her father asked, "If it's so unsafe, why haven't we seen anything about it in the papers?"

"It isn't generally known. We were forbidden to make the news public. Only a few of us know."

For a moment, she thought she had them. Much as they loved her, she knew they sometimes had their doubts about her projects. But about Martha's rock-solid common sense they had no doubts. But then her father asked one question more. "What is your authority for thinking Ohio unsafe?"

With a sinking heart, Hedi knew that she should have begun years ago to prepare the ground. How could she tell them to leave their homes because the Elustreons said so? She knew what they thought about flying saucers.

"Oh, Dad, I don't have time to go into it. I can tell you everything once we're on the way, but we don't have time to do it now. Please, we must go. There's no way to know how soon it will hit, but it might be a matter of hours. We have to go, and I can't leave you here."

"But you can," her mother said calmly, "and you must."

She stilled Hedi's protest. "It isn't that we think you are wrong, but I said years ago that you have your destiny to fulfill and we have ours. All of our life has been here. We expect to die here also."

"Are you saying you want to die?" Hedi asked, the tears running down her cheeks. "Are you asking that I leave you here to commit suicide?"

"Let me try to explain it to you," her father said.

"Your mother and I have spent our lives trying as best we could to make a small bit of this old Earth a little better place. Now you think it is going down the drain, and we must somehow stay alive and start all over trying to build a bright new world. We think we would rather stay here and fight for the old one a while longer."

"But you can't —"

"It may be hopeless, I don't know. But our lives are here. In this house, in this town, with our friends and neighbors. As long as there is any hope at all, we want to stay here."

He looked at her compassionately. "Can you say there is no hope here? Can you promise safety and a useful life for us if we go with you?"

"No, I can't be that certain," Hedi said softly, "but I am so frightened for you."

"We have our faith," her mother answered. "God will give us strength to do what we must do. Now go and do what you must do. If we see that things are hopeless, we will seek higher ground, and should it still be possible, we will come to you in Vermont."

Roy spoke. "I wish you would come with us, but I hear what you say, and you say it with great eloquence." She saw him turn to her. "It's your decision. I had to make mine."

* * *

They left Hedi's small sedan and travelled together in the station wagon. That was Roy's decision. That way, he said, they could take turns at the wheel and drive straight through to Stowe. He had piled luggage on the back seat in order to make room for a makeshift bed in the rear compartment. There he placed the children. Within minutes of being picked up and carried outside, they were asleep again.

Hedi was still weeping silently as he brought the big car up onto the interstate.

"Hardly anybody here," he said. "Just those tractor-trailers. They like travelling at night; it's easier without all the passenger-car traffic. Not many people on the road at two in the morning."

She knew what he was doing, but couldn't make herself respond.

"You know, when I hung up after your call, it took me a few seconds to get over being frightened. Half a minute, maybe. I was hoping you were wrong, but my seat-of-the-pants instinct told me to believe you."

She sensed him glance at her.

"I went to my study and pulled out my 'emergency countdown' notebook, and I worked my way through the list. Didn't take long. I'm trained to deal with emergencies, after all, and there isn't much point in having training if you can't function when the big one hits, right? You listening, Hedi?"

She nodded, then, thinking that he probably didn't see her nod in the dark, said, "Yes. I'm listening." She could say that much, even if she couldn't stop the tears.

"It took me about an hour. I had collected the personal things on our list, I had packed some clothes, I had made certain I had all the cash in the house, and our emergency supply of travelers checks. I had loaded everything into the car, and I was on my way."

She saw him take his eyes off the road for a long moment, searching her face for response. "And I almost turned back."

She waited, unable to meet his eyes.

"I felt terrible. The first thing on my list, of course, was informing the clinic that I was going to be out of town on a family emergency, and I had done that. But then I thought, what kind of thing was that to do? I was deserting my co-workers. I was deserting the clinic itself, after all those years of work and worry. And I was leaving them without so much as a word of warning."

Again his eyes left the road. This time she met them.

"I couldn't do it. It was too cowardly a thing to do. So I stopped the car. I knew I'd have to go back."

His voice was so soft, she could scarcely hear it. "Do you know why I didn't?"

He was waiting for her response. She shook her head. "You thought maybe it wouldn't happen?"

"No. Well, I did try to tell myself that. I said you might be wrong, and if you were, no harm done. But I didn't believe that. My gut instinct is that you are right. No, I got back on the road for only one reason, Hedi. I had promised you. I had promised you, and I intended to keep that promise, no matter what."

A third time he looked at her. "You hear what I am saying, darling? You left your parents because you promised me, and you had to keep your promise. I don't want you to blame yourself for doing what had to be done. Now see if you can't get some sleep. If I get too tired to drive, I'll call you. That's a promise."

"I had all that coffee," she said automatically. "I don't think I can." But she had little idea how tired she was, both physically and emotionally. Within minutes of the time her tears stopped, she dropped into an uneasy asleep.

She awoke to find first light in the sky before them. Roy had driven for four hours, on top of his earlier journey and a day's work.

"You must be exhausted," she murmured.

"I could use some coffee," he admitted. He needed a shave, and his eyes were sunken. "No worse than residency, though," he said.

"Let me drive," she said. "We're only about an hour from the motel I checked into this — yesterday afternoon. We can get some breakfast, call Martha and maybe get a little sleep."

"You think they'll have a room?"

She smiled. Her first smile in many hours. "They do for sure. I forgot to check out, and I've got the key in my pocket."

"If it's only an hour, I ought to be able to make it," Roy said. "You only got about four hours' sleep."

"Four hours more than you had," she said. "Pull over, friend."

He did, and Hedi took the wheel. He had been on the move for twenty-four hours: He was deep in sleep within minutes. An hour later, when she parked the wagon in the same slot that had held her little sedan the day before, she hesitated before waking him. She'd need his strength; it was important not to waste it. But there were too many things to be done.

He awoke without complaint. Of course, as a doctor, he'd long since become accustomed to making do with short snatches of sleep at irregular intervals.

"We're here, I take it," he said. Looking at her tense expression, he asked what she needed done.

"I've got to call Martha right now. I just remembered a few minutes ago, she was planning to fly down to Washington this morning for some kind of meeting. Can you get the children awake and get them to the restaurant and give them breakfast?"

"Shall I order something for you?"

"Yes, but it might be cold by the time I get there. I don't know how long the call will take, and I'm afraid if I wait till after we eat, I might miss her."

Again, listening to rings, waiting for someone to pick up the telephone. Six rings. Eight. Eleven. She can't be there; she'd have answered it by now. Thirteen.

"Hello." Martha sounded a bit breathless.

"Martha, this is Hedi. I was afraid I'd missed you."

"I was in the shower, of course, and I'm standing here dripping wet. Isn't it always that way?" Then what she had heard in Hedi's voice seemed to register. "Something has happened. What?"

"You'd better get dry. I'll hold the phone. Don't take too long."

Hedi sat listening to silence on the other end of the line. If the catastrophe didn't happen, she'd have quite a phone bill. If it did happen, the bill wouldn't matter. Wouldn't exist, in fact.

"All right, I'm back."

"Pretty fast. Listen, Roy and I are on our way to Stowe." She gave her sister a detailed account of what had happened. "You'll have to decide what you want to do, but I hope you'll take no unnecessary risks."

"I can tell you right now that I take your warning very seriously. I don't know how I am going to do it, but I am not going to Washington today, and I must find some way to get my people out of there." Martha paused. "And out of our California office as well. How much time do you think we have?"

"Mr. J said probably less than five days after I received the clue, and the first day is half gone."

"I am going to figure we have two days at the most. Is there anything you want me to do?" Martha asked.

"Hugh Scott should be advised as soon as possible. If you know where he is, you might call him. He should be able to get me at the cottage any time after three p.m."

"How about Mother and Dad?"

Hedi held herself on a short rein. "Martha, I tried, but they wouldn't come. I really did try."

"Maybe I can persuade them to seek safer ground, if only for a few days."

"That would be wonderful," Hedi said. She tried to persuade herself that Martha might have some luck where she had failed.

* * *

Roy parked the car in the driveway by the cottage. "There, thank God, we made it. Now, what would you like me to do?"

"If there are some calls you need to make, perhaps you should make them now. I'm going to run into town and get some supplies, including something for lunch. I'll take Ralph with me. Sally is tired, and I think she'll take a nap. If you run out of something to do, you might try to reach Uncle Jake. He probably won't listen, but at least we owe him a warning."

"And I was warned in a dream about a big storm that might take place. If it does come, your Aunt Martha thinks this will be a safe place to be."

The four of them were having sandwiches and milk in their cottage. The day outside was gorgeous, a snappy early fall day.

"I would like to see a big storm," Sally said. Her father said, "Well, maybe you will get your wish."

"Mommy," Ralph said, "Is that why you came back to get us last night? Is that why you are warning people?"

"Yes, that is why."

"Then why didn't Grandmom and Granddad Carlton come up here and stay with us?"

"I guess they think the storm will not be too bad," Roy said.

"Well, wouldn't Granddad know about it? He knows a lot!"

"He sure does. And maybe there won't be any storm. There isn't any way to be sure. But we didn't want to take any chances."

When Ralph began to worry a subject, he hung on like a dog worrying a bone. "Granddad didn't believe Mommy's dream."

"He wasn't sure, honey. And he felt he had to stay where his friends were."

"Doesn't he believe in dreams?"

"You'll have to ask him. Some people do, some don't."

"I believe in dreams," Sally announced, "and I want to see a big storm." Ralph looked doubtful but said no more.

Roy looked out at the bright-lit day. "Ralph, are you sure there are bears in those woods across the way?"

Ralph brightened. "I'm sure there are."

"Well, don't you think you and Sally ought to protect us? Did you bring your bear gun?"

Ralph looked immensely dignified. "Sally can't hunt bears, she's a girl."

"Can too!"

"Maybe you could teach her. I would feel better, knowing that you'd taken care of any bears out there."

"Okay, Dad, don't worry. We'll get them."

As soon as the children were out the door, Roy's face lost its smile.

"While you were gone, I got through to Uncle Jake's office," he told Hedi. "He is out in Denver goofing off at some medical meeting and will not be back for five or six days. I have finished my other calls. What's next?"

Hedi wrinkled her brow in thought, then felt her tension relax about a tenth of a notch. "Denver might be a good place to be. Maybe we don't have to worry about Uncle Jake for the moment."

She nodded to herself. It was nice to have even one thing settled. "I'm trying to list the supplies we should have in the house for the longer pull. Should have done it a long time ago. Want to work on it with me?"

"Hello?"

"Hedi?"

"Martha. Where are you?"

"I am at Mr. Adams' house. Hugh Scott is coming for dinner tonight, and we will try to decide if we should seek a meeting with the governor."

"I take it you cancelled your meetings in Washington."

"I did. And not only that, Mr. Adams instructed his office staff to send 'Command Performance' invitations to the people on my list. They think they are going to attend an urgent discussion of policy matters in Montpelier. They have been urged to bring their families if possible, as the matter for discussion would impact on spouses and children."

"I'm impressed. How did you do that?"

Martha gave a tense little laugh.

"I went to Mr. Adams with my fingers crossed and laid the entire problem out on the table. I figured he would think I was crazy."

Hedi's thoughts were racing to keep up with Martha's telegraphic delivery. "You had to tell him why you thought our time is up."

"Right. I had to tell the most practical man I have ever met that my big sister had a dream and had her Bible fall off a table, and so I want him to tell everybody the sky is falling."

Hedi smiled. Her first smile in — how long? "Well? Don't leave me in suspense."

"He fooled me. He said, 'So now it's your sister's visions. You may be surprised to know that I believe in visions. Mine were called daydreams, but what matters the time of day? They worked for me.'"

"How about that? I'd say you did well."

"Hedi, do you still think this is it?"

"Y— Yes, I do. And Roy has the same hunch."

"Well, so do I. Listen, I will call Mom and Dad tonight, and will be back in touch with you. If anything urgent comes up, call me here at the Adams house. You have the number."

Hedi had scarcely replaced the phone on the hook when it rang again.

It was Hugh Scott. "I got a private SOS from Martha with instructions to call you, Hedi. I was going to call you anyway. What's your news?"

Hedi told him the story of her experiences of the previous evening, and reminded him of Mr. J's promise of a clue. "It's up to you to decide how seriously this should be taken," she said.

"The fact that Roy and I are up here ought to tell you how we feel about it."

"I am going to call the general right away. Yours is the second clue. Have you talked to Madge Theos?"

"Madge? No. Should I?"

"She has a message for you from her father. He's dead."

"Dead!"

"Last night. He told her he had completed his mission. He turned in for the night and died peacefully in his sleep. Hedi, I must start searching for the general now. We may not have much time. I will be back in touch."

Hedi felt shaken. She saw Roy looking at her with concern as she put down the phone. She repeated Hugh's message. "I am afraid, darling," she said.

"I'm scared to death," Roy replied. He took her in his arms, and for a long minute they held each other close.

"We must remember not to frighten the children," he said.

"Maybe you should bring them in," Hedi suggested. "They've had a mixed-up day. I think I should feed them early and put them to bed."

After the children were in bed, Roy turned on the news.

"Mother Nature provided the feature news stories for today," the TV announcer said. "Severe earthquakes struck in Turkey, Chile, and Mexico. In the far north, there is the most dazzling display of northern lights on record. Charter flights are being organized in both Canada and England to take those who can afford the fee for an aerial view of the celestial fireworks. A similar display has been reported in the south polar region.

"Scientists are speculating that the cause is the occurrence of unusually severe solar storms on the sun, but they are puzzled that these storms eluded direct observation. We will have more details in a moment, but first... these messages."

Roy said, "I can't stand it any longer. I must call my staff at the clinic and give them some sort of warning."

Hedi nodded agreement. "There's Dr. Exter, too, and so many others."

Roy reached for the phone. "Whatever it may be, I believe it's coming," he said.

It was the end of the first full day after Hedi received the warning.

24. The Birds Aren't Singing

Morning brought sunshine and blue skies, accented by the sounds of nature's creatures starting a new day. There was a hint of fall in the air supported by a tinge of color in the forest. How could disaster lurk just around the corner when the whole out-of-doors proclaimed peace and contentment? Perhaps it was all an illusion.

But Hedi prepared breakfast while trying to conceal tears. She was thinking of Martha's futile effort to persuade their parents to flee the coming disaster, and she didn't want her happy, talkative daughter to know her thoughts.

"Both Mom and Dad are anxious that we know how much they appreciate our concern," Martha had said, "but they have their own point of view."

"In other words," Hedi had said harshly, "they aren't moving."

"No. No, they aren't."

"And telling them about Sam Theos wouldn't help."

"Hedi, they never met him. You know what he was, and I do. But they don't."

"Madge called me a little while ago," Hedi had said numbly. "I told her I was sorry about her father's death, that he was like a godfather to me. She said maybe someday I could explain to her why it all happened." Hedi barked out a short, unhappy laugh. "How am I supposed to do that?"

"Take it easy, big sis. Stay cool."

"Yes, of course. I know you're right. You know what else Madge said? She said that years ago she'd seen her father, Sam Woodrow, on his deathbed, and had seen Sam Theos get out of that bed. 'He did remarkable things during a remarkable career,' she said. 'Always he took me with him, and no father could have taken better care of a daughter. Now I have seen Sam Theos die. He believed he was here for a purpose, and he told me before he went to bed that his mission was finished. Wherever he is, I hope he is happy.' I asked her where she thought he was. I just wanted to know what she thought."

"Of course."

"She said, 'I don't know. I never had any traditional religious training, but he said we would meet again, and I believe him. He once told me there was no such thing as death; one only moved from one life phase to another.'"

"'One life phase to another.' I have a feeling we're going to have to cling to that idea, pretty soon."

A brief silence.

"He left me a message," Hedi had said. "Left Madge a note to read me. I wrote it down as she gave it to me. He said, 'Tell Hedi to hang on to her faith, and her Creator will provide the strength and the wisdom she requires. Give Roy my regards also. He is a tower of strength. Tell them we shall all meet again in other times and happier circumstances.'" Again Hedi had broken into tears.

Martha asked, "What are Madge's plans?" In the back of her mind, Hedi wondered if Martha was trying to divert her, as she herself often diverted Ralph or Sally.

"She said the Chief's note told her to leave within 48 hours and contact Hugh Scott at once. She said Hugh had already gotten her an administrative job in his Vermont office. She — she was concerned that there wasn't any funeral service, but she said the Chief had said there wouldn't be time. I told her all his friends would remember him, and he has so many. I told her she wouldn't be far from where we are, so I expected to see her soon."

"'There wouldn't be time,'" Martha had said, repeating again. "That's something else we are going to hear a lot of."

After breakfast, Roy took Ralph with him to purchase the emergency supplies. Two hours later he returned with the station wagon heavily laden.

"Ralph has been a big help," he told Hedi. "And now he's going it help me divide our supplies? Right, big fella?"

"Right, Dad," he said proudly. "One part for the station wagon, one part for the cellar and one part for the shelves."

"You've got it. Let's get to it." Roy winked at Hedi. "Nice to have another man around the house, isn't it? Makes things easier." They watched Ralph borrow the keys to open the tailgate. "C'mon, Dad. We got *work* to do."

By midafternoon, the task was finished and the children were outside in the bright sunshine, playing. Hedi was sitting on the front steps watching them when Roy called her.

Martha was on the phone. "Can you put me up for the night if I hop in the car and come up to see you?"

"Sure. Why ask? We'll be delighted."

Martha sounded tense. "We met with the governor this morning. He is in quite a sweat. He is afraid to take action on the basis of psychic warnings, and he is afraid to ignore them."

"I'll bet."

"He wrote an order placing Lieutenant Colonel Scott in charge of the Vermont National Guard, but he has yet to release it."

"He doesn't know what to do."

"There is much more, but what I need most just now is to consult with you. Since I wouldn't dare suggest you leave your family at this time, I am prepared to come to see you."

"Please do. Of course we can put you up."

Martha arrived just at the beginning of the 6:30 p.m. news. Ralph and Sally immediately climbed all over her.

"Come on in," Roy said. "The experts are arguing over the cause of the electronic fireworks around the north and south poles."

With the children sharing Aunt Martha's lap, the adults tensely sat through stunningly violent film footage of the eruptions of volcanoes in Indonesia and Iceland. Scarcely able to comprehend the forces involved, they watched as thousands of tons of matter were spewed high into the air. "Think of the power that represents," Roy muttered. "Reminds me of Mount St. Helens, back in '80."

The volcano footage was followed by descriptions and some film footage of the damage done by the previous day's earthquakes. This, in turn, was followed by video tape of the spectacular northern lights.

The news announcer projected sincerity and personality through the camera lens. "What's causing all this activity? Some scientists say it may be mere coincidence of timing. Volcanoes and earthquakes, they point out, are natural phenomena, part of everyday life. They remind us that even though several striking events occur in close proximity, this does not mean that the phenomena are necessarily related."

He shifted positions, so that he faced the camera on his right. "One scientist who disagrees is Dr. Richard Ludwig." The camera moved back, bringing another man into view beside the anchorman. "There he is!" Hedi said.

"Dr. Ludwig, you have recently gained considerable attention in scientific circles for your rather controversial theories. Can you tell us what you think is happening?"

Roy laughed. "In two minutes?"

Perhaps Dr. Ludwig was thinking something similar. They could see a trace of his self-mocking smile, quickly covered over.

He made it with a few seconds to spare. He said that it was well known in scientific circles that the earth's magnetic field had reversed itself on several occasions in the past. He thought this might be about to happen again. The process would naturally be accompanied by a great deal of stress. Volcanic activity and extensive earth tremors would naturally be expected to accompany any such field reversal.

"The anchorman looks a little perplexed," Martha said.

Hedi laughed. "I know just how he feels. I remember the first time I heard the same thing."

"Well, Dr. Ludwig, let's suppose your scenario is correct. What happens next?"

"Nobody knows. We have no record of what happened in previous reversals."

The anchorman looked a bit disappointed. "I suppose, then, that you have little advice for our viewers on what to do."

"Those who have a magnetic compass around the house probably should keep an eye on it. If it starts to fluctuate wildly, it might be a good time to seek cover."

"And otherwise?"

Dr. Ludwig shrugged. "The most important thing, obviously, is: Stay calm. Don't panic. Listen for emergency instructions on radio or TV."

"Good advice in any case," the anchorman said briskly. "In a minute we'll be back —"

Hedi, Martha and Roy looked at each other. Roy looked at his watch. "It has been two full days since Hedi received her warning," he said quietly.

"Let's put supper together," Hedi said. "When we get the children safely to bed, then we can talk."

"Somehow the general wrangled another promotion for Hugh," Martha said, "and he issued orders temporarily assigning him to the Vermont National Guard."

"Does he still retain responsibility for liaison with National Guard commands in other New England states?"

"Yes."

"How did Governor Bennard respond to that?"

"He was receptive. The timing was good, because his National Guard commander had just resigned for reasons of health."

"Still," Roy said, "it is pretty unusual to appoint a regular Army officer to command a National Guard unit."

"I think there was some behind-the-scenes action there," Hedi said, looking at Martha.

Martha smiled. "The governor also agreed that Hugh would immediately activate the Little River emergency headquarters."

"What's that?" Hedi asked. "That's a new one to me."

"Little River Recreation Area is a part of a State Forest located just southwest of Stowe. We decided some time ago that it would make a good emergency headquarters. We did the spadework months ago."

"Sounds like you've gotten a lot," Hedi said.

Martha nodded. "Yes and no. Governor Bennard is willing to order any reasonable training exercises for state personnel, because that can be explained away. But he isn't ready to declare an actual state of emergency."

"I can see that," Roy said. "If we didn't know what we know, we'd think it was pretty good common sense."

"That is precisely the present problem," Martha said. "What do we do now? The governor will listen to any proposal that can be supported by logic, but frankly, we ran out of ideas that fall in that category. While Hugh is trying to deal with all the problems that are heaped on his plate, I was sent here to seek guidance and ideas. There must be something we can get him to do!"

"All states have plans for dealing with various kinds of emergencies," Roy said. "Sometimes they have adequate training exercises, but often they do not." He frowned, feeling his way. "Frankly, I do not believe there is time to call an actual training alert, but the leaders at county and township level could be warned of an immediate surprise alert."

Hedi asked, "How can it be a surprise if you inform them ahead of time?"

"By surprise, I mean they will not be told in advance the nature of the emergency, except that it will be statewide, and that a township cannot depend on aid from its neighbors. Hopefully, at a minimum this will cause all units to review their plans and procedures."

"Good," Martha said. "I think I can sell that idea. But there must be something else." She looked, Hedi thought, almost desperate. Hedi closed her eyes and forced herself to breathe slowly. This was what she had trained for.

"There isn't much we can do about surviving the initial disaster, Martha," she said. "That's a matter of being at the right place at the right time. A few of us have had advice on how to improve our chances, but survival is still a matter of placement. And that, unless we have some sixth sense to guide us, is little more than a matter of luck."

She held Martha's gaze. "But the thrust of all my survival training sessions was that there's a lot we can do to improve our chances of surviving the aftermath."

She had Martha's attention — and Martha had the ear of Len Adams, who had the ear of Governor Bennard. This could be the moment when she moved beyond personal survival into a larger arena. She could feel her mind moving efficiently, ticking off item after item.

"Leadership and communication between leaders will be a critical problem. I think the governor and his staff should try to find out where their counterparts in other New England states will be for the next few days."

Martha made a note on the pad before her.

"For communication, we should assume we will have no telephones or electrical power. Most commercial airfields will be shut down, highways will be blocked in many places, and rail lines will be unusable. The most reliable means of transportation as well as communication may be the light piston-engine aircraft... planes that can land on lakes, sections of highway, or on grass strips."

Martha nodded, accepting Hedi's logic.

"I know Hugh will think of this and the military has its own resources, but I think the state should make plans and draft orders to take control of all such aircraft in Vermont." Another note. "And prepare to take control of fuel supplies, too. Fuel is very important, since what you have may be all you get for a very long time."

She took a long breath. "And then there's food. Here's where you're going to have to do some selling, Martha."

She began running through the points the classes had discussed in survival school, so long ago.

"Get the governor to issue an order taking control of every bit of food in the state. That means food in the hands of everyone from the producer to the smallest retailer, and don't forget those supply trucks that may be en route."

"What?!"

"Martha, I'm serious. Get him to prepare an emergency order for the National Guard to requisition all the food in Vermont, and put it under lock and key. That means guards at the doors, and shoot anybody who tries to steal as much as a loaf of bread. Maybe the order can't be actually *issued* just yet, but he should get it drafted, at least. When the time comes, Hugh Scott should have a copy in his pocket: he's going to need it in a hurry."

"Hedi, we can't just take people's food!"

"We're going to have to. That's another item for your list, by the way: compensation. Whoever requisitions the food will have to give receipts of some kind, so that the owners can be compensated when circumstances permit."

Martha looked dubious. "I'm not sure I can talk him into all this."

"Martha, this is vital. When the earthquakes hit — whether it's tonight, or tomorrow, or whenever — when they hit, that's the end of our food-distribution system. Whatever food we have on hand is what we have, and that's it till the next harvest. Have you given any thought to what that means? It means we're going to have to start rationing food immediately. Not when people's personal stocks of food start running out. Not when the grocery store shelves get emptied. Now!"

Martha grunted from the impact. "I see your point."

"And that's not the half of it," Hedi said grimly. "They've got to take absolute control of the means to plant next year's crops. Seeds. Cereal grains. Seed potatoes. We've *got* to be sure that we don't eat next year's seed corn." She looked at Martha severely. "You understand? Even knowing that some people are going to starve, we've *got* to save that seed, or we're *all* going to starve a little later."

Part of Hedi's mind seemed to be back in the survival camp. She seemed to see Sam Theos looking down at her. "Somebody needs to be doing some long-range thinking about increasing our food supply, starting from day one."

"You have any specific ideas I can mention?"

"We'll need programs to make the best use of farm animals. Goats, for instance."

"Why goats?"

"Because goats are tough and they'll eat anything. Almost anything. Pigs and chickens, too. They eat garbage and scraps, and that'll be important. We're not going to have the luxury of holding aside special grains to feed animals. But here, too, we're going to have to be careful. Chickens and eggs are great protein; they'll be a big help this winter, but if we eat all the eggs we aren't going to have any more chickens. And if we eat all the chickens, we aren't going to have any more eggs."

Martha smiled wanly. "That's an old story: Which comes first, the chicken or the egg?"

"In this case they both do."

Martha made another note. "More ideas?"

"Well, the governor could set up a special corps of licensed hunters, to go out and harvest deer for meat. Not just deer, either. Squirrels. Small mammals of all kinds. Believe me, we're going to need the protein."

"There are lots of hunters in New England," Martha said, nodding. "That should be no problem."

"Well, actually, that *could* be a problem. We can't afford to let just anybody get out there and hunt. That's why I said a *licensed corps* of hunters. We want to *harvest* them, not exterminate them."

"Hunters won't like that much."

"No. But it's going to be a different world, Martha. There's a lot of things we're used to doing that we won't be able to do anymore. That's what it's going to take to survive."

"Any other food ideas for the govenor?"

"Well, he might start getting information collected on edible herbs, nuts, and berries — things like that. And if he can find anything on setting up small-scale fish hatcheries — in solar greenhouses, maybe — that would help. We're going to need everything we can think of."

Martha made a note. "More?"

"Medical supplies. Whatever we have on hand is all we're going to have for quite some time. Even aspirin tablets are going to be precious beyond price."

She ticked off several other items before she ran out of ideas.

Martha was looking at her with new respect. "These ideas can't wait for me to get back. I am going to call Mr. Adams and see if he will take them to the governor tonight. Stay near, Hedi. He may want to quiz you on them."

"And after we talk to Mr. Adams," Hedi said, "I suggest we all go to bed. How long has it been since you got some sleep?"

Martha had to make an effort to recall. "More than a day. Less than two. Say 36 hours."

"Perhaps we should divide the night into three shifts," Roy suggested. "Then one of us will be available to answer the phone and watch for any developments in the news."

Hedi took the first shift. It was one a.m. when she awakened Roy for his turn. "The news agencies are getting nervous," she said. "Radio frequency broadcasts are being blacked out by the high static level, and other queer things are being reported, but they can find no one able to give them explanations. Ralph's Cub Scout compass still points north, and Mr. Adams reports that the governor will implement our suggestions first thing in the morning."

"All in all, a good report," Roy said. "Now off to bed with you, and try to get some sleep."

At six a.m., she awoke suddenly, and forced herself out of bed. She found Roy and Martha in the kitchen. Roy poured her a cup of coffee and reported what little he knew.

"I couldn't get anything on the radio. For most of the night, only the cable news station was broadcasting, and fresh news was scarce."

"So you had to stay up for nothing," Hedi murmured. "What a shame."

"I did make note of one announcement. Canada said there would be no more charter flights to the polar region, due to unusual air turbulence and also to problems with various instruments needed for safe operation of the aircraft."

"Magnetic instruments," Hedi said.

"They didn't say, but that would be my guess. There was a report, too, that all communications links to scientific research bases in Antarctica were down, with the single exception of the satellite communication link. And at about 3 a.m., Antarctica reported low-level earth tremors and very turbulent winds." He checked his pencilled notes. "They said their instruments indicated that within an hour, the outside air temperature had jumped some 20 degrees Celsius."

"What?!"

"I know. That about sums up their reaction, too. Everybody is working on the assumption that something happened to the instrument. That would be a jump of — what? — nearly 36 degrees

Fahrenheit. It's virtually impossible. They said they intended to check it."

He looked at his notes again. "But the 4 a.m. report said they had decided that the swirling winds and very dense fog made it too dangerous to send anyone outside to check. At 5, they announced that all contact with the base had been lost."

He looked up at Hedi soberly. "And, a little closer to home, at 4 a.m. I noticed that Ralph's little magnetic compass was very sluggish in returning to its north-south position after being disturbed. Now it's even more so.

"That's about it. I made fresh coffee at 4:30, and the smell must have wakened Martha, because she came stumbling in here a few minutes later, complaining that I should have gotten her up earlier." He smiled at his sister-in-law. "She's as grouchy as you are when she doesn't get enough sleep."

At half past six, the sisters began fixing eggs and toast for breakfast. The children woke up, ate, and hurried outside to play. At 7, the TV news services came alive and the three adults sat at the table eating their meal and watching the portable TV. It made for depressing viewing.

The television producers knew no more than anyone else, but they had record audiences, and all that time to fill. Having no authoritative explanations at hand for the week's frightening news, they began to go with unconfirmed reports and then with the sort of wild speculation normally confined to the silly season. So, their viewers learned that the sun was about to explode, burning Mother Earth to a crisp. And they were told of rumors that scientists knew, but would not tell, that we were on the verge of being sucked into a black hole. And they learned that some felt certain that invaders from space, who had been scouting us for years in their flying saucers, were now in the first phase of an attack designed to conquer and enslave us. They learned that a man named Ludwig thought the earth's magnetic field was reversing; and they learned that others were speculating that the moon had shifted in its orbit and was passing closer to the earth, which was somehow upsetting the earth's equilibrium.

"When facts are few, rumors are many," Martha said. "Everybody knows that something is going on out there. But that is all they know."

"Yes, and the people sense that. You can almost see the panic growing."

"And as usual," Hedi said, "the people are demanding that the government do something, and the government, not knowing what to do, is urging calm and assuring everyone that everything will be OK."

"They will name a commission to investigate," Martha said sourly. "They will be instructed to turn in their report in 90 days."

"Oh no!" said Hedi. The TV had just announced that the president was cutting short his vacation in the Black Hills and was flying back to Washington. They focused on the small screen. "A presidential spokesman said cabinet members and other senior officials were also being recalled for a series of meetings beginning tomorrow," the newsman said.

Hedi realized she had taken her head in her hands. "Oh no," she said again. "I suppose it seems like the natural thing for him to do, but it may turn out to be a tragic mistake. Martha, I don't suppose Mr Adams has any influence on the president?"

"Not that kind," Martha said. She stood up. "I had better be on my way. I have heard more than I wanted to hear anyway. Kiss the children for me."

Hedi gave Martha a hug, and watched her leave. She went back inside. According to the clock, it was just two and a half days since she had received the clue.

Roy came inside, his face white.

"Roy, what's the matter?"

He stood by the door as if dazed. "I was trying to figure out what's so strange about the morning. I know the obvious things. There's no sunshine this morning. The whole sky is a sullen gray. The leaves are hanging lifeless on the trees, without a whisper of a breeze to move them. But everything is so silent. It's oppressive. I couldn't understand why. And then I saw little Ralph at the edge of the woods."

"Hunting bears," Hedi said smiling.

"Hunting bears. He was peering into the shadows, bear gun at the ready, but when he saw me he came running. He said, 'Daddy, our bears are all gone, and the birds aren't singing. Why have the birds stopped singing?'

"And that was it. The birds aren't singing. We'd better get them in here, but I wanted to tell you first, without having to speak in code."

He turned and called out the door. "Ralph! Sally! Come in here for a minute, please!"

Hedi called both children to her. "We may get the big storm after all," she said. "It isn't anything to worry about. If we all stick together, we will be OK."

She searched their faces for understanding. "Now, I want you to stay near the house today. Don't go into the woods. If either your father or I call you, you are to come at once. Don't stop to ask why.

And an answer of 'in just a minute' is not good enough. Do you understand?"

Both children said they did. Sally added, "Mother, I don't really want to see a big storm."

"Well, I hope you won't see one."

"Roy, would you like to help me make some plans?"

"Anything's better than just sitting here waiting. What kind of plans?"

"When I was here looking for this place, I picked up all kinds of information. I got lists describing all of the places offering public accommodations. You won't believe how many rooms are available for nonresidents. Many are open only during the skiing season and are presently closed. And I have detailed geological survey maps of the area."

"What are you going to do with them?"

"I think we are going to need a rescue organization for the local area, and this exists. Every winter it gets real training looking for people reported to be lost in the mountains. We will need centers to provide shelter, food, and first aid to those who have lost their homes, and to provide emergency treatment for the sick and injured. Let's see how well we can match existing physical facilities with relatively safe and accessible locations."

At noon, just as they finished a tentative plan for disaster relief for the valley, Hugh Scott called.

"I am at the disaster control HQ in the Little River area," he said to Hedi. "I need you and Roy to help me. We can take care of your whole family here, so bring the children. Mary is here, and there are other families. It should be as safe as any place you can find. Madge Theos arrived, and I have put her to work."

"We appreciate your offer, and we do want to help," Hedi said, "but we have yet to learn what disaster awaits us, if any. I think it would be better that we are not all in the same place."

"That is what the governor said," Hugh replied. "Another thing, while I have you. On the governor's orders, Lieutenant Governor Duval has been here all day working with your sister Martha on drafting a series of emergency orders, just in case we need them. I expect you know what that's all about."

"I think I do. Thank God for Martha and Len Adams."

"I feel the same way. Okay. If you prefer to remain there, then we need to provide a way for me to talk to you. I have a young officer who is anxious to have his wife and baby with him. I am going to let him go get them and have him leave one of our long-range walkie-talkies with you. It will put you on the same network as the set on my desk. Make certain it is working before he leaves. Now, one question: How much time do you think we have?"

"Roy and I were outside earlier this morning, Hugh, and the birds had stopped singing," Hedi answered. "You remember what that means in terms of earthquakes."

"It means there isn't much time."

"Maybe only hours. Can you tell me what is going on?"

"When you get the radio, listen in, and you will soon know as much as I do. And don't hesitate to interrupt the conversations when you have something to say."

In less than an hour, a young lieutenant roared up in a personnel carrier and showed them how to use the radio.

"As long as you have power, plug it into the house current. After that, you are on the batteries for as long as they last. I brought you one spare battery pack."

Roy tried to check in with Hugh on the FM radio, but he was advised that the colonel was out.

"He's expected back at three o'clock to radio a report to the governor," he told Hedi.

While they waited, Hedi tried to make one more phone call to her parents, but she could hear only a mixture of noise and garbled computer voices.

Hugh wasted no words in his report to the governor. "Communications are rapidly breaking down. Phone service is no longer reliable. Lines are flooded with calls and large numbers of telephone workers, seeing that their efforts to repair service are having no effect, are heading for home to be with their families."

"Colonel, do we know yet what is causing all this?"

"No sir, but I have some late information from General Jerome. About the only reliable long-distance communication left is satellite transmission and the president's red phone. Communication between the White House and the Kremlin has never been so good.

"I am informed that Russia has dispatched six long-range aircraft to find out what is happening in the Arctic region. Two of their subs in northern waters have been ordered to investigate."

"No results?"

"No, sir. Not yet. We have dispatched special aircraft to the Antarctic by way of Argentina. We have one submarine two hundred miles from the South Pole. It reports a massive column of steam, ten miles south of their position."

"What does 'massive' mean?"

"Sir, apparently it extends as far as they can see with respect to both width and altitude. They report it seems to flicker and glow from thousands of electrical discharges within the cloud."

There was a garble of static.

"Say again, sir?"

"Conclusions?"

"Three things are established. Enormous amounts of energy are being released at the poles, particularly at the South Pole. Second, the earth's magnetic field has become weak and irregular, and at times approaches zero. Third, no one knows what is happening or what to do about it."

"Splendid," the governor said wearily. "What does the federal government propose to do about all this?"

"Sir, General Jerome has been urging the Secretary of Defense to get the president and his cabinet out of Washington. I have been urging the general to get out of Washington. Neither of us is having any success."

There was more, but that was the gist of the report. Hugh promised the governor an update at five p.m.

A gusty wind was blowing with increasing force. It was very irregular, blowing first one way and then the other. Roy told the children to come and play indoors. Hedi found that the telephone had become useless.

It was increasingly evident from news reports and short-wave broadcasts that great numbers of people were deserting their jobs in panic. There were stories of massive traffic jams as people sought to get out of core city areas. In some areas, police gave up and joined the mad rush to get home to their families. "I wonder what it will be like when something bad actually happens," Roy said.

At five o'clock Hugh reported to the governor that nothing further had been heard from the U.S. submarine in the south polar region since its captain announced his intention to submerge and explore the waters beneath the steam cloud. Two Russian planes had flown into the north polar cloud and disappeared from the radar screens of the other aircraft. Neither plane had returned. The U.S. planes had not yet reached their destination.

"Sir, we have reports of panic elsewhere. We have lost telephone service in many areas. I suggest that you proclaim martial law."

"Is that really necessary, colonel?"

"It will help immensely, sir. Once that is done, National Guard units can step in whenever other law-enforcement agencies need help to control looting or other disorders. Things may break suddenly. It would be best to be prepared."

The governor sighed wearily. "All right, I agree. I will sign it at once."

Hedi, listening, breathed a sigh of relief. "Good work, Hugh," she said softly.

She fixed the family a meal as it got dark outside. The TV was still by the kitchen table: As they ate, they watched the newscasts become increasingly disorganized. A few stations left the air as though someone had decided to pull the switch and go home.

"The panic is spreading," Roy said. Hedi said nothing.

At six thirty, the radio crackled — Hugh was calling to say that martial law had been declared. All National Guard units had been activated as of six o'clock, and he was trying to communicate the message by every means at his disposal.

"General Jerome promised to leave his office at seven and head for his emergency headquarters in the Poconos," Hugh said. "According to him, the government seems unable to come to any decision on a course of action because of insufficient information."

That was the last they heard from Hugh for a while. At seven, the first shock wave hit, throwing them to the floor and filling the air with flying objects. Ralph began to cry; Sally was screaming in panic. Hedi was desperate to get to them, but she couldn't seem to make any progress in their direction; the floor kept moving under her.

After what seemed an eternity, but was probably less than fifteen seconds, the shock stopped. Roy scrambled to his feet. "God," he said. "I've been a fool! Hedi, get as many blankets as you can. Sally, go upstairs to the bedrooms and pick up every pillow you can find and get back here as fast as you can. Ralph, clear the floor over against that wall. Let's go, people! Move! We don't have much time."

He ran, limping, up the stairs. Hedi, bewildered, shook her head to clear it. "Come on, children, do as your father says. He knows what he's doing, and he said we don't have time to waste."

Before she and Sally could get upstairs, Roy was on his way down, wrestling their double mattress as he came. "Hurry!" he said. "Do it now!"

The children were not used to having their father yell at them. They looked at him in surprise. Hedi watched him struggle to regain control of himself. "Pillows, honey," he said to Sally.

Hedi took her hand. "Come on, honey, let's hurry. We don't want to get in daddy's way."

They got up the stairs. Roy in his haste had left blankets strewn on the floor. Hedi scooped them up and returned to the stairs to find Sally, her face half hidden behind four pillows, making her way cautiously down the stairs. "Hurry, honey," Hedi said. She pushed away an image of Sally tumbling down the stairs after another tremor.

They moved fast and well. When the second quake struck, no more than seven minutes after the first, the family was lying atop two single mattresses, with the double mattress and the guest mattress atop them. "Probably we ought to be outside," Roy muttered to Hedi, "but I'm not really convinced it would be any safer. If the structure stands, we have a chance. But there's so many things I should have thought of."

"Me too," she said miserably. "Flying glass, for one." She thought: Some survival expert.

The second shock passed. They waited, unwilling to leave their soft makeshift cave. Another came, and another, and another, at irregular intervals all through the long deadly night.

25. The Morning After
Day One

"**D**aylight," Roy said wearily. He pushed out from under the mattress. "I'm going to see what I can see. You three stay here."

"Be careful," Hedi said.

"Don't worry. I intend to be."

She watched him stand up and look around. "Roy, how bad is it?"

He was picking his way across the floor, stepping over obstacles she couldn't see.

"Bad enough," he said. Then, perhaps remembering the listening children, he added, "I'd say the worst is over, though."

As if in mockery, another tremor came. Hedi saw him jolted, then lost sight of him as he fell. "Roy!" she screamed.

"I'm — all right," he shouted over the noise of the grinding earth. "Just fell on the damn sofa." Hedi thought how little like Roy it was to swear, though the oath was mild enough in the circumstances.

"I want it to stop," Sally wailed. Hedi turned and gathered her in her arms. "I do too, honey. I do too. And it will. Promise."

The tremor faded, ended. "Roy, I don't think that one was as bad as the ones before," Hedi called.

"No," he said from across the room. "These must be aftershocks. I think they are getting weaker and less frequent."

She could hear him moving around. She wanted desperately to ask what he was seeing, but feared to know.

"Mommy, I want to get out," Ralph said suddenly. "I want to see too."

"Not yet, sugar. Wait till daddy says it's all right."

Roy was suddenly back in sight. "Okay," he said. "You can come on out. Just everybody be prepared to hit the mattress whenever the ground shakes, so you don't get hurt falling. Understand that, Ralph? Sally? Okay, then, come on."

To Hedi he added, "I think if we clear away the stuff nearest to the mattress, we'll be safe enough from flying objects. Anything that ever wanted to go flying got its chance last night."

Hedi cautiously stood up. She looked at the ceiling, now riddled with cracks. "Roy, are we really safe in here?"

"Not particularly. The question is, are we going to be any safer outside. And that's what I want to try to find out next."

Sally had huge tears in her eyes, and she was looking around the room with her mouth drawn down in a great inverted semicircle. Hedi started to ask her what the matter was, and then what she was seeing began to register.

All the furniture had been thrown around or hit by other objects during the night. Not once, not twice, but time and time again. Damage to the sturdier pieces had probably been limited to scratches and rips. (She could see a great triangular tear in the fabric of the sofa.) Lighter objects — decorative dishes, picture frames, table lamps, a coffee table, a planter — had been all but demolished.

Hedi scooped up Sally in her arms. "Oh, baby, it makes you want to cry, doesn't it? All our pretty things." And that did indeed start Sally sobbing.

Ralph had been looking around in dismay, too, until Roy had told him he needed help cleaning things from around the mattress. He was picking up a flowerpot when it slipped from his hand and fell two or three inches to the floor. "Look!" he said in amazement.

Hedi and Roy looked. "Look at what?" Roy asked.

"It rolled!"

It took Hedi a moment to understand. The rounded flowerpot, when set down on the level floor, had rolled downhill. She gasped.

"The ground is tilted!"

"Maybe," Roy said grimly. "Let's hope so." He moved quickly to the window, just at the time another tremor struck. "Get under the mattress," he shouted. "Quickly!"

Hedi assisted the children to safety. "What about you?"

"I'll be all right, don't worry."

She had to settle for that.

The tremor, like the one before, was less violent and shorter than its predecessor. They were out from under the mattresses again in less than half a minute.

"Roy, you okay?"

He looked shaken. "Come on, let's get out of here. Everybody bring a blanket, I'll bring us a mattress or two. Stop at the door, you two. I go out first."

She watched him swing the door open and throw the mattress outside. Then, oddly, rather than step outside, he jumped, dropping about a foot and a half. He turned and said, "Okay, come on," and held out his arms to swing Ralph and Sally out and down. Hedi got to the doorway and got another shock.

"That's why the floor was tilted," she said, feeling sick. The relentless series of shocks had jolted the little cottage half off its foundation. The doorway now stood suspended over space, rather than over the step a dozen feet away.

She took a long step down. "We might have been killed," she said.

He shook his head. "All's well that ends well," he said. "The house hung together and so did we."

"*Did* it hang together, though? Or is it ready to collapse around us?"

Roy rubbed his chin. "It looks a mite tipsy, I admit. And probably the roof will leak some. But it should still be good shelter. The structure seems sound. Lots of houses get pulled off their foundations by tornados and such, you know, and some of them just need pulling back to where they belong and they're as good as new."

Hedi wondered how much of Roy's optimism was for the benefit of her morale. But his next remark made her realize he was not play-acting. The optimism was as innate as the realism.

"That won't be easy to repair," Roy said, pointing. The paved road in front of the house was a mass of cracks. Entire sections had slipped down the hillside. "The only way out of here for awhile will be on foot," he said. That reminded her to look at the wider world around her.

Across the valley two steep, rocky hills were slashed by rock slides. Down in the valley, several fires were burning, and numerous buildings in the village appeared badly damaged. For the first time in hours, she thought to wonder how the world beyond her valley had fared.

Roy's mind had apparently followed the path. "The radio! I forgot all about it!" He climbed back into the house and disappeared within. "I just hope it works," he called back over his shoulder.

Hedi hesitated, then followed him, telling the children to stay put where they were. Sally and Ralph had recovered sufficiently from the shock to realize they were hungry; it was time for her to find the family something to eat.

She got to the kitchen and cleared away enough debris to get the refrigerator door open. She could see Roy rummaging around in the dining room.

The light didn't come on as she opened the door. Well, of course there was no power. They would have to eat first those things that would spoil quickly. She took out a carton of milk and some sliced chicken, found some bread, and (after discovering that all of the dishes were either broken or covered with dust), she located paper picnic cups and plates still in their plastic wrappers.

She put all but the milk in a tablecloth and carried the bundle and the milk outside.

Roy emerged with the radio. "It was under the dining room table," he said. "I wiped it off, and I can't see any damage, but I don't have the nerve to turn it on. What if it doesn't work?"

"Let's eat first, then," Hedi said. "Once we turn on the radio, we'll find it hard to concentrate on anything else for a while. We'll use the tablecloth and we'll have a picnic on the mattress." Efficiently, she made sandwiches and poured out four glasses of milk.

"Let's bow our heads," she said, "and thank God for the food before us, and for each other, and for the fact that we were allowed to survive this terrible time. And let's pray for all the people in the world who are less fortunate than we this morning."

"Don't forget the radio," Roy added. "We need to pray that it works and that there is someone out there to talk to."

It was a fast meal. Hedi noticed that Roy, in particular, gulped down his food in record time.

"Daddy, look!" Ralph said. While still in the living room, he had gathered up his Cub Scout compass from wherever it had slid to. He was holding it now, flat in his palm as he had been taught.

The needle marked North pointed resolutely toward the south.

* * *

Roy moved the switch to turn the radio on. A tiny light appeared, showing that power was available. Bits of noise came from the speaker but no voice. He looked at her soberly.

"It doesn't have an antenna, Daddy," little Ralph observed.

Roy looked sheepish and slapped himself on the side of the face, then pulled out the telescoping antenna to its full length.

". . . Montpelier Station S1. I have Captain Hale's report on damages for Colonel Scott. Do you wish to tape?"

"Tape recorder is on, please proceed."

"Roy, that was Mary Scott! Thank God, she's alive," Hedi said. Roy nodded but shushed her and concentrated all his attention on the radio, staring at it intently, as if it could help him absorb every word.

The situation in Montpelier was not good. Masonry structures were mostly heaps of rubble, even though their steel skeletons still stood. Wood structures had weathered the tremors better, only to fall victim to fire. There was no water to fight fires and few streets passable to fire engines in any case. The state capitol had no electric power and no telephone service. No one had time to count the dead and the wounded.

All was not chaos, however. The National Guard was protecting stores and warehouses from looting. Police and firemen reporting for duty were sent out on foot, by motorbike, and on bicycles to organize the able-bodied in each block to help less fortunate neighbors.

Hedi watched Roy suffer as he heard the report on damage to medical facilities. The section of the hospital housing the operating rooms was in ruins, rendering simple surgery difficult and difficult surgery impossible. Hundreds of injured lay on stretchers or blankets in the streets, waiting their turn for attention.

"We would appreciate any help HQ can give us," the voice said at the end of the report, "but we do understand Burlington is in even worse shape than we are."

"Thank you for the report," Mary Scott said. "The colonel is out looking for help to deal with the critical medical problem. He will hear your report as soon as he returns. Is there any further word on the governor or on Mr. Adams?"

"We have nothing at this time," the voice from Montpelier replied. "Will let you know as soon as we do."

The reports went on and on. "Things are bad," Roy said. "Very bad, everywhere. These must have been the worst earthquakes in recorded history. I wonder if I should break in after this report and tell Mary we are safe and ready to help."

"I think you should," Hedi replied, but Mary saved Roy the trouble. After acknowledging the report she had been taping, she announced she was searching for Roy and Hedi Johnson, last known to be at Stowe, and would appreciate information on their whereabouts and condition.

Roy held down the transmit button. "Bless you, Mary Scott," he said. "We are still at our place in Stowe. We are shaken but well, and it is wonderful to hear your voice. Is there anything we can do to help?"

"You'd better believe it," Mary replied. "I'll get in touch with Hugh as soon as I can. He will be delighted and will call you right away." Signs of weariness and worry showed in Mary's voice. "How's he holding up?"

"To tell you the truth, I don't know how much more Hugh can stand. He hasn't slept for the past forty-eight hours."

"And how about you?" Roy asked.

"Stay by the radio," she said. "Hugh will be calling you as soon as he can."

Roy switched off the radio but left it on call alert. "Let's clean up some of the mess inside," he said. "And everybody keep an ear tuned for a series of beeps: — that will tell us someone is calling."

They carried the radio inside with them, and pitched in to clean up the house. They filled three large trash bags with broken china and other debris. They braced the furniture as best they could, and stored everything else on the floor or in closed cabinets.

It was Sally who first heard the radio beep, and Roy who answered it.

It was Hugh Scott. "Mary found me here in Montpelier," he said. "So glad to know you are OK. Roy, I need help in the worst way. The governor is badly injured, and we cannot take care of him here. A stone wall fell on him while he was helping in a rescue effort at the capital. The clinic at Hanover, New Hampshire, is thought to be the nearest place that might perform the needed surgery, but they are desperately short of doctors. If I send a chopper, can you come here to have a look at him and then talk with Hanover?

"If you think it is the thing to do, we will fly him there, along with as many others as the clinic will take or the big chopper will hold. They will need you to go along on the flight, Roy, and the clinic will likely plead with you to help with some of the surgery. If you will do it, I will send someone to see that Hedi and the children are taken care of."

Roy looked at her, and she nodded. "I will do it," he said to Hugh, "but I want your promise to get me back here whenever Hedi needs me."

"You have the promise," Hugh said. They heard him issuing instructions to someone else in the room before returning to them. "The chopper should be there in about 45 minutes. If they can't find a suitable place to land, be prepared to go aboard in a sling. If you have any medical instruments with you, bring them along. Now, may I speak with Hedi?"

"You don't have to provide a baby sitter for me," she said, "I'll get someone to look after Sally and Ralph. I would like to get down to the village and help set up emergency relief facilities, but the road is impassable. Do you have any units in our valley?"

"We have the equivalent of one platoon in Stowe. One top priority is to get as many bulldozers as they can find, put them in operation, and start opening essential roads. I'll see that they get you out as soon as possible. Okay?"

"Great."

"All right, next item: Lieutenant Governor Duval is at my head-quarters. He is meeting with your sister and surviving state officials to form an advisory council on policy and priorities. I know they want you as a member of that council."

"What happened to Governor Bennard?"

"The last time he was conscious, he declared himself unable to fulfill his duties."

"So it's Acting-Governor Duval now." Hedi remembered the man. He had seemed steady enough. He would need to be.

"Right. Hedi, someone will call you very soon. Keep the radio handy, and be sure it is on talk alert mode."

"Will do," Hedi replied. "Hugh, how does it look?"

"We have a lot of work ahead of us, Hedi. There has been a lot of earth movement in the mountain passes — the main roads into the valley are completely blocked. We're getting equipment to clear it, as I said, but it's going to take some time. A larger concern is that water from blocked streams is beginning to rise. We're going to have to find a way to deal with that, but for the moment we have other things to do."

"Hugh, what's the situation in the outside world? Have you heard from the general?"

She and Roy stood looking at the radio through a long moment. "Hugh, are you there?"

"I'm here. The situation outside is not so good. There was serious, widespread damage, and most communications links are down, so we are on our own for the moment. I have been unable to contact the general, but I am afraid it's much like our exercises at Sam Theos' camp. Hedi, I have to go, I have a million things to do, and I know you do too."

Hedi acknowledged and signed off, feeling numb. "'Much like our exercises.' Roy, you realize what he was saying?"

"Yes I do. He knows how bad it is, or he has some idea, and he's afraid to say, for fear of starting a panic."

"I'm going to check on the Smiths," she said. "We're going to need each other."

* * *

She walked downhill the few hundred yards to the Smiths' two-bedroom house. She found the couple standing outside, slender, wiry Elena holding the baby. As always, burly Gary Smith reminded her of a great peaceful bear.

"She's small, but she's sturdy," Gary Smith said proudly. "The house, I mean, not Elena." Elena grimaced and Hedi laughed. Gary Smith had a joke for all occasions. "It took the shakin' real good."

"How did you manage, last night?"

"I dragged mattresses and covers and all into the baby's bedroom and pulled the crib and all out in the hallway," he told her. "Figured the less stuff in there, the better — that much less stuff to get thrown around. Spent the whole night in there under the covers with the baby between us." He grinned at his wife. "Wasn't near the fun you might think. Mighty rough ride."

"Nobody hurt," Elena Smith said. "That's the important thing."

"Yeah, but now we got maybe the hardest part ahead of us. It's goin' to take a while to get over this. Roads beat all to hell, power lines down, phone lines out. It's goin' to be a mess out there. Hedi, you got any idea how bad the other towns got hit?"

Suddenly Hedi knew how Hugh had felt on the radio. The Smiths had as much right as anyone to know the truth, and they were sturdy, reliable people, unlikely to panic. But there would be no way to control who they in turn would tell, or who would be told third-hand. The ripples would spread rapidly enough as it was; there was no need to speed the process, and good reason not to.

"The news we got from the radio was that everybody around us was hit about as hard," she said. "They say that for now every town is going to have to fend for itself."

"Well, that's all right," Gary said placidly. "Folks here got a long habit of helpin' each other out and makin' do."

About an hour after the helicopter took Roy away, she heard the roar of a bulldozer in the distance. It was nearly dark before it arrived in front of the house. The driver cut the engine.

"Lady, I understand you need to get down to the village. I'm afraid the road we have cleared will be tough going for a car, but your neighbor from just down the road — Smith?"

"Gary Smith," she nodded.

"He has a four-wheel-drive job. He said he would get you to town. Better take your own food, if you have any. Things are pretty tight down there. Smith said he'd be along directly."

He revved his machine and roared on toward the next blockage. She scurried about, getting the children ready, packing a change of clothing for herself and for them, putting together enough food for three days. Before she was quite finished, Gary Smith's four-wheel-drive jeep pulled up to the house.

"Ready? Let me give you a hand with that stuff." He picked up a suitcase in one hand and cardboard box of food in the other, lifting them effortlessly.

"Come on, kids," she said.

"Wait a minute," he said. "You bringin' them to town?"

"Why, sure."

"That don't make sense. They'll just be in your way and they ain't goin' to like sitting around all day in some motel. You let them stay with us."

"Oh, no, I can't do that. Elena has the baby to take care of, and —"

"Right, and I figure she's goin' to need a cute little button like this" (chucking Sally under the chin) "to do some babysittin'. And bein' as I got to get out and help clear the roads with the other folks, we're goin' to need a man around the house to help take care of Elena. And that looks to me like this young fella here. What do you say, kids? Can you help us out?"

The children had visited with the Smiths, and liked them, but they were hesitant to leave their mother.

"They're going to want to be with me tonight," she said.

"Sure, that's natural. Tell you what, kids. You stay with us and help us out durin' the day, and I'll fetch you in to town when it gets to be dark, so you can spend the night with your momma. Okay?"

They were noticeably happier with that arrangement. "Good, then, it's set. And tomorrow mornin' you can decide if you want to stay with your momma or spend some more time helpin' us out."

They agreed to that, and so Gary made a stop at his house before driving Hedi to town.

"Thank you so much for doing that, Gary," she said on their way in. "I hate to impose on Elena, but it will make it easier to get something done."

"Don't think a thing about it. That's what neighbors are for, you know that."

26. The Miracle of Courage
Day One

In the village there was great confusion, but the mayor, the National Guard, and the area rescue unit had combined forces to establish the beginning of an emergency relief organization.

Mayor Ludlum remembered Hedi from Martha's introductions of the year before. "My God," he said when they found him, "this is an incredible disaster. Just incredible. I can't believe it. It is difficult to know what to do first, the needs are so great. I never imagined we'd ever see a disaster of this magnitude." The man seemed stunned, overwhelmed, unable to concentrate. Hedi found herself fighting an urge to mother him.

"Mr. Mayor, I don't want to intrude if I am not needed, but I think I may be able to be of some assistance. I have had a certain amount of training in emergency work."

She took out the sheets of paper she and Roy had filled on the day before the earthquakes struck, and watched the mayor's eager look of anticipation. "He can understand paper," she thought. "It puts him back on familiar territory."

Aloud, she said: "My husband and I made some notes on housing. I suppose shelter is one of the big problems we're going to be faced with."

"Oh, yes, it is. It's terrible. So many people have lost their homes, and winter is coming on —"

His voice trailed off. Hedi realized that the man was close to a blue funk.

"Mr. Mayor, we aren't empty-handed," Hedi said firmly. "There are things we can do. You see these units? They're all closed down except in snow season. They can all be used as emergency housing."

"But how can we contact the owners? Even if we knew all their phone numbers, the phone lines are down."

"I wasn't thinking of asking permission. I was thinking you'd commandeer the units, Mr. Mayor."

Mayor Ludlum wrung his hands. "Oh, I'd hate to do that. These are not just weekend tourists — these are people of substance. I shudder to think of the headlines we could create if we did something like that."

Hedi stared at him. "Mayor Ludlum, do you really think that matters? This is a matter of life and death. If we don't use those units, people are going to die of exposure." Besides [she thought], it's likely to be a long time before you ever see headlines again. About anything.

Still the man hesitated. It occurred to Hedi that he was essentially without imagination. She suddenly realized how to help him grasp the situation.

"Suppose a party of skiers got caught in a blizzard, Mr. Mayor. Nobody would blame them for breaking into an empty ski lodge to save their own lives."

"No, of course not."

"Besides," she said, responding to sudden inspiration, "we shouldn't even need to break in. I bet your police force can pick the locks. If they can't, I'm sure the state police can."

"Yes, yes I suppose they could."

"All right," she said, assuming more than he had conceded, "here's a list of the available housing. My husband and I did some thinking about how it could be used."

"When?"

"Why, right now."

"No, I mean when did you do this thinking?"

"Oh, very recently," she said vaguely, wanting to avoid conversational detours. "Do you have someone you would like to assign to this project?"

As she had expected, he looked at her blankly. "I don't have anyone on my staff with that area of responsibility," he said. "We've never had to —"

"I'd be glad to do it, if you'd like me to," she said. "I can give you a couple of days, at least."

"I don't know," the mayor said. "I'd have to get authorization, and I don't know how we'd pay you."

After living for a dozen years shadowed by anticipation of a global emergency, Hedi found it a little hard to be patient with the man's inability to comprehend how fundamentally his world had just changed. Yet he, however inadequate, was the legitimate holder of local power — she had to deal with him.

"I'm not interested in pay," she said gently. "I'll volunteer my services."

"There might be insurance problems," he said dubiously.

"Well, pay me a dollar a year, and pro-rate it for two days. In any case, you'll need to get *someone* working on this, or people are going to die of exposure."

"Yes, yes, to be sure." They stood there. It was painfully obvious that he had no idea what to do first.

"Mr. Mayor, could we talk to the man in charge of local National Guard units?"

Another blank look. "Yes. We could, certainly. What do we want with him? He's likely very busy."

"I thought that the National Guard might issue an order commandeering all vacant housing units. That might make the situation easier for you, from a legal point of view."

"Ah, yes, I see," he said, brightening. Clearly, any idea promising to allow him to shed responsibility would appeal to him. "But then, what will we do if he declines to do so?"

"If there's any problem at all, I can get in touch with Colonel Howard Scott, the National Guard commander. He'll put the wheels in motion. In the meantime, can we find someone with a four-wheel-drive truck?"

"Four-wheel-drive?"

"Somebody will need to visit these places and see how much damage they suffered. They may not all be habitable now."

"Oh yes, I see. Good idea."

"Then we need to start listing how many people need what, and start allocating what we have to meet the most urgent needs."

"Yes." A sudden decision: "See here, you seem to have thought things out. Maybe I'd better put you on my staff."

Hedi smiled with relief. "Thank you, Mr. Mayor, I'd be honored. But only until we get things organized. I do have other commitments elsewhere."

Hedi wound up staying in Stowe two more days, and might have stayed longer had not Acting-Governor Duval sent word for her to join him at the National Guard headquarters. She took the children with her, since she did not know how long she would be there.

Day Four

She arrived in time to see Governor Duval make Hugh a Brigadier General and appoint him permanent commander of the Vermont National Guard.

"Hugh, congratulations," she said. "You deserve it, and I know you'll do an outstanding job. Can you spare me a minute or two?"

Automatically, Hugh glanced at his watch. "Sure, Hedi. Let's go to my cubbyhole."

His makeshift office had room for a desk, a filing cabinet and two straightback chairs. "Nothing fancy, I'm afraid."

As soon as the door was closed, Hedi came right to the point.

"Hugh, what's happened? I couldn't ask you over the radio, and nobody here seems to know. How bad was it? Which places were hit worst? What shape is the federal government in? Oh, and have you heard from General Jerome?"

He hesitated, and she felt herself pale. She said, "We knew it had to be bad, from what you didn't say on the radio the morning after. *That* bad?"

"Yes. That bad. It's really hard to tell what the situation is: There are too many gaps in communication. But that itself tells you something. We lost all the land lines, of course, but the radios work. If things in the outside world were more or less normal, we'd be hearing plenty of things we aren't hearing. In fact, if the rest of the country were in any kind of shape at all, they'd be sending relief expeditions here. Which they aren't."

He sighed. "And, no, I haven't heard from the general. As to the federal government — I don't know if there *is* any. We aren't real sure what's left of anything — what's left of our government, other governments, anything."

"Hugh, I know you have too many things to do. I'll get out of your way. But I want to tell you this. You are as well prepared, as well suited, to help lead us out of this mess as anybody I can imagine. I'm just sorry so much of it is falling on you."

He had himself back under rigid control. "Thank you, Hedi. You and Roy will find quite enough responsibility falling on your shoulders, believe me."

Matter-of-factly: "I am bringing Roy back here tomorrow. The Governor plans to assign control of all medical facilities to the Guard, and I intend to ask Roy to take charge." He checked his watch and made to stand up. Hedi jumped to her feet. "I'll see you in an hour, I guess," he said.

That would be the meeting to establish an Advisory Council on Policy and Priorities. "Yes," she said. She almost said, "Yessir." Hugh, she suddenly realized, was now far more than the likable young man she had met a dozen years before. In a world where everything had changed, even old friendships would have to change as well. He had become someone of importance: Lives hung on his decisions now. To waste his time now might mean something very near to wasting lives. "I've got to go be sure the children are settled before the meeting," she said. Her exit had something in it akin to flight.

* * *

Late that afternoon, the rains started. Once started, they continued, day after day. Every day, Hedi woke up to the sound of rain. It would be raining when she snatched a few moments for lunch, raining again when she had her sorry excuse of a supper, and raining in between. Among the last sounds she would be aware of before sinking into sleep was very often the sound of rain on the roof of whatever building she was sleeping in. And the rain that fell wasn't even clean; mixed with volcanic dust, it fell like soot. It didn't rain nonstop, of course. It only seemed that way.

* * *

"Excuse me, miss. I require assistance."

The speaker was a man about her own age. Chinese, by the looks of him. Foreign perhaps, — his English was slightly stilted, slightly pedantic. All this she noticed automatically, as she noticed the four-year-old boy clinging to his hand.

"Yes? How can I help you?" Hedi had twice as many things to do as she had time to do them in.

"I am in Chinese Embassy in Ottawa. This is my son. I must search for his mother. I require that he remain here. If I know he is safe, I will be able to concentrate on finding his mother."

"I understand," she said. "Certainly he can stay here until you return. What town was she last in?"

"Washington, D.C. Your nation's capital."

Hedi had thought he meant to leave the boy for a few hours while the father searched the Stowe area.

"I am so sorry," she said, "but you can't go down there. It's too far, it's not safe." She tried to think of how to tell him that anyway, his wife was very probably dead.

"Yes, very far, very difficult. I leave the boy here."

"Oh, no, you can't do that! In the first place, you don't have any way to get there. And you don't have shelter, food, protection — anything you need. You'd be throwing your life away."

Hedi had all the arguments and all the facts. All he had was an unshakable determination.

"In 1943, an uncle walked from Shanghai to Kunming," he said gravely. "Difficult journey. Dangerous. He made it, lived to 84. Please take good care of the boy until I return."

The man's son watched him slowly become a smaller and smaller dot in the road. He watched with great solemnity, but with no tears. Hedi felt her heart go out to this courageous youngster. She made it a point to take him to Fred Crenshaw, who was in charge of finding emergency shelter. She told Fred about the town's latest ward.

"What's this young fellow's name?"

She stared blankly back at him. "I don't know. His father was an official at the Chinese Embassy in Ottawa named Wun. They were here on vacation. The mother was visiting Washington when it happened. His father is on his way to get her." She and Fred stared at each other for a brief second. Then Fred cleared his throat. "Washington, huh? That's a long way. It'll probably take him a long time to get there and back. I'd guess you and I ought to get acquainted, young fellow. My name's Fred. What's yours?"

"Sam," the boy said proudly.

"Sam, huh? Do you have a Chinese name?"

"Sam."

"I see. Well, come on with me, Sam, and we'll set you up with a place to stay tonight so you can start waiting for your father to come back."

Day Five

Roy arrived from Hanover, wrapped in a slick black plastic raincoat, his legs soaked from the incessant dirty, driving rain. He gave Hedi a perfunctory, distracted kiss, holding himself away from her to avoid getting her wet. He kissed her — but just at the moment he had little time or attention for her. "Where's Hugh, honey? I need to see him."

"Come on," she said, trying not to get her feelings hurt. "I can get you in to see him."

Hugh's first question immediately followed his greeting. "How is Governor Bennard?"

"Governor Bennard is off the critical list, but he lost both legs." Roy fished out an envelope from within his raincoat (which, Hedi noticed, was dripping water onto Hugh's linoleum floor). "He asked me to deliver this to you."

Hugh ripped it open. "It is what I expected," he said tersely.

"His letter of resignation, he told me."

"That's right. So Acting-Governor Duval is now governor in name, as well as in fact." He pushed a buzzer on his desk. "Madge, tell Governor Duval's office I am coming across to see him." He looked up at Hedi and Roy. "You will have to excuse me. This cannot wait."

"We understand," Roy said.

"I want to talk to you as soon as possible, Roy. Hedi can give you the general idea. Keep Madge informed of your whereabouts and I will get back to you as soon as I have a minute." He stood up to escort them out, and in a moment was striding down the hallway on his way to transfer the executive power of the state from one man to another.

Hedi, despite herself, looked at her wristwatch. "Roy, it seems like forever since I've had time to talk to you, but I don't have it now either. I've got to be ready for a meeting in a few minutes, and I'm not ready."

"That's okay, honey, I know." Just for the moment, his accustomed grin appeared and erased the wrinkles of fatigue, making him look boyish again. "In fact, I was standing here trying to find a tactful way to tell you that I have too much to do to be standing here. Thanks for making it easier. I'll see you— when?"

She made a gesture of helplessness with her hands, extending them upward and outward. "Who knows? Whenever we're both free. Sometime today, I hope."

"The kids are okay?"

"They're fine, except they miss you and haven't seen all that much of me even when they were here. Honey, I have a million things to tell you, if we ever had time, but I have to go."

"I know, I do too."

A little later, Martha arrived from Montpelier in an open jeep, wet, tired, busy and preoccupied. She went directly to see Hugh and the governor, and it was over an hour before Hedi could get her aside.

For the past six days, Hedi had been pushing thought of her parents to the back of her mind, stuffing it in a cardboard container marked "To Be Opened When There Is Time." But Martha's re-appearance had brought the worries back to the surface.

Of course, she had no word on them. "I've been spending half my time trying to find what is left of the Canadian government," she said, "and let me tell you, it's a major job. It took me three days merely to find Mr. Adams."

"What did Mr. Adams say about the situation in Canada?"

"Well, it turns out that he was in Edmundston, New Brunswick, when it happened." (Hedi noticed that Martha, like everyone else, had taken to referring to the night of horror as 'It,' as though to name it would increase its power and reality.) "He said the damage there was beyond belief, but the loss of life in the interior was not as severe as on the coast or along the St. Lawrence."

"That would make sense."

"He says he thinks that some senior members of the government escaped Ottawa, but if anybody escaped east of the river, nobody has as yet been able to contact them."

"And west of the St. Lawrence?"

"We still don't know. The situation is very confused."

"So what's the situation?"

"That's what I just briefed Hugh and the governor about. The surviving units of local and provincial governments from eastern Quebec and from the Atlantic Provinces have been able to maintain a reasonable degree of order. They are now forming a joint council on priorities. They have asked Mr. Adams to secure the cooperation of those of us here in northern New England."

"What kind of co-operation?"

"Coordination of efforts, to start with. Ultimately, who knows? I don't see that it makes much sense for us to worry about borders at this point. I'd say that concept is about a week behind the times."

Hedi nodded. "The Chief was talking about that a dozen years ago. So what does Mr. Adams want you to do?"

"I'm supposed to sound out the governing bodies in Vermont, New Hampshire, and Maine. If they think the idea has merit, he

wants each of them to choose a delegate to accompany me up
there."

"How would you get there?"

"He has a six-place prop plane he's sending down in four days."

"What if nobody's interested?"

"He said he's going to send it down for me anyway. Even if nobody
is interested in the idea, he wants me up there for discussions."

"Quite a mark of confidence," Hedi said. She thought: Big consequences flowing from a childhood friendship. And those consequences were only beginning to accumulate.

"Martha, what about Jane? I should have asked right away, but I
didn't think of it."

"He says she's okay. I hope our other friends in Vermont escaped,
but of course there's no way to tell."

"No, of course not," Hedi said automatically.

"Where did you go?"

Hedi gave a little start. "Hmmm?"

"You went off wandering, somewhere."

"Oh. Well, yes, I suppose I did. I was wondering how long it
would be until we knew how bad things really are."

Martha looked at her strangely. "What do you mean? Aren't things
bad enough for you right now?"

"Probably the people who really know are telling us only so much
and no more, just as we're doing."

"I don't know what you mean."

Hedi couldn't think how to explain. "Martha, what you just told
me about Mr. Adams and the situation in Canada — am I free to repeat
it to other people?"

Martha frowned. "Certainly not! Roy, of course, and Hugh. Anybody Hugh or the governor designates. But not people in general,
no."

Hedi nodded. "I was just thinking how much we know, you and
I, Roy, Hugh — everybody in positions of responsibility. We know
so much more than everybody else, even though we're all in the
same boat."

Martha's frown became a mask of puzzlement. "Sometimes there
are reasons why you can't tell everything you know. It has to be that
way, Hedi."

"I know."

"Well?"

"I can't help thinking about people like Gary Smith. You know
our neighbor down the way?"

"Big man, looks like a bear?"

"He looks like a bear, he uses terrible grammar, he can fix

anything that ever was made, and he has a heart bigger than the mountains."

"What about him?"

"He doesn't know what is going on outside, and I can't tell him. The other day he said to me, 'Hedi, we got hit bad. So bad, we still don't know how bad. Our roads are out, the telephone is out, the bridges are gone. Now we got these big black clouds that hang in the air and don't seem to go away. What I want to know is, where is everybody?'

"I thought he was talking about people unaccounted for, but it wasn't that. 'You take back when hurricane Camille did all that damage down south,' he said. 'Folks from here pitched in, sent money, gave blood, sent clothes and stuff. We did our share to help. Same thing when Hazel hit. Same with Hugo in South Carolina. Same with the earthquake in Alaska back in the sixties. Same with the one in San Francisco in '89, at the time of the World Series. Now, we didn't ask anybody for thanks; we just did what was right, and the rest of the country did the same. But Hedi, where are they now that we need help? Why ain't the Army in here with medical units? Where's the power equipment we need to clear up this mess? Where's the food and clothes when *we* need it?'"

He had looked at her pleadingly. He had said, "Hedi, there's women and babies need *help* and need it now. It's goin' to be winter before long, and we got to get organized. Where *is* everybody?"

"Martha, I knew why nobody was sending help, and I'm sure he was thinking that I knew and that I wasn't going to tell him. And this while he and his wife were taking care of my babies every day. That hurt."

Martha's eyes on hers were calm and watchful. "What are you saying, Hedi?"

"It's their life too. Maybe they have a right to know."

"It isn't going to do them any good to know how bad things are, if telling them results in making things worse. What they know is bad enough. They have to deal with earthquakes, fires, blocked highways, clouds blocking the sun, shortages of everything and isolation too. Already, it is all many of them can do to contain a deep, bone-chilling fear. Do you want to tell them what we suspect, as well, and turn fear into panic?"

"I'm not sure that the fear of what is known is ever as bad as the fear of what isn't known."

"You say that now. But try telling people the real story and see how they react. Try telling Smith that most of the world's population was probably wiped out in the first few hours."

"Don't underestimate Gary Smith," Hedi said staunchly. "He's tough."

"I don't doubt it. But what about everybody he talks to? Are they all tough, too?"

"Martha, I know everything you're telling me. I've already been through it."

"I know you *know* it. The point is, you have to do what's right. Just at this moment, you don't have the luxury of all these feelings."

Hedi shook her head stubbornly. "What you say is logical enough, but I'm not sure you're right. Don't underestimate people's ability to deal with adversity. Provided the leadership is there, the people will measure up."

Martha looked doubtful.

"Martha, think of World War II. Look at the difference between England under Chamberlain and under Churchill. Same people, same situation. In fact, the situation was worse under Churchill than under Chamberlain. But what a different reaction, when the people had a leader with courage and confidence. The English responded with unshakable fortitude. Can you imagine them surviving the Blitz under Chamberlain? Or Lord Halifax? With the leadership paralyzed with fear, how could the people possibly have responded?"

"Maybe you're right," Martha said.

"I know I am. The greatest danger facing us, now that we've survived the initial disaster, is that we'll be destroyed by fear — by our fear of taking bold action."

"Well, it is the leadership's responsibility to prevent that from happening," Martha said. Three busy days later, she left for Canada.

Day 10

"I don't think I like this," Roy told Martha. "Are you sure it's safe to fly in this kind of weather?"

Martha made a sour face, and laughed. "No, I'm not sure. Not sure at all. But I have a hunch that this is the only kind of weather we are going to have for a long time. Roy, Hedi, it looks like they're ready to go now. I've got to get aboard. I hope you find your place in good shape when you get there."

"I'm sure we will," Hedi said. "No matter what it looks like, it'll be good to see it again." She hugged Martha in the rain, wondering if she would ever see her sister again. "Mr. Adams couldn't have sent a better envoy."

Martha hugged her again. "Thanks, Hedi." They released each other, and Martha climbed into the little plane. Roy helped slam the door and they backed away. Almost immediately, the little red and white airplane was taxiing, turning, pausing, then accelerating down the little strip of marked-off highway that was one of their chief connections to the outside world. The wheels were kicking up great sheets of spray.

"Please," Hedi breathed. The right wheel hit a puddle, throwing a great globe of water into the air around it; she would have been willing to swear that the plane stumbled. But maybe she was wrong: The next minute, it was up in the air. Thirty seconds later, it had disappeared into the clouds.

"Well, your sister is off to Canada."

"And she got her approvals," Hedi said. She was steeling her heart against any future news of Martha's death in a crash.

"She did," said Roy, moving toward the car they'd come in.

"I'll bet she's dissatisfied with the job she did, though, knowing Martha."

"She got everything that could be expected: New Hampshire, Vermont and Maine."

"Even if it did take her two days to find somebody in authority in Maine."

He shrugged. "That doesn't count against her, that's one in her favor. It wasn't easy."

"She wanted to get Massachusetts, too."

"With Boston swept off the face of the Earth? As we make contact with towns and cities, we'll bring them in one by one — provided there's anything left to gather. Come on, let's get in out of this damned dirty rain and get going before Hugh finds us and calls us back."

"Oh, that won't be a problem. He agreed that we could stay and help at Stowe for a few days after we got our things."

"Yes, he did. But we also agreed that when we got back, we were his. And I have a feeling that after about a day and a half go by, Hugh is going to look up and say, 'Madge, where are they? They promised they'd be back to help. Get them on the radio, would you?'"

"He might at that. You're right, let's get going." And so they got into the car, got the kids, and drove back over newly cleared roads to the cottage in Stowe.

27. Night of Terror
Day 12

For eight days, since Day Four, the rain had been coming down, accompanied by a continuous series of tremors and quakes. At times it seemed the Earth's crust trembled as if frightened by the turmoil beneath it.

She looked up to see her husband standing in the door, the water running from his raincoat. The water should be forming puddles, but strangely it was running rapidly across the floor to the opposite wall. "Oh Roy, I'm so glad you're here", she cried. "I didn't hear the car."

"I had to leave the car down the road." She could see that he was thoroughly alarmed, and trying not to let his alarm show through. "Take Ralphie, grab your raincoats and a flashlight, go out the back door, and head for the wood lot. I'll get Sally and be right behind you. We must try to get down to the village. And hurry!"

The Earth was shaking; she could feel the house tilt. She heard it groan as if it too were in pain. Little Ralph had already taken the flashlight from the table. She reached for him, and together they swept coats from the rack in the hall, and ran for the back door.

Outside, the rain beat in their faces, and the ground beneath their feet trembled like jello. They gained the edge of the woods without speaking and stopped to wait for Roy. The light from his electric lantern was just behind them; a moment later he appeared out of the darkness carrying four-year-old Sally, still wrapped in her blankets and still trying to understand this rude awakening.

Roy paused inside the shelter of the trees. "We thought this kind of soil doesn't form mudslides," he said shortly. "The rain and the constant quakes have changed all that. The soil is nothing but thick slurry."

She was filled with silent terror; he sensed it; moved to defuse it in son and wife. "I was afraid that by morning we might have trouble getting down to the village, and if Aunt Martha arrives tomorrow, we certainly want to be there, right?"

She read Roy's message correctly, and her heart turned to ice within her, but six-year-old Ralph accepted it at face value. Grasping his mother's hand, he aimed the flashlight into the pitch darkness of the woods and announced bravely, "I will go first, Mother, and warn you if there are any bears in there."

"I left the car near the Smith cottage," Roy said over the noise of wind and rain. "We'll have to find it in the dark. I'm going to angle downhill toward the road. If we get separated, don't leave the woods. If you come to a clearing, stop and let me check it out. It might be a deathtrap, even if it looks just fine. Ralphie, you hold tightly to your mother's hand, and she will hold tightly to mine."

This is not an exercise in survival, she told herself. This is for real. This is happening to me and my family. Happening to my precious little Ralph, chattering so bravely about bears because he knows there are no bears.

Out of nowhere came a cloud of foreboding that left her numb, and at that moment the Earth tossed as though in pain, then rumbled with rage, sounding much like a heavy train passing. It was then that buildings crumbled, and rock slides swept down the mountains, destroying everything in their path.

They were at a clearing. "I think I see the road", shouted little Ralph. He shone his light across an open area and leaped forward in his excitement. She was barely able to keep hold of his hand as he pulled her into the clearing.

"Come back," Roy yelled. "Both of you come back." His grip tightened around her wrist even as she felt the ground give way beneath her feet. She clung with all her strength to her son's hand, but it was torn from her. "Mother, help me," he screamed, and disappeared into a moving wall of mud.

The mud was up to her knees; it was sweeping her feet from beneath her. "Let me go," she yelled at Roy. "Let me go. I have to get him."

"You can't save him. Think of Sally," he yelled. One hand clenched in a death-grip around a thick branch of an oak tree, he held her wrist with a superhuman effort that left (she realized later) deep bruises. The tree held, and Roy held, and after an eternity, the slide, its deadly damage done, passed on.

Little Ralph was gone. That is all she knew. She wanted to lie there and die, but Roy would not let her.

"You're the expert on survival," he yelled over the noise. "And that's what we have to do. Hedi, we have to survive. There are people depending on us!"

She thought, Yes, I'm supposed to be the expert on survival. I was so certain that this cottage was in a safe site. Mudslides in these hills? Never. Rockslides, yes, but mudslides, no. Some expert.

Sally was crying and calling for her brother Ralphie. Roy pulled Hedi to her feet, almost roughly. "We have to find shelter for Sally, and it's too dangerous to try for the village in the darkness. We'd better climb up to the crest of the hill. It must be less than a half mile away. I think we can get there without leaving the shelter of the woods. When daylight comes, we'll look for a safe way down to the village."

He took her hand, and she followed silently, thanking God for him. She knew that by herself she would die.

They made it to the crest of the hill and found a large tree. Roy spread her raincoat on the ground and had her sit on it, using the tree trunk as a prop, then wrapped Sally in the one blanket that was still reasonably dry and laid her beside his wife. He put the other raincoat over them, and the two wet blankets on top of that. Then he crawled under this cover on the other side of Sally and leaned against the tree. Huddling as close together as they could, they cradled Sally in their arms and waited for daylight.

Sally gradually warmed up and stopped shivering. Her sobbing also tapered off, and with a big sigh she fell asleep. Roy and Hedi did not. Crying for their lost child, they prayed for strength and understanding. After a while the rain stopped, but moderate quakes continued, each bringing down a shower of water from the tree leaves. It was a long night.

The first dull red in the eastern sky announced the approach of another day. Roy slipped out from under the soggy cover, moving carefully to avoid waking Sally. Hedi got up and joined him, moving a little away from their sleeping child.

Roy nodded toward the red dawn. "By the look of things, we'd be in for a day of sunshine, if it weren't for all the volcanic dust. As it is, though, I'm afraid it'll be years before we see another clear blue sky."

Hedi, absorbed in the bitterness of her loss, was in no mood to talk about dust and sunshine, and didn't dare talk about the only thing that remained in her mind.

The growing light began to reveal the extent of the devastation, and Roy swore softly to himself as it sank in. Their cottage was gone, presumably smashed to bits and buried at the bottom of the long slash on the hillside made by the slide. Dozens of similar slashes could be seen on their hill, and on other hills within their field of vision. Their car was gone. Worse, the Smith's cottage was gone too, likely swept away by the same slide that took little Ralph. Again the tears came, but Hedi knew there was no time for them.

In a few minutes Sally began to stir, and soon she was standing at her mother's side, looking up at her from a mud-smeared face and clinging tightly to her leg. Hedi put her hand on Sally's forehead, and thought she sensed the beginning of a fever. She thought the little girl must be hungry, but Sally said nothing and so neither did Hedi.

Roy pointed downhill. North of where the Smith cottage had stood, a small tree-covered ridge ran up to the top of the hill. It appeared to extend for a quarter mile or more below the spot where Roy had left the car.

"We should be able to walk along the crest of this hill and make our way down through the woods to within a few hundred feet of the valley floor. Then maybe we can find a safe path to the village. If the village is still there."

He rummaged through his pockets and found a package of mints. He gave one to Hedi, took one for himself, and gave two to Sally. Then he picked her up and started north along the ridge. Hedi picked up their raincoats and followed. It took about an hour to work their way down to a spot opposite the former location of the Smith cottage.

Roy shook his head. "No sign of the cottage, no sign of our car." He shook his head again and fed Sally two more mints.

He looked to be sure that his wife was not lost among black thoughts. "Last night when I was in the village, I started hearing reports of mudslides. That's when I headed out of there. But about 50 yards past Smith's, I came to a spot where half the road had slipped away, and the other half looked none too stable. I backed up and left it at the Smith's."

His face took on a haunted appearance. "I took a minute to tell them about the danger of slides. Their car wasn't working, and they were wondering about the wisdom of starting out on foot. I told them I'd give them a lift as soon as I got you and the kids back to the car."

They stood there near where the cabin should have stood. "Maybe they didn't wait," Roy said without conviction. "Maybe they set out on foot."

Another minute passed. "Come on," he said heavily. "We still have to get out of here."

After 20 minutes, they came to a place where the little wooded ridge angled sharply to the south before resuming its downhill path. Here the ridge had diverted the slide, which had reacted by throwing debris and a considerable amount of mud into the edge of the woods. Roy stopped to consider how to proceed — and they heard the sound. They stared at each other, unbelieving, but they heard it again and again until there could be no doubt — it was a baby, crying.

Less than twenty yards away, they found it, lying mud-covered, cold, wet, hungry, and enraged in a somewhat battered baby bed wedged between two trees

The baby, sensing that now someone could hear him, screamed at the top of his lungs.

Hedi held her hands to her mouth, in horror. "It's the Smith's baby," she said.

"How can you tell?"

"The bed. That's the baby bed we loaned the Smiths six months ago for their little Peter."

And suddenly, finally, she was filled with fury. She found herself shouting at the helpless baby. "By what miracle do you live, when my son was taken from me?"

The baby stopped crying and looked up at her with wide, solemn eyes, as if overwhelmed by the enormity of the question. For a moment they stared at each other, and then her heart melted, and she lifted him carefully out of the bed and wrapped him in her raincoat.

They heard voices. Making their way to the other edge of their strip of forest, they saw the road below them. There, near the place where the road had fallen away, stood a van with a rescue team from the village. Crying and laughing at the same time, they scrambled down to meet them, and in short order they were driven to the relief center in the village. Hedi was anxious about the children. She hoped that food, a bath, and dry clothes would enable them to escape illness.

Hedi had helped select the location for the relief center. It was a lovely motel, built three years before to accommodate skiers in the winter and tours of 'leaf gazers' in the fall. It was of frame construction, and consisted of a central building and twenty-five separate units, each containing an efficiency apartment with one master bedroom and two additional spacious guest rooms. It was built on a meadow about one hundred feet above the village and nearly a mile from the nearest significant hill.

The center, having been advised by radio of their arrival, was ready for them. They got a quick check by the doctor on duty, then a bath and dry clothes, followed by a hot meal.

IV. Struggle

28. No Time For Grief
Day 14

After two days' fruitless searching, Hedi and Roy admitted to each other that Ralph's body probably would never be recovered. "We've got to get back to work," Roy said bleakly. "We're going to be needed."

"Yes," said Hedi, thin-lipped. "I hope I do better for the others than I did for us."

Roy held her with one arm, his other arm around little Sally. "Honey, thousands of people died in the last few days. You weren't responsible for them dying, and you aren't responsible for Ralph dying. It was never something within your control."

"I could have found a cottage in a different location. I could have double-checked the 'expert' who told me we can't have mudslides in New England. There's a lot I could have done. Should have done."

Roy was a man of great good sense. He said nothing, but held her close.

"It would have made more sense to move to Hugh's headquarters when he asked us," she said. "I should have seen that. We'd have been closer to where we should be, where we're needed. But I wanted the comfort of being in our own house, even half-wrecked."

"I know," Roy said quietly, "but there's no use second-guessing ourselves. I keep thinking about Gary and Elena Smith, wondering if they would be alive today if I hadn't told them we would give them a ride. But what can we do about it now? We have to go on."

"Yes, we do," she said numbly. "I know it. But it's not much of a start for a so-called survival expert. I can't help wondering what else I'm doing wrong; who else I'm going to lose."

"You can't think that way, Hedi." She heard his voice harden. "When I lose somebody on the operating table, either it's because I did something wrong or because there was nothing else I could do. Maybe somebody else might have done better, but I was the one actually there. If I did something wrong, I can't undo it — all I can do is make damn sure I never make that mistake again. And if it was something beyond my control, well, it was beyond my control. You do your best. That's all you ever *can* do."

She shuddered, as if shaking herself out of her numbness and despair. "You're right, my dear, I know. It's just hard."

"You don't know the half of it yet, I'm afraid. 'Hard' isn't the word for it. But, Hedi, you wanted to be a leader."

"I never did," she said automatically.

"Well, that's right, but you have been marked as a leader, like it or not. Mr. J certainly saw you that way. So did Sam Theos. And lots of others — including myself, if you recall. Why else do you suppose I followed you out of Ohio? You have been given the opportunities and the training, and here is the emergency. Hedi, I'd say you don't have any choice. Like it or not, a leader is what you have to be. And the first thing you learn when you're in a position of responsibility is to carry on with the job at hand, regardless. Leaders feel stress like everyone else. They can't dismiss it, but they must be able to manage it."

"I understand," she said quietly. "I'll try, Roy. I'll really try. I guess we'd better get on our way to headquarters."

Day 15

"I have two related announcements," the governor said. Huddled around his desk, crowding the little room that served him as an office, were various elected and appointed officials. Hedi stood with Roy behind the governor.

"I am hereby appointing Lt. Colonel Roy Johnson chief medical officer for the National Guard and for the State of Vermont. I am appointing Colonel Johnson's wife, Hedi Johnson, special assistant to the governor."

The governor was a good-hearted man. He knew what he was asking.

"I am certain you all know their capabilities and dedication. For any of you who may not know, I will say that Dr. and Mrs. Johnson lost their eldest child, their only son, in a mudslide three days ago." He turned to Hedi and took her hands. "On behalf of all our hard-hit citizens, I extend my heartfelt sympathy to you both. I know you will find it particularly trying to have to go back to work without proper time to grieve or accustom yourself to your loss. I feel it excusable to demand this of you only because, quite simply, we have no choice. We desperately need your talents."

She knew he was sincerely moved by their loss. Surprisingly, it seemed to make no difference. She still felt utterly numb, utterly alone.

He turned back to the officials around him. "Of course, every person here has suffered severe loss, these past two weeks. I trust that the selfless example set by the Johnsons will remind us all of the particular consideration we owe each other."

The governor, Hedi knew, had inclined toward giving them a few more days to adjust to Ralph's death. Hugh had ruled otherwise. As military commander under a thousand impossible responsibilities, he had insisted that they be pressed into service. As friend of long standing, he had come to them to tell them in person, telling them that if the living were to be saved, there was no time to grieve for the dead. "I fear that it will be a long time before we have time for personal grief," he had said. This was telling them only what they already knew. Hedi had prepared to throw herself into whatever had to be done. Fortunately, there would be more than enough work to be done. Losing herself in work shouldn't be hard.

But she had scarcely settled herself at her desk in the governor's outer office, which she would have to share with his private secretary, when Hugh Scott came bursting in. "Did you hear? General Jerome is alive! He did escape from Washington after all."

"What?" Hedi found it hard to believe. "Where has he been?"

"He has been trying to contact us, apparently, but between the static on AM and the gaps in the short-range FM relay, he couldn't get through. Sandy," he said to the governor's secretary, "ask Governor Duval if I can have a word with him, please."

Turning back to Hedi: "Ten days ago, he sent up two men in a plane to find us. They were caught in a bad storm over southern Vermont, and crashed on a mountain top. The pilot was badly injured, and the copilot had to find shelter for him in an abandoned cabin.

"I don't know the whole story, but the copilot finally found his way to one of our National Guard units near Bennington. They sent a squad for the injured pilot, and they are forwarding the copilot here. He is named Browning, a captain in the Signal Corps, an electronics engineer. He says he has the keys that will tap us into one of the military satellites. And when he gets here, I guess we'll learn something about what has happened to General Jerome."

Day 16

Captain Browning looked from the governor to Hugh Scott, then looked around at the dozen key officials arrayed around the conference tables. The tables were the folding type used, until nearly three weeks ago, for church suppers and bingo parties.

"Fill us in," the governor said. "Nobody here has any idea what has been going on in the outside world since the earthquakes struck. All we know is that it has to have been bad. We got a satellite dish working the other day, but as far as we can tell, there isn't a communications satellite in use at the moment. At least, if there is, we haven't been able to pick up the program."

"You must understand," Captain Browning said, "that I'm almost as out of touch as you have been. All my information is ten days old."

"Well, tell us what you know."

"Yes, sir. Most of what I know isn't good." He paused, organizing his material.

"Tell it in the order you found it out, if that will help," Hugh said. "Where were you that night? And what happened?"

"Sir, not long before the earthquakes hit, I was in the Pentagon with General Jerome, listening to one of our pilots over Antarctica. He had been sent over the South Pole to try to get a fix on all the electrical and magnetic disturbances being reported. They had patch ed him into the Air Force communication network and through to the Pentagon, so we heard it first-hand. He reported seeing gigantic clouds of steam rising from the ocean and said he was having a lot of trouble with his instruments. And then you could hear him gasp. He said it looked like all of Antarctica had exploded, like the whole continent had been blown right out of the sea. Then we lost him."

"Nothing more?"

"No sir."

"All right. Then what?"

"General Jerome sent an aide to the White House with a tape of the pilot's report. The president was meeting with his cabinet at the time. Presumably they were listening to it when the earthquake struck Washington."

Governor Duval: "When was that?"

"About seven, sir. It struck from the west, as far as we can tell."

"I see. Go on. What happened to Washington?"

"Sir, I was leaving with General Jerome and five other members of his staff when the first earthquake hit. I don't know what happened subsequently."

"How did you get out?"

"Helicopter, sir. General Jerome had ordered it readied earlier. I believe he hoped to stay long enough to persuade the president to seek safety, then escape himself at the last minute. His final attempt to persuade the president was shortly before seven. He had the helicopter waiting in the parking lot, and we were just lifting off when the first earthquake struck. It felt like we were being thrown into the air."

"I see," the governor said grimly. "I take it the president did not leave in time."

"To the best of our knowledge, sir, that is the case."

Captain Browning seemed to think he needed to defend his superior officer. "He tried his level best," he told them. "He stayed in Washington to the last possible moment. Beyond that. Even then, the only reason he finally gave us the okay to take off was that it was so clear that the president and his cabinet weren't going to budge. As it is, he swears he's going to go back and search for someone who can claim the right to succeed to the presidency."

"I presume he has more sense than that," Hugh Scott snapped. "He has more important things to do than going back to die with his commander-in-chief."

Captain Browning shook his head. "I don't know, sir, he's pretty determined. I guess you know what he's like when he sees his duty in a certain direction — there's no turning him."

"When he sees the shape we're in up here, maybe he'll change his mind about his duty," Hugh said. "Go on. Is there anything left in Washington worth returning to?"

It seemed to Hedi that Captain Browning was choosing his words with particular care. "Sir, it is difficult to say. We left immediately after the first shock, and we didn't get much of a last look. And when I left the Poconos, links with existing reconnaissance satellites had not yet been re-established, so I have no later data."

Madge entered the room and handed Hugh a note. As he read it, the governor cleared his throat and spoke. "Things are bad," he said. "We knew they must be. Let us take what comfort we can in knowing that we are not alone. Others are in the boat with us, and everyone is trying to keep the boat afloat."

Hugh leaned over and showed the note to the governor, who nodded. He stood up. "I am advised that Captain Browning is needed to provide code and procedure to access the military satellite, so we will adjourn at this point. After we have talked to the Poconos, we will know more closely where we stand, and I will reconvene this meeting." He made a grim joke. "I am confident that everyone here can find one or two odd jobs to keep them busy in the interim."

As Hedi left the room, she met Martha, just arrived from Montpelier. She could not talk to her about Ralph. They held each other wordlessly for long minutes while Hedi fought angrily against further tears that could do nothing to make things better. When they did talk, they confined themselves to the details of the overwhelming catastrophe that had engulfed their country and their world. Yet Hedi must have been longing for Martha's presence — it seemed to her that scarcely five minutes had passed before the meeting reconvened.

* * *

"Captain Browning has succeeded in making contact with the Poconos," Governor Duval said succinctly. "I will allow him to summarize the present situation as he understands it."

"Yessir. At the time I contacted headquarters, General Jerome was unavailable, being in Harrisburg meeting with the governor of Pennsylvania. However, he had instructed his staff to prepare a situation report, which I will summarize."

He picked up a sheaf of notes.

"Washington was hit by a series of earthquakes, as you know. Within a few hours, the tremors were followed by tidal waves."

Hedi remembered the lectures from so long ago, when the talk of earthquakes and tidal waves had seemed serious, but somehow theoretical and remote. She knew the answer, but she had to ask. "How much damage?"

"You have to understand what we're dealing with. In deep seas, undersea shock waves have negligible height, but move at speeds of as much as 600 miles an hour. When they hit the shallower water of the continental shelf, their forward motion is greatly slowed. That energy is converted into towering waves."

He hesitated, then went on. "According to the reports we received, by the time the waves hit the coast, they were 400 feet high. Higher, some places. The Eastern Shore slowed them down some, but there was plenty of force left for Washington. Maybe one person in a thousand survived. The city is a ruin."

Hedi found herself speechless.

"Not Washington alone, of course. Baltimore, Salisbury, Wilmington, Philadelphia, New York, Boston — you name the city, if it was on the seacoast, it's probably gone. And not just in this country. The situation report states that the satellites show the whole world in about the same condition — devastation. Apparently the continental plates fractured. Certainly ocean floors were shattered from pole to pole."

"What this is going to mean is anybody's guess," the governor broke in, "but obviously it isn't going to be pretty."

"No, sir. According to the report, initial estimates are that a quarter of the world's population may have died in the first ten hours."

They sat there for a long moment in an appalled silence. Finally, Hugh Scott asked the captain to tell what he knew of General Jerome's post-emergency planning.

"Yes, sir. As you know, he established his command post in Pennsylvania. That was one of 12 emergency centers to be established. All were on high ground, all but two were located well away from seacoasts."

"Very well. How did they fare in the event?"

"Sir, the center near Atlanta survived. It informed us that Asheville, North Carolina, was badly damaged but still functional."

"Is that center actually located in Asheville itself?"

"No, sir. About 12 miles away."

"All right. Go on."

"Sir, we were able to re-establish communications with the center at Colorado Springs, and the Commandant of the Air Force Academy there had established contact with the center at Butte, Montana. Together with this establishment, six centers are accounted for. At the time I left on this mission, we had no information on the other six, sir."

"What about NORAD's underground command headquarters for missile defenses?"

"Yes, sir, that survived. We count that as Colorado Springs."

"All right." Hugh's fingers were drumming again. "Captain, perhaps you'd give those assembled here a resume of the situation as sketched by the general's staff."

"Yes, sir," Captain Browning said. "As the Eastern Pennsylvania armed forces command sees it, we are faced with three immediate, critically important problems." Hedi could see that he had prepared himself to give just such a report before just such a group.

"First, the oceans are rising at an incredible rate. The average of four east-coast measurements so far is a rise of 55 feet." Hedi heard gasps, but she was not surprised. She had heard it all long ago.

Governor Duval: "In 16 days!"

"Yes, sir. The rise appears to be continuing at two feet per day. These numbers do not include the effect of the giant tidal waves which continue to batter the coastline following undersea disturbances.

Governor Duval: "Captain, why is the sea rising? And how high will it rise? Do we know?"

"Sir, the short answer is that no, we don't. But we know that on the night this horror began there was a stupendous amount of energy released in the polar regions, especially at the south pole. There were millions of cubic miles of ice on that frozen continent. No doubt enormous chunks of it — perhaps all of it, and maybe the land too — were blown into the sea. There could easily have been enough to account for an immediate rise of 55 feet."

As if from a distance, Hedi heard the low exclamations, the curses.

"In addition," the captain went on remorselessly, "the thin crust in the deep ocean trenches appears to have split open, disgorging billions of tons of lava onto the sea bottom. This also raises the sea level with respect to the land."

"How far?"

"Sir, no one can guess how far, but we know it would have a double-barreled effect. For every million cubic miles of lava that pours out of the Earth's mantle, somewhere an equal volume of the Earth's crust must sink down to fill the space that had been occupied by the lava. Thus in some cases we may have trouble knowing whether the sea is rising or the Earth is sinking. Our intelligence staff has heard estimates that from one tenth to one half of the Earth's surface will be flooded. One thing is agreed — we know of no way to stop it."

"Go on," the governor said grimly.

"Sir, the second critical problem stems not from nature but from our people themselves. Hundreds of thousands of fear-crazed and starving survivors are fleeing low-lying coastal areas. Like an army of locusts they are devouring the countryside, and all efforts to stop them have been futile. The commandant of West Point reports that his facility is about to be surrounded and overwhelmed by an endless horde fighting their way up the Hudson. He has ordered his staff and the cadet corps to evacuate under a tear-gas cover. They are ordered to attempt to reach high ground in the Catskills.

"Third, senior military officers are desperate for instruction and guidance from their commander-in-chief, but there *is* no commander-in-chief. Sworn to support the United States Government, they find there is no such government. Faced with overwhelming practical problems, they find no solutions, no prospect of solutions, and no one with authority to craft solutions.

"To cite but one of their problems — how are they to feed their troops? If they cannot feed the troops, obviously they cannot maintain their force in being. But how are they to do so? What last month was one of the strongest currencies in the world is today of questionable value, if indeed it has any value at all. Should they issue new currency? If so, what will they back it with? If not, do they simply confiscate what they need and make it legal by decree? Or do they disband and join those fighting blindly for personal survival?"

The captain looked around at a circle of sobered faces. "The report stresses that a solution must be found, and quickly, or the federal forces will be lost as a major factor in preserving order and supporting government by the will of the people."

Hedi saw Hugh meeting her eyes and she could not resist nodding. Things were still proceeding as advertised.

Evening, Day 16

Hedi had been told she was required in Hugh Scott's office. To her surprise, Roy was there, and Martha, and Hugh and Mary Scott (working the recorder), and Captain Browning, and no one else. Hugh motioned her in with an urgent gesture. "Shut the door and sit down. We are about to get patched in to General Jerome."

Hedi sat next to Roy. She whispered, "Where is he?"

"In the Poconos."

"Where's the governor?"

"Some emergency, I don't know what."

"Shhh," Hugh said, and in a few seconds the voice of the radio operator in the Poconos came into the room, via a piece of communications hardware 22,000 miles overhead, a satellite that a few weeks ago had been aging and somewhat behind the times, and now was technology that would not be replicated for decades, if ever.

General Jerome wasted no time coming to the point. "Hugh Scott and Hedi Johnson and I have been thinking for many years about how to handle just such problems as are now piling up about us. Out of that talk, and much thought, and with historic experience to guide us, I can state flatly that the fact that we are alive is no indicator that we can ride out this storm on our good luck. Quite the contrary.

"In truth, the worst is yet to come. Our stock of aviation fuel is running low and none is being produced. Supplies of automotive grade gasoline are all but gone, and not a refinery is in operation. Electric power generation is limited to emergency generators, and these will soon be out of fuel. Winter is approaching, and we have only wood to use to supply heat.

"The banks are closed, and we have no government to ensure that money has value. We are on the verge of starvation, with no way to distribute what little food we have. Worst of all, the earth continues its violence, and the seas continue to rise. And the federal government is gone."

"Gone?" Hugh Scott said it for all of them. "All of it?"

There was no sound but the hum of the radio.

"Oh, no," Hedi whispered.

"They wouldn't listen." Abruptly, they heard the general's sudden, uncharacteristic burst of anger. "I don't know what the hell scene they thought they were playing — going down with the ship or something. Or maybe they thought it couldn't happen to them, they were too important. So now they're gone and we are left with this hell of a m—"

They heard him pull himself abruptly under control. "Sorry. Anyway, that's how matters stand. We don't know for sure that no part of the government survived. That's only an assumption. Communications are too fragmented to be certain."

"But, sir, I thought we were tapped into the satellites again."

"We are. But you have to understand, we don't have the capabilities we had before. The communications satellites are still in orbit, but if you want to talk to them, you have to have trained operators, you have to know the proper codes, the proper frequencies, you have to have the proper equipment, you have to have power to operate the transmission and receiving apparatus. It is a vast mosaic of people and equipment. Do you know how much of that survived?"

"Not much, I suppose," Hugh said.

"Cape Canaveral didn't. Houston didn't. Vandenberg didn't. The stuff at Cape Cod didn't. When the tidal waves hit, we lost it all. At the moment, we are relying on NORAD. The earthquakes didn't knock it out, the tidal waves were hundreds of miles away, it was protected from the fires, and anyway it was set up for a prolonged siege underground. That's what it was designed for — to survive a nuclear attack, and still be able to carry on afterward.

"But anybody who can get to NORAD via short-wave radio wants information, and they all want the same kind of information: did this survive, did that survive, have you heard from A, can you pass a message to B. It's an overwhelming load, and they don't have time to do it all. They try to do the most important things first."

"Priorities," Hedi thought numbly.

"In the circumstances, it is essential that we move quickly. I asked to talk to you for two reasons. First, you will understand what I am talking about, and I want your advice. Second, I look on you as friends and want to explain why I am about to return to Wash-ington."

Hugh broke in: "Sir, I thought the city was destroyed. Isn't it?"

General Jerome, it appeared, was clearing his throat. "Ah—, well, the city appears to be largely under water. But there seem to be people on islands of high ground and in some undestroyed buildings. Perhaps in these groups I may find one or more officials with a legitimate claim to be in the line of presidential succession."

Hugh Scott was drumming his fingers impatiently on the table. Hedi had never seen him do that before. "That's madness," he said flatly.

Martha reached over to push the transmit button. "General, this is Martha Carlton. I beg you not to return to Washington." Hedi was surprised to see tears running down Martha's cheeks. "It is unlikely that you will find the people you seek, and even if you did, the mobs would wreck your helicopter fighting over who would climb on board, and they would tear you to pieces if you sought to stop them. It is a suicidal mission. Don't try it. We need you."

"Thank you, Martha, for your concern," the General replied, "but my mind is made up. I know the risks, and I will take such precautions as I can. But if we had someone in the line of presidential succession, the additional legitimacy this would confer upon our efforts might be of immense importance. It might mean the difference between a united, successful effort to survive and division into several pygmy governments going their separate ways. Any chance, however remote, seems worth taking.

"Please understand that I was very serious when I swore allegiance to my country and my president. Trying to help protect this wonderful land of ours has been my love and my life. It was my job to persuade the president to flee the impending danger that I knew was coming. I failed that assignment. Now I must make this one last try, regardless of the odds against success."

"Then this is good-bye?" Martha said.

"Perhaps. I hope not."

But this, Hedi knew, was exactly what General Jerome was saying.

Looking around her, she knew that everyone in the room knew it too. They were frightened. So was she.

"The time has come to look reality in the face," the general said. "From here I am able to contact some thirty-five senior officers and influential civilian leaders, and I want to give them my advice before I leave on my mission. In the event I do not return in three days, my deputy General Estes, Governor Howe of Pennsylvania, and the commandant of the Air Force Academy will issue a joint call for a national conference."

Hedi heard Roy speak. "General, with all due respect, I don't think there's time to call a conference for the purpose of creating a new national government. We need effective action *now*. We have all we can do to maintain order and use our limited resources to the best advantage. We don't have energy left for political conferences." Hedi thought of Gary Smith, the first time she had been able to visualize his face since Ralph had gone.

"Was that Roy? Roy, the problem is one of legitimacy. That is precisely why I intend to go out on what may prove to be a wild goose chase, on the off-chance that I can bring home the bacon."

"Sir," Captain Browning said, "maybe legitimacy isn't the problem we think it is. However the government is put together, it will have to be tough. With the problems we face, we can't afford some of the old niceties."

The fact that a captain felt able to offer suggestions — and implied criticism — to a general underlined for Hedi the extraordinary nature of this radio conference.

There was an interruption in reception. "— if I cannot find someone with a legal claim to leadership of this nation, I think it quite likely you will have to face a move to establish a military dictatorship."

"No!" For the moment the strength of her feelings carried Hedi quite out of herself. She was speaking before she knew it. "We need a tough government, true. And it may have to take actions that are harsh and arbitrary, yes. But it must exist and exercise its power by the will of the people. Anything less is not worth preserving, and I will have no part in it." She thought of Mr. J's law. "It isn't any accident that our old world is being destroyed. If we are going to build a New Earth, it's going to have to leave behind the worst of our past and preserve the best. There is no doubt about the category in which dictatorships fall."

Hugh Scott was nodding his head vigorously. "Hear, hear! General, Hedi's right as usual."

"And I fully agree with her, as you should well know. But what would you do to prevent it?"

Hugh looked to Hedi.

"Do what's being done here and in eastern Canada," Hedi replied. "Let military units place themselves at the disposal of the most responsible government they can find. If there's a state government, it makes sense to integrate the federal forces with the National Guard of that state." Rapidly, inspired, talking without the necessity of thinking out what she would say, she sketched out in a few words her thoughts on preserving forces in being while preserving the principle of representative government.

Hugh Scott and Martha chimed in to support her, and at length the general conceded the practicality of her ideas.

"It wouldn't be a permanent solution," Hedi said. "But with luck it will buy time to establish a national government. Someday, perhaps, even a world government."

"The only thing I would add," Hugh Scott said, "is that I do believe a high-level staff unit should be formed at once to provide information and advice, and to control very special U.S. military assets such as the communication satellites."

"Thank you, my friends," the General said. "Those are good arguments. I hope they will persuade all who listen to this tape, as they persuade me. Sam Theos always told me I could count on you." There was a moment's silence, a low hum carried from Pennsylvania to Vermont by the shortest electronic route available, a mere matter of a 45,000-mile round trip. "Hedi? Roy?"

"We're here," Roy said hoarsely. He seemed to know what was coming.

"Hugh told me about little Ralph. I can only say I am very sorry, my friends. I know what you are going through. I lost my only sister and my two nephews that I loved dearly. Try to remember that everybody around you has lost people too, and remember that there will be a time for mourning later."

Hedi saw Roy's face start to dissolve, then resume its impassive mask. But his voice quavered, just a little, as he thanked Jerome.

"Thank you, Jim," she choked out. "Take care."

"Good-bye," he said. "God bless you all." There was a click, and a heavy silence filled the room.

29. Coping
Day 19

"All right," the governor said. "I think we are all here. Ladies, gentlemen, I have urgent business to set before you. We in this room, though fewer than 20 in number, represent the entire remaining civil and military leadership of the State of Vermont. It is up to us to set priorities and devise a plan of action.

"We have no time to waste, and precious little margin for error.

The present state of extensive disruption and disorganization is such that our foresight, energy and ability are our people's only hope. Should we fail to find ways to overcome the deadly perils ahead, no one else will retrieve that failure. There *is* no one else.

"After three days in the field, out among the people, I can only tell you that I found the realities of life nearly three weeks after the earthquakes more sobering than I would have imagined even one week ago.

"People are desperately trying to stay alive by any means possible. No doubt, that is how it is everywhere — in other states and in other countries.

"Wherever some authority is able to maintain order, as here, the survival effort has some success. This is true even if the authority is no larger than a town council. Otherwise, there is nothing but chaos and death.

"We are receiving reports of what is occurring on our borders, both in New York State, and in other parts of New England. I must say these reports are very troubling. We here should give thanks for our good fortune in having so many resources available to us. To speak only of food, consider that more densely populated areas began to run short of food within 48 hours of the initial disruption. Like ourselves, they had no possibility of obtaining supplies from outside. But they had far less to work with.

"In fact, in many heavily populated coastal areas where damage was greatest, the initial destruction was followed by mob rule and then by chaos. This was bad enough, but after the initial hysteria burned itself out in death and exhaustion, the pattern we are seeing is that some strong individual will succeed in converting a mob into a gang. These gangs are fighting one another for food and for control."

"Let 'em kill each other," someone murmured.

"But that isn't what is happening," the governor replied. "The strong ones grow larger, and the weak ones, faced with surrender or starvation, become the servants of the victors. No doubt, you see the danger. If any one gang grows large enough, and its leadership is strong enough, it may develop a disciplined fighting force and even a form of government."

"Oh, Mr. Duval," another said, "what kind of a threat is a disorganized mob, when we have the National Guard and contingents of various armed forces?"

"More than you would suspect, I fear. Let me tell you what has been happening in Pennsylvania. I know that may seem a long way away from us, at the moment, but just last month it was only a few hours' drive, and there will come a time, with God's help, when it is again. In the last few days, I heard the same story again and again from our people who are trying to deal with the flood of refugees in the southern portion of the state. I talked to some of those refugees myself. I got on the radio to the governor of Pennsylvania, though we found ourselves talking half in a sort of makeshift code, for fear of who might be listening. Listen to what has been going on down there."

The governor proceeded to tell them. In those first desperate days, millions in the New Jersey and New York City area tried to escape death by fleeing west. Those who were spared destruction by the initial tidal waves saw that the seacoast would drown, and so fled west.

Hedi had heard enough tales to imagine the picture. The only thing most of that mass of fleeing humanity would have had in mind was movement toward safety on high ground. Some would have had bicycles, which would give them an advantage over others. A few would have had automobiles, and they would make some progress on clogged and broken roads, until their gasoline ran out. Most would have had only their feet, and many would have been slowed down by their women and children and, for a time, by their aged or ill.

"That so many would flee was inevitable. But that they would turn into violent, destructive mobs, was not. And, indeed, subsequent events made it clear that those mobs did not form and move at random. They were formed, and they were herded, deliberately. They were part of a maneuver aimed at achieving power for one man or one small group of men. A successful maneuver, apparently. Probably most of the mob never did know what was happening."

She could imagine that, too. If you were in the middle of the group, or on the westward side, all you would notice, probably, is that the people to the east of you were pressing you more and more urgently. You would have to press forward more quickly as well, pressing the people ahead of you. You wouldn't have any choice. By the time the crowd had turned into a mob, and the mob had turned into a stampede, you would be just like everybody else, shoving desperately to stay on your feet, trying to protect your loved ones, if you had any, until they were trampled. Doing some trampling yourself, in turn.

"The crowds were driven into the small towns along the west bank of the Delaware River. By midnight, six towns were burning. By dawn, they were pillaged and devoid of life. We are told the herding was done by fewer than 20 men, directed by a man in a helicopter," the governor said.

"Not so hard," Hugh put in. "One man in a helicopter, directing the action and ferrying his men from place to place as need be. A few men with shotguns loaded with birdshot, to move people in the proper direction. A couple of tear-gas canisters...."

"Perhaps. At any rate, when morning came, the men who had looted the town — and I leave *that* scene to your imagination — found themselves in towns with no food left. A few hours after dawn, maybe having come to their senses, they tried to leave. Or maybe they were searching for another town to devour. It doesn't much matter. They found themselves surrounded by men with tommy guns — the same ones who had herded them earlier, apparently — who proceeded methodically to mow them down."

"Good God!" Hedi said. "Why?"

"Object lesson. A few hours later, the ringleader gathered up some important citizens of the larger communities a little further west, and gave them a tour. He wanted to show them two things: What the mobs had done to the town, and what his men had done to the mobs."

"He wanted to show them that he could turn the mobs on, and he could turn them off," Martha said grimly.

"Precisely. After the tour, he offered them a deal. He would protect them from invasion from the east as long as they helped protect him from foes in the high country to the west."

"Meaning the National Guard, I take it," Hugh said quietly.

"Mostly."

"They weren't fool enough to believe him?"

"They believed him, Hedi. For one thing, what choice did they have? He was organized and they weren't. He was also more ruthless than they were. The way they saw it, they had no choice."

"I hope they're happy with how it worked out for them."

The governor looked at her with an odd expression on his face. "So far, he appears to have kept his word. As long as they do what he wants, they are not harmed. Those who didn't accept his offer got a repeat demonstration, with their towns used as examples."

"Who is this monster?"

"We don't know," Governor Duval said, "but to me he sounds like a gangster. What he is doing is straight out of the old protection racket."

"That would explain the ready-made army, too," Martha said.

Hedi said, "I'm surprised the Pennsylvania National Guard — or even the Highway Patrol — doesn't come down out of the hills and disperse this rag-tag army of hoodlums."

"I think these hoodlums are more organized than you make them out to be, Hedi, and the National Guard have enough on their plate where they are."

He saw the doubt on her face. "Suppose we had the same kind of thing to face here. General, if I asked you to field a force sufficient to disperse an organized army, what would it cost?"

"Even if we didn't have to fire a single shot, there would be a price in lives," Hugh said reluctantly. "We would have to commandeer food, fuel, material — lots of things. Manpower, particularly. Right now, we have all we can do and more, just to see that our people live through these first few weeks. I don't see how we could justify a campaign against anything other than an immediate threat. A grave, immediate threat."

"It can't be any better in Pennsylvania, Hedi."

"But is this gang, then, to be left in possession of territory because it is inconvenient to root them out?"

"'Inconvenient' is a misleading term," the governor said. "'Impossible' is closer."

Hedi couldn't leave it alone. "Think of the helpless people within that territory," she said. "They are our fellow citizens."

"I am aware of that," the governor said a trifle sharply. "But they happen to be fellow citizens beyond the reach of our assistance.

"Which brings me to the point. The only alternative to mob rule and gang rule is lawful government. That depends, in turn, on the existence of some unit of former government, and at least a few of its lawful officials. In the beginning, it may be necessary to govern with the use of martial law or its equivalent, but if we cannot make provision at the start for the people to vote for those who will exercise authority, we risk losing individual freedom and representative government."

Governor Duval paused and wiped his forehead with his handkerchief, a curiously homely gesture, Hedi thought. "You know, all my life I have heard politicians, including myself, talking about freedom and democracy. We used to put the words in our speeches and our party platforms because people expected us to, and they expected us to because that's what they were used to hearing. But the words are more than just words. They are a kind of shorthand for our way of life."

He looked around the table. Hedi had been unimpressed by the man's political or mental stature when he was lieutenant governor, but working with him day by day, she had become increasingly aware of the value of his sincerity and simplicity. Now, with every word he spoke, he seemed to grow. "My friends, it is a good way of life. It has its problems, and we have to work on those, but all in all it's the best way of life, I think, that the world has ever known. We can't let it go down the drain for lack of trying."

He proceeded to give them their charge. "In four days' time, I intend to call into special session the Vermont legislature. By that time, I want you to have prepared for me a report setting out our priorities and spelling out a plan of action. I will make several requests of the legislature. I want it to give its retroactive approval of my martial-law proclamation. I want it to redetermine the size of the legislature, and provide provisional procedures for filling vacant legislative vacancies. Perhaps most importantly, I want it to support the action plans that will be developed right here in the next three days."

"Sir, what if you cannot locate enough members of the legislature to form a quorum?"

"Then we'll go with what we have. This is no time to be excessively scrupulous. First we'll get the legislature functioning again, as legally as possible; then, as soon as we can, we'll call elections. One set of elections will remove a mountain of irregularities. The spirit is more important than the letter."

"Particularly in emergencies," Martha said.

"Precisely," he said appreciatively. "One thing more, and then I will leave you to your work. I want you to bear in mind that the net effect of what you accomplish here may extend far beyond the borders of our state or region. General Jerome's final recommendations to his staff were that a national convention be called at Colorado Springs to establish a national provisional government. As a first step toward that convention, he recommended that a small group of leaders be invited to Colorado Springs to plan for it.

"The planning-group meeting is tentatively scheduled for 16 days from this date, or Day 35 since the night of the calamities. By that time, I want to have this state functioning as a model of what may be accomplished."

"Mamma, can you stay home with me today? I'm bored!"

Hedi, her hands full with changing the baby, answered her daughter through the safety-pins in her mouth. "Honey, I'm sorry, I can't. I'd like to."

"But you *never* stay home any more!"

She got the second pin in the diaper and lifted Peter from the dresser that served as changing table. "There, baby, all dry." Lifting him to one shoulder, she stooped down and gathered snuffling Sally to her with her left hand. "Honey, I know. It's hard. And you don't know how much I miss you all day."

"Daddy's always gone too."

"I know, honey. But right now we can't help it. After a while it will get better, promise." At least she wasn't crying for Ralph. There had been some scenes that Hedi had wondered if she could live through. She had said to Roy, "I want to be all grown up and comforting for Sally, but how can I, when I feel like all I want to do is go crying to my own mother?" Who is very probably dead, she had added silently.

"Honey, in a few days things will get better and your father and I will have some time. In the meantime you will have to be brave and help take care of Peter."

"But I want *you*."

"I know, honey. I know."

Day 22

"Let's get started. Hedi, would you summarize the panel's conclusions?"

"Yes, sir. In the three days since you assigned us the task of setting priorities and devising a plan of action, this panel has convened six times. After extensive and often heated discussion, we have more or less unanimously agreed to submit several plans for your approval. Shall I summarize the discussion?"

"Let's hear the recommendations first, so I get a clear idea of what you want me to do. Then we can go around and hear minority views."

Hedi consulted her legal notepad.

"First, we think you should propose to your counterparts in New Hampshire and Maine that a board of governors be created for the three state area."

"Why?"

"We think it would facilitate coordination of policies. Properly implemented, it should reduce staffwork by eliminating redundant efforts. Several people indicated that over the long haul it should produce significantly less friction among the governors, by providing a common, agreed-upon mechanism for setting policy."

"Majority rule?"

"That, or unanimous decision. We left the question open. In a group as small as three, we think the problem is larger in theory than in practice."

"All right, I'll think about it. Go on. What are the board's immediate priorities?"

"We came up with several extremely urgent tasks:

"One, the treatment of refugees fleeing from the coastal areas. Two, rationing of critical items of food, clothing, heating fuels, medical attention, and shelter. Three, establishing a common currency. Four, drafting laws as necessary to replace old federal legislation that is no longer enforceable. Five, appointing a committee to draft an interim area Constitution."

"Quite a handful," the governor said. "Good; that's what I wanted you to do. Let's look at the list. What's the problem with refugees? Let's just treat them as fellow citizens in need. Disaster victims. Which they are."

"Yes, sir," Jim Morris said. Morris, thin, crew-cut and 40ish, was sharp, if somewhat unapproachable. "But somebody's going to come up short. We don't have unlimited supplies of anything. The more liberal we are with refugees, the greater the chance that our own people suffer."

"They are *all* our own people," Harry Karpen said sharply. He was an older man, usually soft-spoken and polite. Hedi liked him.

"We just don't have enough!" Morris shot back. "If we are limited to taking care of only a given number — and we are — we ought to take care of our neighbors first."

"Who is my neighbor?" Hedi asked innocently. Morris flushed angrily. "That's all well and good, but *somebody* is going to come up short. Why should it be our own people?"

"I see the point at issue," the governor said. "We can come back to it." He glanced down at the notes he had scribbled. "Let's move on. Rationing?"

"Whoever has the power to ration has the power of life and death," Karpen said shortly. "We think the governors need to consider the matter carefully."

Governor Duval set his jaw. "That's easily decided. That power belongs to the lawfully elected representatives of the people, and nobody else. And it will be checked by the lawful representatives of the people, to assure that no one uses his delegated authority to take advantage. Hedi, make a note — we need to set up ombudsmen, so that our people have a quick, easy method of bringing abuses to our attention. Check with General Scott on that: The military system of inspectors-general may serve as guide." Another glance at his pad. "Common currency?"

"This problem grows more acute by the day," Morris said. "To date we have made do with existing United States currency. Basically, we are asking our people to trust us to come up with a way to back that currency with value."

"The freeze on prices appears to have worked."

"To date. But we cannot expect it to work much longer. The historical experience with price freezes is that their effectiveness erodes rapidly, and with increased velocity. The extraordinary nature of this emergency has called forth reserves of public-spiritedness that has helped us to limp through this period. But I can say with considerable certainty that these reserves, like any reserves, are in danger of depletion."

The governor nodded. His fingers, Hedi noted, had begun playing with his pencil, rolling it back and forth on his pad. "I assure you I have given the problem considerable attention. This is not the time to go into the difficulties involved." He sighed. "I agree, however, that whatever we do ought to be done in a unified fashion. We haven't time to spare for the complications that currency differences would cause." He smiled. "I think you realize that a common currency implies a common sovereignty. I will have to present this point carefully to my fellow governors, lest they think me too presumptuous."

Another glance at his pad. "Drafting laws to replace federal legislation need not detain us. Federation will bring such legislation in its wake automatically. As to appointing a committee to draft an interim area Constitution," — another smile — "if my fellow governors are with me to this point, they will already have agreed to this implicitly."

He rolled his pencil back and forth for a few seconds. "Very well. I agree in principal to all of this. Whatever specific decisions we come to on the various items, it is of first importance that the area governments act with a common purpose."

He turned to Hedi. "Mrs. Johnson, I would like you to represent me in implementing this. This is to be your top priority project. Pursue this full-tilt. When you find an obstacle in your path, try to remove it by persuasion, compromise, concession; whatever is appropriate. If the obstacle does not move, I expect you to come directly to me or to whomever is appropriate. This federation must go through, and the sooner the better."

He looked around for dissent, and saw none. "Very well. What's next on the agenda?"

Hedi consulted her notes. "It was agreed that liaison with surviving government bodies in Eastern Canada would be appropriate."

"Yes, I've already thought about that. Martha Carlton informed me a few days ago that Len Adams, whom I believe most of you know, has been sitting in on discussions among Canadian authorities aimed at accomplishing much the same things we are discussing today. If it is agreeable to this body, I thought that Miss Carlton would be an appropriate person to serve as liaison with the Canadian group, particularly in view of her long-standing relationship with the Adams family." Hedi, like Governor Duval, looked around the table and saw no dissent. "Fine," he said. "Miss Carlton, consider yourself so appointed. While I'm at it, I might as well tell you and this body that I decided last night to appoint you director of communications, as well."

"Thank you, sir," Martha said. "What did you have in mind for me to do?"

"Right now, get us on track with the Canadians. Later, who knows? I'm sure we can find something to keep you busy. Our people out there are going to want to know — going to need to know — what's going on. It looks like it's going to be a long time before we get radio and TV back on the air. Paper for newspapers and magazines is going to be in short supply for a long, long time: We will need the timber for other purposes. I'm going to depend on you to come up with ways for us to communicate. Wall posters, relay teams, organized rumor mills, I don't know. Find something. When you solve that problem, come back and I'll think of others.

"Oh, and that reminds me. Mrs. Scott, in addition to your other duties, which I fully realize are extensive enough, I've dreamed up another project for you to implement when and as you find time to do so: creating a technical library. I want you to find, collect, and preserve every scrap of information that may conceivably be of use at some later time. We cannot afford the luxury of assuming that what is known will be preserved. For all we know to the contrary, the past few days may have opened enormous gaps in our technical and scientific knowledge. I'd rather err on the side of caution by preserving things that have been preserved elsewhere, than take the chance of losing something irretrievable by assuming that it is safe elsewhere. You understand what I have in mind?"

"Yes sir, I think so."

"Good. I'm giving you an enormous job, I realize. But it is enormously important. Hedi, what's next on your list?"

"As part of a general agreement on coordinating policies in the three-state area, we concluded that a unified military command is desirable."

He nodded decisively. "General, if my fellow governors agree, that will be your baby. We will expect you to maintain order and defend our boundaries from whatever external threat may present itself. Once our legislatures are functioning again, you will be expected to assist civil police to enforce the law when need be; in the meantime you will enforce whatever emergency decrees are proclaimed while we are under martial law. Should Maine and New Hampshire disagree, you will still have these responsiblities with respect to Vermont. Any questions or comments?"

"Only one, sir. When you say we are to protect our boundaries, does this mean precisely the former state boundaries?"

The governor understood the question. There was a moment's silence while he considered it. "Use your common sense, of course. I'd say that in relation to Canada, use extreme tact in dealing with neighboring authorities. As to Massachusetts and New York, you will have to feel your way as you go along. If a neighboring township or county has maintained order and requests our assistance, my inclination would be to extend that assistance unless there are overriding considerations. Is that how you see it?"

"Yes, sir, more or less. In earlier sessions we discussed the threat posed by gangs that appear to be forming into quasi governments. Should these gangs become a threat great enough to require a military response, questions of tactics and strategy may play an increasing part in decisions to extend or withhold assistance to various localities beyond our boundaries."

"I understand, and we will have to deal with those situations as they arise." Back to Hedi. "More?"

"No, sir. That's the gist of it. There are details we could talk about, of course."

He brushed that aside. "No, we all have more urgent things to do. Does anyone who was in the minority in any of these decisions feel strongly enough about their position to want to raise the question here and now? Very well. I consider that this panel has done what was asked of it. Mrs. Scott, I will ask you to prepare a document outlining these plans; I want to forward them to General Estes for further distribution prior to the planning meeting on - - what would the date be?"

"November 7," Hugh Scott said. "Or, dating from the night of the earthquakes, day 35."

"Day 35. All right, I suppose that's as good a dating scheme as any. General, I want you and Martha Carlton to attend that planning conference in Colorado Springs. Miss Carlton, prior to your departure, I expect you to have engaged our Canadian counterparts in discussion of their participation in the planning meeting and the convention itself."

"Sir,—" Hugh Scott said.

"General, I understand the pressures on your time and the responsibilities you bear. Nonetheless, I am firm in my mind about sending you. Your responsibilities here will not diminish with time; they will grow. There will never be a time when we can better spare you, though God knows it will be difficult enough to do so now. You will prepare your subordinates to function without you until you return. If they are uneasy under the responsibility, assure them that I will see that they receive whatever cooperation they require."

"Yes sir, but —"

"No 'but', general." Perhaps sensing that this came close to being a public rebuke, the governor added another sentence. "Colorado Springs may be crucial to our future, general. It is imperative that we have forceful, effective, authoritative representation. You speak the language of those who will be running the conference. I cannot spare you here, but I damn well can't spare you there."

Hugh Scott nodded. "Thank you, sir, for your confidence. Have the conference members indicated how participants will travel there?"

"The Air Force is going to fly you there and will fly you back. If you'd gone a month ago, probably you would have travelled first class and it would have taken you five hours, portal to portal. As it is, I expect you'll be riding in a one- or two-engine propeller-driven airplane that will take — well, who knows?"

An afterthought struck him. "The fact that the Air Force is allocating fuel from its dwindling reserves ought to indicate the importance Colorado Springs places on this conference."

30. The National Conference
Day 35

"Governor," Martha said, "you would have been proud. General Estes named our document 'The New England Example,' and representatives from all regions were studying what we were doing and making plans to recommend similar action when they returned home."

Another meeting of the de facto government of the State of Vermont, this time to hear a report from Martha and Hugh Scott, just returned from the first national conference.

"Sixteen governors were present," Hugh said. "Four more were represented by senior state officials. In addition, seven senior military officers were invited as delegates. Three civilian leaders had been selected as delegates by local officials in areas where state governments did not exist. The three areas represented comprised fragments of seven states."

Martha summarized the political decisions arrived at: the compromises, the half-measures, and ultimately the bold, far-reaching attempt to form a structure that could retrieve disaster.

"I cannot stress too much the catalytic effect of distributing 'The New England Example' before the conference began," Martha said. "As a result we heard presentations on 'The Denver Example', 'The Carolina Approach', and 'The Montana Plan,' and I described what I called 'The East Canada Plan'.

"Out of this exchange came many little ideas that I think will be of great value. The idea for initially using ration coupons as currency, for example. The bicycle express service for delivering all but high priority mail and messages. And as you will see in our attached report, there were many others — common-sense solutions to pressing everyday problems."

Martha gave them a summary of the political situation; where law and order had been maintained, where anarchy seemed to have the upper hand, which area appeared to have been given over to what might be termed organized anarchy, or, more simply, tyranny.

"Unfortunately," she said, "the sheer extent of physical destruction seems to make reconstruction of our federal government as it was almost an impossibility. Although the structure we set up seems very similar at first blush, in many ways it more closely resembles the old Articles of Confederation that preceded the original Constitution in the 1780s."

"I don't understand that idea," the governor said. "Why are we moving backwards?"

"Sheer necessity," Martha said succinctly. "Much of what was our country is underwater. The substantial portions that are left are separated from each other by great expanses of water, inadequate means of conveyance, and fragmentary means of communication. In practical terms, it's every region and district for itself. The fact that we were able to agree on a loose confederation is more a tribute to the nation we were than an expression of present realities."

"A tribute to what we were, and a statement of intent to become once again one nation sometime in the future," Hugh said. "But it doesn't seem physically possible, right now."

"Why not? Maybe you'd better spell this out in small words," the governor said, frowning.

Martha deferred to Hugh. "Partly, it's because of the weather changes," Hugh said. "Clouds of volcanic ash prevent the Earth from radiating excess warmth into space. At the same time, all that lava is releasing vast quantities of heat. Net effect: Even though we are living in a twilight world of frequent dirty grey rains, the climate is becoming warmer."

Hedi spoke up. "A good thing, too, Roy says. He says if we'd had our usual amount of subfreezing cold, we'd have had massive loss of life from exposure."

"That's true enough, but all that undersea lava is still generating new warm ocean currents, and the thermal gradients continue to re-route old ones. This, in turn, is causing major changes in air currents, breaking up jet streams and forming new ones. The result of all this is that local weather changes continue to be violent and unpredictable. Besides that, we're seeing tidal waves of terrible power continually rising up from the continental shelves and smashing ashore. Smashing onto an ever-receding shore. Storms at sea are frequent and violent, and it's liable to be a long time before surface craft have a reasonable chance of crossing the oceans safely. As to air transport, nearly all our long-range jets are gone, many damaged or destroyed, others grounded for lack of fuel. In any case, landing facilities for jets are few and far between, with Colorado Springs one of the few exceptions."

Jake was in Colorado. Martha had seen him, said he worked 18 hours a day, maintained a determined optimism, and encouraged those around him to keep their minds on the long run. "We'll get past all this, some day," Martha had quoted him as saying. "And the question then will be: 'Have we preserved the best of what we had?' If we don't keep our eye on the ball, we may wake up one day and realize that all this suffering was for nothing. But if we keep our minds on what we're doing, what we're going through can be an offering we're making for the sake of the next generation."

"The present is bad enough," Hugh Scott said, "but the experts seem to think we haven't yet seen anything like the worst of it. They concentrated on two simple questions: How high will the sea rise? And how fast will it rise?

"Early data apparently was very confusing, due to the uneven settling of the land masses. Fortunately, the satellites in synchronous orbits were affected only slightly by the chaos on the Earth. Using information from these satellites, scientists were able to obtain the first accurate sea level measurements by Day 30 — that is, 30 days after the earthquakes."

"Yes?"

"These readings were not comforting. They showed a rise of 87 feet in the first 30 days, with a current continuing rise of 19 inches per day."

This was appalling. No worse than what had been predicted long ago in Sam Theos' camp, but still, it was catastrophe.

"For how long?"

"We pushed the geologists on that. They kept saying that it was too early to be able to make a good estimate, but they finally came up with a ballpark guess of 200 feet by the end of Year Zero. A rise of another 100 feet by the end of Year One is possible due primarily to the continued eruption of lava on the sea floor."

The officials looked at each other in blank dismay. Yet General Scott came next to a matter of even greater concern.

"A huge fault is dividing North America," he said bluntly. "A crack of unknown depth is widening at a rate averaging fifteen hundred feet per day. In some places it increases in width by as much as three miles a day. The ground along the borders of this chasm is sinking at rates averaging 25 feet per day."

"Why?" the governor asked tersely.

"Sir, we don't know. One geologist presented a theory. He said there was a time, hundreds of millions of years ago, when the entire vast expanse of our continent between the Rocky Mountains and the older Appalachian chain was covered by a great inland sea. In those days the oceans were not so deep, and the land masses were not so high. The Earth was rounder and in better balance."

"So?"

"In the geologist's opinion, the Earth had come full cycle and was now trying to regain its ancient shape."

"I don't see the connection."

"He thinks land is sinking into the earth's hot mantle, where it is remelting to replenish the enormous streams of lava being discharged on the ocean floor. One result is the opening of faults running from the Gulf of Mexico to the Arctic Ocean, and along the St. Lawrence to the North Atlantic. Along the sides of these great fissures the land is sinking, with huge chunks breaking away and falling into the crevice, making it ever wider. We seem to be witnessing the creation of a great inland sea."

"Hmm," the governor said non-committally. "It doesn't sound like there's anything we can do about it." Hedi by now knew how the governor's mind worked: If nothing could be done, then no matter how important the development, it was more profitable to turn attention to something that could be affected by human activity.

"Sir, there is nothing that can be done to prevent or slow the earth-molding activity; the point is, this is one more phenomenon tending to split up what was one country into quasi-independent districts."

"Yes, yes, I see that."

"The fault runs roughly along the Mississippi and Ohio river valleys to the Pittsburgh vicinity. There it branches into two prongs: one that has found its way to the North Atlantic, and another which is seeking the Arctic. Tragically for tens of thousands of people, the fault does not follow the Ohio's great bend to the south, but cuts more directly across from the Cincinnati area to Pittsburgh. Those people trapped between the fault and the river were in desperate circumstances. The earthquakes destroyed every bridge on the river, leaving them no way to cross the fast-flowing flood waters."

Hedi felt Martha's eyes on her, and knew what was coming.

"On Day 39," Hugh Scott said — reluctantly, because he had already talked with Martha — "the satellite showed the final chapter of the tragedy. The chasm swallowed the last strip of land between the fault and the river."

That was where she had left her parents a few weeks earlier. She looked up and faced Martha, and knew the truth.

The governor made an apparent effort to shake off the depressing vision. "All right," he said resolutely. "We have already lived through a lot of bad news, and we always knew we were going to get more. Let's move on. Martha, how does this affect the national structure the conference proposes? We know the conference issued a call for a provisional Congress. How is it supposed to work?"

Martha resumed speaking as calmly as though they had been discussing the geography of the Jurassic Era. Hedi thought: No one who didn't know that Martha had just listened to a report of the death of her parents would have guessed it.

"Delegates to the provisional Congress would be seated from each state or equivalent political area," Martha said. "The number of delegates from each state or area would be determined initially from a rough estimate of population. The provisional Congress would undertake the creation of an interim national government, electing a president from among its members. Any state or area sending delegates to the provisional Congress would be deemed to be thereby pledging the support needed for it to carry out its work."

"What about places that weren't part of the union? Canada?"

"Any area or government in North America will be invited to adhere to the union or to send a non-voting observer delegation."

"All right. How do they intend to get around the constitutional requirement of a three-fourths' vote by states on new admissions? Or are we going to do it now and straighten out irregularities later?"

"The delegates concluded that the Congress should create a commission to draft a Constitution for the new nation."

The governor frowned. "Why? What's wrong with the old one?"

"We felt that conditions had changed too drastically for us to continue under the old Constitution."

"You're going to have to explain that. I happen to think it's a damned good Constitution, made to be elastic enough to change with the times."

Martha seemed to be picking her words with care. "Yes, sir, it is. But we felt that the disruption of our civil life has been too extensive to be dealt with under the existing structure. Too many of its unspoken assumptions have been swept away."

"Give me a 'for instance'."

"For instance, the only existing means of communication are now in the hands of the state — meaning the military, mostly — and are likely to remain there for the foreseeable future. Provision of housing, food, and clothing — to say nothing of non-necessities — *must* be coordinated by authorities at various levels if we are to survive. In the circumstances, it is incumbent upon us to take the greatest pains that we do not deliberately or inadvertently create a self-perpetuating oligarchy, or some form of absolutist rule, or a military dictatorship. The old Constitution didn't have to provide particular protection against those dangers because the conditions of civil life itself provided a certain protection."

"More than that," Hugh said, "we're going to see much greater local autonomy than before. In most matters of practical everyday life, each district is going to be on its own. Again I say, in the long run, this Congress' major accomplishment may well be that it kept the various districts loosely tied together, against the day when conditions will allow them to reunite."

"All right," the governor said, nodding slowly. "I sent you two because I trusted you. I'll continue to trust you until I see some reason not to. But I want to tell you that I'm going to have plenty to say about various drafts of this new Constitution. I recognize that in the shortest term, it seems almost frivolous to be spending time and energy on crafting and re-crafting political documents. As pressed as we all are, I feel that way myself sometimes. But it is now, when conditions are fluid, that we must take greatest care to keep our eye on what we want to create. In these times, we will do things in a matter of weeks or months that we will not be able to undo, for better or worse, in years, if ever."

Martha cleared her throat. "Speaking of which," she said, "it became quite clear that you were absolutely right to insist that General Scott attend."

The governor glanced at Scott curiously. Hugh preserved his unflappable demeanor, but Hedi seemed to see that he was a little less comfortable than usual.

"The conference decided to recommend that each district place military units under the control of elected authority," Martha said.

"What military units are those?"

"Any that have not been integrated with National Guard units."

"All right. So?"

"It might easily have been otherwise."

The governor shifted in his chair. "Miss Carlton, ordinarily I find you quite direct and to the point. Would you kindly tell us what is on your mind?"

"Yes, sir. It was just as General Jerome predicted it would be — a lot of the delegates felt strongly that we need military governments, with a promise of free elections at a later date."

"Dictatorships, you mean."

"That's it, exactly. They argued this would provide the most effective way to make and implement decisions. They said it would be the best way to ensure survival. Some said the only way."

"Yes?"

"The rest of us argued for majority rule and individual liberty, but in the context of the immediate problem of survival, our arguments didn't sound as persuasive as they should have. It sounded like we were romantics, arguing for a luxury we couldn't afford. I really think that if General Scott hadn't been there, we might have lost. Hugh, I hope I'm not embarrassing you."

"General Scott will have to bear with any embarrassment he may feel," the governor said drily. "I want to hear."

"You have to understand the prestige he started with. Nobody there knew Martha Carlton. Nobody much, anyway. But they knew Hugh. Two of the military men knew him personally, and the rest knew him as someone who had been very close to General Jerome. They knew General Jerome, I assure you!

"Anyway, because Hugh is a professional military officer, now the commanding general of the Vermont National Guard, I think most of the delegates — those who didn't *really* know Hugh — assumed they knew where he would stand."

Martha positively beamed. "Governor, he was magnificent. He stood up and he ticked off his points cool as a cucumber."

Hedi wondered: How long will it be before I taste cucumbers again?

"From the first sentence, he didn't leave them in any doubt where he stood. I've got it here, I've been waiting to do this." She pressed 'play' on the tape recorder on the desk in front of her, and turned up the volume so all could hear. Hugh's voice, tinny and distant among the background noise of many bodies moving about in a large room, filled the air.

"The fallacy of the argument for a military dictatorship is twofold," Hedi heard him say. "First, history is littered with the broken promises of dictatorship now and democracy later. If you doubt this, I invite you to prepare a list of such promises that have been kept.

"Second, and more important, the goal of survival at any cost is wrong. All of you who are members of the armed services, and many others holding public office, have pledged your personal survival to defend your country and its dedication to life, liberty and the pursuit of happiness. General Jerome took that oath, and gave his life in the effort to find and rescue a lawful national leader. He did this in defiance of considerations of his own survival. Can you doubt which side of this argument he would have taken?

"I want to state my own views as strongly as I can. My first priority, and the prime goal of my associates in Vermont, is the survival of those great principles from our past that produced free societies and nurtured individual liberty.

"If survival means reverting to the dark chapters of our past — to the suppression of human rights and the bondage of entire nations — then it is not a worthwhile goal. At any rate, it is not a goal for which we wish to fight.

"Nor is it necessary. Instead we support a proposition that has inspired and supported every struggle man has made to gain freedom. We join with our neighbors in New Hampshire who say, '*Live Free or Die.*' For as long as we live, we intend to live free."

Martha clicked off the tape recorder. "The record shows there was no further debate on the matter," she said, her eyes shining. "Instead, Governor Howe of Pennsylvania rose and moved that General Scott's statement be recorded as expressing the view of the conference, and his motion was passed on a voice vote."

Governor Duval turned to his military commander. "Thank you, Hugh," he said simply. "I knew you'd come through."

Hedi and everyone in the room broke out in applause.

31. Priorities
Day 103

Roy took her into his arms. "Honey, I am glad to see you."

"Me too," Hedi said emphatically. "And you can't possibly know how much I mean that."

"Oh, I think I do. It seems like a year since I've seen you."

"You warned me that being married to a doctor was no bed of roses," she said, burrowing her head into his shoulder, "but this is more than I bargained for."

This was heaven on earth, to be back in Roy's arms with time enough for more than a hasty kiss and a few words in each direction. It was more than happiness, it was luxury, it was a gift, calling for her little joke. They kissed and held each other and said nothing, fearful — on Hedi's side, at least — that any word might somehow lead to an interruption.

At length, Roy spoke. "Is it fair to leave Martha with the kids tonight?"

"Fair? I think if I'd tried to stop her she would have brained me. They're as close as she comes to having children of her own: I think they fill a need in her."

"She certainly is a treat for them, that's for sure."

After a while they separated. Roy sat down on the bed and began unlacing his shoes. "The provisional Congress is off to a good start, I take it?"

"Martha says so." Hedi kicked off her own shoes and sat on the bed near him, letting her toes luxuriate in their new freedom. "Sounds like they did a lot, anyway. They decided on their rules of procedure, they elected a provisional president, appointed a commission to draft a constitution, and started creating emergency legislation to deal with the most critical problems. Of course, a lot of what they're doing is jury-rigged, but what else could you expect? When you consider the alternatives, we're doing fine."

"Alternatives like what?"

"Like anarchy and tyranny, mostly. The reports we're receiving from refugees are awful. There must be scores of little crime bosses fighting each other up and down the seacoast — what's seacoast now, I mean. We're very lucky not to have to fight that sort of thing up here."

He grunted. To Hedi he seemed distracted, not entirely in the room. But it had been so long since they had had time together, she couldn't be sure. He said, "What kind of turnout did they get?"

"Delegates from 24 states, Martha says, and four areas representing what's left of 11 others. Three areas of Canada sent observer delegates."

Roy was unbuttoning his shirt. "Did Len Adams make it, then?"

Hedi smiled. "He functioned as technical advisor, Martha told us. This at the request of both the Eastern Canada and New England groups."

Roy's smile matched hers. "'Technical advisor.' Fixer, you mean."

"Well, he's always very useful. Speaking of which, I could use a little help with this zipper, friend."

Afterward, they lay on the bed together in lazy contentment.

"Did you hear about Governor Bennard's new role?"

"No! I thought he was still on invalid status."

"Not any more. You must have done a terrific job of amputation. Apparently, learning how to get around on crutches is no longer challenge enough for him, and he's anxious to get back in the swing of things. Governor Duval talked to him a few weeks ago — didn't I tell you any of this? — and he agreed to be appointed spokesman of the District of New England."

Roy was lazily rubbing a thumb along her neck. "What in the world are you talking about, my love?"

"Roy! I *must* have told you this!"

"If you did, I don't remember. I may have had one or two things on my mind."

"I know," she said contritely. "I know you have. It's just that I live surrounded by all this, and it's hard for me to remember that you don't. We decided — I mean, the governor and Governor Benbow and Governor Jacobsen decided — that New Hampshire, Maine, and Vermont should act together in the Congress as well as here at home. So we're going to go under the name of the District of New England. Other areas are talking about joining together too, to form similiar district governments. Governor Howe of Pennsylvania has introduced a resolution in the provisional Congress to encourage this. It's his idea that all such districts formed in what was North America should eventually get together to form a regional government with powers to coordinate or control matters of common interest."

"I am so glad to see Governor Bennard remain active. He is a courageous man. When I had to help take his legs off, I wasn't real sure he was going to live out the week, let alone — what is it? three months, now?"

"Yesterday was January 13th," Hedi said. "Day 102. Going on four months."

"A little more than two months till spring," Roy said moodily. "If it comes. All that damned dust in the air...."

He sat up and reached for his robe, then stood up and, belting it around him, began to pace the floor. Hedi, lying on her side watching him, felt a pang. This was what it had been like in those impossibly remote days before the earth changed. He would be worrying over a patient, or a question of support for some new service he wanted to provide, and he would begin to pace as he talked it out with her.

"Long time since I've seen you do that," she said simply.

He interrupted his pacing, stood looking at her. "It has been," he said slowly, getting her unspoken point. "It seems like that was a different world, doesn't it?"

"Not 'seems,' I'm afraid, darling. Was. What are you worrying over?"

For a long moment he remained still, looking at her and through her. "Yes, it really was. Already it's starting to seem like a dream. Blue skies, white clouds, plenty of everything you'd ever need."

Hedi thought of how that would sound to Martha. "Let's not romanticize it, though. It wasn't much fun to be poor, or old or sick or alone and not be able to afford what you needed."

"No. No, I won't romanticize it. I saw too much of life in the inner-city hospitals to do that." His head dropped and he went back to pacing. "All the same, Hedi, I swear I don't know how we're going to cope."

They had never used false optimism as a tactic to encourage each other. "I've got to admit, sometimes I don't either," she said.

He was pacing back and forth by the light of the little candle they had allowed themselves. "It's just like the problems you used to tell me about, the ones you'd set for each other in survival camp. There's only so much to go around, and when it's gone, it's gone. It's like that with everything, I know, but it seems to me it's worse with medical care. You can grow more food, and make more clothes, or find more, and improvise shelter somehow. At least you know that the demand is going to remain more or less the same."

"I don't know about that. Some people die, but plenty more want to move in. Too many. More than we can handle."

"Yes. But in medicine, the demand keeps getting worse."

He walked the three steps to the opposite wall, turned on his heel, walked three steps back, turned again and walked, turned and walked.

"Hedi," he burst out, "I don't see how we're going to make it. Three months ago, we had a remarkably good health care system in this country. We don't have it today. And we aren't going to have it again any time soon. Probably not in our lifetime. Even if we happen to be lucky enough to live out our normal lifetime. What used to be normal." Pace, pace, pace. "We can't afford the resources. It took too many highly skilled people. It took too much money, too many manufactures, too much of everything that we can no longer afford. We just can't do it."

Hedi knew he needed to talk; she concentrated on waiting him out. "And so?"

He sighed, and stopped pacing again. "And so we're in a situation where we have too little food, too little shelter, too little clothing, and pathetically too little medical resources. And in addition to that, we have people working themselves too hard, often under unhealthy conditions. All perfect conditions for promoting the spread of disease. Count on it — new strains of germs and viruses are developing, and resources to identify them and devise treatments are not going to be available. Millions are going to die in epidemics."

Hedi sat up, holding the sheet over her. "That's what our scenarios always came to," she said. "Many die at first, then the survivors keep dying off to disease and discouragement and hardship. And you've known that for more than a decade, and so you've long since come to terms with it as one of the unavoidable facts of life. But tonight you're all stirred up. Something has changed. What?"

He stopped pacing, came to sit on the bed. "You know I love Hugh Scott like a brother, but sometimes I wish he wasn't quite so West Point."

"You had a set-to with him?"

"Oh, not that. We didn't come to words, exactly. We just don't always see eye to eye."

She waited.

"Have you ever met Dr. Steven Woodbine?"

"I've met him to speak to, of course. But I can't remember having anything much to say to him."

An echo of his boyish grin. "Unless your conversation revolved around immunology, I'm not surprised. He's the most single-minded individual I've ever met, even including Sam Theos."

"Including Dr. Roy Johnson?"

Another grin. "Touche. Well, Dr. Steven Woodbine wangled some of my time today. He wants me to go to bat for a proposal of his. He wants us to put a substantial portion of our medical-research reserve into immune-system research. Something like 65 percent of it, in fact."

For a brief moment, Hedi was struck speechless. "He what?!"

"You heard me. He thinks it's the key to our health problem."

"Of all the self-centered, narrow-visioned things I've ever heard.... Does he know that people are starving? Does he know how little extra we have in every field? Does he have any idea how stretched we are?"

"I think he has an idea," Roy said mildly. "He's out there every day, Hedi. He knows the score. Nobody's working any harder than he is."

"Then I don't see how he . . . ."

"Hedi, I'm tempted to go to bat for him."

That stopped her.

He got up and resumed his restless pacing. "You know we can't match the medical system we had before Day Zero. It cost too much: in money, in materials, in skilled personnel. We don't have any of the essentials, and we aren't going to. And if we did, we'd have too many other things we needed to do with them. But we can't just let people die. Woodbine thinks maybe we don't have to."

Pace, pace, pace.

"He's convinced that the immune system was designed to protect us from all types of infections and disease. And as an automatic defense system against known invaders, it's a marvel of perfection. The problem is, when faced with a new challenge, or an old one in a more severe form, it doesn't always work."

"Defective genes."

"Yes, sometimes. Defective or missing. There could be many causes. Up until Day Zero, genetic engineering promised solutions to such problems. But today we're no more able to continue that research than to launch a new communications satellite. Anyway, much of it isn't genetic. Much of it is from an invading virus somehow tricking the system into attacking itself, destroying itself and the human body it was supposed to protect.

"Traditionally, the system is viewed as a thing apart, reporting to no higher authority and taking instructions only from its own control center. It seems to be an independent but friendly visitor residing in our bodies. Woodbine thinks the system's independence is the flaw: When overwhelmed by a new situation, it has nowhere to turn for intelligent help. Instead, it relies on mindless trial and error."

"That seems to have been good enough to save the human species from extinction so far."

"It has. But the fact that countless random experiments eventually produce a solution is small comfort to those who die from the experiments that fail."

There was no answer to that, of course.

"We'd learned how to help the system somewhat. Smallpox vaccine, for instance. But in instances where the immune system has been deceived into attacking the cells it should be protecting, the problem becomes more difficult. They brought AIDS under reasonable control, but look at the cost of the research-and- development program that did it. We can't afford anything remotely comparable, that's clear."

Roy was standing still again, looking at her, looking through her. "He thinks that the immune system can be made to march to the drumbeat of a higher authority than its own remarkable control center."

"Thinks? Or hopes?"

Roy laughed. "The first thing he said, as soon as he sat down, was this: 'As I understand it, we are striving for something more than physical survival of the species. That means the authorities must allocate resources to projects such as the one I am proposing.'"

"That sounds cool enough."

"Oh, he's not lacking in self-confidence. I suppose that people don't get where he is — where he was a few months ago, I mean — without that kind of confidence."

"But he needs your support."

"Well, sure. Changed circumstances."

"Does he know what he's asking of you? What giving him support might cost you?"

Roy came and sat down on the bed again. "I asked him why he thought he could make the immune system responsive to us, rather than to its built-in program. He said because he believes that the universe has meaning."

Hedi felt herself go very still, and saw Roy notice.

"He said he believed that all physical things first exist as a thought created by a mind. He said that since all minds can access a common pool of knowledge, it doesn't matter if we're talking about an all-knowing Creator, a universal mind, some smaller mind, or a combination of minds. He said, 'I believe this immune system was created for a purpose by a mind with a purpose. I believe the mind, working through the brain, has the ability to maintain and control all bodily functions.'"

Roy got up again and paced back and forth, more slowly now than before. "And on a hunch, I tend to agree with him. Although it is a puzzle why the system ever fails to exercise its abilities."

"Perhaps it's a skill minds have to be taught. Something like playing the piano — a few people seem to come to it naturally, but most people have to learn."

"Perhaps." She noticed that he was pacing a little faster. "I told him that if he did receive support, he'd have to be prepared to face unpleasant attacks. The woman in the village with a sick child who cannot find a doctor is likely to become bitter about the parasites on the hill playing all day with test tubes and gadgets. And if the child dies, we might have to set armed guards to protect his laboratory. I asked him if he was prepared to face that."

"What did he say?"

He hesitated, as you would expect, and he started to say something, and stopped, and finally he said it would be difficult, but if he had to face it, he would."

"Roy, I've got to meet this man. He could be important."

"I thought you'd think so."

"Are you going to support him, then?"

"Well, I can't seem to decide." He lay down on the bed, hands beneath his head, staring at the ceiling. "It means going to see Governor Duval and General Scott."

She began to see the light. "And you went to Hugh to feel him out."

"Yeah, I did." More studying of the ceiling. "I told him what Woodbine had in mind, and I told him what it would cost in lives. Told him that since we don't have any extra resources, anything we give to Woodbine, we take from somebody else. And not somebody else who can spare them: somebody else with urgent needs; somebody else who's going to suffer for lack of them; somebody else who's maybe going to die."

"Surely Hugh understood that. We were made to face that reality long ago, when we were youngsters."

"Oh, he sees it, all right."

Long pause. "Well, Roy, are you going to count the cracks in the ceiling or are you going to tell me?" Immediately, she regretted it. "I'm sorry. I didn't mean that."

He turned to look at her. "That's all right." He seemed to rouse himself. "He sees the problem. What he *doesn't* see is why I'm torturing myself about it, as he puts it. He says I should decide yes or no and then put it behind me."

"Do you want me to defend him? He practices what he preaches."

"I know he does, but I can't. I can't help thinking about it."

She tried to draw him to her. "I know, honey. I'm the same way."

He resisted her pull, continued staring at the ceiling. For a long, long moment he lay there unmoving.

"You'd be pulled into it, you know. As executive assistant to the governor, you couldn't very well be left out of the decision. And Martha, too, assuming she is, or will be, district director of communications. Some of it would fall on the two of you, as well."

"That's all right," she breathed. "We'd have to do what we thought was right. What else could we do?"

Another long moment of silence. The guttering candle was flickering wildly now, throwing insane shadows in all directions. "Nothing," he said. "There isn't anything else you could do."

Surely, she thought, by now he has memorized every crack in the ceiling.

"Hedi, if he's wrong, a lot of people are going to die for nothing."

She dared say nothing.

"Even if he's right, a lot of people are going to die because of this. Even if he's right."

He turned to her, shifting his entire body to lie on his side. "I think he is right. I have a hunch. But it isn't going to come overnight, and it isn't going to come cheap. I'll do it," he said, "and I'll hope for the best. But people are going to die because I made this decision, Hedi. Right or wrong, people are going to die." He rolled onto his side and buried his face against her, shuddering.

32. The Dark Side
Day 363

"**W**e could be doing worse," Hedi said drily. "From what we hear, in other parts of the world, fear and ignorance have turned men into animals."

"Not men only, I think." (Duval, governor of the District of New England, equally dryly.) "I'd hesitate to get between a woman and her survival, or the survival of her children." With only Martha present in the room besides themselves, Governor Duval and Hedi were free to swap jests, free from the formality that entered the room with strangers. It was pleasant, reminiscent of old days at the clinic. She smiled.

"Governor, that statement demonstrates the discretion you have become famous for. But you know what I mean. Probably hundreds of millions have died in rioting and chaos in the past year. Pardon me, 362 days. We've kept that from happening here."

"So far, at least."

"So far," Martha echoed. "But every day gained is another day toward recovery."

"Yesterday," the governor said, "I would have agreed with you. Today? Well, let's see what we think after we hear from General Scott. And here he comes."

Hedi thought: Hugh comes into a room like a battleship maneuvering among tugboats. Then she wondered where that analogy had come from. And wondered if there were a battleship, or a tugboat, left on any of the world's waters.

Hugh, moving deliberately, as was his habit these days, placed some papers on the table in front of him and very deliberately sat down. Hedi thought again, as she had many times before, that he had schooled himself to move deliberately in the days of panic, so that his very body language would reassure rather than give alarm.

He very courteously — as was his wont — acknowledged Hedi's and Martha's presence, and addressed himself at first primarily to them.

"I requested of Governor Duval that you be present to hear this: Martha in your capacity as communications director of the Congress, Hedi in your new capacity as alternate delegate for the governor. And also, more informally, because I value your counsel and trust your discretion."

He looked at the governor, who nodded.

"You will recall the governor telling us about the man behind the rioting in Pennsylvania, and that damned new dukedom being set up down there under somebody named General Red Beard. At the time, we decided there wasn't much that could be done about it.

"Day before yesterday, a man named Cernetich worked his way up the chain. Said he wanted to talk to the top military man; had something urgent to tell him; wouldn't talk to anybody else. Took him nearly a week of pestering before he persuaded my staff to let him see me — and even then, when Marty and John brought him into my office, they stood right there, ready to yank him out of there if it turned out he was wasting my time."

The governor broke in. "Hedi, Martha, this is just about as new to me as it is to you. General Scott started briefing me on this man's tale and got far enough that I realized I wanted you both to hear it. Go on, general."

"Cernetich — if that's his right name — purports to be a defector from Red Beard's ranks."

"What makes you think we can trust what he says?"

"Hedi, I *don't* think so. I don't know either way."

"That's why we're here," the governor said. "So that the two of you can help us evaluate the information. Go on, general."

"He says Red Beard is the son of a third-string New Jersey crime boss known as Pete the Protector. He says the old man had been assigned a district lying between the old Interstate routes I-76 and I-80, running from Union to the Delaware River."

"All gone now," Martha said.

"With the exception of numerous small islands, yes, the area is now covered by the sea," Hugh said. "Apparently Red Beard — he was called Duke in those days — wanted to be the biggest of all the bosses. According to Cernetich, Duke is very intelligent. Persuaded his father to send him to college, it seems."

Hedi said, incredulously, "College?"

"Don't laugh. He wasn't planning to become a teacher. The word is that he studied the lives of the powerful — how they acquired power and how, in many cases, they lost it. Apparently he can talk at length about Bismarck, Napoleon, Alexander the Great, Stalin, and Hitler. Maybe he wants to be just like them."

"He sounds like an idiot," Hedi said.

"He isn't. He's no fool — always provided that Cernetich's account can be trusted, which, again, is the question."

"What's this Duke look like?" Hedi had no idea what prompted her to ask the question, but she yielded to the impulse.

"Cernetich describes him as a massive man, strong as an ox. He has flaming red hair and a bushy red beard."

"This isn't my social stratum," Martha said, "but I had the impression that beards are unusual among hoodlums."

"I think you're right," Governor Duval said, "but nobody in his circle would be likely to object to it."

Hugh drilled on toward his objective. "Anyway, that's about all we know for sure about this Red Beard, except that he seems to be doing well in the fighting that's still going on up and down the seaboard. He seems to be doing pretty well at eliminating the competition, though he has a long way to go yet."

Hugh paused and laid his hands flat on the table. "Unfortunately for us, Day Zero found him in an excellent position to exploit the opportunities it offered him."

"I wonder," Hedi said pensively, "why it is that great challenge, great hardship, ennobles some and turns others into wild beasts. Look at our people. We were nearly as hard hit here as anywhere, but our people rose above their fear and set about doing what they could for themselves and for each other. Why?"

"That's New England," the governor said shortly.

"Hedi and I are not New Englanders," Martha said. "And anyway, what does that say about other lands that seem to be preserving themselves? I gather that civilization is surviving in parts of South America and Africa and Asia."

As with so much else in those days, the question was unanswerable.

"There must be *some* common factor," Hedi said, "if we only knew what. The severity and nature of the challenge? The presence or absence of leaders? The amount of preparation? The intervention of some unknown force? Think how much good could yet come out of this, if we learned nothing more than that."

"No doubt," the governor said, "But first things first. General?"

"I think we would be well advised to prepare ourselves against any future moves by this General Red Beard. I think he poses a threat to our society that we must counter. That means siphoning off some resources into military preparation."

"Oh, Hugh," Hedi said, "didn't we have this discussion nearly a year ago? We decided at the time that we couldn't afford it."

The governor shook his head. "Not so. We decided that the threat was not urgent enough to justify an expedition to wipe out this rats' nest. But we are in better shape now than we were then."

Hedi said "Are we?"

"In the past year we have repaired a good deal of infrastructure," the governor said. "Our situation isn't nearly so desperate as it was then."

"Isn't it?" Hedi found the words bursting forth as if on their own. "We've cleared the roads," she conceded. "We've thrown wooden bridges across the most important river crossings. We've set up the bicycle expresses and the horse-drawn delivery of heavier loads. But what a tiny bit that is, against so massive a need!"

He smiled affectionately at his energetic, impulsive assistant. "We have accomplished much more than that, Hedi — as you should know, having had no small part in the process. We have restored a skeleton of telephone service between towns. We have begun to put small wood-burning electric generators on line. We have managed to get a year's crops planted and harvested, despite all the obstacles of reduced sunlight and lack of artificial fertilizers. We have a long way to go, but what we have accomplished is not negligible."

He paused, a deliberate pause for emphasis. "Not to mention the fact that we have preserved our society. We don't have mob rule here, and we don't have dictators either. That's worth noting. And worth preserving."

"But we're still living off our seed corn! Roy tells me we're beginning to lose people to the kinds of diseases that follow long deprivation and exposure. Pneumonia, for instance. Emphysema. People are contracting tuberculosis, governor! The other day, he had a child die of scarlet fever. Every kind of medicine we had is rationed. Many are running short. Where are we going to get new ones?"

Martha said, soothingly, "Hedi, the governor knows all this."

Hedi bit her lip. "I know. I'm sorry. But it just tears me up to think of putting money into guns and soldiers when we haven't half started on the recovery process. After the disasters, we were supposed to build a New Earth. What are we doing here but repeating the patterns that led to the destruction of the Old Earth? We see a criminal and a gang of hoodlums and right away we're thinking in terms of armies."

"Now, Hedi, I know the thought is distasteful, but this man's testimony makes this Red Beard look far more formidable than simply a gangster."

"I agree," Martha said, "even if this Duke, this Red Beard, is a criminal by background and inclination, I don't see that we can safely ignore him. Hitler and Stalin were criminals, and they made plenty of trouble before they were through. He seems to have the same kind of warped genius."

"He does seem to," Hugh said. "And very likely he has the same kind of ambition. The significance for us, and for our citizens, is that this development cannot be taken lightly. At some point the existence of basically malign organizations could become a lethal threat to us and to our way of life."

"It's like a bad dream," Hedi said.

"A bad dream dreamed long ago," Martha said. "Isn't it just like the old Earth?"

"There must be a way to break the cycle," Hedi said fretfully. "If not, what's the use of all this?"

"Maybe that's the test," Martha said matter-of-factly. "I suppose we are required to figure out how to create the new Earth, rather than expect someone to hand it to us."

"These are interesting speculations," the governor said, "but I fear we will have to pursue them at another time. General, I am unwilling to agree to diversion of resources to military purposes at this time. I believe the danger is remote enough to be put on the back burner. In the face of what we know as of today, I cannot see going before our citizens and asking them to die to strengthen our military defenses — for dying is what it would amount to. What I suggest, instead, is beefing up your military intelligence organization. And I recommend some careful contingency planning: If we do have to prepare to counter an active, organized force, rather than disorganized mobs, what resources will it require?"

Hedi thought their meeting was about to break up, but Hugh picked up another paper from the stack before him.

"I know you are aware of the physical changes that have taken place in the past year," Hugh said without preamble, "but I want to sketch out the military aspects of the situation, since, unfortunately, matters have come to that."

He picked up the top paper from the stack in front of him. "The latest figures I have for the new effective sea level places it at 227 feet above the pre-Day Zero figure. This is the net effect of continued discharge of lava on the sea floor and continued sinking of the land."

"I'm told the rate of increase in sea level may be slowing down a bit," Hedi said.

"Yes, that's what they think. But the point at the moment is the military effect of the changes in landforms that have already occurred."

Hedi noted how smoothly he returned to his line of thought. For some reason, a vivid image of Gary Smith downshifting his four-wheel-drive jeep flashed across her mind's eye.

"The Y-shaped crevice dividing North America continues to widen, forming a huge inland sea. In many places it was more than fifty miles across as early as Day 90. The banks are still crumbling and sinking, and the oceans are still rising. No one can say how wide that inland sea might ultimately become. With the ocean unsafe for sea travel, and land communication slower and less versatile than it was before Day Zero, that inland sea may become very important to us militarily some day. Anybody who controls a large, relatively protected body of water is a menace to all the land surrounding it. A menace, or a protection, depending on who does the controlling."

To Hedi the entire discussion smacked of the ways of the old Earth that she had thought they had escaped, as partial recompense for the losses she and others had suffered.

A fresh reminder of those losses was not long in coming. The following afternoon, she was working at the endless paperwork her job entailed when she heard Martha's voice. "Hedi, do you have a minute?"

Martha's voice, but Martha's voice with a tone in it that Hedi had not heard since the days after Tim had been killed. Hedi looked up sharply. Her sister stood there, outwardly composed, introducing her to the stranger beside her. A stranger would have thought Martha calm and unruffled.

Martha's words hadn't registered. "I'm sorry?"

"Mrs. Hodges made her way here from the midwest, across the inland sea. She's trying to find her sister. When she heard my name, she asked if I knew a Glen Carlton, in Ohio. She knows what happened to Mother and Dad."

Hedi clutched the edge of the desk and closed her eyes. Then she opened them again, matching her sister's calm. "Is that right? Can you?"

She looked more closely. Mrs. Hodges looked to be in her fifties — her fifties as influenced by the past year's hardships. Presumably many of the lines on her face had been put there in the past 12 months. She wondered, fleetingly, how the woman had made her way past the million obstacles between Ohio and New England, then dismissed the question. She stood up. "Let's go into the small conference room."

"My sister and I have assumed that our parents fell victim to the fault that opened along the Mississippi and Ohio Rivers," Hedi stated calmly. "We know that the fault cut directly across Ohio, from Cincinnati to Pittsburgh, cutting off the territory between itself and the Ohio, to the south, which is where our parents lived. And we know that in the days immediately following Day Zero, the fault was widening at a rate of as much as three miles a day. We know further that every bridge on the Ohio went down in the earthquakes, and so we assumed that, barring a miracle, our parents had died there. Do you have information to the contrary?"

"No, ma'am, I'm sorry, I don't. They're dead, sure enough."

Hedi had thought she had long since abandoned any hope that her parents had survived. Watching herself as from a distance, she found that some faint spark had remained, until this very moment.

Martha had had more time to adjust. "We would be grateful to hear anything you can tell us," she said.

"That's what I want to do," the woman said. And, after a false start or two, she did.

The widening chasm had created a torrent of people fleeing south, making their way along the broken roads. At first they carried a little food, a few precious or useful belongings. But as hour succeeded hour, possessions were abandoned along the road. Soon the road looked as though it had been travelled by an army in retreat. Which, Hedi thought, in a way it had.

Unlike the mobs that were looting eastern Pennsylvania at the same time, these crowds were orderly, if fearful. They marched to escape a tangible physical threat, with — in most cases — no time or inclination to quarrel with, or molest, one another.

In most cases.

"My husband and me and our son and his wife and my two grandbabies were on our way on foot with the rest of them, carrying what food we could. On the second day, we were attacked by two men wanting our food. And what else they were wanting, God knows.

"There was a terrible fight before we druv 'em off, and my husband's foot got broke by a stone so's he couldn't walk. He wanted us to leave him, but of course we wouldn't. We made him a crutch, and he hobbled along, but it was slow going. When we stopped for the night, it was clear we were losing ground.

"When I woke up in the morning my husband was gone.

"Danny — that's my son — said he couldn't have got far on the bad foot, but we spent four precious hours tryin' to find him and we couldn't." The woman's eyes were dry: She'd long since shed her tears for her husband, Hedi realized. This wasn't a new story she was telling, but a very old one.

"Finally we had to give up, or we'd get caught and Larry would ha' died for nothin' at all. I told Danny and all to go on without me, but he never would do it, so we kept on, me tryin' my best not to slow 'em down."

The five refugees had traveled most of the night, fearing to stop, not knowing how quickly the chasm behind them might be spreading toward them.

"Two days later, when we reached the river, we got the bad news. There wasn't no way across."

Her eyes widened a bit as she relived the scene.

"There was people trying all sorts of desperate things. Some of 'em was tryin' to swim, which the way the waters was, was death, certain. Little Jimmy — that's Danny's oldest — found himself a steel drum, and tied himself to it and jumped in, thinking to get acrost that way. His father told him not to, but he was 15 and he had a mind of his own. He done it anyway."

She gave out a sigh. "I knew he was going to get drownded: That current pulled him out of sight in a matter of seconds. But we didn't know for sure, and we couldn't just forget about it. So we made our way downstream, just on the odd chance he might make it back to shore."

Another sigh, but a different quality to this one. "We never did see him again, but goin' downstream lookin' for him brought us to what was left of this little town, where they'd got a cable across the river where the bridge had been, and made this ski-lift sort of thing to get people over to the other side."

The 'ski-lift sort of thing' was actually a four-person aerial tramway, fashioned from pulleys and cables. Since the only power available was manpower, the price of crossing was to take one's turn pulling on the cables that moved day and night to help others across. The family got in line.

"It took two days before it came our turn to cross. While we were waitin', and workin', we heard how the thing got set up. Right away, right after the worst quakes, before the heavy rains started, some of the townfolk snaked a cable across the river and fixed it on each side to the concrete of the old bridge. It was your father took the lead doin' it, they told us. And it seemed to be him, more than any other, that knew what to do whenever the cables got themselves jammed up."

She sighed again.

"Your father wanted to send your mother over — we heard that when we were waitin' — but she wouldn't go without him, and he said they needed him where he was. So they put in me and Billy, he's my youngest grandbaby, in with this older couple, and we went over, swayin' and bumpin', with that terrible stirred-up water just a couple inches under us, seemed like. Danny was back there takin' his turn at th' cables, Susan stayin' with him. That's his wife."

Yet another sigh. Hedi scarcely breathed.

"It was just after we got over that we felt the ground shiftin', and saw the abutment start leanin' toward the river. The cables sagged and then they jammed on the pulleys. Everybody on both sides of the river was frantic, tryin' to get 'em clear again. They was still workin' on it, after dark, when the whole works toppled into the river and we had to head for the hills."

Any screams were lost in the roaring, as water and earth were swallowed up by the great hungry chasm.

"The way I see it, it was your dad saved our lives," she said. "I just wanted to tell you thanks, and I'm sorry he didn't make it safe."

Hedi thought of Ralph, and of Gary Smith. She had a clear picture of Roy, weeping at the lives that would be lost. She thought of her mother, saying that the survivors would need young folks, not old, to build their new world. Then she thought of refugees being herded into mobs by men with shotguns, and felt a cold anger growing within her, an iron determination. Then, mercifully, she wept.

33. Breakthrough
Spring, Year Z 5

Five years of unceasing work and care had aged Roy visibly. The lines around his mouth and eyes were deeply ingrained, now. "No use telling you to take some time off, I suppose," Hedi had said to him.

He had smiled at her through his fatigue. "Sure, honey. When you slow down, let me know and I will be right behind you. I warned you about the doctor's life — and his wife's."

She had looked at the grey on his temples and had wanted to cry. "If we'd never had a Day Zero, you might have learned to slow down."

He had maintained his smile. "If there hadn't been a Day Zero, we wouldn't have seen nearly as much of New England. And you wouldn't be a rising young star in the government."

"Not so young anymore, I'm afraid."

"Fishing. Always fishing. If my calculations are right, you are all of 37. Good for another four or five years, at least."

So she had gone to her boss with a suggestion, and the governor had seen the sense of it and had told his secretary to schedule an appointment for Dr. Johnson that afternoon, and had told Hedi to attend as well. In so many words, he had ordered Roy to take one full day off each week, beginning the following day. "I've cleared this with General Scott, and he is prepared to make it an official order if necessary," he had said.

He had waved away Roy's protest. "I know what you are about to tell me, and it won't wash. There are no indispensable men, doctor. And if there were one, it would be doubly important for him to refresh himself, lest he become no good to himself or anybody else.

"Now, what I am telling you is only common sense, and it is exactly what you yourself would order for someone else. I want you to promise me that you will do it. Take some time with Hedi. Take some time with your children. They're growing up every day, and you don't want to miss any of it. Take some time by yourself. But get away." And so here they were getting ready to start hiking through the mountains, out on a family holiday for the first time in five years.

"Ready, kids? Let's go, then. Sally, lead the way." They set out, nine-year-old Sally and five-year-old Peter in front, Roy and Hedi following behind. For quite a few minutes, they walked without having much to say, listening to the children chattering, pointing out to one another birds and squirrels and objects of interest.

Hedi looked up at the heavens. "Does it seem to you the skies are a little clearer this spring?"

Roy walked along, visibly more relaxed than she had seen him in a long time. "Maybe. I think so. Stuff's still settling out of the atmosphere, I suppose."

"I sure wish I could see the kind of blue sky I remember. The kids probably can't remember that at all."

"No," he agreed. They walked in silence for a while. "No, there's so much they can't remember. But, hopefully they'll live on into better times."

That seemed to remind him of something. "Speaking of which, do you think it would violate Governor Duval's injunction against doing business if I told you some good news?"

"I could use it, after last week."

"La—? Oh, your Uncle Jake. I know you'll miss him."

"I wasn't thinking about Uncle Jake, but yes, I'm going to miss him. We haven't seen him in all these years, but somehow when Martha told me he'd died, it made the world different."

"One more link gone," Roy said.

"I suppose that's it." She glanced at him, then glanced away. "That's why I talked to the governor about you, you know. I'm convinced that Uncle Jake would have lived years longer if he hadn't been so overworked."

Roy shrugged, shifting the old army backpack he was carrying their lunch in. "Hedi, everybody's overworked, especially doctors. It couldn't be helped." He brightened. "But that brings me to my good news. It looks as though Dr. Woodbine has made his breakthrough!"

"Not really?!" Hedi had been hearing about the Woodbine project off and on ever since Roy had made his decision to help get official support. She had watched Roy's attitude toward the project fluctuate between hope and discouragement as new progress or new obstacles had surfaced. She had listened to his fears and misgivings, knowing that he could not voice them to the team itself for fear of discouraging them. "*The* breakthrough? The big one?"

"Yes. At least, we think so." Several times, as the team had gained in understanding of the nature of disease and the operation of the immune system, they had made breakthroughs of more or less importance.

"You've saved many lives already," she said. The very day around her seemed to be brightening with her mood.

Roy was smiling; he looked, for the moment, almost carefree, as she had not seen him look in years. "Yes, we have. Every ailment we learned how to treat by biofeedback and mind control freed doctors for more difficult problems. And skilled medical personnel, even more than medicine and drugs, are in short supply. As you well know. But up until now, the goal of establishing mental communication with the immune system remained elusive." His face darkened. "That's why the epidemics have cost us 40 percent of those who were still alive on Day Two."

Hedi didn't want anything darkening their day together. "But you say he's made the breakthrough we've been waiting for?"

Roy had a strange, unreadable expression on his face.

"Roy, what aren't you telling me?"

"Watch out for those brambles, kids! You don't want to get all cut up." Turning to Hedi: "Everything is so overgrown. If you didn't know this used to be a two-lane road, you'd never guess that that's what these patches of broken asphalt were for. It reminds me of what I've heard about the shakes country in Tennessee, where Davy Crockett grew up. You ever hear about that?"

"No, and I don't want to hear about it right now, as you know full well, Roy Johnson. What aren't you telling me?"

He smiled. "I'll tell you a story about Dr. Woodbine."

They walked along on the broken road in the mid-morning, surrounded by the songs of birds and the chattering of the children.

"It seems that about six months ago, Doctor Woodbine was discouraged and thinking seriously about resigning his post. He was stuck on three aspects of the same problem: locating the immune system control center, studying the messages it was receiving and sending, and learning what needed to be measured and how to measure it. Four aspects, really.

"So one night, after a long and frustrating day, Dr. Woodbine lay awake trying to come up with a fresh idea, and for some reason his Uncle Albert began to intrude in his thoughts. You met his uncle. Do you remember? Albert Parker?"

Hedi cocked her head. "There was a Dr. Albert Parker who attended the survival camp one summer. He was in holistic health."

"That's the one." Another grin. "You weren't the only unusual person he met there. Another was a holy man from India named Cheng Tu."

Hedi smiled. "I hadn't thought about Cheng Tu in a long time. I wonder if he survived."

"I don't know. For that matter, nobody seems to have heard from Dr. Parker either, not since Day Zero. But for some reason, this night thoughts of Uncle Albert kept running through his nephew's mind, no matter how hard Woodbine tried to keep his mind on the question of finding a new approach. 'If ever a man needed help instead of hindrance, I am that man,' he thought, but he couldn't keep his mind clear. Finally he gave up and fell asleep."

"And had a dream!"

Roy nodded. "He supposed it was a dream, but whatever it was, he saw his Uncle Albert walking beside a lake in earnest conversation with an elderly man dressed in the old garb of the Far East. He asked them what they were talking about, but they appeared not to hear. After a short time they stopped walking, shook hands and parted company. The older man continued his walk along the lake, but Uncle Albert stopped at a little beach, picked up a stick and wrote something in the sand; then waved good-bye and faded from view. Guess what he wrote."

"Make your mind blank," Hedi said. But after a few seconds she gave up. "I don't know, what?"

"Woodbine had to strain to see it, but gradually it came into focus, spelled in capital letters in the sand: 'THE LETTER'. And then he woke up."

"That was it?"

"That was it. 'The letter.'"

"What letter?"

"Well, that's what he wanted to know, naturally. He puzzled over it for a while, and then went back to sleep for a couple of hours.

"When he woke up, he remembered. There are a lot more redwing blackbirds around than last year, don't you think?"

"Roy Johnson, stop it! I'm in no mood to be teased!"

He laughed out loud, the first time she could remember him doing so in — in a long, long time.

"Sorry, honey, I just want to drag it out as long as possible."

"'Bad news is soon told,' Martha says. So I suppose this is very good news."

"It is. For some reason, when Woodbine woke up, he remembered what he had long since forgotten. He dragged out a large cardboard box from the corner of a storage closet, dumped it on the floor, and started rooting through a pile of Old-Earth notes and documents."

In the course of five years' reconstruction, they had gotten into the habit of referring to the world before Day Zero as Old Earth, and calling themselves the New Earth.

"Near the top of the pile (it had been near the bottom of the box) was a letter his Uncle Albert had written him when he graduated from medical school. Skimming through the usual congratulations and warnings of the hard work yet to come, he found the account of his uncle attending a survival training camp in Maine. The letter went on to list the people he had met followed by a detailed account of a conversation with Cheng Tu, the enlightened holy man. It seems that Uncle Albert had asked him a series of questions about acupuncture, Yoga and about remarkable abilities attributed to the holy ones in the monasteries of Tibet."

"And he quoted Cheng Tu's answers!"

"Woodbine showed me the letter when he told me about the dream. I borrowed it." He pulled it from his jacket pocket. "Here. Read for yourself."

Uncle Albert had summarized Cheng Tu's answer thus:

"Thousands of years ago it became known to a few people that the involuntary functions such as heartbeat, breathing, and temperature were not involuntary, but were subject to the control of the mind. For many centuries the Yogi techniques for controlling some bodily functions have been taught. This control was developed after years of practice, prayer, and meditation. Other mystics were teaching methods of mind control over matter to those few of the faithful willing to spend a lifetime in the learning. Now some of these abilities are being developed very quickly using biofeedback. Using the brain as its agent, the mind can control all bodily functions. I know this is true even though I do not know all of the techniques for exercising these controls. All physical things in the Universe were created by the mind and are subject to the mind. Only our ignorance leads us to different conclusions. Remember this fact, for it is a universal truth, and some day it will be useful to you. The power to control is there. You only need to discover the technique.

"A key to discovering some of the techniques is the study of acupuncture charts. Some of the old ones are best for this purpose. They show control center locations and the pathways of primary messages to and from these centers. By inserting needles at the proper junctures of these pathways one can block or intercept these messages. Of course, sometimes the object is to open up a pathway that has been blocked by other means. It occurs to me that by combining some of the ancient knowledge with your modern technology, remarkable results might be obtained."

Hedi re-folded the letter and handed it back to Roy, who put it carefully back in his pocket. "This may prove to be an historic document," he said.

"Dr. Woodbine took it seriously, then?"

"Dr. Woodbine said he had never believed in dreams, but then he had never experienced anything like this. The next day he gathered his staff around him and pointed out their failure to make satisfactory progress toward their primary goal, and asked if they would support him in one last 'long shot' effort. He proposed that they proceed on the assumption that the immune system *was* subject to instruction and correction from a higher level of consciousness. First, they would direct their total effort toward finding the location of the immune system control center, and then trace the messages it was sending and receiving in the belief that at least one message pathway would lead to a higher control center within the brain's domain. The second phase was to learn what had to be measured in order to apply the biofeedback technique. He told them of the acupuncture approach he proposed using, and gave them twenty-four hours to think it over."

"I take it he got them to go along with it."

"One member of the staff resigned, but the rest pledged full support. And now they know they're on the right track. They are getting results. Woodbine tells me they will be teaching trainers in another few months, he hopes. A year, tops."

"Oh, Roy, that's so wonderful! Does this mean we can look forward to an end to epidemics?"

"Looks like it." He grinned again, and looked, if possible, even happier than before. "And that may not be the most important result! He thinks automatic monitoring of the immune system will increase lifespans."

"Will it? How much?"

"He's much too cautious a doctor to say how much," Roy laughed. "The most he will say is 'significantly'."

"Well, but Roy, this is wonderful news. Why hasn't the Governor heard it yet?"

Another laugh. He seemed to get more lighthearted by the moment. "What makes you think he hasn't?"

"Well, I certainly think I'd know if he had!"

"Getting pretty indispensable, are we?"

"Roy, answer the question!"

"The short and simple answer is that he probably received his briefing at the same time you just did. At least, that's when Woodbine's appointment was scheduled. So when you get back you can exchange congratulations."

They walked along in companionable silence, watching the kids, listening to the birds, enjoying the greenery around them.

"Roy?"

"Mmm?"

"This is your victory, you know."

"Woodbine's."

"You know what I mean. I was there when you made the decision. If you hadn't dared take the chance, this never could have happened."

"Maybe some people are dead who would be alive otherwise."

"Yes, maybe. And certainly many, many people will be alive who otherwise would die." She tugged him to a halt and kissed him. "That's for being brave enough to do the right thing and smart enough to know what the right thing was. I know what it cost you to do it."

He returned the kiss. "Thanks, honey."

They resumed walking. After a moment, Roy shook his head. "It really was a strain," he admitted. "All those casualties piling up, the epidemics coming one after another, people everywhere in pain and suffering, and this team of doctors off on one side, working on something nobody knew would work. And then we started having battle casualties too, from this damned war with Red Beard's pirates that looks like it's going to go on forever." He took a few more steps. "God," he said, shaking his head again, "you don't know how bad it was. But now I think maybe the worst is over."

They had finished their picnic lunch and were on their way home when a thought struck him. "What happened last week?"

"What do you mean?"

"You said you could use some good news, after last week? If it wasn't hearing about Uncle Jake, what was it?"

"Oh, Red Beard again. Lately it seems like it's always Red Beard. We had to move more resources into arms production. It's so depressing."

Roy shook his head in sympathy.

"He just keeps getting stronger, and I can't understand why. Why would anybody rather live in a dictatorship than a democracy?"

"I gather they don't have much choice."

"Well, they must have a choice about being officers or not! About actively helping this man terrorize his population?"

"Hitler doesn't seem to have had a whole lot of trouble staffing his armies."

She could feel herself getting depressed. "I wish we still had our nuclear navy," she said. "One sub would make all the difference now. We wouldn't have to maintain an army of coast- watchers to guard against his damned navy."

Roy shrugged. "They couldn't do the maintenance. Even cannibalizing parts and concentrating the experts on the one ship, it finally got to be too much. It has been three years — more — since they scrapped the last one. The subs helped a lot at first, especially in communicating with foreign shores. But they weren't much help fighting pirates."

"I've heard that, but I still don't understand it," she replied.

"They are just too big: five to six hundred feet long. That's more than the average ocean going vessel. In the shallow, constricted waters controlled by Red Beard's river-boat navy it would be like trying to operate a battleship in Walden Pond."

"Couldn't they stand off shore and blast his strongholds?" "And have everything for miles around destroyed by the nuclear blast? And radioactive fallout does not distinguish between friend and enemy, you know. Would you order such an attack?"

"I suppose it wouldn't make sense to mount naval guns on the sub's deck?"

"The simple answer is that any long-range artillery and ammunition we have can be used much more effectively to defend our land positions." Roy paused. "At least that is what our friend and my commanding general Hugh Scott tells me."

"So, what have we done with the subs? I know quite a few of them escaped the tidal waves and made it into the inland sea."

"The fuel elements have been removed from the reactor cores and stored in a safe place. This leaves the subs useless except for scrap, and that is exactly what we have been turning them into. As for the nuclear fuel, we don't know of anything to do with it now, but it would be of no use to Red Beard either, so we might as well hang on to it." Roy waited to see if Hedi was satisfied with his answer.

Hedi was not. "Why not admit we don't know of a safe way to destroy it?"

Roy smiled. "The answer to that is bound to be classified."

She frowned. "The real problem is that Red Beard's group was well-organized from the start. They captured arsenals, they captured a population, they put together a conscript army, they systematically went about wiping out their rivals at a time when everybody else was too preoccupied to resist effectively.

"But that was only their head start. If he and his original band of cutthroats were the only people we had to worry about, we'd be home free by now. They'd be a forgotten annoyance, like the desperados they put down in the southwest."

Gangs in the Denver area had never gained control of large territories in the way that Red Beard's army had, but nearly three years had gone by before federal authorities had succeeded in suppressing banditry. At times the conflict had approached the level of guerrilla warfare.

"The problem is, they *aren't* the only ones we have to worry about. They seem to find plenty of people to join them. And I can't imagine why. They don't have to live like animals. They could live like us. But they don't want to!"

"Hedi, isn't that just the Old Earth? If everybody had been interested in justice and peace and mutual benefit, maybe none of this would have happened. You know that. You knew it before I did. There are always plenty of people willing to live in an oppressive society, provided they get to be among the oppressors."

34. Decision

Summer, Year Z 6

"Unfortunately," the governor said, "the short-term effect of General Scott's success seems to have been the creation of a more immediate danger."

For more than a month, Red Beard's forces had been trying to push west along old Interstate 90, clearly intending to drive a wedge from their base to the inland sea. Hugh Scott's outnumbered troops had fought a long series of delaying actions, reluctantly trading territory for survival, trying to do so as slowly as possible. Finally, in the mountains just west of the Connecticut River, they had been reinforced by troops sent by Pennsylvania, whose interest in keeping the pirates out of the inland sea was as great as New England's. Fighting with the assistance of fresh troops, and using to full advantage favorable terrain, Scott had inflicted a decisive defeat on the lowlanders.

"They fell back eastward to the Connecticut River because they had to," the governor told his council of war. "But this Red Duke seems to have had this push north among his contingency plans. Or maybe this is what he always intended to do as soon as he pushed General Scott across the river. Either way, they're coming north, and we are caught with most of General Scott's forces in the mountains to the west of Springfield. Our situation is desperate."

"Typical of Red Beard's method of warfare," Hedi said distastefully. "Hiding behind innocent men, women and children."

"Effective, though," the governor said.

Two-thirds of the Red Duke's army was herding in front of them a mob of 75,000 half-starved, half-crazed wretches gathered largely from the Connecticut River valley south of Springfield. Goading the mob on toward the north, shooting any that tried to turn back, the Red Duke's forces had created an army of locusts, devouring everything in their path.

"Now he has sent us this damned ultimatum," the governor said. "And I do not see that we can ignore it."

Taciturn, hard-bitten Andrew Davis, the governor's district police chief, opened his mouth long enough to say two short sentences. "No negotiations," he said. "Wash 'em away."

The governor closed his eyes for just a moment. "Baldwin, are the explosives in position?"

His imperturbable staff assistant was sitting behind the governor in a chair backed up to the wall. "Yes sir."

"Davis, have we warned our people to get out of the valley and into the hills?"

"All we could reach. Some were trapped behind enemy lines.

Some won't leave their homes no matter what. Only one choice. Blow the dam."

This was a revolting suggestion. Hedi was glad to hear Martha object. "But what about the poor devils in front of the pirate army? It isn't their fault they're being herded."

"No," the governor said heavily. "And not our fault that their very existence is a gun pointed at our head."

"Sir," Martha said, "how can we drown these people, including many of our own, when we have an invitation to talk? Is that the act of a free nation?"

"It's undoubtedly a trick," the governor said shortly.

"I think everyone here recognizes that as a possibility —"

"A strong probability," Davis said.

"— but perhaps that's the kind of risk we have to take, being what we are. And talking will buy time, if nothing else. Time for Hugh to get his troops back into position."

They argued the point back and forth for several tense minutes. Finally the governor placed his pencil on the table in front of him. "All right. We'll take the risk. I fully realize, Mr. Davis, that in accepting this offer of a parley, we do put ourselves somewhat at risk. But perhaps the principle involved justifies the risk. If there is any chance at all of averting this attack by honorable means without killing thousands of innocent men, women and children, we must attempt to seize it."

"Well, then," Hedi said, the question becomes: Who will meet with him?"

"Why, I will, of course."

"No, sir," Hedi said automatically. "It can't be you."

"Why not, pray?"

The answer was so obvious it took her a moment to find words to phrase it in. "We can't be sending our governor to deal with — with these pirates."

"Well, we are agreed that somebody has to meet with him." Governor Duval looked around the table at his council of war, looking for support.

"Yes, governor," Hedi said stubbornly, "but not you."

"I am the one that will bear the responsibility. It would give me a chance to size him up. Why should I not be the one to go?"

"Because you are the governor of the District of New England," Hedi said, not for the first time. "For you to meet him face to face would imply recognition of him as a rival head of state."

"Oh, come," he said mildly. "That's making a lot of a simple parlay under flag of truce. I am not much inclined to stand upon ceremony when the chance exists to save lives."

"I agree with Hedi," Martha said. "Why should we elevate him so much?"

The governor shifted restlessly in his chair. "If we leave off theory and return to actual fact, we wouldn't be elevating him one bit. The man is in effective control of a sizable territory, and has been for half a dozen years. He has an army, well-armed enough, and well-trained enough, that it is all we can do to hold them off. He has created a state. We may not like it. We may wish it were otherwise. We may hope that state will not endure — may, in fact, do all we can to see that it doesn't. But the hard fact is that at the moment his state exists, and we have to deal with it. He rules the east coast as far south as the old Baltimore area. More to the point, we have to deal with the fact that he's right at our gates, and we need to make time by talking. Need the time more than he does."

"Yes, sir. Someone needs to meet with him. But I repeat, it can't be you. The governor can't meet on equal terms with a man who calls himself the Red Duke and chooses as his flag the skull and crossbones."

"The flag he flies cannot be a sticking point," the governor said, dismissing the argument. "The Jolly Roger is nothing but a gesture of arrogance, a stupid gesture in my opinion."

"It is that very arrogance that must not be rewarded by the sight of our governor coming to dicker on equal terms," Hedi maintained.

"Get General Scott on the radio," the governor snapped.

Alert as always, Baldwin was speaking into the field radio within seconds. "A moment or two, sir," he said, looking up.

The governor said nothing and everyone else in the room waited, watching Baldwin sit with his ear to the headset, eyes looking off at the floor a little distance in front of him. It would be a serious crisis indeed that would disconcert John Baldwin.

"One moment, general, for Governor Duval," Baldwin said into the mouthpiece. He stood up and handed the set to the governor. "General Scott, sir."

The governor set out the argument in a few crisp sentences. "You're out in the field, general. You know the situation. Do you share Mrs. Johnson's opinion?" He listened. "Do you think so?"

Hedi felt herself straining to hear Hugh's end of the conversation, absurd though she knew that to be. "I don't know about that. One moment."

He lowered the headset. "General Scott concurs with Hedi. He says it would be bad for morale. He suggests that he himself leave his troops and meet Red Beard, instead."

"Remind him," Hedi said, "that Red Beard stated he would talk only to an official of the government authorized to give orders to the generals. I think it is dangerous to ignore that warning. We are running out of time."

The governor looked around the table, inviting comment. Then he repeated Hedi's opinions to Scott. "I have to agree with her, Hugh, and that seems to be the consensus of opinion here."

"I'll go," Hedi said suddenly.

Martha said, "You?!"

The governor dismissed the idea. "No, no. We can't very well do that."

"Why not?"

"He might not think you were on a high enough level for him," the governor said, temporizing.

"I am executive assistant to the governor of the District of New England, and can be empowered to negotiate for him. What more would he need?"

Martha, Hedi noticed, was pale, almost ashen. But she was long used to leaving out personal considerations when making hard decisions. "Hedi's right, governor. She has the experience and you can give her the authority."

"But we can't very well send —"

"Send a woman?"

"That's right. For all we know, Red Beard would take it as a deliberate insult."

"Why? I wouldn't be going there to fight him, just to negotiate with him. And you can't argue that I'm indispensable. I feel that I have been useful, but I know I am not indispensable."

"General," the governor said, "Hedi Johnson wants to be the envoy to Red Beard. I don't much like the idea. Do you?"

Hedi, with the others, waited, trying to imagine Hugh's end of the conversation.

"No, I don't. If I could, I'd name them."

More listening.

"Yes, I admit, I'm old-fashioned enough for that to be a consideration." She noticed that the governor had one hand pressed hard against the tabletop in front of him. Slowly, very slowly, it relaxed. "No. No, I suppose we can't. No. All right. Over and out, general." He very deliberately handed the headset to John Baldwin. "All right, Hedi. You're it."

She was it, and it was time to find out if she were up to the responsibility. The valley below was shielded from view by half a mile of forest, but she knew that to the south thousands of wretched human beings were being pushed north by the pirate army — the disciplined mob — that was using them as pawns.

To the north, there would be her own side's armed men and

women, a thin line in the hills on either side of the vast reservoir, determined to prevent capture of the dam for as long as possible, the earthquake-made dam that had stopped up the river and created this natural defense. This natural weapon. She shuddered, then told herself that surely it wouldn't be necessary to use it.

She had argued her case forcefully, even vehemently. Red Beard, she had said, would surely settle for half a loaf, rather than none. "Even though we can't overthrow him, he can't overthrow us, either," she had said. "Why should he jeopardize his own regime in a hopeless attempt to destroy us? I say he'll come to terms." He had carved out his petty kingdom, and he knew by now that he could more than hold his own against the forces that could be arrayed against him. And he had to know that the democratic governments found his existence distasteful, but knew the limits to their own strength.

Her own logic had convinced her, and she had prepared to go out to parley. But Martha and Baldwin had asked for a quiet moment alone with her, and had come straight to the point.

Martha spoke first. "Hedi, I know you think you can reach agreement with Red Beard, but you absolutely must be prepared for failure. Baldwin has provided a way for you to carry our ultimate weapon with you, just in case instant action is called for."

Baldwin handed her a small black device that would easily slip into her jacket pocket and explained its purpose. "We have tested the system," he said. "It will work."

Hedi, knowing the logic of her own position, had been on the point of refusing, when at the last second she thought of Ralph. Her logic and her careful preparation hadn't been much help to Ralph. New England didn't have mudslides — except that when all conditions changed, all bets were off. "Okay," she'd said humbly, "you win. I'll take it. I just pray I don't have to use it."

"So do I, big sister," Martha had said in some relief. "But it's better to have it and not need it than need it and not have it."

She stood on the edge of the clearing, watching the massive red-bearded man make his painful and awkward way uphill toward her. While still quite a distance away, he waved his followers back to the forest and continued alone, leaning heavily on a cane. Hedi was impressed by the strength of a man who could pick his way uphill with his foot in a cast. No point in making him wait.

"I'm going," she told John Baldwin.

"We'll keep you covered. Good luck."

"Thanks," she said, adding silently: I'm going to need it. She stepped from the shelter of the trees into the clearing, and stopped at a level point about halfway down the hillside. She was uncomfortably aware of the near presence of Red Beard's hostile followers, now out of sight in the trees behind him. She sensed their weapons pointed at her.

"I am not afraid," she told herself. "The world is a lot bigger than Red Beard." She clung to the memory of Mr. J, so many years ago.

Red Beard made his way to her, limping and resting heavily on his cane, yet looking as though he owned the mountain and everyone on it. The man's personal authority was immense. Hedi felt herself struggling not to be overwhelmed by it before he said a single word.

"Who are you?"

Well, useless to expect manners from a pirate. "I am not afraid of him," Hedi told herself. "I won't let him intimidate me." Aloud she said: "I represent the governor of the District of New England—"

He snorted. "I know that. Who are you? What's your name?"

"Hedi Johnson."

"What's your rank?"

"My rank? I am executive assistant to the governor of the District of New England."

His mouth turned down at the corners. "Executive assistant. I ask them for somebody with authority and they send me a paper- pusher. Do you have the power to give orders to your General Scott?"

"I am authorized to act for the governor of the District of New England." Then, putting as much coldness and indifference into her voice as she could muster, she said, "Can we talk about the matter at hand?" Infuriatingly, she couldn't quite stop her voice from quavering.

His extra inches of height gave him a psychological advantage — he was able to look down at her, as well as on her. It gave extra emphasis to his contempt.

"All right, chickie. Here's my offer. It's my only offer, so pay attention. First point, these troops you have hidden in the woods lay down their arms. Second, your so-called government officials report to me and I decide which ones stay and which ones go. Third, your officials receive my terms for the orderly surrender of all your troops. In return, I keep my troops in leash."

The effrontery left Hedi open-mouthed.

"What's the matter? Have you exceeded your authority already? Do you have to go running to your boss, hiding out in the woods somewhere, and ask him what you do next?"

Hedi drew herself up straight, forcing herself to meet Red Beard's stare squarely. "Surely you must know that the surrender of our forces is not under consideration. I was sent to offer you a sensible alternative. Lay down your arms and join us in a peaceful effort to survive."

"Fat chance," he said. One side of his mouth was drawn up in a mocking smile. He was laughing at her.

"We would give you and your men a promise of personal safety if you did so."

"Very impressive. I know I could rely on it."

"You could. It's an honorable offer."

"Sure. And all we'd have to do is spend the rest of our lives with our tails between our legs, following every little rule and regulation you set down. You'll have to come up with a better offer than that."

She said, "You could turn your army around and send it home, and then we could sit down and negotiate a truce."

That made him roar with laughter. "Now, *there's* a terrific offer! I have the army that can wipe you off the boards, I have the mob in front of the army that can turn your little tin paradise into a grave-yard, I have the ability and the will to rebuild our country on strength instead of daydreams — and I am the one who's supposed to sur-render. That's what you call an offer?"

He raised his right arm and gestured with the cane, sweeping the hills from one side to the other. "From the time I let you go, I'll give you just 30 minutes to stack arms and come down in single file, or I'll make you wish you had."

Despite herself, Hedi was shivering inside. It was critically impor-tant that she convince him. "Please," she said. "You don't know the alternative. We didn't come here empty-handed."

His contempt was heavy and convincing. "Time for the big threat, now. All right, what's the 'or else'?"

"We have no intention of submitting to tyranny. We're willing to live and let live: I've told you that. But sooner than surrender our government and our people to you, we'll blow up that dam and wash you away."

Abruptly his face darkened with anger. "You think you can bluff *me*? Blow up that dam and you drown your own citizens along with the rest of the mob. You think I'm too stupid to realize that?"

"That wouldn't stop you."

"No, but it stops *you*, or you would have done it already."

"We wanted to demonstrate our humanity. We didn't want to do it if we had any alternative at all."

"Yeah? Well, you don't."

There was no further point in trying to reason with someone who wouldn't be reasoned with. Hedi met his gaze in calm defiance. "We will do whatever we must. We will not live as slaves."

Red Beard, quite evidently, was not used to being talked back to. His face seemed almost to swell and blacken with blood as his rage overmastered him. He swung his cane sharply. As though it were happening to someone else, Hedi heard the crack as her legs snapped. As she crumpled to the ground, he swung again, and her kneecap exploded in a white-hot burst of pain. She saw him running nimbly back toward a little ridge, breaking in different directions to avoid the hail of gunfire from her troops above her. She saw him reach safety, apparently unhurt. From the cover of the trees, he could work his way back to his troops.

A trick!, she thought bitterly. A trick from first to last. A phony cast, a cane sheathed with lead — an unarmed man with a concealed weapon.

She lay still to escape the bullets passing over her head. She was starting to hurt, but knew that the pain was nothing to what it would be when the shock wore off.

She fumbled in her jacket and pulled out the garage-door opener Baldwin had given her. She held it for a long moment. Baldwin had said it had been checked. If she pushed the button, it would work. And tens of thousands would die, including many of their own people.

In a matter of seconds, she fought a bitter battle in her mind. Mr. J had taught her that death wasn't everything. And the people of New England were better off dead than living under Red Beard. But were they? Did she have the right to make that decision? Suppose it were Roy down there where the water would run? Well, that was an easy question. She had no doubt Roy would prefer death to slavery.

Red Beard's insults still rang in her ears. He had probably crippled her. If she blew the dam, would it be because it was the right thing to do, or because she was letting anger rule reason?

Action and reaction: Not the thing itself, but the spirit in which the thing was done.

But could she kill?

The debate must have taken less than five seconds to play out: Time was important now. Red Beard's troops would be stampeding the mob to shield them from the fire of New England forces. Soon it might be too late for her to act. For that matter, within minutes she might lose consciousness from the pain and shock of her injuries. Then who would blow the dam?

Already her head was throbbing with pain that made it hard to think. Her mental eye produced, all unbidden, a picture of another day. Hugh Scott and Sam Theos and she on the camp's boat, talking with one Maximum Fact Banker. "Physical survival is not enough," she thought. "This is more important than individual lives." Societies lived with the consequences of the actions and thoughts and emotions of their peoples. Her legs and kneecap were throbbing, now. Closing her eyes against the pain from broken bones and from what she had to do, she pushed the button, voting.

35. Not Alone
Summer, Year Z 6

Hedi, both legs in casts, was lying flat on her back in her hospital bed, trying to read and finding it slow going. She was glad of the interruption when, out of the corner of her eye, she saw the nurse open the door and put her head in.

"Decent? You have a visitor." Turning behind her: "You can go in, sir." And in came Hugh Scott, closing the door behind him on the noise from the rest of the hospital and the nurse's curiosity.

Hugh pulled up a straight chair to the side of the bed. "Always working, I see," he said lightly. "You always were that way."

Hedi put down the paper she had been reading. She found her eyes filling, apparently for no reason at all. "Hugh," she said.

"Yep, me," he said comfortably. It was one of their little jokes from another time. He looked at the papers around her on the bed. "Doesn't the governor ever let you rest?"

"He says he needs me to keep up with matters so that I'll be fully informed when I return. That's why I have this room to myself: they keep bringing me confidential materials."

"More like a broom closet than a room."

"It's small," she conceded. "But it's nice not to have to share it. All this reading is kind of a chore, though. I have to hold the pages up in front of my face, and my arms get tired, so I have to rest every few minutes."

"Doesn't sound like much fun."

"Well, in fact, being an invalid, I've decided, is a damned nuisance. Roy says I should remember that it won't last forever. I tell him it already has."

"You might look at it this way, Hedi," he said gravely. "It could have been a lot worse. Suppose Red Beard had snapped your spine. He is well capable of it."

Hedi swallowed. "Oh, Hugh, don't even think it. That makes my stomach turn over." She saw again Red Beard's eyes.

"Want to talk about it?"

She started to say no, then found it pouring out of her. "I never did tell Roy," she said. "My injuries upset him enough." She told Hugh of Red Beard's intimidating presence, his arrogance. "He was so contemptuous, Hugh. He thinks we're so soft."

"Not any more he doesn't, I'll bet. Thanks to you."

She closed her eyes, seeing in her mind's eye the wall of water roaring down the valley, sweeping away everything in its path.

She opened her eyes, to find Hugh calmly watching her. "Self-reproach?" he said gently.

"Hugh, it was the right thing to do. I know that. I'd made our offer and he scorned it. If I didn't blow the dam, he and his troops would have made mincemeat of us. There were too many of them, and he is absolutely ruthless. I did what I had to do. There was no other way. I know that."

"But — "

She bit her lip. "But thousands of innocents died in that flood, Hugh. Died at my hand."

He sighed. "Yes, they did. That's partly why I came to pay you a visit. That, and to express my thanks on behalf of New Earth to a truly heroic individual."

Absurdly, her eyes were filling with tears again, and her throat was tightening up. Hugh took her hand.

"Hedi, you and Roy are so much alike. Do you remember how he agonized over helping Dr. Woodbine get permission to do immune-system research? He knew — he absolutely knew — that his decision was the best decision he could make in the circumstances. He knew that his motives were good, his information was as good as could be expected, and his judgment was as good as anyone's. Better, really."

"I know where you're going with that, Hugh."

"I know you do. And you also know that I'm right, but it doesn't stop you from brooding over what can't be helped."

He squeezed her hand. "Don't think I am calling you down for it, Hedi. You and Roy cannot help being the conscientious individuals you are. Those scruples are part of what makes you so valuable to the New Earth. But I figured you would overdo it, left to yourself."

She saw a hint of an incalculable something up his sleeve.

"Roy has told you the same thing, am I correct? And you agreed with him and it didn't make any difference to your feelings?"

She smiled at him through her troubles. "You know us pretty well. I think that's why I have all this paperwork to wade through. I think it's the governor's way of trying to keep my mind off what I had to do."

"I wouldn't be surprised if that's part of it."

"Hugh Scott, I can tell something's up and you're holding off telling me. That's unchivalrous, particularly when you're dealing with an invalid!"

He smiled at her, happy to hear the echo of old banter. "Some invalid," he said. "All right, I know that you, being a woman, cannot help being impatient, so it's up to me to come to the point." He released her hand. For some reason this brought up an image of Sam Theos, standing on the camp boat, smiling at them.

"First, I'll tell you what you already know. Red Beard isn't dead, unfortunately, and neither is his little kingdom. But you cost him thousands of trained troops, which is why I have time to pay you this visit. He's going to be years rebuilding his strength."

"Years. But how *many* years?"

"Yes, precisely. I hope for two or three, at least." His eyes were positively twinkling now. "And by the time he's ready to come at us again, I think he will find himself in for a big surprise. Another effect of your battle. By the way, I overheard somebody the other day calling it 'the battle won by a woman,' and I told them a more fitting title is 'the battle that Hedi won.' I wouldn't be surprised if the name sticks. You don't realize it, lying here goofing off, but you are famous."

"Famous," she echoed. Famous for pushing the button that killed thousands of innocent people. The thought made her queasy.

Hugh's smile broadened. Hedi thought of Roy's face when he'd told her that Dr. Woodbine had finally made the crucial breakthrough. "And you don't know what else you accomplished."

"No, and I can see I'm liable to die of old age before I find out."

"Invalids have such bad tempers," he grinned. She couldn't remember the last time she'd seen him in such boyish high spirits. "Okay, here's the scoop. You remember your Revolutionary War history? What was the significance of the Battle of Saratoga?"

"Hugh!"

"It brought the French alliance, which made possible the ultimate victory over the British. Congratulations, general — we have won our foreign alliance. Thanks to you."

"Hugh, what *are* you talking about? Who's left to help us?"

"The Elustreons."

"The—"

"Good lord, I've done it, I've rendered you speechless. A lifetime goal accomplished."

"The Elustreons!"

"Seems you gave them a scare and they decided it was time to step in."

"Hugh Scott, you tell me the whole story this minute, and don't leave out a single detail."

"You remind me of your sister," he said smiling. "Martha said exactly the same thing, in nearly identical words. Very well —."

She interrupted him. "I had almost forgotten about them. It has been so long, and we had so much to do, and it became evident that they weren't going to help."

"No, Max said from the very beginning that our survival depended on our own efforts."

"I didn't think that meant we were on our own."

"Well. At any rate, they have been watching us. You'll be happy to know that our efforts generally meet with their approval. But Max says —"

"You've talked to Max?!"

"— Max says they are quite chary of direct intervention."

"Yes, I remember. Hugh, tell it in order."

"All right, let's see." He rocked his chair back on two legs, leaning it against the wall, and looked up at the ceiling.

"At the time you blew the dam, I was on my way up to you with two companies of men. I would deny this to anyone else, but I don't mind telling you: I was frantic. Even though Red Beard had lost the battle the week before, he had retreated in good order, and he held the river crossings. I didn't much like the idea of trying to force them.

"I could not risk a full-scale assault, and yet I dared not move my army north toward you and leave my flank open to attack. Worse, his move north might be a feint, designed precisely to draw me off so that he could resume his push westward."

He shifted his gaze back to her. "We New Englanders obviously concentrated on keeping him south of New Hampshire, Hedi. But strategically it is vital to all the states to keep him from the inland sea. Only the very gravest considerations would justify leaving that artery at risk."

"You had the Pennsylvanians."

"I did. And you can believe they were concerned about the threat westward."

"They didn't want you heading north?"

"They certainly did not. Nor was that mere selfishness. Strategically they were absolutely right. If I had taken our forces north and Red Beard had managed to make a quick move west, the Pennsylvanians would have been too few to stop him."

He was looking at the ceiling again. "The problem, basically, was lack of mobility. Red Beard was operating on interior lines. He could shift his forces one way or the other and leave us scrambling to keep up. Well, as I said, I left General O'Neill in charge of the combined forces —"

"General O'Neill?"

"Commander of the Pennsylvania National Guard. I left him in command, and I was hurrying north with two companies of men."

"Not much," Hedi commented.

"All we could spare, and all I could move quickly. I had the men continue on the road 'til after midnight, but the road petered out and we couldn't make our way overland in pitch black darkness. The best we could do was try to get a little rest and be ready to go with first light. I intended to start off without breakfast and go all day if necessary, rather than risk arriving with my men well-fed and well-rested, only to find that the decisive battle had been lost. I had Jackson's foot cavalry in mind: I thought we could always rest later.

"We hadn't brought tents or baggage. My men were sleeping in their clothes, lying where they dropped. I was ready to do the same, but then I had to answer the call of nature, and I decided to go off a little way to be by myself. Preserving distance from the men I commanded, I suppose.

"I went a few yards into the woods and lo and behold, there's Max."

"He just happened to be standing there."

"Max doesn't 'just happen to be standing' anywhere, as you well know. And yes, I'm sure he put the idea into my mind in the first place.

"Right off, he told me that I needn't push my men quite so hard, that you had saved us from immediate danger."

"He'd been watching."

"Of course. They keep in touch with things, even if they don't necessarily contact us. In fact, he says they have watched with particular concern the challenge posed by this Red Duke. They think he is the most serious challenge we face."

Hedi pursed her lips. "Imagine," she said wryly. "Earthquakes, hurricanes, tornadoes, tidal waves, shortages, exposure, epidemics — and the most serious threat to the New Earth is a one-time crime kingpin."

Hugh's expression acknowledged the irony of it. "Yet it makes sense, in a way," he said after a moment. "What is it but the worst of the Old Earth's ways? Force, domination, selfishness, ego."

"Well, we must prevail over all that," Hedi said firmly, "or what's the use of all this suffering?"

"Perhaps you will not be surprised to hear that the Elustreons are in agreement."

She looked at him. "What's the bottom line, Hugh? I know full well you're hiding something."

"Not hiding, exactly. Savoring."

"Well?"

"They have a stake in this too, you remember. We on Earth get to do the voting, but the issue affects far more than Earth."

"I remember," she said, thinking back to Mr. J and Sam Theos' survival camps.

"We gave them a good scare, Hedi. For a terrible moment, everything we are fighting for hung balanced on a knife-edge. If not for you, Red Beard might have prevailed."

"Surely it wouldn't have been as final as all that?"

"Max seems to think so. Nobody knows, of course, because it didn't happen. But he laid out a scenario for me. Red Beard overruns the troops at the dam; he sweeps on northward, destroying everything that lends cohesion to our government; he then moves west, coming down from the north, and either sweeps my troops and the Pennsylvanians out of existence or throws us far back into the

Pennsylvania plain. Either way, he establishes himself on the Inland Sea and destroys any challenge to himself from the north."

"I knew the situation was dangerous," Hedi said, "but I hadn't thought of it in such catastrophic terms."

"Max did. And that's not the worst of it. Max pointed out that Red Beard's triumph would very likely be seen by many in government as evidence that democracy was all very well for good times, but an unaffordable luxury in tight places. In the face of the threat posed by Red Beard's very existence, many would argue that the times called for a strongman, military or otherwise."

"Oh no! That's just what we *don't* need!"

"Yes, I know it and you know it and General Jerome knew it - - but once let Red Beard get on the Inland Sea and see how many people still agree with us. It was a dangerous moment up there at the dam, Hedi."

"Yes," she said, "I suppose so. That must be what the governor meant —"

"Meant about what?"

"He was just hinting, I think. Either that, or he was thinking out loud. He said maybe it was just as well that we'd had a close shave — it might bring some people to their senses."

Hugh nodded. "I know where that's going. He and I have had many a discussion about it. Voluntary assistance among districts and groups of districts was all well and good as an interim measure, but it's time we moved beyond it. If we'd had a strong federal government, the way we used to, we in New England wouldn't have had to beg, borrow and steal men and resources enough to hold Red Beard at bay. We could have finished him off long ago. It isn't anybody's fault that we had to give up the federal government at Year Zero, but it seems clear that the time has come for closer co-ordination."

Hedi thought of the governor's few words, spoken at her bedside the day before. "He's going to call a constitutional convention, isn't he?"

"Well, the present system has brought us about as far as it can. Your battle made that clear. We need something stronger."

Hedi chewed on her lower lip. "I wonder if we're strong enough to carry it off. New England in Z 6 isn't Virginia in the 1780s. We're not strong enough to be critically important to the other districts. We might have a hard time carrying the day."

"Oh, I don't know that that will be a large problem, necessarily," Hugh said innocently.

"And transportation is such a problem. The distances count for so much more than they did in the old days. Why are you smiling?"

"Your injuries must extend to your head. The Hedi I remember would have picked up on it when I said we gave the Elustreons a good scare. They don't think the danger is past, Hedi."

She had been too caught up in reassessing the danger she had helped avert to connect his later words with his earlier ones. When the realization hit, she raised a shout.

"They're going to help!"

His smile was even broader than before. Or was it that his eyes were sparkling so merrily? Or was it that he was out of his chair? Or that his fists were clenched with excitement?

"That's it exactly. They intend to give us assistance. And Hedi, *you* did it. You could have lost the battle, and instead you won it for us. And I would not be at all surprised if you won the war."

This was wonderful news. Now she could look at her broken legs swathed in plaster and she could smile. It was worth it! It was cheap at the price!

"This means survival," she said. "With them on our side, we'll finish the pirates in a matter of days!"

Abruptly, Hugh sobered. "Whoa. Not so fast."

"Hugh, don't be silly. How long do you think the pirates can hold out in battle against the Elustreons?"

"There will be no battle. The Elustreons will not engage in warfare."

"Oh, I know that. They won't even appear on Earth. But surely Max is worth an army in himself."

"Hedi, you misunderstand. The Elustreons are resigned to the necessity of us fighting the pirates, but they will not assist us in any military way. We do our own fighting."

"Oh. Well, all right, we've fought our own battles up to now, I guess we can keep on."

"You understand, this is a matter of deep-seated principle with them."

Did she understand? "Yes, I suppose I do," she said reluctantly. "But if they won't help us fight, what *will* they do?"

"Of that, I am not sure. All I do know for certain is that Max said they would provide us with 'material assistance.' What that means, you can tell me."

Hedi shook her head. "It's a puzzle," she said. She felt herself brightening. "But if Max said it, you can take it to the bank. No pun intended. Whatever it is they have in mind, I'm sure it will be valuable. As long as they believe we're right, they'll help us prevail, somehow. Hugh, this means we're not alone."

Hugh's smile reminded her of the proverbial cat that ate the canary. "That's exactly what it means."

36. Allen's Story
February, Year Z 18

Mary Scott said, "You might call it the final legacy of Hedi's victory at the dam." It sat there before them on the table, an 80-page spiral-bound student blank book from the old days, 6 inches by 9 inches, with a bright blue cover. Hedi and Martha and Hugh and Governor Thompson of the District of New England had all taken turns leafing through the pages, looking at the cramped script that had been entered day by day by the well-mannered, soft-spoken, inconspicuous little man who had worked for so many years, unsuspected, so close to Mary.

"The man is dead," the governor said. "Are we quite sure he died a natural death?"

"I was with him when he died," Mary said. "He came down with H-5 flu in December. Along with a few thousand other people. Pneumonia followed, and the day before yesterday, it finally took him away."

The governor looked grim. "Surely he could have been cured?"

"Priorities," Hugh said. "The man didn't have enough points to warrant the necessary drugs. The fact that he was on my wife's staff did not, by itself, qualify him to jump ahead of others on the list. And, in lieu of drugs, it was up to him to get his own immune system to cure him."

"But in light of what he could have told us —"

"Governor, no one suspected. And he chose not to mention it. Perhaps he had his doubts about how we would treat him, if he let us know who he had been. Or perhaps he feared that if he once told anyone, the news would get back to Red Beard, and he would be a dead man anyway."

"Possibly he had no further wish to live," Hedi said gently. "Or perhaps he did wish to live, but not if it meant depriving someone else of the means to live."

"He doesn't seem to have been quite that altruistic earlier in his life," Governor Thompson said, drily. His irony reminded Hedi of her years with Governor Duval, now serving as secretary of natural resources in the government of region three.

"Quite obviously, he'd grown," Mary said.

"Perhaps you'd better tell us the story from the beginning," the governor said. "When did you first meet this man?"

"It would have been about a dozen years ago. A little after the battle that Hedi won. He was one more refugee, one of countless thousands of refugees."

"How did he wind up working in your technical library?"

"He was a refugee, and I needed another person to work at shelving and cataloguing."

"Cataloguing?"

"Under supervision, at first. He picked it up rapidly, though."

"In other words, as a refugee, he was assigned the normal year's probation, working at semi-skilled labor while he demonstrated his willingness and ability to live under our rules."

"That's right."

"And you didn't find it surprising that after his year's probationary period expired, he remained at the library rather than seeking a position offering a chance of advancement?"

Mary shook her head, a very small, precise gesture. "In the first place, I rarely gave him any thought. He was one employee of many. Beyond that, the position seemed to suit him. He was a loner, with neither family nor friends. He seemed the sort who ask only a quiet life, and are well content to get it. Besides, in time he did become a librarian/researcher. Not the most exalted of posts, perhaps, but not negligible either, nor devoid of intrinsic interest."

The governor nodded his understanding. "So you found his contentment reasonable. Very well. And he continued to work with you from that day to this."

"That's right. And after he died, I found that he had left me this." She touched the notebook in front of her. "Apparently he'd kept it squirreled away in his little apartment."

"I don't understand. How did you know he'd left it to you?"

"The night before he died, he wrote a note and left it with my name on it. He gave me the note when I came to see him, just before he died. He said this was the only thing he could do for the New Earth to pay a little bit of what he owed."

"All right. I'll read this little book when I can. For now, tell me what it tells us about Red Beard. How did they hook up in the first place? And what was his real name?"

"George Allen. He met up with the Red Duke as a young man just out of a two-year institute that taught various skills, including piloting light aircraft."

"He was a pilot, then."

"According to his own testimony, he was a would-be soldier of fortune, with no compunctions, willing to do just about anything if it promised to lead him toward riches. Apparently he worked for an offshore oil company for a while. In any case, he was knocking around accumulating experience when Red Beard — he was called the Duke in those days — signed him on."

"Why?"

Mary shrugged. "Looking for intelligent, unscrupulous henchmen, I suppose."

"No, I mean why did he sign on?"

"He says that Duke was paying twice what Allen could get on a legitimate job. But it doesn't take much reading between the lines to imagine that he saw Duke as his ticket to the big time."

"To my mind," Hugh said, "the value of this book is that it gives us a unique close-up look at Red Beard, inside information unlike any we have ever had."

"Let's look at it," the governor said non-committally.

"You know that Red Beard was the son of a third-string New Jersey crime boss known as Pete the Protector. We learned the outline of his history years ago."

"I know."

"Allen confirms what we had, but he says much more. He says Duke wanted to be the biggest of all the bosses. According to Allen, Duke is very intelligent, and directed that intelligence to thinking of ways to amass power and wealth."

"We knew he'd been to college."

"That's right. He came home with his ambition whetted. He learned his father's business by running the western half of his father's district — the area bordering on the Delaware — while his father took it easy. He more than once demonstrated his ability to break bones with his bare hands, and he was an artist with a lead pipe, too."

"A sadist," Hedi said.

"Apparently not," Mary said. "From all reports, he was completely unmoved by the suffering of his victims, but he did not take pleasure in it. It was all business with him. Allen says Duke often said 'Everything should have a purpose, so don't let me catch you wasting working hours smashing windows just because you like the tinkle of breaking glass.'

"He worked his father's territory for seven years prior to Day Zero, building an organization of which Al Capone would have been proud. He spent a lot of time teaching the finer skills of the master criminal to those he felt had talent. He conducted regular classes for those who ranked as captains, lieutenants, or sergeants, explaining his rules and describing his long-range ambitions for himself and his loyal supporters."

Martha said, sardonically, "Rule number one, of course, was that anyone violating his basic rules came to an abrupt end."

"Of course. Beyond that, the principle was always the same — the organization was in the business of acquiring power and wealth. If need be, it used other people ruthlessly to achieve those ends, but fun and games were not permitted during working hours. Poor judgment was not tolerated at any time, and disobeying the Duke was very poor judgment. Allen was one of Duke's staff, one of five captains. Except for Duke himself, he was at the top."

Hugh said, "Unfortunately for us, Day Zero found the Red Duke in an excellent position to exploit the opportunities it offered him."

"I want to hear about that," the governor said. "How did he get into a position to do so much damage?"

Mary said, "I thought you'd want to read his account. I made copies. She picked up the governor's book, found the proper page, and handed it to him. He began to read:

Duke called his five captains together at the lodge in the Poconos. He said he wanted us to help him figure out what was going on.

"I thought his territory was in New Jersey," the governor said, looking up.

"It was," Mary said. "Go back about three pages. He explains that this was a ski lodge just west of the Delaware that the Red Duke had picked up. The previous owners signed over the place in return for his not giving the authorities certain information he had stumbled onto."

"Blackmail," the governor grunted.

It was real nice. It even had two choppers — a two-place and a six-place. The boss made the lodge parking lot into a landing pad and put in fuel pumps and storage tanks, and he stocked the place with canned food, firearms, ammunition, that kind of thing, all picked up the same way the boss picked up the lodge itself.

"Sounds like he was worrying about a siege," the governor said.

"I get the impression of planning, rather than worrying," Mary said. The governor returned to Allen's account of the conference at the lodge.

We were watching TV. We listened to the experts, and we could see they didn't have a clue. Then Morgan stood up and says he's going to go take a good look at the foundation.

Duke says, "Why?" Morgan says he wants to see how well the building will stand up to an earthquake. Morgan was a small-time civil engineer before Duke recruited him.

Duke sat there a minute, stunned. "Earthquakes!" he shouts. "Morgan, what happens to bridges in big earthquakes?"

"Most likely they fall into the river," Morgan says.

"Morgan," Duke says, "you go ahead and check out this building. If it's okay, you find a couple of more places nearby that we can put our people in. The rest of you, start contacting as many of your people as you can find. I want everybody on this side of the river that can possibly make it. Tell them to bring their families.

"Tiny, as soon as you call your people in Jersey, round up as many men as you can and start collecting boats. You rent, buy, or borrow anything you like the looks of."

Tiny grins and says, "Whether they want to or not, right?"

"No rough stuff yet. We don't know for sure what's going to happen. Maybe nothing, for all we know. We don't want to bring a lot of heat down on us. Anything you steal, you steal after dark."

He says, "Now listen. Tiny, take half a dozen machine guns and mount them on your best boats. Tommy guns and automatic rifles will have to do for the rest. If we find all the bridges down tomorrow, I want to be in control of the river from Port Jervis all the way to Philadelphia. Tiny, you are going to be an admiral."

"Allen," he said to me, "go warm up the big chopper. We have got to get my wife and kids here before they get stranded on the Jersey side of the river."

We were all thinking maybe the Duke just went off the rails, but when he tells you to do something, you do it. I headed out of there fast, him on my heels. "I'll be back before dark," he says over his shoulder.

"I don't understand why his wife and children were in New Jersey if he was in the Poconos," the governor said.

"He had them on a farm on the Jersey side of the river," Mary said. "Duke paid a man to manage it as a legitimate operation. Allen says Duke's wife didn't really know what Duke did for a living."

The governor looked at Mary severely.

"Oh, he says she had the general idea. But he says she didn't know the details, and Duke made sure she didn't find out. He makes her sound something of an innocent."

The governor looked dubious.

After we got through the first couple days' shaking, Duke rounded us all up again. He was all excited. "This is our big chance," he says. "From right now, nobody's talking bigger rackets. We're talking our own *country*, with our own citizens paying us taxes. From now on, we don't *buy* the law, we *are* the law." We don't exactly know what to make of what he's telling us, but you can believe that nobody disagrees. "It's going to take a little time," he says, "a little patience, but we're going to do it." And he starts telling us how we start.

"We know how they started," the governor commented, lips thin. "They terrorized the towns around them into imploring the authorities to leave Duke's little empire alone."

"That's right. You can tell that Allen still can't conceal his admiration."

It worked out pretty much the way he figured it. The Delaware turned into a tidal river, getting wider every day. After the first two days, there wasn't a bridge left standing across it. What was left of the old bridges were standing in the middle of the river, and every day the shores got farther away. So we didn't have anything to worry about from that side, not with Tiny's gunboats working. And we didn't have to worry about any of our new citizens deciding they liked life better on the other side, either. We had that river from Port Jervis to the sea, and nobody went across without Tiny's say-so. Same with those on the islands that had been hills before the sea started coming up.

"We could have dealt with Tiny's riverboat navy," the governor said unhappily, "if the Coast Guard had been operational. But they not only lost most of their cutters, they lost all of their operational bases in the first series of tidal wave assaults."

Hedi felt herself frowning. "I don't know how big this Duke's gang was, but it couldn't have been all *that* big. Not big enough to set up his own little empire."

"That was a matter of recruiting, to hear Allen tell it," Mary said. "No problem, when you know what you're doing."

Say you need new hands. And you always do, right? When you have hungry, desperate people, there isn't anything in the world simpler than signing them up. You find somebody who looks hungry and healthy and you ask him what he'll do for a steady supply of food. If he says "anything" — him or her, it doesn't make any difference with Duke — if they say "anything," you try 'em out some way. You put them in a mob control unit, maybe — see if they fire on women and children. If they pass the test, they get food and shelter.

The governor looked up. "I'm surprised they could get skilled people to work for them."

Hugh said, practically, "Morgan was an engineer. Allen was a pilot. Duke was a college man himself. There isn't any necessary correlation between education and morals, or compassion. And it wouldn't take a whole lot of people with skills to keep the workers working. Certainly they've proved that in the past few years."

"Oh, yes," Hedi said, her lips set in a grimace of distaste. "And it was proved many times over, all throughout history."

"In any case," Mary said, "we all know that the Red Duke came to dominate what was left of the other gangs that infested the northeast. It took him three years, but he did it."

"So what happened? How did Allen wind up living among us? I take it you are convinced he was not spying?"

"Oh, yes," Mary said. "Over the years he had more than one opportunity to move into sensitive positions. He always turned them down. Said he wanted a quiet life."

"I guess he did," Hugh said, not without humor. "If he walked out on the Red Duke, he had a choice between a quiet life and a short one."

"So what's the story?"

"After Day Zero, Duke installed his wife and children in a country estate and kept them virtual prisoners. According to Allen, Duke didn't want them to know just what he was doing."

"She must have known something," Martha insisted. But Hugh shook his head. "If nobody dared tell her anything? How's she supposed to find out?"

Mary referred to her copy of the manuscript. "'Duke had always put me in charge of seeing that his wife and children were taken care of when he was busy somewhere. After E-Day — [that was their word for Day Zero] — I was still in charge of taking care of them, only now I had to be sure they didn't escape. He was always busy, going here and there, setting things up. It wasn't long before I was seeing a lot more of Maria than he was. I think he still loved her, in his way, but I was falling in love with her in a whole different way. She was different than the kind of women I knew. She spoke real quiet, and always was saying please and thank you and noticing any little thing you might happen to do for her. And I liked the way she was with her kids, like she really liked them.'"

"So he fell in love with her," the governor said coldly, clearly disbelieving what was being read to him. "Pretty risky business, that, wasn't it?"

"You might as well call it suicide," Martha murmured.

I couldn't seem to help it. It got so I couldn't stand to see him with her, the way he talked to her, the way he acted with her. He can't stand people saying no to him, and that's what she started doing. He intends to be king, and they're going to be the crown princes and princess, and she would be the queen. His wife wanted no part of any of it. Then when Ramond, his oldest son, was ten, Duke decided he must begin training him to be a future crown prince, so he took the boy to his lodge.

Maria rarely saw her husband in those days, and when she next saw her oldest child, she was horrified. "They are turning him into a beast," she told me, "and now Duke talks of taking the other boy when he is ten, and even our daughter a year later. He says I must stay here, that I can have no part in their training. I will fight him with my bare hands before I let her go." I wanted to help, but there seemed to be no way to do it.'"

"So what finally happened?"
"Finally Allen offered to help her escape."
"Escape? Escape where?"
"Here." She pointed out the page.

When he took the second son, I asked her if she wanted to bring the girl and run away. I told her I could take her to a place where she would be treated kindly, and I would stay there and take care of her if she wished. "I cannot desert any of my children," she told me, "and I will not run away." Then she took my hand and held it for just a moment. "Please be careful. He would kill you for what you just offered. You have been kind to me, and I do not want your blood upon my hands."

When Duke did come back to get the girl, Maria fought like a tigress. I was not there, but the pilot who flew the chopper told me how Duke tore the girl from Maria's arms, how she followed him and grabbed the chopper's skids as it took off, and how Duke kicked her loose, letting her fall perhaps ten feet to the ground. He didn't bother to go back to see if she was dead or alive.

I took off before the Duke knew I had gone. I found her lying where she had fallen. I think her neck was broken. She was dead. The servants had fled, frightened at the thought of being questioned about what they had seen.

"So he jumped in the chopper and escaped, fearing that the Duke would eliminate all witnesses of his wife's murder," the Governor surmised.

"And took Maria's body with him," Mary said.

"Why? I don't get it."

"He knew the Duke would never be sure what happened. He hoped that not knowing if Maria was dead or alive would drive him crazy. He says he carried her to the chopper and headed for enemy country. Here. He got as far as a mountain top somewhere in southern New Hampshire, and buried her there. He says, 'I thought someday the sun and the moon will get through all this ash in the skies, and will cast their light upon her grave.'"

They sat quietly, absorbing that.

"He says he ditched the helicopter in the Inland Sea, made his way to shore, picked a new name, and started a new life as a refugee, terrified that the Duke would find him."

"So now we have a better idea what we're up against in this Red Beard," Hugh said.

The governor sighed. "I know what you're driving at. Conscription, again."

"Governor, believe me, it isn't because I like the idea. But it's necessary for us to defend ourselves."

"Well, I've fought you tooth and nail on this issue for months, but now I'm afraid you're right. Hedi, have the attorney general draw up legislation to that effect; I'll introduce it to the legislature in person, using this journal as my explanation."

Hugh suddenly looked exhausted, as if he'd just finished running up Mount Washington. "Thank you, governor, I appreciate it. I know what it costs you."

"Mr. Allen may have done more to repay us than he suspected," Hedi said.

37. Massacre
Year Z 31

The door between the office of the governor and the outer reception office in which her secretaries worked was usually left open. Hedi preferred it that way: The chatter outside did not interfere with her concentration, and the sound of human voices made her feel less isolated. But even when she was sharply focused on the papers before her, some portion of her mind noted what was going on outside her door. Thus, one day she heard her secretary say, "Yes, she is, colonel," and she knew before the buzzer sounded that it was Roy outside.

She jumped up from her chair, and met him before he was fully inside her office. She gave him a hug, closed the door behind them, indulged in a long kiss. "Roy! I'm so delighted to see you!"

"Glad to be here," he said, smiling down at her. "Does the governor greet all her guests this way?"

"Only very special guests. Guests in uniform, particularly."

"I'll have to start keeping track of Hugh Scott's visits, I suppose," he said. "Listen, Hedi, I am here on borrowed time. I only have about half an hour."

"Well, I'm glad to see you anyway, even for half a minute."

"Is that speaking as governor to Hugh Scott's chief medical officer?"

"It is indeed, friend. And as the chief medical officer's lonely wife, too. Where are you off to?"

"The base hospital at Mount Washington. We had to abandon the forward field hospital north of Springfield, Massachusetts, and shift much of that load to the Hanover, New Hampshire, facility. They are

now overloaded with battle casualties, and I am involved in determining what staff and equipment can be spared from the base
hospital to help them out."

The Lowland Pirates had mounted yet another offensive, penetrating as far west as the Connecticut River near Springfield, then
driving north along the river. To Roy, as chief medical officer, had
fallen the job of reallocating medical capabilities to handle the
increased load of wounded. "I need to see how heavy the workload
is at the base hospital. I had some able assistance from Sally in the
build-up at Hanover, by the way."

"Is Sally going with you to Mt. Washington?"

"Can't. She's too busy at Hanover. The staff is terribly overworked. They cannot afford to lose the services of a surgical technician just now."

"No, I suppose not. Roy, when is Hugh going to hit back?"

"In his own good time," Roy said calmly. "He knows what he's
doing." Scott had been giving ground slowly in the valley while
readying his forces.

"But surely he could have counterattacked by now."

"Well, naturally the pirates are fighting hard. The ocean has taken
so much of their land, they're desperate. They *have* to win, or
they're finished."

"But we have thrown everything we have into the defense and
haven't been able to stop them. How much further can Hugh retreat,
without giving up our heartland?"

"All I can say is that I'm confident Hugh will beat him." Roy
shrugged. "But right at the moment, it's Red Beard who's on the
offensive, not us. We have to stop him before we can throw him
back."

"Speaking as governor to chief medical officer, Roy, what are you
telling me? Is there a specific problem we can help you with?"

"Not at the moment. I want to see what the base hospital can
spare in the way of staff, supplies, and equipment, that's all. But I
should tell you that if this campaign lasts too much longer we will
be asking you to go to the legislative assembly for authority to take
an even larger chunk of the District's medical capabilities away from
the civilian sector and give it to the military."

Her memory turned back to Sam Theos. If some must die, which
ones will it be?

"I know what you're thinking, and we both know that the
decision must be made by the government — by the governor and
the assembly."

"And we'll face that decision, Roy. It's up to me to see that we
do. That's why I'm holding the assembly in continuous session. I
confer daily with the assembly president. We'll see that Hugh Scott

gets a prompt answer to any request he makes. He may not always get the answer he wants, but he'll get an answer."

"There was another reason for stopping by. I thought you might want to know where your wandering husband is."

She kissed him again. "Always," she said.

This was a rare moment to relax together. They spoke of this and that.

"You know, Madam Governor," Roy said after a while, "it struck me the other day: Since the night the Old Earth died, an entire generation has grown up. This is all they know. They take all this to be normal life."

"I suppose they do."

"Not a bad life, really, do you think? I mean, I wonder how it looks to them."

"They've had plenty of hardships."

"But maybe they don't feel them the way we do, not knowing anything else."

"Maybe not. *I* certainly do, sometimes. Think of all the little conveniences we lost."

"I do, sometimes. But then I think of other things we lost. Graft. Pornography. Child prostitution. Drug addiction. Juvenile delinquency."

Hedi could not help smiling. "Don't forget mail fraud and tax evasion. You make the Old Earth sound like hell."

"Sometimes when I think about it, it sounds that way. I'm glad Sally and Peter didn't grow up amid all that. It balances out a lot of hardships they've had to endure."

"Has Sally been talking to you about hardships?"

"No, not at all. I guess originally I was thinking about Steven Woodbine."

Hedi shifted positions in her chair. "Roy, you're losing me."

"Let's put it this way, Madam Governor. Thirty years' hard work has not sufficed to build the New Earth, but we *have* laid the foundations. If Woodbine's observations are accurate, and if his projections are sound —"

"And they always are."

"— 'and they always are' is right — well, we're looking at a tremendous increase in life expectancy. Maybe a hundred percent increase for those who learned the feedback technique as children. Maybe 50 percent, he thinks, for old-timers like us."

"I know all that," she said simply. "I'd know it as Dr. Johnson's wife, if not in any other capacity."

"Of course. But the upshot is that here we are in Z 31, better off in at least one way than we would have been if the Old Earth had survived. In the Old Earth, you and I would be nearing retirement age. In the New Earth, the sixties are the prime of life for our generation. We're almost exactly at the middle of what you might call our expected life span. For the kids, with a life expectancy of 160 or so, the sixties will be like late youth. Early middle age. Think how much they'll be able to accomplish in their lifetimes."

He was driving at something. She waited him out, as she had so often in their long marriage.

"Hedi, have you ever stopped to realize how much Red Beard has cost us in 30 years?"

"I always know ahead of time when it's going to rain," she said briefly. "My kneecap aches."

"Honey, I figure he cost you a lot more than that. Cost all of us. Think of all the lives, the resources, the time and attention we have been forced to lavish on countering him and his delusions of grandeur...."

They went on to speak of other things until Roy glanced at his wristwatch and got up to leave.

"Got to go," he said.

Hedi gave Roy a last hug and a kiss, and they went out the door into the outer office. At the outer door, he turned and waved to her. She wondered if the coming years would spare him his steel-gray hair, which she thought looked so distinguished.

* * *

Again she was at her desk, and again she was reading reports when her attention was captured by words from the outer office. But this time the words were Hugh Scott's, spoken from his field headquarters. Before he had said ten words, Hedi was in the outer office, staring at the radio that monitored Scott's transmissions.

"This is General Hugh Scott, speaking to all military and civilian personnel in New England. I am speaking on both the military and commercial radio networks. By the emergency power vested in me I am calling a general alert! Repeat, this is a general alert! This is to every loyal citizen of our district. New England needs you, and needs you *now*. I urge every man, woman and child who has a weapon and knows how to fire it to come to our common defense.

"The Lowland Pirates have managed to outflank our northern defenses and launch a surprise attack on our base hospital at Mount Washington. Heavy fighting continues even as I speak. In the name of the District of New England and in the name of the New Earth, I order every armed person in the vicinity to get to the Mount Washington area by any means available and help defend our sick and wounded, and, beyond that, our homes."

The hospital? Roy!

But she had no time to think of Roy. Hugh's voice had scarcely faded from the airwaves before he called her on the secure telephone.

"Madam Governor, I apologize for acting before consulting you, but we had no time to lose. Did you hear my appeal on the radio?"

"Yes. What happened?"

"We got a call. From one of the hospital guards, I think. The pirates are attacking the base hospital, and all we have there is a military police company to defend it. They must have slowed down the pirates long enough to get the call out. Good thing they did, or we would have had no idea what hit us.

"I've told Colonel Davison to keep someone on that radio every minute repeating my call until we've thrown the pirates back from the base. I want every civilian in the area heading out to Mount Washington, and the radio's the way to see it gets done. If Foch could use taxicabs, we can use radios.

"Hedi, I'm getting ready to fight. I'm betting my bottom dollar this attack is only a diversion, and I want Red Beard to think we're falling for it."

He waited for an answer, but there was none. The telephone handset lay on the desk where she had left it, and she was running toward her gravity car which always stood ready on the landing pad near her office. In a matter of minutes, the governor, her pilot, and two unarmed security guards were on their way to the base hospital. Sometimes the Elustreons' prohibition against transportation of arms aboard gravity cars was a damned nuisance, and Hugh would have disapproved of the governor putting herself in danger. In fact, he might even now be trying to learn what she was doing. It wouldn't take him long to make the right guess. Then he would do everything in his power to stop her. This is why she had taken off while he was still talking. "Don't answer any radio calls until we reach the hospital," she ordered the startled pilot.

By the time the gravity car made its landing near the main hospital building, the pirates were already being pushed back from the hospital grounds by the unlikely collection of soldiers and civilians that had answered General Scott's appeal.

Before they had the doors open, a young captain recognized the governor's gravity car and came running up, saluting as he came.

"Ma'am, you need to be careful here. We're running the lot of 'em out of here, but there's still a lot of fighting and dying going on. We wouldn't want to give 'em a clear shot at you."

"Thank you, captain, but I've no time to argue," she snapped. "My husband, Colonel Johnson, is somewhere in there. Can you help me find him? If not, I will go alone." Without waiting for an answer she turned and started toward the main hospital building.

"God help me if you get hurt, governor, but I'll help you look, and forgive me for saying so, ma'am, but I admire your guts."

They found Roy still alive, but just barely. He was lying in a pool of his own blood, and Hedi could see that he knew death was very close. "Been holding on," he whispered. "Knew it would be you."

She knelt in the blood and cradled him in her arms.

"Killed a man," he whispered. "God forgive me." He threw his glance at a man sprawled nearby. "I knew him as Captain Martin." Then, so feebly that Hedi had to strain even harder to hear him, he spoke a few sentences — scarcely more than broken phrases — that would haunt her for many years to come. The message delivered, he closed his eyes. "My love to Sally. Peter."

His eyes opened, but the effort of focusing was beyond him. "Stick with the cause.... Little Ralph and I nearby.... Love..." And with that, he was gone.

For a long time she held him, not willing to let him go. The captain made a discreet departure, standing guard at the entrance of the ward.

* * *

Time had passed. The sounds of shooting and shouting had died down. Suddenly Hedi became aware that someone was behind her. She turned to see a patient with both feet in heavy casts dragging himself across the bloody floor.

"I was under the bed," he said, seeing her surprise. "You knew the Doc?"

"He was my husband."

"He saved my life. He distracted them long enough for me to roll out of bed and hide underneath it. I saw everything."

"Tell me what happened."

"That pirate officer" — pointing at the body near Roy's — "and two of his men came in this ward. The two men had clubs. They rolled patients out of bed and kicked and beat them unconscious. Then the officer shot them through the head. They seemed to like hearing the victims scream with pain and beg for mercy.

"Doc rushed in and tried to stop them. The leader laughed and shot him in the stomach. Doc kind of doubled up and sank to his knees. The leader leaned over him, taunting him, laughing.

"That was his mistake. Doc jerked his legs from under him, grabbed his gun as he fell, and shot him. But then the other two turned their guns on Doc and must have shot him a dozen times. I don't know how he lived until you came."

"He lived because he was determined to," Hedi said.

"If you say so. He was your husband, you say? Well, he was a kind man, a good man. He wanted to save lives, not take them. But for a moment, there, he was a raging lion. He was a better man than any I know, lady, and right now I would swap places with him if I could."

The man's voice was kind, his words obviously sincere. "You sound like a good man yourself," Hedi said heavily. The man's sincerity helped counteract the bitterness of what Roy had told her before he died. "Captain!" When the captain came, she gestured to the wounded man. "A survivor. Let's get him back into bed. Is the danger over, here?"

"The pirate forces are retreating toward the coast," the officer said evenly. His face was an expressionless mask. "The discipline of our army is not at its highest just now," he said. "Besides being a mixture of regular troops and civilians, it has seen what happened here."

"What are you saying?"

"Our forces are not disposed to be merciful. Not many pirates will make it back to their ships," he said. "And there will be few prioners." They stared at each other for a long moment. Finally Hedi spoke. "Thank you, Captain," she said. "I understand."

The captain hesitated. "We will take care of things here, Ma'am. We have to make a full report on all casualties, and I expect we will soon be hearing from General Scott."

* * *

She was on her way back to the capital when Scott finally reached her. "You know what happened?" she asked.

"Yes. It is a critical loss to me, an even greater loss to you. I could not possibly be more sorry." She heard the small break in his voice that was more eloquent than his words.

"He gave me a message for you, but that must wait until we can meet in private."

"Is there anything I can do to help you now?"

"Not now. I've called my secretary to locate Peter and Sally so I can talk to them as soon as I get back to my office. I want to tell them first hand what happened. After that I must go somewhere and cry."

Hugh spoke very softly now. "I have spoken to the captain at the hospital. It was an unwise risk the governor took. The general had to try to stop her, but I'm glad he failed. And, Hedi, like the captain, I admire your guts."

* * *

Hugh paid a flying visit to see Hedi the following day, and she gave him Roy's message.

"That explains the massacre," Hugh said grimly. "Geographically, that base was about as secure as any could be — that's why we put it there. The White Mountains to the east, us to the west, and well-manned positions to the south. And only the sea to the north."

Everything from the old coastline to the base of the mountains at the northern end of the range had flooded long before. Of course there were hundreds of islands, and these gave the pirates' ships a measure of protection from the tidal waves, but not from observation. "Between the observation posts on the ridges and the regular scouting patrols along the eastern coast, we should have been secure. Nobody could mount an attack by land or sea without being seen in plenty of time for us to move defending troops into position. That's why I have always been free to concentrate our forces in more vulnerable areas. Now we know that the attack on the hospital was a diversion, but it was a diversion in force that could have inflicted great damage had it not been repulsed."

Two weeks passed — two weeks of exciting news from the battle fronts. Then Hugh called with an invitation. "I can tell you that the battle is won, Madam Governor, and in another week I believe I can tell you the war is won."

"That's wonderful news, Hugh. Tell me more."

"I can do better than that. I have turned command over to my able deputy, General Oliver, and he has agreed that I take the day off to conduct a tour of the theater of operations in our flying field headquarters, all for the sole benefit of our Commander-in-chief. That means you, Governor Hedi Johnson. Will you grant me the honor?"

"You know that I will, General Hugh Scott. When?"

"One hour from now, if that's OK. I'll pick you up at your office."

Hedi advised her secretary of her plans and then leaned back in her chair to reflect. Hugh had staged an old trick and Red Beard had fallen for it. First there was the radio security code deliberately leaked to a known pirate spy. Then he had pulled combat units out of the valley with fake orders to report to the Mount Washington area. Then the air waves were full of pleas from well-coached company and regimental officers begging for ammunition, for medical assistance, for transport equipment, and above all for replacements for their exhausted troops.

With Scott's men in the valley falling back rapidly, and weapons and other equipment being abandoned, Red Beard had smelled enemy blood, and had urged his men forward for the final kill.

At first they met little resistance; then they ran headlong into a fresh reserve brigade that Scott had thrown into the battle.

Fifteen miles to the south, Scott's remaining reserve division teamed up with the troops he had pulled out of the valley. With a skillfully executed pincers movement from both sides of the river, they cut the over-extended pirate lines in two. One brigade attacked the forward pirate units from the rear, cutting them to pieces. Scott's remaining troops turned south, creating chaos in the Red Duke's lines of supply and support. The confusion they created was immense. What might have been a defeat became a panic.

And now here it was. The Battle of The Valley was ending with Red Beard's army fleeing east and south, bleeding itself white as it ran. Hugh Scott had made sure that all his troops knew of the massacre at the base hospital. Hedi finished writing the message she had been working on. She gave it to her secretary to type and returned to her desk. A tear trickled down her cheek, then another, and then another as she fought against surrendering to the lust for vengeance. But visions of Roy's broken body continually interfered.

Roy was dead! Oh, God! Roy was dead, and she was alive! As clear as anything, she could remember the young idealist, utterly devoted to his dream of saving lives. What kind of young lovers spent hours talking not about themselves but about a vision of better health care? But that's what they had done. They had emptied the restaurant and used up the night, and she had asked him in for a cup of coffee.

Oh, Roy! How am I supposed to live, now? First little Ralph, and then my parents, and now you? How can I bear it? What am I to do?

But now Hugh was speaking to her. "Are you ready to go, Madam Governor?"

The general's flying headquarters was a gravity liner equipped with the best communications equipment, mapping systems, and telescopic cameras available. Soon they were at 20,000 feet. A video screen showed a slowly changing map of the land below them and Hugh was speaking.

"I beg your pardon, General?"

"I said, he seems to be losing as many men to desertion as to us. Our troops are inflicting casualties and taking prisoners — but all who can escape are high-tailing it."

Hugh's face was a curious mixture of elation and grief.

"So it is a major victory."

"We are well beyond a victory now, Madam Governor. We are now into free pursuit. This could be the beginning of the end."

Her breath caught. "Do you really think it could be?" If it was the end, maybe she could lay down the burden of office and — And what? She had wanted to spend more time with Roy.

"Madam Governor, I have been waiting 30 years to strike a blow of this kind. If we can keep him from regaining his balance, we can prevent his deserters from returning to the ranks. We can make this more than a setback for him; we can make it total defeat."

She thought of Roy's body as she had last seen it. She reached out and gripped Hugh's arm. "Whatever you need, Hugh, ask. Whatever the cost, we'll pay it. Everything we have is yours for the taking. But do it. Defeat him. End this war."

"Hedi, if God wills it, we'll have him before the week is out. We will assure that Roy's death, and the deaths of so many others, were not for nothing. And then we can set about the process of rebuilding."

"Rebuilding."

"Rebuilding. As we have wanted to rebuild. Now you can pursue your dream of world government. In that campaign your weapons will be different from mine. They will be diplomacy, sound ideas, careful planning, stimulating ideals, and there is no one better equipped to lead such a campaign than Hedi Carlton Johnson."

Yes, they would set about rebuilding. How Roy would have wanted to be a part of that. Oh, God! Was there no end to sacrifice? She thought: "I feel so alone — so helpless, yes, and so weary. What shall I do?" Then, as though in answer, a new awareness shone through her grief. Roy was already a part of it. He would always be a part of it, as would all those others who had died or who had lived to help lay the foundations for this moment. A fresh and gentle breeze blew through the corridors of her mind. It ruffled her hair and brought to her the faint scent of roses — Roy's favorite perfume. Suddenly she was at peace with herself. The burden of pain was still there, but with the strength born of understanding, she knew she could carry it.

Hugh was regarding her silently. Now he spoke. "Where have you been? It was some distant place."

"You should know, Hugh Scott. You were there with me listening to Cheng Tu, the enlightened master, explain to a very young college girl and a brash young lieutenant how the God of love and mercy answers our prayers. Now, what were you saying when I so rudely left you?"

"Thank you for reminding me of that," he said. "It puts more emphasis on what I was about to say."

"Yes?"

"Our problem now," Hugh said, "is to resist the desire for vengeance. If we do not stop them, our troops will kill every pirate in sight."

"I've thought of that." She handed him the message she had written while waiting for him to pick her up. "Here. Broadcast this when you think fit."

He read it:

"To the officers and troops of the security forces of the District of New England:

"My sincere congratulations and heartfelt thanks to each of you. You have won battles before, but now you have won the war. Now at last we can get on with the building of a better world and a better life.

"You have endured hardship and suffered personal loss, and I well know and fully understand the temptation to seek revenge, but for thirty years we have fought for our principles — for the right to travel the high road — and we have won. Now I invite you to join me in enlisting the vanquished in our cause. To do otherwise invites future conflict. Indeed, it is a time to celebrate our victory, but enough blood has been spilled. And vengeance is not a principle that becomes us.

"—Hedi Carlton Johnson"

"Will that help, Hugh, do you think?"

He looked up, and she could see that he was stirred. "It's exactly what they need to hear, Madam Governor. I am proud to be associated with the person who could write this, in your particular circumstances." He paused. "As I was proud to be associated with Roy. He was a great man, truly a hero, a man faithful unto death."

"Thank you," she said simply. She smiled at him. "And now, General, let's get back to work. Even in victory, there are things to be done."

38. One More Campaign
Year Z 36

"Efficient as always, Hugh," Hedi said, looking around his bare office. "Packed and ready to go, with time to spare."

From where she sat in the comfortable upholstered guest chair, she could see Hugh sitting ramrod-straight behind his bare desk. "The secret of success, Hedi, as I know you know from personal experience, is delegation of responsibility. My chief of staff is supervising the loading of staff personnel and equipment on the gravity liners."

"Minus weapons, of course."

He smiled. "Of course. We have to hold to the conditions the Elustreons laid down. But Region One will supply ammunition and weapons, and nothing touches the gravity liners for moving personnel and equipment."

Hedi looked fondly at her old friend. "I've come to say a private good-bye before you leave on your last campaign."

"By God, I *hope* it's the last campaign."

The last organized resistance of the Lowland Pirates had ended. Red Beard and his command were all dead or missing. Region Three, New America North, was at the beginning of what came to be called the Period of Stability. Hugh Scott, commanding general of the

Region Three security forces (responding to a plea from the government of Region One, New America South) was taking an army of volunteers to fight in the upper reaches of what had been the Amazon River. Their old friend, Duval, now governor of New America North, supported the venture and granted Hugh an extended leave of absence.

"One more rat's nest and that's it, Hugh?"

"That's about the size of it. This bunch in New America South is a lot like our own pirates. The New Earth doesn't need them."

"Amen. Maybe this will be a final farewell to the ways of the Old Earth, do you think?"

"A little premature for that, I'd say. We have to defeat them, first. That's more than the government down there has been able to do in more than 30 years."

"But you'll do it, Hugh. Everybody knows it."

"Everybody knows it, but nobody can tell me how I will accomplish it," he said, smiling.

"Neither can you, but you know as well as I that you will."

"With God's help, yes," he said simply. "Then we can concentrate on overcoming natural obstacles, rather than human ones."

"After you have destroyed the last pocket of criminals on the New Earth," Hedi said innocently.

Hugh looked at her sharply.

"I suppose you know that highly placed persons in Red Beard's organization continue to throw themselves on the mercy of the government," she said.

"Northern New England, you mean?"

"No, the one we just organized — the government of New America North."

He was watching her closely. "They have been doing that since the Red Prince was reported missing and presumed dead."

"Yes, well, they're doing it in great numbers now."

"And?"

"You know the 'and'. The government is treating them with mercy. Cautiously, but mercifully. They know they're on probation. They'll follow our laws and they'll conform to our standards of behavior, or else. We're not going to let them distort the free, democratic, enlightened society we're trying so hard to build. But nobody in the government seems to be thinking too hard about the danger of enemies boring from within. Are we doing right, do you think?"

"The government?"

"You and I."

Hugh looked at her. She looked at him.

"You know what Roy told me before he died."

"I am unlikely to have forgotten."

Lying in his own blood, seconds from death, Roy had glanced at the body lying near him. "I know him," Roy had said. "... Captain ... traitor... with Pirates... killing — patients... Tell Scott... Must be others... find them."

"You swore me to silence. You said you'd look into it. So I kept silence, Hugh. And you know I've never asked you in all these years. But with you going away, I need to know. Did you make any progress on it at all?"

Hugh sat silently. Hedi could see that two impulses were warring within him. She waited patiently for one to win.

"I have learned one thing," he said reluctantly. "Two. The traitor Roy shot had been in command of our northern observer base: I have no doubt he betrayed his own men by leading them into an ambush. And his name was not Captain Martin — his identity papers were forged or stolen."

When she realized that no more would be forthcoming, she frowned at him. "That's it? That's all you've been able to find out in all this time, Hugh?"

"That is all to date, Hedi, I regret to say. I wish we knew more."

"Have you found any other traitors?"

"Not to date."

"Well, then, can I take it you no longer object to my telling the truth about how Roy died?"

Hugh's hands were folded neatly on the desk in front of him. "Hedi, I am sorry, but yes, I do object. It would be better all around if no one knows but we two."

"But why?"

"Surely it is obvious that our chances of finding any other traitors in our midst improve if they don't know we suspect their presence. If we ever want to avenge Roy — or, put it another way, if we ever want to assure that he did not die in vain — we need to keep this to ourselves. We may find something yet."

Hedi found herself chewing on her lower lip. "It makes things hard," she said, almost to herself.

"Sally?"

Hedi nodded. "The subject is a continual source of friction between us. She wants me to put more effort into finding out who betrayed her father. No, I never even hinted anything to her, she's convinced of it because of what she knew about the set-up. She can't understand why I'm not moving heaven and earth to find the people responsible. And I can't tell her. She thought the world of Roy."

Hugh looked down at his hands. One thumb was rubbing the other. Someone who didn't know Hugh might have been tempted to think him far away.

"My Lucy is 11 now," he said. "Growing up fast. God knows how old she'll be by the time I get back from the Amazon." He unfolded his hands. "I can imagine how much she'd miss her father, if something were to happen to me."

"See that it doesn't," Hedi said shortly.

Hugh looked as though he were trying to construct an adequate response. A knock on the door forestalled him.

"Come in!"

A downy lieutenant stepped into the room. "Colonel Baker's respects, and all troops are aboard, sir."

"Very good. My respects to Colonel Baker and I'll be there directly." The lieutenant disappeared behind the closed door.

"Hugh? About something happening to you. Mary would miss you, too."

"I know," he said. "I've said my good-byes from time to time. This morning, most recently." Abruptly, he stood, and she, thinking he was ready to leave, rose to her feet. But he walked around the desk to her and took her hands in his. "Hedi," he said awkwardly, "I know how much you miss him."

"No you don't," she said bleakly. "You couldn't possibly."

"Well, I'm sorry all the same. I'd give anything if he were still here among us."

"He is," she said. "I've often felt his presence." Silently, she added, "But I've much more often felt his absence."

Hugh's stern, weathered face folded into unfamiliar lines, softer, younger than the mask he showed his troops. "I'm glad, Hedi. I hope you never lose that sense of his presence. And I expect by the time I come home you'll be in the national government. I've got to go now. Give me a hug good-bye."

She embraced him, and his masculine presence was a vivid reminder of Roy, taller than she, broader. She felt her eyes stinging.

"Good-bye, Hugh. Be careful. Even after you clean out the last rat's nest, we're still going to need you. Come back to us."

"I will, Hedi. And you take care of yourself. Give my love to Sally and Peter."

Then they walked out his office door, and she watched his strong hand close around the doorknob and pull open the outer door. "I'm not going outside," she said. "That was good-bye enough for me." He nodded. "Good-bye, Hedi. Take care."

V. Resolution

39. Seven Symbols
December 22, Z 96

In that quiet period that often precedes the dawn, it began to snow. It was not the hard stinging snow driven by the winds of a winter blizzard, nor the wet, heavy, spring snow that breaks tree limbs and tests the strength of the schoolhouse roof. Instead it was soft and fluffy, and in the absence of wind it clung to everything it touched in a friendly, hesitant way as though to say, "I like it here, but if you don't want me, just shake me off or whistle for a breeze, and I will float away and leave you alone."

When Hedi awakened early on Saturday morning and looked out her bedroom window, she saw the silent flakes drifting down in such numbers that she could barely see the boundaries of her yard. She got up immediately, donned her robe and slippers, and with the aid of her crutches, made her way to the picture window in the den. En route, she reflected on how great it was to be able to get around the house without having to call someone to help her, or be restricted by the limitations of a wheelchair.

From her chair by the window, the Grand Lady watched the snowfall gradually diminish and the range of her vision increase. Bit by bit, the expected scene unfolded until she could see the entire valley and its surrounding hills covered with a pure white blanket of snow, except for the lake, which was not yet frozen and which looked almost black by contrast.

At least once each year Hedi watched winter work this special magic on the earth. It was a time when the scars caused by man and nature were forgiven by the Creator and briefly hidden from view by this marvelous blanket of white. So quiet was the early morning, and so beautiful, that even the wind was afraid to whisper, or the trees to shiver.

Now as she watched, living creatures began to stir. Dozens of wood fires sent their plumes of moisture and threads of thin blue smoke out of as many chimneys. A snowplow appeared on the road below, breaking the silence, and a bad-tempered blue jay began to enumerate his complaints. Gaining courage, the wind moved gently through the trees, sending showers of fluffy white crystals drifting down to the forest floor.

Hedi did not resent these intrusions. She knew it was intended to be thus. One experienced these moments of pure beauty and inspiration, and then, enlightened and strengthened, one needed to come down from the mountaintop and get to work.

With a sigh, she turned from the window just as Sam entered the room with her breakfast tray. "Good morning, Grand Lady," he said. "I thought I would find you here."

"Good morning, Great Wun," Hedi laughed, enjoying her well-worn joke. "As usual your timing is perfect. Have you had your breakfast?"

"Yes, I peeked in and guessed you would rather not be disturbed, so I went ahead and fed my own face. I hope I made a good guess."

"I think you always make good guesses," she answered. "Now sit down while I eat, and let's make plans for the weekend."

After they had combined their shopping lists, Sam asked if there was anything special she would like to do. He noted that once this light snowfall was cleared, no further problems with travel were expected for several days.

"If that proves to be true, I'd like to visit the Chapel In The Lake during the church hour tomorrow."

"I will be delighted to take you," Sam replied.

Sunday, December 23

No one knew how many residents of the valley died during those early months of Year Zero. Some bodies were found and were buried in marked graves. No doubt some of the missing left in search of loved ones in other areas and were not heard from again. Some had been buried in rock slides such as those that closed off normal drainage from the valley, causing the lake to form. Many — at least 50, and perhaps as many as a hundred — had been swept away by the mudslides that claimed little Ralph and the parents of Peter Smith Johnson, and these would still be buried beneath the lake bottom.

In normal times, a massive excavation would have been undertaken to recover the bodies, but in Year Zero there was neither equipment nor labor available for such an undertaking. Those who were still alive needed all of their time and energy to survive. Years later, when the level of the lake had stabilized and resources permitted, the good people of the valley undertook the creation of a memorial to show that the lost ones had not been forgotten.

Several former hilltops were now small islands in the lake. One of these was a lovely little island only about 200 yards from the western shore. The water between it and the mainland was of reasonable depth, and the memorial committee had chosen it as the most appropriate site. A footbridge had been constructed from the mainland, and in the center of the island, surrounded by towering pines, a chapel had been built in memory of the known and the unknown who lay beneath the lake.

It was built in traditional New England architectural style and painted the traditional white. In more recent times the town council had been able to provide stained-glass windows. It was here that Sam Wun brought Hedi Johnson that Sunday morning in December.

The chapel was small, being used mostly for prayer and meditation. Hedi sat midway between the altar and the back row of seats.

She listened intently as the minister read selections of scripture and gave a brief prayer. When he had gone, Hedi sat in deep thought, while others finished their meditation and departed quietly.

She slipped to her knees and besought the Creator to watch over her lost son, wherever in the universe he might be. She then said a prayer for Roy, and asked for guidance in continuing the work they had started together... work toward a better world... work for which he had given his life.

Finally, overwhelmed with her own loneliness, and with tears running down her cheeks, she prayed for help and understanding.

It was then that it happened.

First she felt a presence, the presence of someone dear to her.

Then she sensed, rather than heard, the kind, thoughtful words so typical of Roy.

"I will always be near when you need me. As for Ralph, he is no longer here. He is working now to help you and is preparing to pick up the torch when you finally lay it down. There are others who stand ready to help, including our Sally, who will surprise you.

"Mr. J sends you a token of his esteem, something to remind you he stands ready to help if needed. Use it to call him. If a person you love needs strength and advice, give it to that person with instructions to find a quiet place, hold the token tightly and ask for help and understanding. He will answer the call and give help if he can.

"New problems lie before you, but you are equal to the task, so do not worry, and remember that I love you and am happy in the knowledge that in good time we will be together again."

Hedi felt a light touch on her arm and a squeeze of her hand. A breeze ruffled her hair; then the presence was gone. She found that tears were drying on her cheeks. She dabbed at them.

When, filled with new resolve, she stood up, she found it awkward to maneuver into the aisle while keeping a proper grip on the crutches. Fortunately the ever-alert Sam came forward from the back of the chapel to help her.

He leaned over and picked up something from the floor.

"Your handkerchief, Grand Lady," he replied. "You dropped it when you entered the aisle."

"But I only have a piece of tissue, and it hasn't been out of my bag. Besides, this isn't a handkerchief," she said. "It is round like a shoulder patch, and has some kind of design on it. Let's take it outside where the light is better."

Outside, Hedi held the circle of cloth in the palm of her hand. It was pure white and appeared to be woven from lamb's wool. Seven symbols in royal purple were displayed evenly around its circumference, but with a vacant space at the top that could accommodate an eighth symbol. Another design appeared to be woven into the white background with very fine gold wire, but to see its detail one would need a magnifying glass.

"Have you any idea where it came from? Or what it means?" Sam asked.

"I don't know how it got in my hand or what the symbols mean," the Grand Lady answered, smiling happily, "but I know where it came from."

Back at her home, she told Sam what she had experienced.

"I was in the back of the chapel the entire time," he said. "I neither heard nor saw anything until you dabbed at the tears on your cheeks, and stood up to leave. Then when I came forward to help you, I saw you drop what I thought was your handkerchief."

Sam paused. "There was one other thing. When I leaned over to pick up this bit of cloth, I thought I caught the faint scent of roses. I thought it came from your hair, and now I seem to smell it again. Is the Grand Lady wearing perfume?"

"My sense of smell isn't what it used to be, and I assumed it was my imagination, but I thought I did smell roses. They were Roy's favorite flower, and his way of saying 'I love you'. He liked me to brush a little of the fragrance on my hair, and often he would do it for me. When he left me at the chapel, I thought a little breeze ruffled my hair, but it must have been his touch, leaving the scent of roses as his signature.

"Many times I have felt the comfort of Roy's presence. But this is the first time since his death he has talked to me in that kind but firm way I know so well. At the end, I felt the light touch on my arm and the quick little squeeze of my hand, touches that pictured Roy Johnson to me as clearly as if I had turned to find him sitting beside me."

"It is an exciting event," Sam said. "I am deeply honored that you shared it with me."

"It was a wonderful experience for me, Sam, but like so many things my husband did, it also had a purpose. And to uncover that purpose — to find its full extent, anyway — we will have to discover the meaning of this circle of cloth."

Sam thought about what she had said. "Are you saying you do know a part of his purpose?"

"Let's say that I know one purpose was to comfort and encourage me," Hedi replied. "Find us a magnifying glass, and we'll see what we can make of this magic piece of cloth with its mystical seven symbols in royal purple."

Magnification showed a stream of tiny gold arrows flowing in a clockwise direction from the vacant space at the top of the circle to the first symbol, and then in decreasing numbers around to the sixth symbol, beyond which there were no arrows. Instead a diminishing stream of tiny symbolic lightning bolts flowed from the vacant space at the top of the circle in a counter-clockwise direction, ending in a trickle at the second symbol.

The Grand Lady and the devoted Sam Wun spent the rest of the day trying to interpret the meaning of the seven symbols, but nothing seemed to make sense.

"It must contain a message of great importance," Sam said. "Perhaps it is in some sort of secret code. We have experts in that sort of thing in World Intelligence, and with your permission, I would like to challenge them to solve this one."

"You are welcome to try, as long as you don't start another story about my mystical experiences. You may photograph the symbols if you like, but the actual circle of cloth is to remain in my possession."

"Will you tell your daughter about this?" Sam asked.

"It will be the third week in January before Sally gets here. I will tell her then, but not until we have discussed all the other things on my agenda. She is rather sensitive about her father's death, you know. Subconsciously she seems to hold me responsible for it, and I don't know what her reaction will be. She may just conclude that her mother has gone off her rocker again."

40. Sally
January 15, Z 96

Sally shook her head. "I don't know what you asked me up here to talk about, mother, but I wish you'd get down to business. I can tell that something big is cooking, and you are driving me crazy letting me smell the roast, but not letting me taste the meat."

Hedi looked intently at her daughter, now a woman of one hundred years with cause to be proud of her own accomplishments. She had never asked her mother for help. Had, in fact, always seemed anxious that Hedi's fame not rub off on her. Hedi remembered a line from Old-Earth television where the young bride said "Mother, I'd rather do it myself." That fitted Sally to a tee.

Of course, Sally was always her father's daughter. That's why she had become a surgical technician — so she could serve with her father during the wars with the Lowland Pirates. They were always very close.

And Sally had always been bitter about her father's death. She blamed the surprise attack on the base hospital and the brutal massacre of its staff and patients on treason. Or if not treason, criminal negligence. She had never understood why Hedi had not used her considerable power and influence to see that more was done to identify the guilty one and bring him to justice. The fact that an intensive investigation had continued for years without reaching conclusive results made no difference to her. She wanted her mother to devote the region's full resources for as long as it might take.

Suddenly it dawned on Hedi that she had never fully explained to Sally why she had not pushed the search even more. This was something she should do at the first appropriate opportunity.

Sally's voice broke in on her thoughts. "Sorry to interrupt you, but I wanted to call you back before you got completely out of earshot. Want to tell me what you were thinking about?"

"Yes I do, but not now," Hedi said. "All right. You want to know what I really want to tell you. I am about to make one more try at solving the problem of classified information. I must stress: It is essential to the success of the project that our intentions not be disclosed prematurely."

"I am all ears," Sally said. "You know I would be delighted to see you succeed. I'm all for declassifying information. As you know very well, I can't see why *any* information is still classified."

"I know this will be difficult to discuss with you," Hedi said.

"... because the subject is classified," Sally said. "I know. I have heard it more than once."

"Heard it and rejected it. That's the other reason it will be difficult."

Sally shrugged. "Mother, you know how I feel, and how Eric feels. Nothing has happened to change our minds."

When the wars ended and the Period of Stability began, Sally applied for university training in the field of mental health. (And she had applied in Region Two, Hedi reflected proudly, to assure that she would not benefit from her mother's growing influence in Region Three.) While at the university, she met an associate professor named Eric Becker, who was not only the best educated person she had ever met, but a man with a purpose in life. He had a compelling devotion to the concept of individual freedom coexisting with a system of social justice. He believed there need be no conflict between his personal rights and the rights of the rest of society. He had studied all of the examples of success and failure that history could provide, and believed he had an approach that would work. He burned with the desire to sell his ideas to everyone.

Sally had been immediately attracted by his thinking, and he was immediately attracted by Sally.

It was not a whirlwind courtship. The loss of her father still hurt, and Sally was afraid to become too attached to anyone. Eric had persevered, however, and in due time they were married. It was a good match, Hedi conceded, despite the fact that Eric was some twenty years older than Sally. But then (she reminded herself) a

20-year age difference no longer meant quite what it had meant in Old-Earth days.

"You have run away from me again," Sally said, "but this time I can guess what you are thinking."

"And I can guess what you are guessing," Hedi replied. "You and Eric gave me a hard time for many years over the matter of classified information."

"It is a vital point," Sally said stubbornly. "Eric believes, and so do I, that individual freedom of speech and action are compatible with social justice, if there is trust and understanding. But to have trust and understanding, there must be full and open communication. This was not possible if discussion of certain important matters is forbidden by law."

"In principle, I agree with you."

"But when you were a member of the World Council and we were fighting to have all information declassified, your voice was not raised in our support."

"Full disclosure isn't always possible."

"I can see that, in theory. But if it isn't possible, the people need a rational explanation of the need for secrecy."

"I told you then and I tell you now, I agreed with you. I never opposed your efforts."

"No, your voice was not raised in opposition either. In fact, no one on the Council publicly disagreed with our position. They just kept on voting it down, and explaining that they were acting in the best interests of the New Earth."

"I know it isn't very satisfactory, Sally, particularly without an explanation."

"Eric finally gave up that approach and concentrated on teaching his philosophy. He says that in time, the written word will prevail."

"I hope it will," Hedi said cautiously. "I can tell you that the need for secrecy in certain areas has always been one of my greatest frustrations. Still is. I hope I can find a way to explain it to you."

Sam entered the room "Excuse me, Grand Lady. A telephone call for Sally Becker from Eric Becker."

"Perhaps you'd better take the call in the next room," Hedi said. Moved by a sudden mischievous impulse, she added, "I know how you youngsters like your privacy."

To her surprise, Sally smiled.

When Sally returned, she was obviously disturbed and excited.

"The call must have been important," Hedi said. "Is there a problem?"

"I'll tell you about it after lunch," Sally said.

"It's OK to talk in Sam's presence, if you wish. Another thing on my list to tell you is that Sam is now an officer with World Security Forces, and has been assigned by order of the president to protect me from all harm."

Sally looked startled. "In that case, he should hear all of it." She massaged one hand with the other, a gesture Hedi had watched her make for more years than she could remember. Always, she did that before taking a plunge of one kind or another.

"Just before I left home I had a call from Simon that started me wondering. He was off to an enthusiastic start as Region Two director for Aunt Martha's genealogy project, but had run into a puzzling situation. A man claiming to represent a very prominent person in Region Two presented him with a chart of that person's family tree dating back to Z-Minus-60. Simon was invited to examine it, and if he found it complete, he would not need to waste his time and the taxpayers' money doing further investigation. If he had any question about completeness or accuracy, he should call, and the missing information or validation would be supplied.

"Simon called me for advice. He said the material was remarkably thorough and complete, so much so that it added to his uneasy feeling about the whole affair. He did not want to mention the prominent person's name over the phone.

"I told him to call his boss, Aunt Martha, as that was what bosses were for. This he has done, and has followed her advice. The result has him very upset. Not being able to reach Aunt Martha right away, he called and unloaded on his father. Now Eric is excited and wants to dash out and fight someone, if he can figure out who to fight. I urged him to calm down and let Simon and Aunt Martha handle the problem."

"What did Martha advise him to do?" Hedi asked.

"She told him to contact the messenger, note the high quality of the work and thank him for the assistance. He should then add that while no problem was expected, he was obligated under the terms of his appointment to audit at least ten percent of the material against other sources of information. Simon followed this advice and was happy with the response. He was assured again that the charts were accurate, and that help would be gladly provided with any audit that might be required."

"Keep 'em guessing," Hedi murmured.

"Simon slept peacefully last night," Sally said, "but this morning he was called by the prominent personage himself. I am not clear on exactly what followed, because Eric was so excited, but Simon is said to feel that in a very smooth and careful way he had been offered a bribe if he stayed in line and threatened with bodily harm if he made waves in the wrong places. Simon will keep trying until he reaches Aunt Martha, and Eric feels you will hear from her before the day is done."

"Let's wait until we hear from Martha or directly from Simon," Hedi said.

"I am beginning to think we may have enemies after all," Sally said. "What do you think, Sam?"

"I believe it to be a strong possibility," Sam answered, "and it is most important that we keep our suspicions secret while seeking to learn the facts. I do thank you for sharing your story with me." Then he excused himself, saying he supposed that they had other things to discuss.

Hedi cleared her throat. "To continue our discussion of the classified information problem, I think it might help if I review a little history."

"It was the year Z 72 when I accepted the appointment to be the New Earth's second Grand Councilor, replacing Judge Mark Enslow. One condition was that he be engaged as consultant to the Judicial Council, and in that capacity he was of invaluable assistance to me until his death some fifteen years later.

"Shortly before he died, Mark told me that he considered the problem of classified information and the secret of the gravity car as the most important problem remaining to be dealt with. 'I wish I could advise you what to do,' he told me, 'but all I can do is urge you to keep trying. If solutions are not found, sooner or later internal dissension will grow to the point of threatening all that has been done.'

"I knew what Mark meant, and I promised to keep trying. I did try, but workable answers continued to elude me. It was my greatest frustration, and finally I resigned my post to give someone else a chance."

Hedi sighed. "Now it is clear, my dear Sally, that I cannot escape responsibility that easily. Win, lose, or draw, I must make one final attempt to deal with a rising tide of suspicion that citizens feel toward their government. I am now engaged in laying the ground-work for that effort. I know that there will be powerful opposition, but I will be able to depend on some powerful support."

"I'm not very powerful, Mother, but please put me on the list of those who want to help," Sally said earnestly.

Hedi looked thoughtfully at her daughter. This was not the way she had expected Sally to react. Roy was right; Sally was surprising her. Once more Hedi had the old feeling that destiny was about to have its way with her.

41. Understanding
January 16, Z 96

Martha's voice on the telephone was brisk and devoid of emotion. "Sally, I have been talking with my people in Region Two and wanted to let you know that Simon is doing a fine job. One prominent citizen there has saved him a lot of work by providing a complete history of the family and its many branches, going back more than 150 years. Simon was worried because the rules say he should audit at least ten percent of privately furnished material, so I suggested he check the last 20 years against government birth and death records. That will be easy to do and will meet the technical requirements. Of course we would both be very much surprised if any discrepancies are found."

Hedi could see that Sally was confused. She jumped in before Sally could say the wrong thing.

"It's nice that people are trying to help Simon with his job," she said innocently. "I told Sally and Eric he would do just fine, but when he ran into this little problem they were concerned because they're anxious for him to do a good job for you. We're glad to know it's not a significant problem."

"I do appreciate your calling," Sally said, finally getting her cue. "Is there any reason you shouldn't tell us the name of the family who are trying to be so helpful to Simon?"

"I understand they would not like to be seen as trying to curry favor with the government, and since I am not calling on a security line, I would rather not name them on the phone. No doubt Simon will tell you when he sees you. Now, unless you have other questions, Sally, I have a question for Hedi."

"I'm quite happy," Sally answered.

"What I need from you, dear sister, is an honest statement on how rapidly you are recovering from your surgery. It is the president who wants to know. I had a brief chat with him this morning. He doesn't want to push you at all, but would like to know if the doctor's estimate that you could go back to work on a part-time basis six months after the operation still holds."

"Yes, it does," Hedi answered. "In fact I am doing so well, I could return to the capital earlier if there is a need for it. What does Carlos want?"

"There is no great rush. He wants to schedule some appointments with people whose judgment he trusts. He is wrestling with the question of whether he should run for a second term and wants advice. I'll tell him what you said, and no doubt he will be in touch with you. I have to run now. Take good care of yourselves."

"Good-bye, and thanks for calling," Sally said. When Hedi had turned off the speaker, Sally said, "Now would someone please tell me what is going on here? Obviously you two were talking in some kind of code, and I was floundering in an effort to figure out what to do. I must say you don't lead a dull life. Are you always involved in stuff like this?"

"Not always," Hedi laughed, "and I think you did very well in entering into the spirit of the conversation. What your Aunt Martha was saying is pretty clear. Simon's experience with the prominent family is very significant in Martha's view, so much so that she has talked to the president about it. He may want to talk to both of us, if he thinks it ties in with my activities. In the meanwhile it is important that we not rock the boat. We must do nothing to alarm the prominent personage, or we may never learn what's going on — if anything *is* going on."

"She said all that?" Sally queried.

"She said all that," her mother answered, "and I expect she is hoping that you will help calm Eric down. It is necessary that all of us act as though nothing out of the ordinary has happened."

"I will call him tonight and tell him Martha has assured me that everything is all right," Sally responded. "Now can we get back to your story? I have some questions to ask once we get to the question period."

Hedi paused. "You may recall that in succeeding me as Grand Councilor, my old friend Ho Sun insisted I continue to head the ombudsman activity. Ever since the establishment of that organization, its reports show increasing interest in the matter of classified information. I saw interest turn to suspicion of the government, and more recently to active resentment. At some point, this will turn into confrontation."

Sally, she saw, was listening.

"For a long time I felt that only the key facts about the gravity car warrant continued classification. There were some who agreed with me, but others felt we should never assume the absence of external enemies. A small but effective group has held the balance of power. They claim that it must be all or nothing. Unless the gravity car is declassified, they oppose all declassification. I have never been able to understand their position, but I'm ready to accept it now, in view of the greater danger represented by this growing unrest.

"I hope I can swing enough votes to carry the day. But I know that when the evaluations are finally made, all facts will need to be available. The people will then have to decide what they believe. It's not as simple as you may think, and we may need several years to properly set the stage. Among those who agree with me are the president, your Aunt Martha, and Grand Councilor Ho Sun. Now you have it." Again, Hedi sighed. "I suppose you have some questions."

"Like just about everyone else, my first question is — why can't you tell us about the gravity car?" Sally asked without delay. "I can understand why the government might want to forbid everyone else from producing or owning these remarkable contraptions, but what would be so bad about explaining in a general way how they work, and who invented them in the first place?"

Hedi bit her lip in frustration. "I know you find it nearly impossible to accept, but we do not have permission to say who invented them, and we cannot explain how they work."

"Then tell me why you cannot reveal such a harmless thing," Sally demanded, a note of disbelief in her voice.

"Because," Hedi said very softly, "we do not know how they work."

"But surely Peter knows, as well as all the others who put them together and service them. The president must know. You must know."

"None of us know. I can tell you no more. I have said too much already, and may have violated the security laws, in a technical sense at least, by telling you as much as I have."

"I will not repeat it to anyone," Sally promised. "Of course even I find it hard to believe that none of you know, and if you told the general public what you have just told me, hardly anyone would believe you."

Sally paused as the significance of this idea sunk in. "That must be why the problem is so frustrating," she said. "If you tell the truth no one will believe it."

"That's the large part of the problem," Hedi conceded. "I can say no more."

Sally stayed with her mother for two more days, and they finally talked about the sensitive subjects they had avoided for so very many years. She told of the trauma resulting from her father's death, and Hedi knew the time had come to explain as best she could the circumstances surrounding his murder.

"Of course you know the historical facts concerning your father's death," she said. "After all, they're part of the history taught in the schools, and they are correct as far as they go."

"Is there something more?" Sally asked very softly.

"There is. You remember that the pirates attacked the base hospital by sea. Everybody has heard of the story told by a captured enemy officer — a story of a daring patrol of mountain climbers who worked their way up the mountain and into a position behind our northern observation base on a dark foggy night.

"He said they attacked before the fog lifted and killed all of the base personnel, some twenty persons in all. Then they waited for the patrols to come in and wiped them out one by one. His story was well-documented with detail, including a description of how they broke our code and were able to send in 'all is well' reports while they were unloading their ships and organizing for the attack."

"I never believed the story," Sally said, tight-lipped.

"And you were right not to," Hedi said.

"But you always said..."

"Sally, I'm trying to tell you now. That attack was the work of a traitor or a spy. I know it was, because your father told me so, and because I saw the man's body."

"Why didn't you tell anybody?"

"I did tell one person. I didn't tell anybody else because your father told me not to.

"You've heard his last words, many times. I'm sure I don't need to repeat them to you. But there were a few others I never passed on to you. He told me that the man he'd killed was a traitor. He said I should tell Hugh Scott, and no one else, that there must be others."

Unexpectedly, after all this time, Hedi found her eyes stinging. Perhaps it was because she could see the unshed tears in her daughter's eyes. "His last words were for you and Peter, you know."

"I know," Sally choked out, and then they were sitting together, both crying silently.

"Here," Hedi said at last, pushing the box toward her daughter. "Tissues. Very handy things to have around, sometimes."

Sally was squeezing her hand. "What a terrible experience it must have been for you. I'm sorry to have forced you to relive it, but I am so thankful that you have told me."

"There's a little more. I did tell Hugh Scott, and no one else. The general also felt that we would find more traitors before we were done. 'The traitor we know is dead,' he said, 'and if there are more, we have a better chance of finding them if they think we don't know.' I suppose it no longer matters, but I have kept these things to myself, as General Scott advised. If he discovered any of the other traitors, he did not live to tell me about it. One wonders if he was killed because he was close on their trail."

She sat silent, remembering her friend. "Hugh did learn that the traitor Roy shot had been in command of our northern observer base, and no doubt had betrayed his own men by leading them into an ambush. He also learned that the man's true name was not Captain Martin, his identity papers having been forged or stolen."

"But, Mother, when you were in power, why didn't you look for these traitors?"

"Honey, we did. We looked as well and as quietly as we could. But after a while, when we found nothing, we concluded that there was nothing to find. The New Earth has only so many resources.

Without some sign that we weren't on a wild-goose chase, I couldn't justify an open-ended expenditure of those resources."

Hedi bit her lip. "I must say, I was never fully convinced that we were truly free of traitors. My left brain said: They're gone. On all the evidence, they're gone. My right brain disagreed, but had no evidence to go on until very recently."

"I'm so glad I came, and I'm so glad we talked," Sally said. She stood up. "I must get back now, and try to calm Eric down until you go public with your project. Once he knows and understands the facts, you will have another fighter in your corner."

Hedi took a deep breath. "There is one more thing before you go," she said. "I have a message for you from your father."

Sally stood speechless for a moment and then dropped back into her chair.

"Don't say anything until you hear the story," her mother said, "and let me call Sam to help with the telling, since he was there."

Half an hour later Hedi and Sam had finished describing the experience and laid the strange circle of cloth on the desk for Sally's examination. "I no longer know the nature of your beliefs on such things," Hedi said, "but you have heard the story. You may laugh now, if you wish."

"I'm not laughing," Sally said. "I only ask that you let me help Sam try to discover the meaning of the seven symbols."

Sam did not wait for the Grand Lady to answer, but with a little bow to Sally, he said, "Sam would be honored."

42. Looking for Clues
March 18, Z 96

W ith the temperature hovering around freezing, the heavy wet March snow that had fallen during the night clung to the tree limbs, bending some to the ground and breaking others with its weight. The Grand Lady appeared to be watching the scene outside her study window, but actually it was not an inspiring picture, and she had given it only brief attention. Instead, her mind was busy reviewing the events of the past several months and making plans. It was time she got back to her office in the capital to make her annual review of the ombudsman reports and prepare a summary for the president.

A polite tapping on the door interrupted her thoughts. It was Sam, and she sensed excitement beneath his placid exterior.

"I have a routine message from World Security granting me three days leave for rest and recreation in recognition of my arduous task of protecting the Grand Councilor-at-large. My replacement arrives tomorrow."

"And your replacement will be your cousin Tu Wun, now widely known as Agent Countdown," Hedi suggested.

"As usual, the Grand Lady is right," Sam said. "Would you care to risk another guess?"

"If you insist. But it will only upset you if I am right and it will upset me if I am wrong," she replied. "You will help me by letting your mind go blank.

"That's good! Now into that void introduce one thought... the real reason your cousin is coming."

After a pause: "That's splendid, Sam. You're very good at sending. But you really should try to improve your receiving skills."

"I should know better than to ask, but what did I say?"

"You said Tu Wun was bringing me a message from the president. Knowing that, it's easy to guess that you'll choose to travel to the world capital for your rest and recreation, taking with you my reply. Did I overlook anything of importance?"

"Nothing except telling me how you do it," Sam replied.

"Some call it nonverbal communication. I learned about it from an ancient enlightened holy man at the Old-Earth survival camp of Sam Theos. Some day I'll try to explain it to you.

"But enough fun and games. I have a feeling important developments are in the air. Ralph Woodbine is coming to talk to me this morning. He said he wants to talk history, but his tone of voice told me he has something more exciting to report. I suggested he be prepared to stay overnight if necessary."

"An excellent idea," Sam replied. "I hope he can stay until my cousin Tu arrives."

Hedi saw Ralph land his father's gravity car and hurry toward the house. Even at that distance, he looked like a man who had not slept. She went back to her desk in the study, but before she could sit down, Sam was announcing his arrival.

"Grand Lady," Ralph said, "I shall be forever thankful that I was able to see you so promptly."

"All right," she said crisply. "What did you learn?"

"As mother said, Grandmother Scott's letters contain those speculations and convictions she did not wish to disclose publicly; they were for her daughter's ears only. Mother let me make copies of the ones I thought most pertinent, and I will leave a copy of them with you."

"Thank you; but summarize for me."

"One letter states that the last few pages of General Scott's diary, the ones that were torn out, contained his belief that the Red Prince and most of his official family were not dead, but had found a hiding place somewhere in Region One — New America South. Others had concealed their identity so well they were able to blend in with the general population, and in many cases they had attained positions of influence and power. General Scott believed most of these were in Regions One and Three.

"Another letter expressed Grandmother's belief that although her husband had had a premonition of death while recovering from his wounds, he was not murdered while in the hospital as some thought, but died as a result of a blood clot in accordance with the medical reports. She wrote that Major Rogers, the last person known to see the general alive, was completely trustworthy, and was hot on the trail of the Red Prince. She believed he was probably ambushed and killed by the Prince's agents. She said Hugh had told her of Major Rogers' assignment the day before he died. At that time he also asked her to read the last few pages in his diary."

He looked at her intently.

"A third letter expressed an opinion that has me winging. Grandmother Scott believed that Grandmother Woodbine learned a great deal more about all of this from some source than she told. Mary Scott thought she remained silent because she feared harm would befall herself or her family. Due to her poor health, Grandfather Woodbine is fiercely protective of Maria, but with your permission, I will discuss the problem with my father and see if he has any ideas."

"By all means talk with your father about it," Hedi replied. "All of our information points in the same direction, but none of it is conclusive. I have just learned that Tu Wun will be here tomorrow with a message from President Fernandez. I suppose Carlos would like to know when I am going to start the review of the ombudsman reports, but there are easier ways of finding that out than sending a messenger, so there must be something more. Can you stay over until he arrives? Then we can consider the news you bring along with whatever he may have to contribute."

"I can stay over," Ralph replied.

* * *

Tu Wun handed the Grand Councilor-at-large a note from President Fernandez. She glanced at it, then read it aloud. "I understand you are planning to start your annual review of the ombudsman reports in the near future. Please let me know when you have established the date of your arrival in the capital, as I would like your advice on a personal matter affecting my future career."

"I will prepare a reply," Hedi said "but first I would like to hear the rest of the president's message."

"You assume correctly that there is more," Tu said. "First, the work of World Security has done little more than confirm Ralph's conclusions. The direction of the protest movement comes from someone located somewhere in Region One. I think we can argue that it could be a remnant of the Red Prince organization, and we feel that the location is on the mainland rather than on one of the thousands of islands located in the Region. Beyond that we have nothing to go on as yet. The ombudsman review could provide useful information."

"The review will take about two months of full-time work," Hedi replied.

"There is one thing more," Tu said. "I was told to advise you that your son Peter has requested a meeting with the supplier of the gravity cars to discuss our problem and report the planned drive to declassify the information pertaining to them. The president does not know what to expect, but suggests you be prepared for an emergency meeting to determine our policy. I am not privileged to know who the supplier is so I cannot comment further on the matter."

"Who will deliver my answer to Carlos?"

"It is arranged that Sam will deliver the written answer and any verbal answer," Tu replied.

"I will have a note for you in half an hour, Sam," Hedi said. "In the meanwhile listen carefully to the story Ralph has to tell and relay it to the president. Tell Carlos that Ralph and I will tackle the problem of obtaining possible information from Maria Woodbine. Also tell him I am prepared to respond to any call he may make for an emergency meeting."

Sam departed for the world capital shortly after he heard Ralph Woodbine's story.

* * *

"I have an hour or so before I must leave," Ralph said. "I have the start of an idea of how I might approach my Grandmother. Would you like to discuss it?"

"Indeed I would," the Grand Lady replied.

"Everyone says Maria Woodbine talks very little to anyone. She infers that paralysis makes it difficult for her to talk, but I think she talks quite freely to Grandfather Woodbine when no one else is around. I know she reads a great deal, and she listens a lot. When I go to talk with Grandfather, she always wheels her chair in to listen.

"I see this as a way to talk to her by talking to him. I have a reason to talk with him because I want to start work on his life story. Based on past conversations, I have written a condensed summary of his most impressive work, the work that led to the control and repair of the immune system. I plan to ask him to review it, and then as time permits we will expand it into a life story. I know Grandmother will be there listening as Grandfather and I talk. The trick will be to turn the conversation in a direction that will cause her to reveal whether or not she has knowledge of the Red Prince."

"I think you have a good start on an idea," Hedi said. "You might consider telling them that you believe the Red Prince is still alive, and that you intend to prove it.

"Of course this is pretty strong medicine, and you had best talk it out with your parents first."

"Certainly it is a place to start, and I will go to work on it," Ralph said.

43. A Message
March 30, Z 96

"**I** had a call from Martha last night," Hedi told Sam. "It was very strange. One of the pots we had simmering on the fire must have boiled over."

"Would the Grand Lady care to tell me what she said?"

"She didn't say much — just that she knew I was moving to the world capital temporarily, and knew there was plenty of room on the gravity liner picking me up. She just wanted to tell me she'd hitched a ride so we could exchange gossip on the way back."

Sam nodded thoughtfully. "We had scheduled a staff gravity car, not a liner."

"And they were going to pick me up at two o'clock. Martha said they would arrive at one. And she said something quite out of character. Did you notice it?"

"I think so. Your sister said she came along in order to exchange gossip — and the clue is that even if she were guilty of gossiping, she would never admit it."

"Precisely," Hedi said. "In fact, a brilliant deduction."

The liner landed quietly beside the cottage at exactly one o'clock. Hedi went out without delay: A World Government gravity liner always attracted a lot of attention, and she wanted to get it on its way as soon as possible.

She met Martha half way to the liner. "I just want to speak to Sam," Martha said, giving her a peck on the cheek. "Go ahead and get aboard. The captain is waiting for you."

The liner had extended its power lift, a device used for VIP's and for cripples. Hedi supposed that she qualified on both counts and stepped onto the lift platform.

She stepped off into the cabin, to be met by a very distinguished gentleman in a captain's uniform greeting her with a graceful bow. "Welcome aboard, Grand Councilor-at-large," he said. "My superiors send their respects, and I am delighted to finally meet you."

For a moment Hedi was speechless. Then she said, "You are Max

Fact Banker, the robot envoy. We have met twice before. Don't you remember?"

"Ah, but that was my father. He is now retired and also sends his regards. I am Max Fact, Jr., a new generation robot. Today I am having a little fun operating this liner. It was a way to contact you without arousing suspicion." As gallant as any diplomat could be, the new Max escorted her to her seat. "As soon as your sister returns we will take off; then we can talk," he said.

Martha returned in short order. "I had to run in to deliver a message to Sam Wun from his cousin, the security officer," she told Hedi shortly. "An expert is being sent to see if your home is still free of bugs. My office in the capital is also being checked. Several devices have been found in your office and in Ho Sun's office and apartment."

While Hedi was absorbing that fact, the liner took off, lifting straight up and climbing rapidly above the thin clouds.

"Seeing Max Jr. was a surprise," Hedi said.

"I've had a ball talking to him about the Elustreons," Martha said. "He is more human than a lot of humans I know. The people of The Five Central Planets must be remarkable. I wish I could visit them."

Out of the corner of her eye, Hedi saw the door to the flight deck open. A tall, handsome man appeared. She got out of her seat and they threw their arms around one another.

"Peter! Oh, Peter!" she exclaimed. "I am so glad to see you. But what are you doing here? And who else is on board to surprise me?"

"Your friend Ho Sun and a security officer who happens to be Sam Wun's cousin from Region Four. I believe you know him. Officially, he is present as a gravity-liner pilot. As you must suspect, we have important things to discuss."

"I knew they were important, but now I sense they are urgent."

Peter was always serious. His expression now became downright solemn. "As always, Mother, you have a feel for the facts. 'Urgent' is a good term. 'Critical' might be more accurate. We would like to meet with you and Aunt Martha in the conference room on the flight deck as soon as you are ready."

Martha was right behind Hedi. "We are ready," she said.

"Since Ho Sun is the senior World Government official present," Peter said, "I believe it would be appropriate for him to chair this meeting. Time is short, so I suggest we stick to the major questions."

"I agree," the Grand Councilor replied. "Yesterday the president dropped into my office to suggest that I be present on this trip. He told me that three nights ago the envoy had appeared on the presidential gravity liner with an official message from his government for the president and Peter Johnson. I understand the envoy is here to repeat it for our benefit."

"That is correct," Max said. "My superiors are aware of an organized movement to force your government to declassify all remaining documents and make them available to the public. Most of the participants in this movement have honest motives, but the organizers have only one objective... to learn the secret of the gravity cars. They intend to use gravity cars to seize power and convert the World Government into a dictatorship."

"They couldn't learn to manufacture them, of course," Peter said.

"No, but you heard me tell the president that the threat of them seizing existing vehicles may force my government to intervene."

"How?" Martha asked.

Max, Jr. appeared to temporize. "You know that an attempt to disassemble the critical components of a gravity car would cause it to self-destruct. This would take place with great violence, causing destruction of any structures and people in the vicinity."

"Yes, we have been told that," Martha said tensely. Hedi could see that Martha, too, was waiting for the other shoe to drop.

"But this you have not been told: We are able to destroy these vehicles by remote control if necessary."

Hedi found herself holding her breath, waiting to see where Max, Jr. was leading.

"My superiors do not wish to cause loss of life, however. Therefore they have ordered me to convey this request: All gravity vehicles in your possession are to be returned within the next three years."

This brought Hedi to her feet. "Do we have the right to appeal this decision?"

"I will need to know the grounds," Max, Jr. said calmly.

"Your superiors must know that it will be most difficult to come up with alternatives to the gravity car in such a short time. And we'll need time to gather popular understanding. If we don't handle this carefully, we could wind up facing civil war. If the Elustreons wish to avoid bloodshed, they will not trigger such an event."

"One moment," the envoy said. Hedi knew the envoy of the UFCP's was receiving additional instructions from his superiors.

Presently he said, "The Central Committee of The Union of Five Central Planets has great respect for the persons sitting at this table, and will listen to any appeal they care to make. They also feel responsibility for your well-being because they have subjected you to great risk by entrusting the gravity car to your control. It is one of my duties to continue to ensure your protection."

"Continue?" Ho Sun asked. "Have there been attempts?"

"Yes," Max replied. "Of course, Peter has been at greatest risk. My security forces have taken care of four attempts to kidnap him, and two attempts on his life. We have ways of making people and things disappear into space. It is unnerving to have one's agents continually disappear without a trace, and the efforts to harm Peter have stopped for the moment."

"You are very efficient," Peter said. "I only knew of one attempt to kill me."

"That's one more than *I* knew of," Hedi said ominously.

Peter looked slightly sheepish. "Didn't want to worry you, Mother," he muttered. To Max, he said, "Could your government see giving us five years? It may be that we could handle it in five years."

"Such a request would receive full consideration, but it should be accompanied by a plan of action with a reasonable chance of success. Perhaps it would be best to leave you alone for a little while to discuss this problem I have so abruptly dumped in your laps."

He looked around at their grim faces. "Please be assured that the Elustreons wish to be helpful. You should be aware, however, that they learned long ago that great harm sometimes flows from good intentions, when one society meddles unduly in the affairs of another. Please call me when you are ready." He let himself out of the stateroom.

Ho Sun looked at the minister of transportation and gravity-car czar.

"Peter, you suggested we might be able to handle the problem if we had five years instead of three. Would you be good enough to tell us what you had in mind?"

Peter nodded. "Naturally, ever since Max briefed the president and me, I've been thinking about what we could do. I think our best approach is to expand light-plane production. We've done a lot of the groundwork in the past 15 years. In fact, our past efforts put us in a pretty good position."

He raised his eyebrows. "A suspiciously good position, you might almost say. Sometimes I feel like the outline of what happens to us is already laid down somewhere, and all we're doing is filling in detail."

Hedi smiled at him. "I've often had the same feeling, Peter, but that's not my understanding of how things work."

Ho Sun said, "Peter, do proceed, if you please. What do you have in mind?"

"Well, sir, you know we've spent a lot of time, these last 15 years, building Old-Earth versions of the single-engine light plane, redesigned to burn alcohol."

"Yes, of course. We needed to counter growing public demand to use the gravity car for pleasure and sporting purposes."

Peter nodded again. "And petroleum products are too scarce and expensive; we had to go with alcohol. Well, we're past much of the experimentation stage. If we had the airports and decent hardened runways they had a hundred years ago, we could produce large transport aircraft. But we don't."

"There was never the need," Ho Sun said.

"Not when you can land the largest of these things in my backyard," Hedi said.

"Perhaps the outlines of my idea become apparent," Peter said. "We have built a few twin-engine propeller planes designed to carry six to ten persons. These could be built in large numbers, if needed. Given time, we can develop large multi-engine aircraft to replace many of the uses of the gravity car."

"Not jets, I suppose," Martha said.

"Old-Earth jet aircraft remain beyond our capability," Peter said with regret.

"The technical knowledge is lost?"

"It isn't that. The problem is, the materials and equipment going into one of those old jets was produced by hundreds of specialized high-tech industries. We can't afford to restore those industries. Even if we could, we don't have the hundreds of thousands of skilled workers needed to man them.

"Besides, we lost most of our oil fields and refineries in the Year Zero. How would we restore that industry, too?"

"You have convinced us," Ho Sun said. "But in the past you have told me that alcohol is not the answer, either."

Peter shrugged. "Our alcohol is mostly a product of agriculture and, as such, it competes with the production of food for our people."

"Grimmer and grimmer," Hedi said. But she smiled as she said it: She had faith in her adopted son.

"Well, with all of this in mind, we have been working to develop a hydrogen energy system. We hope to skip over the Old- Earth jet engine and go directly to ram jets, or to rockets, for high-speed long-distance transport."

"I seem to recall," Martha said, "that the earth once supported a population of the present size without benefit of any mechanical transport whatever. They made extensive use of the oceans and other bodies of water; they developed some pretty efficient sailing ships. Things were a lot slower in those days, but what's wrong with that?"

"There is nothing wrong with it, Aunt Martha, provided the people will accept the added safety hazards, the higher costs, and the much longer time required in getting from one place to another. But let me remind you that travel on the high seas is more dangerous now than it was when Columbus set sail for America. Mother Nature still mounts ferocious storms; massive tidal waves destroy any ship caught between deep blue water and our limited number of safe harbors. After nearly a century, they still come rising up from the continental shelves at a rate of 25 to 30 a year. We can rely on water transport to a greater extent than now, but it will not be a popular substitute for the great gravity car freighters and the fast liners we now have."

"What other hope can you hold out?"

"I believe we can develop land transport and the old prop plane technology to the point of getting by without the gravity car on the short hauls. I think it is possible to do this in five years, though I would much prefer to have ten."

Ho Sun shifted uneasily in his chair. "You say there is something we can do. This is encouraging. But you point out the magnitude of the task. This is discouraging." He turned to Hedi. "Perhaps the wisdom and perception of the Grand Councilor-at-large can help us."

"God help us if that's all we have to lean on," Hedi said. "The big problem that I see in Peter's approach is motivating the people to once again tighten their belts and give these projects priority over improving their immediate standard of living. But how can we possibly obtain their support without being able to explain to them where the gravity cars came from, and the promises we made in order to get them, and the reasons why we must now give them up? Unless we can bridge this gap in understanding, I can imagine violence in the streets."

"What's more," Peter said, "I can see the people demanding to know how Peter Johnson could have had control of the gravity cars for all these years and be so stupid as not to understand how they work or how to build them."

"Speaking as one who has never before been involved in an official discussion of the gravity car," Martha said, "I can say that I, for one, do not understand why we are not allowed to explain how it works or why we should be forbidden to manufacture our own."

"I suggest we make a list of questions for the envoy," Ho Sun said, "I will start with the one Martha just asked."

"Ask if they have any technology they are willing to reveal that will help us bridge the gap caused by this abrupt withdrawal of the gravity vehicles," Peter proposed.

"Good question," Ho said. "Give me some more."

Hedi found herself looking at the ceiling of the small room, an old habit. "We need time to consider how to respond to the UFCP," she said. "A detailed study of the reports of my ombudsman organization should indicate the breadth and depth of public dissatisfaction. I would need three or four months to complete such an analysis."

Ho Sun said, "President Fernandez and I have put together a small but very competent intelligence group to identify some of the leaders who are promoting the public protests. We have a few leads now, but it will take some time to fully penetrate the upper level of authority in the organization. One thing you should know. At least one of them is a member of the World Council, and we know her name. We believe there is a second member but do not know who it is. I tell you this to indicate the care you must exercise in discussing these matters."

"Martha and I think we also know the name of the woman you just mentioned," Hedi said to Ho Sun. "When there is time, I suggest we compare notes."

"We should be pooling our findings," Martha suggested. "For example, in my genealogy project I have already run into forged birth and death records. I would like to concentrate on a few names that are suspected of being a part of the underground. Perhaps I might find evidence their records have been tampered with in some fashion. Perhaps my work might serve to identify other suspects."

"A good idea," Ho replied. "All things considered, I believe we should ask Max for six months to consider our response." Hedi, Martha, and Peter indicated their agreement, and Peter called Max on the flight bridge, asking him to return to the conference room.

The envoy listened without interruption while Ho Sun summarized the group's discussion and stated their questions. He said, "The UFCP's Central Council understands your problems and your need for time to assess them. Your request for six months' delay in giving your response meets with their approval. Peter Johnson's question about bridging technology will be taken under advisement, and an answer given within thirty days. In answer to the questions raised by the highly respected Martha Carlton, you are entirely free to reveal all you know about gravity car technology and to build them if you can. My government asks only for the return of the vehicles it supplied."

"But I don't know anything to reveal," Martha said.

"We have told Peter Johnson all that wisdom permits. He is free to pass it along to you," the Envoy replied.

"We thank you and your government for the understanding shown," Ho Sun stated. "If there is no more business to discuss, the meeting is adjourned."

"I have one more item of very important business," Max stated. "In order for you to feel the emotions flowing from a living person, this message is coming to you from the chairman of the central council. I am serving as a receiver and transmitter of the message."

There was a brief pause and then a voice they had never heard before came from the lips of Max Fact, Jr.

The voice... if it was a voice... was rich in understanding and kindness. Behind it one sensed a being of great knowledge, knowledge tempered by the wisdom of maturity and the experiences of living. It saturated the room and surrounded the earth people with its message.

"To Hedi, and Martha, and Ho, let me say we have watched as you prepared to meet the challenges of catastrophic change. We watched you survive the first day of the catastrophe, while one quarter of the earth's people perished. We watched you gather your strength to endure the horrors of the month that followed, when half of those remaining died from the violence and from exposure and starvation. We watched as you became leaders and organizers in that first year; a year that saw the oceans rise and the land sink; a year that ended with only one tenth of the Old Earth's population alive.

"We saw you blend compassion with the necessity for survival in the period of struggle and doubt that followed, a period of suffering and death stemming from man's inhumanity to man. You picked yourselves up from the depths of despair when friends and family were taken from you. You continued the fight, and you led in the successful effort to preserve the constructive advances made by thousands of past generations.

"For all of this we admire you, and we are grateful. You have done your job. You deserve an alternative to leading another struggle with the forces of destruction which have managed to hide in pockets of rot that still exist in your bright new world. Please listen with care to our envoy as he presents this alternative. It is a project of much importance; do not make a quick decision. Wait and include it in the overall response you will give us six months hence. Now may the Creator bless you and grant you wisdom."

They could feel the presence of the chairman fading from the room; then out of the silence came the envoy's voice, "When you are ready, I will complete my assignment," Max said.

"We are ready," Ho Sun said.

"One hundred thousand years ago, the Elustreons discovered a planet with an oxygen atmosphere and a carbon chemistry not too unlike that of planet earth. In size it is slightly larger than your earth, and its surface temperature and atmospheric composition are within the range of human tolerance.

"At the time of discovery, it was completely covered with water, but internal forces and mild volcanic activity caused land to appear above the sea a few thousand years thereafter. It is relatively unmarred by meteorite impacts, and it spins smoothly on an upright axis. It rotates around its sun on an almost circular orbit once every four hundred of your days. It is a beautiful and peaceful planet. Marine life is well developed and vegetation is beginning to appear, but birds and mammals have not yet evolved.

"The Elustreons have long studied this planet. They would like to colonize it with the best of the Earth's birds and mammals, and with carefully selected earth people. They would like to place the three of you in charge of the project. You would be free to select up to one thousand earth people to help you, and these could include your loved ones. No one would be taken without his consent, and of course transport and other technical support would be furnished by the Elustreons."

Martha could no longer restrain herself. "It sounds so exciting, but I cannot see how it could work. We are now very advanced in years, and it would take a very long time to get us there. We would all be dead."

"Not at all," Max replied. "The advanced state of medical technology achieved by the Elustreons would enable them to assure you of another two hundred years of life. A recent breakthrough in the physical sciences now makes it possible for us to travel in time's third dimension. This changes the entire complexion of space travel. My father, the first robot envoy, was in transit to the earth for over one hundred years. Fifty years ago I was sent here in just four months, and I understand that today you could be taken to this new virgin planet in a matter of about six weeks."

"How fascinating it would be, but I have responsibilities here. It will be a tough decision," Martha sighed.

The envoy paused for a moment and then said, "My government does not belittle your value in dealing with the crisis developing in the New Earth, but you have other strong leaders who should be able to handle the problem."

"It would be dishonest to consider ourselves indispensable," Hedi said, "but your government may not fully appreciate the delicacy of the timing, and the promises we have made to others."

"I have passed along all of the information I have," Max replied, "but of course there may be facts of which I am unaware."

"I think we are overwhelmed by the questions you have raised and need time to think," Hedi said.

"This is understandable," Max replied. "We have agreed that you need more time, but before I go, are there any questions you wish to ask?"

"There will be a thousand when I have recovered from the shock," Ho Sun replied, "but at this moment I can think of nothing."

"You will have another chance in three months. I will arrange it through Peter." Abruptly, with a smile and a wave of his hand, Max was gone.

Peter broke the silence that followed. "We will be landing at the capital in ten minutes, and I plan to stay out of sight." He gave Hedi a hug. "See you again soon."

"There's much work to be done," Hedi said. "There has to be a way to outsmart these termites in our society." She turned to Ho Sun. "How do we keep in touch with each other, and how do we go about conferring with the president?"

"I will arrange for us to see each other every week or ten days," Ho said. "The president is taking responsibility for making contact with us in ways not likely to arouse suspicion."

"This has been the most exciting day I have experienced in a long time," Martha said. "You know I will not abandon the ship or desert my friends as long as I am needed here. Nevertheless, I do find this new planet idea fascinating."

44. Maria Woodbine
June 17, Z 96

For as long as she had known him — which was all of his short lifetime — Hedi had known that Ralph Woodbine was by nature serious-minded. But his expression today went far beyond serious-ness. He looked shaken. His first request, before even sitting down, was that Sam be allowed to remain in her study while Ralph told her what he had learned. Hedi nodded and motioned them to sit.

"Now I have heard my grandmother's story," Ralph Woodbine said simply, "and I came immediately to you. I fear that her story may have great significance to our World Government and to you per-sonally. I am embarrassed that, despite your warnings, I so badly underestimated the ruthless strength of those trying to destroy our young democracy."

That seemed beyond comment. Hedi waited. As always, Ralph proceeded in an orderly fashion.

"As we discussed, I told the story of the Red Prince to my grandfather, in Grandmother Woodbine's presence. She sat in si-lence and without emotion until I got to the part about his abuse of his wife, Maria. Then she began to tremble, and motioned to Grand-father to take her to her room. I told him the rest of the story, and he said he would tell it to her when she was feeling better."

"When was that?"

"Two weeks ago. I told Mother about it, and she went up the following week to check on the situation. Grandmother had nothing to say, but Grandfather said she had been unable to sleep since I was there, that she seemed unable to get the story of the Red Prince off her mind. Mother said that I had sent a copy of the story to the president, asking if he objected to its publication. She said that the president wanted to talk with me about it, and then added that I thought the Red Prince was still alive.

"Mother told them she had urged me to tell them the story before they heard it on the news. Again Grandmother became agitated and was taken to her room. Nothing more was said about the matter that day, but Mother called me at the university two days ago and said Grandmother wanted to see me as soon as possible. Mother picked me up that night, and by sunrise Maria Woodbine had finished telling us an incredible story. One that leaves me feeling sick at the brutal treatment my grandmother received."

Woodbine glanced at Hedi's security officer. "The first thing to say is that Grandmother Woodbine told us where to find a copy of the missing pages of General Scott's diary. It is...."

"Stop where you are," Sam ordered. "Such knowledge places all of you in great danger. With your permission, Grand Lady, I wish to call my cousin in security. He will arrange for special protection. We have a code. They have enlisted my assistance should anything of this nature arise." Hedi agreed, and Sam was gone. She paced the room, and Ralph sat in silence until he returned.

"I apologize," Sam said, "but I felt there was no time to lose. Please proceed, Mr. Woodbine."

"The second thing is that my grandmother did not crash into a ravine and break her back. She was tortured and pushed over an embankment because she would not reveal the whereabouts of the Scott papers."

"Dear God!" Hedi gasped. "They will come back and kill her if they know she has talked."

"She has lived with that fear for many years, not for herself alone, but for her entire family." Hedi watched Ralph wipe his eyes. "Shall I fill in some of the detail?"

Hedi turned to Sam Wun. "I think Noe Singh should be alerted to this at once, and she should advise the president. I want to be certain they are available as soon as we hear the rest of the story. They should advise us on what means of communication we should use."

"Even as we speak, this is being done," Sam said. "We should have instructions within the hour."

"Please proceed, Ralph."

"As you know, Grand Lady, Maria Woodbine was dedicated to serving the people of the New Earth," Ralph continued. "She was skilled in the political arts and was an enthusiastic proponent of workable approaches for making this earth a better place. She served two terms as governor of this region, the post you once held; then she was elected to the World Council.

"One evening while she was working late in her office in the world capital she heard a knock. She opened the door and was astonished to see a man crouched in the hallway next to one wall. 'Please turn out your light and let me come in,' he said. 'We are both in danger if I am seen with you.'

"Naturally, she asked who he was and why she shouldn't call the security guards.

"He said, 'I am, or I was, Major Thomas Rogers, special aide to General Hugh Scott and probably the last man to see him alive. You must believe me. Please let me in and hear my story, then you can have me arrested if you wish.'

"She let him in. She turned all lights off except a small night light, but she could still see that the man was poorly dressed, needed a bath, and appeared half starved. He had lost one eye and his hands looked as though all of his fingers had been broken. There were other scars on his face and head, and one leg appeared to be crippled in some fashion. He belonged in the hospital, she thought, not in her office. Before she could speak, he began to talk.

"He said that General Scott, while in the hospital, had sent for him. He said the general had a premonition that he might not recover from his wounds. He said the general told him he had given his diary to his wife, and had told her to turn a copy of it over to the World president. He handed the major six pages cut out from the back of the diary. They were filled with the assumed names and the location of leaders of the Lowland Pirates who had gone into hiding, as well as the names of many of their secret agents.

He told the major — at least, that's what the man told my grandmother — that he was ready to spring the trap on the lot of them as soon as he could learn the whereabouts of the Red Prince, the ruthless ruler of all the pirate bands."

"But the Red Prince was reported to have drowned in a storm at sea," Hedi said.

"The general believed he had gone into hiding. The major's final assignment was to locate him and learn the name he was using. In the meanwhile he was to memorize the contents of the six pages, hide them in a safe location, and personally advise Hedi Johnson of the hiding place."

"Why me?"

"He said General Scott said that his own wife and other family members would be watched too closely. Also, your official position afforded you better security protection."

"He never contacted me."

"No. The man told Maria Woodbine that he had memorized the information, but had been caught before he could hide the papers. He only had enough time to destroy them. He had been taken to a distant place that served as the enemy's headquarters, a place remote and well guarded. There they tortured him, trying to learn if there was a missing chapter in Scott's diary, and if so, where it could be found. He had insisted he knew nothing about it, but they never quite believed him.

"They argued, in his presence, over whether they should kill him or continue to try to break his will. There were long periods when they left him alone, but in complete solitary confinement.

"He said he had been held prisoner from that time until three weeks before, when he had escaped."

Sam's face spoke eloquently of his skepticism. Ralph picked it up and nodded his head.

"I know, that was my reaction, too. And Rogers said he too, thought the escape seemed a little too easy. He suspected that they had let him get away and were following him in the hope he would lead them to the missing papers. He told of hiding all that day in the shrubbery of the World Capital Park and watching the laying of the cornerstone for General Scott's memorial statue. He had heard Maria Woodbine introduced as a World Council member from Region Three and as the mother-in-law of General Scott's daughter, and he listened as she made a short speech about the general's achievements.

"He said he came back that night, having recreated the information from memory, wrapped the papers in a piece of building plastic he found nearby, scratched a slit in the still-soft mortar on the left side of the corner stone, placed the packet in the slit, and smoothed over the surface with his finger.

"The man begged Grandmother to see the World president at once and urge him to retrieve the papers. If she could not reach the president, she was to tell the story to the Grand Councilor.

"'I do take your story seriously,' Grandmother Woodbine told him, 'but first let me get you to a hospital.'

"'Chances are neither of us would get there alive. I suspect they are right on my heels and may even now be searching this building. They will likely catch me, but I promise you, they will not take me alive. For your safety, I must leave quickly. Please do as I ask before it is too late.' Then the man dragged himself out of the office. Following him to the door, Grandmother watched him limp rapidly down the hall and disappear into a fire escape exit.

"She left the building at once, but she did not try to reach the president. Instead she lay awake all night trying to decide what to do. Perhaps it was some kind of hoax, and the president would laugh at her for telling such a cock-and-bull story."

The communication console chimed, breaking into Ralph's story. A red light glowed, indicating a top secret message; then a picture appeared on the video screen. The message 'Sam ack., by V, only print' appeared on the screen.

"Do you know what it means, Sam? If so please answer it," Hedi said.

Sam touched a panel marked 'ACK RED' on the console. "They

want the vital info by video with no sound," he said. "I will print the message and leave it on the screen for one second... not time to be read but plenty of time to be photographed."

They watched as he printed a message on a piece of cardboard and positioned it in front of the video camera. He set the camera for one second and then dialed a number code into the console. Again the red light glowed, and the message 'send' appeared on the screen. Sam touched another panel on the console, there was a brief flash of light, and the screen read 'received'.

The message on the card read "Remove mortar left side cornerstone Scott's Memorial. Papers likely fragile. Info top secret. Observe max security."

"Go on, Ralph," Hedi said quietly.

"My grandmother continued to wrestle with the problem all the next morning before thinking to check a reference book on General Scott's life. It disclosed that Hugh Scott did have an aide named Major Rogers, and that he had disappeared after the general's death in Z 38. She picked up the phone and called the president's office, only to learn that he was out of town and would not be back until the following day. Uncertainty seized her again, and she did nothing until late afternoon.

"Then she called the president's office to request an appointment with the president the following morning. She was advised that the appointment secretary had gone home, and to please call again in the morning. Maria made one unsuccessful attempt to reach the Grand Councilor. It was now quite dark and she decided to go home and try to get some sleep. She left her office and made her way to the parking garage.

"As she walked toward her parking place, she was seized by three men who gagged and blindfolded her and drove away with her in her own car. They were well outside the city before anything was said. Then she was warned to be quiet, and the gag was removed.

"'You can save yourself a lot of pain and trouble by doing two simple things,' one of her captors told her. 'We know that a vagrant who sometimes claims the name of Major Rogers came to your office yesterday. Tell us what he told you and give us what he gave you, and we will drive you back to town and let you go unharmed.'

"'No such person came to my office,' she said firmly. 'I don't know what you are talking about, but I am outraged at being treated in this fashion.'

"'You put on a good show,' the man said. 'I suppose we must take you to meet our leader, and that will be a meeting you are certain to regret. I give you one minute to change your mind.'

"Her answer was an attempt to tear off her blindfold, but her arms were quickly pinned to her side. She felt the jab of a needle; then she lost consciousness.

"When she came to, a woman in a doctor's coat was bending over her. 'She is coming out of it,' the woman said. 'She can understand you now. Call me when you want her checked again.'

"She was aware that several people were in the room, but she could only see the one man that sat beside the hospital cart on which she lay. He asked what the man calling himself Major Rogers had told her and what he had given her. Again Maria denied having seen such a man.

"'Very well,' he said, 'we are going to put you on our specially designed rack, and unless you start talking in time we are going to slowly break your back. It will be very painful, and you will never fully recover from it.'

"The cart was pushed into another room, and she was lifted onto a curved metal surface, shaped like half a wheel. As she lay on her back, straps were fastened around her wrists, and her feet tied to a footrest on the wheel; then she was stretched over the curved surface until the stress on her spine became very noticeable.

"Someone told her she was running out of time, but she still thought they were bluffing. In any event, she was determined not to talk. Then she heard the whir of a motor and her spine was bent slowly backward over the wheel until she screamed in pain. It was too late to stop them now. She felt something snap in her lower back, and she became unconscious."

Hedi could hear that Ralph was making an effort to keep his voice steady.

"When she came to, with the woman doctor working over her, she was in severe pain but felt nothing from the waist down.

"Again the same questions and the same threat, but she was determined to die before she would talk. She only wished it would happen quickly. Again they made good their threat, and she felt the blinding pain as her spine snapped in another place. This time when she awoke her entire right side was paralyzed. Again she refused to talk. 'Stubborn bitch,' the doctor said. 'His Highness said all women named Maria were stubborn.'

"The man who had done the talking now moved into view. 'Listen carefully to what I say,' he told her. 'The third treatment will be the last. You will not be able to talk after that. You have about two minutes to change your mind. During those two minutes remember one thing. If we ever discover that you have lied to us, every member of your family will get exactly the same treatment we have given you.'

"He told the others: 'Remember we don't want her to die before we get her back to the capital. His Highness wants it to look like an accident.'

"When she became conscious again, she was in a hospital bed with her husband beside her. She had been found among the rocks at the bottom of a ravine with her smashed car nearby. It took Dr. Steven Woodbine and the best surgeons of the New Earth three years to get Maria back to where she is now, paralyzed from the waist down."

Ralph fell silent. The tears had dried on his cheeks, but he was white with fury. "May the Creator forgive me," he said, "but if I could get my hands on the animals that did this thing to my grandmother, I would kill them."

"There are many scores to be settled with the Red Prince, if he still lives," said the Grand Lady. Each of her words were covered with frost, and her normally friendly blue eyes had turned the color of granite. Ralph Woodbine was astonished at this new facet of his heroine's character. For the first time he understood why there could be cause to fear an aroused Hedi Carlton Johnson.

45. Reports
June 20, Z 96

The government gravity liner rose silently from the Grand Lady's side yard. It showed no lights, and was barely visible in the misty rain. Up it went, through the thick clouds, and into the star-filled skies above. Then it headed for the world capital. Fifteen miles up and two hundred miles from land, the lights came on and President Carlos Fernandez left his seat to sit beside her.

"Good to see you, Hedi," he said. "This cloak-and-dagger business is to disguise my presence on board. Other precautions have been taken in our effort to avoid suspicion that we are on to something. At the same time, certain people need protection. Ralph has returned to his job at the university, but the two new graduate students assigned to him actually work for Noe Singh. The morning news will report that Maria Woodbine, wife of the famous Dr. Steven Woodbine, has slipped into a coma and is in critical condition at the Woodbine Memorial Hospital. Let them think she'll soon be out of their way."

Carlos smiled at Hedi. "Of course it is only natural that Lucy Woodbine should be constantly at her mother-in-law's bedside. The news media will report that. What they will not report, because they will not know, is that the nurses were carefully selected by Tu Wun, a senior security officer we borrowed from Region Four."

Hedi smiled with satisfaction. "Maximum security for both of them, without giving anyone a clue as to why. Very nicely done, Mr. President. And Hugh's papers...?"

"The copy Major Rogers made from memory is quite legible despite its age. We have struck the mother lode, Hedi. The information is there, and I hope we can be smart enough to bring these master criminals to justice."

"We owe it to the courage and determination of a man we had forgotten," Hedi said soberly. "He's the real hero. We should see that he receives proper credit."

"It's hard that he should be suspected all these years of having been a traitor," Carlos replied. "But when he disappeared the night Hugh Scott died, it did look that way. I suppose we will never know what did happen to him after his visit to Maria Woodbine forty years ago."

Hedi felt her brow wrinkling in thought. "You said you hoped we were smart enough to bring the criminals to justice. Is there any doubt about it?"

"Ho Sun reminds me that we are a government of law. We can no longer line traitors up and shoot them by presidential decree or by order of a commanding general. The serious crimes we know about happened many years ago. The statute of limitations will have expired on most violations; witnesses will have died or forgotten important details. No doubt we can pull most of their fangs, but punishment to fit their crimes will be difficult, if not impossible."

"Does the Red Prince still live?"

"We think so."

Hedi spoke calmly; her voice betrayed neither anger nor hatred, only unyielding resolve. "Well, if he still lives, he and his followers must learn that the universal laws have no statute of limitations. They cannot be broken. Sometimes the reaction is deferred, sometimes it occurs during one's life on earth. All actions are permanently recorded on the fabric of time, and that testimony is never forgotten. It is to everyone's advantage to learn these things, and I believe I can assist in the teaching."

If the Red Prince regards her as a frail and aging woman, he is in for a great surprise, the president thought.

Peter Johnson's voice came over the intercom. "Mother, can you and the president join me in the small conference room on the flight deck? It will be more comfortable here."

As soon as they joined Peter, Carlos said, "Tell your mother what has been learned since the discovery of the papers hidden by Major Rogers."

Peter took his mother's hand and squeezed it. "Rogers not only left us the names of the principal traitors known to General Scott in Z 38, but he added additional information. When he escaped in Z

56, the Red Prince was in good health and in firm control of the underground organization he had established. Rogers had been imprisoned at the Prince's headquarters, and was able to describe it and give its approximate location."

"Tell me more," Hedi said.

"If you think there's more, you're right," Peter said. He looked from his mother to the president and back again.

"As you know," Peter said, "we were to have met with Max, Jr., this coming Friday to discuss the gravity car and the matter of the planet they wish us to colonize. The president thought it might be better if we delayed that meeting in view of current developments, and I contacted Max with that suggestion.

"Max already knew what is going on, as you would expect; he suggested we meet as soon as possible to discuss it, while delaying discussion on the other matters. He said he was prepared to offer additional assistance. If possible, he would like to pick up Mother and Aunt Martha from the roof garden beside Aunt Martha's penthouse apartment at half past midnight tomorrow night. He will see to it he is not observed. I am to pick up the president, Ho Sun, and, if the president agrees, Noe Singh, at midnight.

"Our trip will be billed as a meeting with the governor of Region Four. Ho Sun will arrange for the governor to request the visit. The two liners will meet at an agreed point, and my passengers and I will transfer to Max, Jr.'s ship."

"I am anxious to agree with these suggestions, but we should have a plan and a list of alternate courses of action to suggest," Carlos said. "We have not yet had a chance to get together and discuss the problem, and I do not wish to play the fool before the envoy of the UFCP. Do either of you have a plan to propose?"

Hedi broke the silence that followed. "Peter, do you have any idea what assistance Max is prepared to offer?"

"I know of two things," Peter replied. "First, we were able to determine that Major Rogers was imprisoned on a massive rock formation in what used to be the country of Venezuela. It is a peninsula on the north coast of the Great Amazon Sea. It is protected by a dense rain forest on one side, and on the other three sides, sheer rock cliffs drop down to the water below, the sea formed when the rising waters of the Atlantic Ocean filled the Amazon river basin.

"The area used to be controlled by the Lowland Pirates of Region One, and the hideout was probably discovered by a pirate ship cruising its northern coast. Max says the headquarters are in a maze of very ancient caves in the heart of the mountain. He says the Red Prince is alive and in charge. He claims to know three entrances into the caves, one of which the Red Prince has never found."

"How does he know all this?" Carlos asked.

"You will have to ask him," Peter replied, "but they have a marvelous system for obtaining information. Which brings me to the second part of his offer. He is authorized to lend us one of their surveillance gravity liners equipped with special intelligence-gathering devices. It would be operated by robot technicians, who would also see that we did not violate any of the rules laid down by the Elustreons. With that liner and its equipment, we could pick up a whispered conversation in the heart of a mountain."

President Carlos Fernandez looked happy. "Nothing would please me more than leading our security forces through that secret third entrance and bagging the whole lot of them," he said. But Hedi saw the pleasure fade as he considered the difficulties.

"But they'll have plenty of weapons, and the Elustreons won't let us carry weapons in their gravity vehicles. I cannot picture us attacking a cave full of armed pirates unarmed."

"An attack by land or sea would be equally difficult," Peter pointed out.

"And it would require full support from the regional government," Hedi said.

"At the moment, I am not prepared to trust any of the senior regional officials, not even the governor," Carlos said glumly. He looked again at Hedi and gained new hope. "But something tells me the Grand Councilor-at-large has an idea."

"Perhaps I do," the Grand Lady replied, "but two things are required to make it work. Even then there is a risk it will not be successful."

"Tell us more," Carlos said. "There is also grave risk if we do nothing."

"First, we must be satisfied that our enemy has no suspicion of what we have learned. They must be completely absorbed with the problem of the gravity car. Second, we must all be fully committed to the plan. We must know it by heart, and once launched, there must be no turning back."

"What kind of approach do you have in mind," Peter asked?

"In my youth on the Old Earth," Hedi replied, "it was known as *the sting*."

For the next half hour the two men listened as Hedi outlined the essential elements of her plan. An excited discussion followed.

"Count me in," Peter said at last. "I wouldn't miss it for all the earth."

"You have my vote," Carlos added. "Suppose I brief Ho Sun and see if he thinks Noe Singh should be a member of the strike team."

"I am willing to abide by Ho's judgment," Hedi said.

"Agreed," Carlos said. "Hedi, I will depend on you to brief Martha.

Peter, I leave it to you to set the stage with Max. As envoy of the UFCP, his reaction is crucial."

"I will set the stage," Peter replied, "but the plan should not be revealed until Aunt Martha and Ho Sun are in agreement. Actually, I don't think any of us should make a final decision until Max has officially stated what assistance the Elustreons are willing to offer."

"It is absolutely necessary that there be no leaks, and Hedi and I must take every precaution in briefing Martha and Ho," Carlos said. "After we hear what Max has to say, we will ask for a private meeting to discuss the matter. Then, if we all agree, we will invite Max to join us and tell him what we plan to do."

* * *

The Elustreon surveillance liner, its photon absorption devices and electromagnetic fields shielding it from detection by any method known to earth science, hovered motionless over the headquarters of the Red Prince. The envoy of the Union of Five Central Planets had explained that the massive slab of rock rising from the sea below them was one of the most stable formations in existence.

"It appeared above the water's surface early in the earth's history," Max said. "And while the ocean has lapped at its base from time to time, there is no evidence it has ever been covered again. The reason there is so much information available about this particular mountain is because the early Elustreon space explorers used its caves as a base. In those days highly sophisticated robots had not been developed, and when outside their space ship, the living astronauts wore space suits to provide the temperature and atmosphere needed to sustain their lives. The caves in this mountain were undamaged by earthquakes, and could be sealed to hold an ammonia atmosphere of the right temperature and pressure for Elustreons. This was done, and for several thousand years the base was used, off and on, by Elustreon astronauts.

"Now let me show you some of this ship's capabilities," Max said. "Remember that while the defensive systems are freely available for use by my crew, the offensive spy systems are controlled by a monitor of the UFCP's Central Committee and are released only for purposes approved by that committee. The systems I will show you are approved as long as you adhere to the rules specified by my government."

Max nodded to his robot technician, and a picture began to form on a large screen. It showed a flat-topped mountain covered by dense vegetation. Sheer rock cliffs plunged to the sea on three sides, and a river rushed through a V-notch it had cut in the top of the mountain and fell with a thunderous roar into the seawater below. Another mountain range to the east could be reached by traversing a large rain forest.

"Our video cameras are very sensitive, and you are seeing this picture using only the dim night light," Max said. "Now we will switch to a gamma radiation system that will penetrate the ground cover. Our computer will construct a picture for us, and we will enlarge a small area near the center of the screen and just above the river.

"There. Looking through the cover of vegetation, you can now see the outline of a trap door. It is pivoted in the center, and unless wedged shut from underneath, one person can open it. This is one of the entrances to the caves, and it is often used by those who would overthrow your government. The entrance most used, however, is very difficult to reach except by gravity car. It is an opening in the north cliff, about half way between the top of the mountain and the sea. It is of adequate size, but it can only be seen from the air and from a very limited and dangerous area of the sea."

Max paused for a few seconds. "Our detectors have picked up an approaching gravity car," he said. "It appears to be headed for the cliff entrance. I will now switch to one of our most advanced technologies — forming focused images with beams of neutrinos. With this system we can see through solid rock of any thickness." The picture on the screen faded and a new picture began to form. It showed the vertical line of a cliff and the cross section of a tunnel leading from its face into the mountain.

"Watch!" Max exclaimed. "The gravity car is approaching."

In a matter of seconds it appeared in the picture, grew larger, and slowly entered the tunnel. The picture tracked the vehicle until it arrived in a large chamber. There it stopped, and two men got out and stood quietly facing a stone wall as if waiting to be recognized and admitted. The picture zoomed in for a close up, and Hedi gasped. "It is Juan Sebastian," she said, "and the other man is the pilot of the gravity car assigned to him by the World Government."

"Juan is the executive clerk of the World Council. He is in charge of all Council administrative matters and knows everything that goes on," Ho Sun added.

"Almost everything," Carlos corrected. "He is cleared for all information except secret minutes of the Council's executive committee meetings."

"I think I will soon have information confirming that he is also the half brother of the very important person in Region Two who threatened and then tried to bribe your grandson Simon," Martha said to Hedi. "The pieces are beginning to fall together."

"We have been looking for another traitor on the Council," Noe Singh noted. "I think our man is this executive clerk."

Looking back at the screen, they saw a door open in the stone wall, and the two men stepped inside; then the picture disappeared.

"We must be back in the capital before dawn, and we are running out of time," Max said. "You have not yet told me if you have a plan that requires the use of this ship."

"Will the envoy of the UFCP give us a few minutes to discuss these questions?"

"Certainly Mr. President. Peter knows how to call me when you are ready."

"Before you go," Peter said, "may I ask about the audio capabilities of the ship? It would be a great help if we could hear what was being said in those caves."

"Actually I was listening," Max replied. "There is a carrier wave that comes back with the picture, but it communicates with us in thought language. If you use the ship, we will program the computers to convert to your kind of audio so you can hear what is said."

"Could you tell us what you heard?" Hedi asked.

"The conversation between the two men in the gravity car had to do with your appointment secretary, Grand Lady," Max replied. "The man you called Juan was instructing the pilot to keep Alice happy at all costs. He said the information about your lunch and dinner appointments was proving very useful."

After Max departed for the flight bridge, Carlos said, "We are short of time, so I will ask those in favor of Hedi's plan to raise their hands." He looked around the table. "The vote in favor is unanimous," he announced. "I will ask Hedi to outline the plan to Max on the way back to the capital."

* * *

When Max returned, the president told him the World Government was pleased to accept the generous assistance offered by the UFCP. He said that the Grand Councilor-at-large would present their plan for dealing with the Red Prince during the return trip.

The envoy replied that his government was pleased to be of service. Then he asked if there were any more questions before leaving the domain of the Red Prince.

"Noe Singh and I would like to have a look at the third entrance to the caves, if that is possible," Peter said.

"I thought you might ask," Max replied. "It is underneath the waterfall, and is only about twenty feet above sea level."

Even as he spoke the picture appeared on the screen. The tunnel from this entrance sloped upward into the mountain. The stone door at its end had been left open, and the picture took them through a series of three large chambers. At the end of the third chamber a stone stairway spiraled upward in a vertical shaft.

"The Red Prince is unaware of either the third entrance or the caves below his palace cave," Max said. "It is amusing that his princely throne sits squarely on the stone that conceals the spiral staircase. Now if you have seen enough, I think we should get this ship under way."

As the ship made its return journey, Max Fact Banker Jr. listened attentively while Hedi outlined the key points in her plan. With Peter's help, she called attention to areas where more information was needed in order to reduce the risk of failure. "The use of this ship will be invaluable in reducing the guesswork," Peter said, "but of course we are dealing with human emotions, and I think tempers are going to be pretty hot. One can never be certain what another person will do under severe stress. Of course I am leading up to a question."

"Please state the question," Max said.

"While the odds are in our favor, success is by no means assured. We will obey the rules governing the gravity car, but the Red Prince and his crew have access to many of these vehicles, and one or more of them might be destroyed before this is over. Should that happen, what will your government's attitude be?"

"The goodwill of your government is very important to us," Carlos added. "We would like to take aggressive action, but we cannot afford to lose your support."

To the extent that a robot can look surprised, Max looked surprised. "Please give me a few minutes," he said. "The chairman of the Central Committee wishes to respond personally to your questions. He will speak through me."

Again it seemed to Hedi that another personality had entered the room. Then the chairman began speaking through the lips of Max, Jr. "Of course we expect you to observe the rules we established for the use of our equipment. After that, it is the view of our government that you bear the responsibility of protecting your people and preserving the values you and they hold dear. You must decide how best to accomplish this goal. We think your plan ingenious, and we wish you well, but we neither endorse or oppose it."

After a brief pause, the Chairman continued. "I am also entitled to my personal opinion. I can best express it by using one of your informal old-fashioned statements: *Go get 'em, tigers.*"

"OK, big sister," Martha said to Hedi, "you can start purring now, but don't flaunt your stripes. You aren't the only tiger on the block, you know."

46. Strategy
June 21, Z 96

"The lunch was delicious," Martha said, "and I have enjoyed your company. Now suppose you tell me what you really have on your mind."

"I must admit," Hedi replied, "I do have another matter on my mind. The annual review of the ombudsman reports is complete, and my report to the world president is due next Thursday. He won't be happy with it."

"Can you tell me why?" Martha asked.

"I suppose it's safe to talk here," Hedi replied, lowering her voice and looking about the crowded restaurant. "I know I can trust you to keep quiet until my report is made public. It will show there's much grumbling — sometimes loud complaints — about the government's continued security classification policy, especially about the gravity car."

"If there were an election on the issue, who would win?" Martha asked.

"Perhaps the government would win this time, but don't bet on next year. The complaints come from all parts of the world. They are loudest in the cities and on university campuses, especially in Regions One and Three."

"I think I smell a big public-relations job coming up," Martha said.

"It seems to me we must face this problem and insist that the World Council take action without further delay. This will be my recommendation to the president. I expect, before it is over, there will be much you can do."

"Just let me know. In the meanwhile, my lips are sealed. Do you think we should go? I am expected back in my office shortly."

"First let's take a short walk in the park. I need the exercise, and it is a very pleasant day."

"Be glad to."

The sisters walked toward General Scott's statue in the center of World Capital Park. Without moving her lips, Hedi said, "I'd be pleased if our conversation in the restaurant was overheard. I had Alice, my receptionist and appointments secretary, reserve our table for lunch."

Martha smiled, a very small smile. "I don't like to be catty, but my guess is she could be seduced and subverted by anyone's male agent, if he appealed to her as sexy."

"If we sit here on the wall enclosing the fountain, the splashing water will make it difficult for anyone to overhear us," Hedi suggested.

Martha smiled. "This wouldn't have done us any good against the spying equipment they had in the old pre-Zero days."

"No. That's one branch of technology we can do very well without. I'd rather rely on our good friend Hugh Scott here to watch over us. I wish he could speak and tell us what to do."

"I surmise you have something more to tell me," Martha said.

"Indeed I do, little sister," Hedi replied, "and I hope there is something you can do to help right away. Usually I read the Regional Director's summary reports — they are quite detailed and lengthy — plus random samples of the district reports. This year I read all of the district supervisor's reports, plus a sampling of the individual ombudsman reports. I found that about three fourths of the Region One district reports contained sentences with identical wording."

"Meaning someone higher up is directing them."

"Or that the reports had been doctored. They all stressed a high level of discontent and urged declassification of information about the gravity car. There were some reports from all regions that incorporated this same wording. I will give you a tape before we part that you can run on your video decoder. It shows the key charts and lists the names of all regional directors and district supervisors. I have put little check marks by the names of all the district supervisors who used the identical wording. Perhaps your genealogy records will disclose some interesting relationships."

"Is there anyone you recognize?" Martha asked.

"Isobel Perize, for one."

"The Isobel Perize who's a member of the World Council?"

"That's the one. We believe she's one of the leaders. And you'll be interested to know that the regional director of Region One is named Alberto Perize. I hope your records will show if there is any relationship with Isobel."

"I will get to work on it immediately. You know I have found a number of birth and death records that have been altered. I can quickly check these names against your check marked list. I will be in touch."

Thursday June 27

As was his custom, President Carlos Fernandez invited Ho Sun to sit with him while he heard the annual ombudsman report. The room in which they met had been carefully checked for bugs by the deputy chief of Internal Security, a lady named Noe Singh, who had previously been chief of operations of Region Four's security forces. Ho Sun had recommended her for the post, and had complete confidence in her ability and in her dedication to the ideals and objectives of the New Earth's World Government.

In her capacity as chairperson of the ombudsman organization, Hedi presented her report in a calm and businesslike fashion. She listed all of the significant citizen complaints and the frequency of each category of complaint by district and by region. She then consolidated the regions on a bar chart to show the world picture. By a margin of five to one, the chart showed declassifying information about the gravity car and relaxing controls on its use were the major concerns.

"In view of the frequency and increasingly strident tone of the voices being raised," Hedi concluded, "it is my recommendation, Mr. President, that you insist that the World Council face this problem. They should either direct the government to make public all available information or explain in simple language why such information should remain secret."

"And what position should the president take?" Carlos asked.

"I hope the president will push for declassification and that the Grand Councilor will also support that view," Hedi answered.

Ho Sun did not look surprised. "I am prepared to push for declassification," he said.

"Not so fast," the president injected. "When is the Grand Councilor-at-large going to give us the rest of it? I know there is more somewhere."

Hedi smiled. "That is the end of my official report, Mr. President, but I do have an informal report that I would like to share with you and Ho."

Ho Sun said, "Would you object if I asked Noe Singh to join us? If my guess is correct, we will be depending on her for a lot of help before this matter is put to bed. I think it best if she heard the story directly from Hedi."

"It makes sense to me," Carlos replied.

"Bring her in," Hedi said. Ten minutes later Hedi was presenting the information she had given to Martha the previous week.

She came to the end of her report. "My sister Martha advised me yesterday that Alberto Perize is the nephew of Isobel Perize. He is the son of her brother Ramond."

"Who is dead?"

"Who is reported to be dead. Martha has suspicions about the death certificate."

President Fernandez looked at his deputy security chief.

"I am embarrassed that I did not know this key piece of information," Noe Singh said. "This makes me suspicious of our own security organization in Region One. The biography they routinely provide on all high-ranking officials who are citizens of Region One should have disclosed the relationship."

"Have you told them that we suspect Isobel of being a high-ranking member of a subversive organization?"

"Fortunately, I am not in the habit of confiding in anyone," Noe Singh said with a slight smile.

"That's all to the good," Carlos said. "Now we know Juan Sebastian is also an agent of the Red Prince. Have you found any others in such high places?"

"We are working on it," Noe Singh responded. Turning to Hedi she asked, "Will you pave the way for me to approach your sister? I would like to ask her help in establishing a number of relationships."

"I am meeting her for an early dinner tonight and will tell her of your interest. I am certain she will be glad to help," Hedi said.

47. Setting the Stage
July 27

Two weeks before the World Council met for its regular August session, President Fernandez very publicly named a special committee to consider declassifying all information concerning the gravity car. The committee was composed of Grand Councilor Ho Sun, who was named chairman; Sidney Graves, World Councilor from Region Two and chairman of the World Council's executive committee; Governor Lin Lee of Region Four; Regional Ombudsman Director Alfred Ford of Region Three, and World Councilor Isobel Perize from Region One. Executive Director Peter Johnson and Grand Councilor-at-large Hedi Johnson, the two people who knew most about the history and operation of the gravity car program, were named advisory members.

The government-supported World Information Services and the independent news media organizations went wild trying to learn what lay behind the president's action.

The committee met a week after its formation was announced. The only public announcement was a statement by Ho Sun that the president had addressed the first meeting to explain why a recommendation by the committee and subsequent action by the World Government was urgent. He also reported that all meetings would be held behind closed doors and that Juan Sebastian, executive clerk of the World Council, would keep the minutes of the committee proceedings.

Rumors said that both President Fernandez and Grand Councilor Ho Sun favored declassification. Both declined to comment on the report.

The committee met for the next three days under tight security and a complete news blackout. Then Chairman Ho Sun announced a two-day weekend recess to allow the members to rest and to digest the testimony of the two advisory members. He also announced that the news blackout would continue.

August 2

The surveillance liner hovered over the underground domain of the Red Prince, waiting for the arrival of Isobel Perize. "She is still thirty minutes away," Peter Johnson said as he watched the image on the large view screen. "She is pushing her gravity car as much as she can, but this ship we're on can travel much faster than anything the Elustreons turned over to our control."

At another station, one of the robot technicians presented Noe Singh with a detailed analysis of the underwater conditions and the rock formations beneath and behind the waterfall. "It will be difficult to get in, but not impossible," she said as she joined Peter, Hedi, and Martha at the big screen. "Perhaps while we are waiting, someone can enlighten me on the early history of the Red Prince. I have read the recent account reported by Ralph Woodbine, but what do we know beyond that?"

Hedi summarized the career of the man. "His ambition was to be called 'Your Imperial Majesty, The Red Emperor, Ruler of the World,'" she said grimly. "Apparently he harbors it still."

Martha added: "When he found he could not conquer the Earth by force, he ordered his key followers to adopt assumed names and go underground. Three of the key leadership groups obeyed his orders. His own immediate family took the name Perize. The maiden name of the wife he first loved but then abused and killed when she defied him, is thought to have been Perize. The second group adopted the family name Rogers, and the third group took the name Sebastian."

Martha paused to check the view screen. "The Red Prince had three children. Isobel we know. I think Ramond still lives. But the third child, Martin, is dead. Recent information suggests Martin was the spy and traitor who, as Captain Martin, led our troops into a trap and then attacked our base hospital. If so, it was actually Martin Perize that led the slaughter of the patients, and who shot Roy Johnson, Hedi's husband. The present head of the Rogers clan is the rich dowager of world capital society, Beverly Rogers. Her son is Conway Rogers, Region Two's influential business tycoon, the one who tried to intimidate Simon Becker in his capacity as regional director of my genealogy project.

"Beverly's husband appears to have been killed in an internal conflict with Juan Sebastian, Sr. over who was second-in-command to the Red Prince. Or maybe it was a quarrel over a more personal matter. In any event, it seems clear that Beverly moved in with Juan after her husband's death, and bore him a son named Juan, Jr. I understand that no love is lost between Conway Rogers and his half-brother, Juan Sebastian, Jr. The elder Sebastian was killed in an accident while traveling in Region Two some 45 years ago. We now know that the documents which state Ramond Perize was drowned in a shipwreck were forged."

"We may soon know what did happen to him," Peter said. "Isobel's gravity car is approaching the cliff entrance."

They watched as the vehicle entered the opening and stopped in a cave at the tunnel's end. Isobel Perize and her pilot got out and stood waiting to be recognized.

"Let's switch to the Prince's Great Cavern and see who may be waiting for her," Peter said.

"This could be the first act of a very interesting show," Hedi ventured, as they watched the picture developing on the screen.

"There he is!" she exclaimed, "the one pacing back and forth in front of the dais."

The Red Prince was a little stooped now and somewhat gaunt. His hair and beard were thin and straggly, but they were still red. There could be no doubt that in his youth he had been a big and powerful man. There was no sign in the lines of his face that he had ever smiled. It currently showed an exasperation that threatened to explode into anger, and the other people in the room were staying well out of his way. He wheeled as a side door opened and Isobel entered. "Where the hell have you been?" he shouted. She opened her mouth, but he overrode her. "Never mind... just tell me what happened. For three days the news knows nothing. The meetings recessed at six p.m., they said. The committee will meet again on Monday, they said. Big deal, I say. I want to know what is going on. For over sixty years I wait for this and now no one tells me anything!"

"If you will listen, Father, I will tell you what is going on. But you aren't going to believe it."

"Tell me anyway," the big man demanded. "No, wait so your brother can hear. Come here, Ramond, and hear what your sister has learned. At least she knows something, and that is more than your spy system has produced. The rest of you get out. I will send for you when I want you."

Followed by his son and daughter, the Red Prince entered a private study and sat down.

"That's his son Ramond. No doubt about it," Martha breathed. "Except that he is younger and has sandy hair and beard, he is a carbon copy of the old man."

"Let us hope he also has his father's quick temper," Hedi said, but she did not explain the remark.

Isobel began her story without delay. "We have been listening to the president, to Hedi Johnson, and to Peter Johnson tell how in Z 6 General Hugh Scott was contacted by an envoy from a distant planet. The envoy was a robot, but represented a race of living beings called Elustreons who wished to help the highland forces under Scott in the fight with our coastal people. The envoy offered to lend a fleet of magical gravity cars for use in transportation and communication. They did not wish them used for combat, however, and under no circumstances were they ever to carry a lethal weapon — not even a hand gun. It was also understood that the vehicles would be returned on demand, and all information about the deal would be highly classified. The envoy would only meet with Hugh Scott,

Hedi Johnson, or Martha Carlton, all of whom were known to him from Old-Earth contacts. In later years, Peter Johnson, Ho Sun and Carlos Fernandez have been added to the list.

"They were told that any effort to disassemble a gravity car to learn how it works will cause it to explode, and we know this to be true. The Elustreons have demanded return of all gravity cars and liners within three years. There was a lot of talk about how to get along without these vehicles, but I have given you the meat of the revelations to date. We are to hear more next week."

The Red Prince looked thoughtfully at his two children. "And what do you think of all this, Ramond?"

"They are spinning a web of old rumors and fairy tales to deceive you," Ramond stated. "It means we have aroused the people and they are demanding answers. Once the truth is told, we will know the secret of the gravity car, and nothing can stop us from seizing control of the government. They are willing to dump all of the gravity vehicles in the sea rather than let us get our hands on them." He grew vehement. "We should seize as many as possible. Now! We'll arm them and take over the government. We can melt the phony robot down for scrap. It is time to stop listening to this insipid sister of mine and take some action. I know her game; she can never take your place unless she can discredit me."

Isobel's face turned white with anger. "And what do you want, dear brother? You would put a knife in your father's back if it would gain you his power."

"Say that again and I will kill you!"

"Shut up, both of you," their father shouted. "I will make the decisions, and until more information comes in, we will do nothing."

In the surveillance liner Peter Johnson noted the time. "Mother, this family quarrel may go on for some time, but I think we have heard the decision. I must get you and Aunt Martha home before you are missed. We will transfer to my ship, and Noe Singh will stay here to observe and record the drama being played out below. These were the president's instructions."

August 5

For the next three weeks Ho Sun skillfully led the committee through the delicate and often explosive aspects of the problem before them. He made certain they understood how possession of a modest fleet of gravity liners armed with lethal weapons would enable a would-be dictator to rule the world. He said this was a matter of concern to the Elustreons, a concern intensified by the current clamor for declassification. "Since they also feel the time has come for the New Earth to stand on its own feet, the obvious answer is repossession of the gravity vehicles they lent us," he said.

At Ho's request, Peter outlined his Five Year Plan for replacing the gravity vehicles with other types of transport. He said the Elustreons would agree to a five-year phase-out if it was part of a workable plan. Of greater importance, they had offered the World Government the know-how to convert solar energy to electrical power with an efficiency many times that of any process known to earth scientists. An extension of this technology would convert the solar power to hydrogen, making the hydrogen system an economical energy source for the world's needs.

He said the period of conversion to new energy sources and modes of transportation would be painful, but that the long-term benefits were very exciting and would pay handsomely for the sacrifices made.

Peter's enthusiasm over this energy technology was the first optimistic news provided, and the committee was obviously excited. Even Isobel abandoned her poker face long enough to register interest.

It was Hedi's lot to bring everyone back to earth again. "Except for one problem," she said, "the answer to our problem is simple. We only need to come clean, tell people the whole truth just as we are doing with this committee, and ask them to accept short-term sacrifices to their standard of living. The problem is: How do we get them to believe us? That will be difficult, but I hope not impossible. Asking them to make the sacrifices without explaining why will not work. The people are in no mood to buy the 'We are your leaders... trust us' approach. Other approaches I can think of are dishonest as well as ineffective."

"I agree with Hedi," Alfred Ford said. "As a regional Ombudsman Director, I am fully convinced we must lay the whole story out on the table."

* * *

Ho Sun worked the committee for long hours six days a week, and asked them to remain in the capital on the seventh day for possible consultation. Members were provided with a complete list of gravity vehicles, showing the type of vehicle, the organization or individual it was assigned to, the reason for its assignment, and a detailed record of its actual use over the past five years.

They took a field trip to see the central station where each gravity vehicle was inspected and cleaned on a regular schedule, and they reviewed the monthly reports made by Peter Johnson to the envoy of the Union of Five Central Planets. But they did not meet any robots.

At the end of the third week, the meetings were recessed for two days of rest. Ho promised them that during the following week Peter would tell all that he knew about the construction and operation of the gravity car. As a final and unexpected development, the envoy agreed to meet with the committee and deal with their questions.

August 24

Hedi and Martha remained in the capital that weekend while Peter and Noe Singh observed activity in the caverns of the Red Prince, and President Fernandez joined them in the surveillance liner for the crucial period Friday night when Isobel Perize and Juan Sebastian arrived to report to the Red Prince.

Video disk recordings of significant activity in the caverns were delivered to Hedi by noon on Saturday, and again at midday Sunday. The two sisters reviewed them as they arrived.

On Saturday morning Noe Singh had arranged for them to take a lesson from a security specialist on spotting listening devices in a restaurant. Special attention would be given to radio mikes hidden in flower arrangements. Hedi also had Alice, her appointment secretary, reserve a table for dinner with Martha on Saturday night.

Sunday night she would dine with Peter in her apartment. Later that night there would be a very secret meeting with the president, Ho Sun, Martha, Peter, and Noe Singh to review final plans for implementing "the sting" and deciding on alternate approaches should the primary plan fail. It would be a very busy weekend.

The two sisters had watched the highlights of Friday night's drama for two hours. "It was quite a battle," Martha said. "I thought blood would be spilled before it was over. At what point does the Red Prince exercise his authority and put an end to the debate?"

"The moment it becomes a rebellion," Hedi replied. "There are laws and traditions in the Red Prince's world, too. This is still a family fight. One becomes a member of the family either by birth or after many years of loyal service. However brutal the Red Prince may be with outsiders, he is good to the family. He is even tolerant of their opinions, allowing them to argue and shout and even threaten, but there is a line they must not cross. A prince does not remain a prince for long unless he can instantly detect when that line is crossed."

"Can you tell?" Martha asked.

"Not well enough to play in the fast lane," Hedi replied, "but I can recognize some of the signs. Remember, Ramond asked his father, 'When are you going to stop listening to *my insipid sister*? The first time he asks 'When are you going to stop listening to *your insipid daughter?*' you will see a marked change in the Red Prince's reaction. Now I think we had best rehearse our lines for tonight's dinner show, so we can lie to the pirates by telling the truth."

* * *

At dinner, they talked about the information given to the committee concerning the gravity car problem.

"What will Peter tell them next week? Will it be the whole truth?" Martha asked.

"We do not know the whole truth, and would not understand it if we were told. Peter will tell them no lies, but neither will he speculate about things beyond his knowledge." Hedi made a point of looking at the diners around her. "But this isn't a good place to talk about such sensitive matters. Suppose we take a walk in the park when we have finished eating, and I will try to be a little more helpful."

As they were leaving, Martha commented again on the delicate beauty of the three small pink roses that graced the table. "I wonder if they would mind if I took one?" she said.

"I think not," Hedi replied. "Which one do you want?"

"I think they are all alike. You pick one out for me."

"How about this one? It seems just a little fresher."

"It looks good. No, don't pin it on me... I'll just carry it," Martha said.

"There is one thing Peter will avoid," Hedi said, when they reached the fountain and found a vacant park bench. "Gravity vehicles are scheduled in for inspection every six to twelve months, depending on type of service and hours of operation. Part of the servicing includes injecting a special liquid provided by the Elustreons through a valve in the gravity pack. We don't know the composition of the liquid, and it is always handled and injected by one of their robot maintenance technicians."

"I thought that liquid was necessary to recharge the gravity pack."

"No. The general public also thinks the vehicles are called in to replenish their energy supply. Peter says none of this is true; that unless mechanically damaged, the gravity pack with its membrane seal is good for a thousand years of service. The liquid is part of a test they run to determine if anyone has tampered with the gravity unit. The test is not part of Peter's responsibility, and the envoy declines to confirm or deny Peter's deductions. Since there is no reason for this matter to influence the committee's decisions, Peter feels he should not speculate about it."

"I have one more question," Martha said. "Can the Elustreons destroy any vehicle they choose by remote control?"

"We don't know how they would do it, and we have never asked them to prove it, but they say they can, and I believe them. Only one has ever blown up, and we don't know what caused that. We know that it was very violent."

"Time to go home and get some rest," Martha said. "Next week will be a busy time."

They had walked a short distance when Martha stopped abruptly.

"Stupid me," she said. "I left my rose on the bench. Wait here and I will go back and get it." She was back in less than five minutes. "It's gone," she said. "Who do you suppose would have wanted it?"

Hedi smiled. "We must have selected the right rose."

Sunday August 25

The dinner with Peter on Sunday night was intended to be a time to relax and just have a mother-son kind of visit. Before leaving, however, Peter said, "We have all agreed that once the operation is launched you will be calling the shots, but if you decide you must face the Red Prince again, I want to be with you."

"Thank you, Peter," she replied, "but this is a thing I must do alone. Besides, you are going to be needed elsewhere."

A few hours later, at their final council of war, Carlos Fernandez made the same request as Peter and received the same answer. "I may be the only person old Red Beard will believe," she said. "He knows I do not bluff."

After that, they reported on their respective assignments. Noe Singh spoke first. "At dawn, two noted Oriental research botanists will ignore warnings of danger and launch their rubber raft for a trip down the Lost River in search of rare botanical specimens. With luck, they will make landfall near the Red Prince's surface entrance Tuesday night. Our surveillance shows that the guards protecting this entrance take refuge from the hoards of biting insects by ducking into the entrance cave at dusk every evening and closing the stone door behind them. Our intrepid explorers will case the area before dawn, hide out during the day on Wednesday, and be ready to block the entrance shortly after nightfall Wednesday night. They will have wedges of special design to jam the door, fast-setting cement to reinforce the wedges, and a couple of tubes to be set in the cement. Should there be too much activity on the inner side of the door, they can blow tear gas through the tubes. They will also have a canister of old-fashioned dental laughing gas they can inject if they wish to strike a lighter note. I can assure you, Hedi, that your man Sam Wun and his cousin are having a ball with this assignment."

"My assignment was to deal with the cliff entrance," Peter said. "We know that the Red Prince has called a meeting of leaders — he calls it his High Parliament — to meet in the Great Cavern on Wednesday afternoon. The cliff entrance tunnel and cave will be jammed with gravity vehicles used to bring them there. On instruction from our command center, one of our largest gravity freighters will move in. It will hover against the cliff above the tunnel opening and lower a steel mesh net to block that exit. A second freighter will be standing by should anything happen to the first."

"My second assignment was to work with the commando unit of

the Naval Security Force to develop access to the third entrance beneath the waterfall," Noe Singh said. "They have found a path for their mini-sub around the turbulence of the waterfall. They have anchored ladders and a walkway to the cliff, providing access to the entrance tunnel. As we speak, a powerful hydraulic jack is being assembled at the top of the spiral staircase. The other items Hedi requested will also be on hand by Wednesday."

"I think it is my turn," the president said. "Two years ago some of our young air security officers were inspired by old World War Two records to form a Piper Cub Commando Club. Peter has helped by selling them prop planes with equal or better capabilities than the original Pipers. They have been fitted with replicas of the old shoulder-held anti-tank rocket launchers. Bomb racks for dropping a variety of ten and twenty-five pound bombs have been fitted under the wings. In addition to the pilot, they will carry a gunner armed with a Tommy gun. Six of these planes will be standing by on a sandy beach thirty miles south of the Red Prince's mountain to deal with any unexpected attack from land or sea."

"My assignment is to the surveillance liner," Ho Sun said. "Carlos will be with me, and our job is to provide information and emergency support to all units and to relay orders and requests from and to our field commander, Hedi Johnson. Hedi and Noe Singh will make use of the secret third entrance, and will be operating from the cave just below the Great Cavern of the Prince. Martha will be in charge of the communication center and will do the talking."

"Splendid!" Hedi exclaimed. "With this kind of help, my job is the easiest of them all."

"Except," Ho Sun said grimly, "that you are the one most likely to be killed."

Monday, August 26

Peter began his presentation to the committee by saying he was an engineer, not a research scientist, and it was necessary for him to grossly oversimplify things in order to picture how a gravity car works. "Although, you will be astonished at what I am about to tell you," he said, "you will be even more surprised by how much I do not understand.

"I think all of you know, or once knew, that the atoms of all elements are composed of combinations of electrons which have a negative charge and therefore repel each other, protons which have a positive charge and repel each other, and neutrons which have no charge at all. Outside the atom, the neutron is subject to the very weak force of gravity, but is relatively free to wander about as it wishes, passing through solid materials with ease. Inside the atom such wanderlust is restrained by something the scientists call 'binding energy.' I don't know what that is, but we have known for a long time that it exists and can be measured. We can contain atoms which contain neutrons, but we have no leakproof containers for free neutrons.

"Probably you have heard of neutron stars. If a very large star loses its electrons, protons, and other charged particles, the remaining neutrons are so numerous that the sum of their weak gravitational attraction packs them together in an incredibly dense mass.

"If we could fill a bucket with densely packed free neutrons, it would be so heavy that gravity would likely pull it right down into the earth. Of course we have never tried this, because we've never figured out how to contain free neutrons in a bucket. But after eight hundred years of research, the Elustreons did.

"I don't understand the containment system, but envoy Max Fact Banker, Jr., has given me what he calls a crude analogy. Suppose we took a helium atom — which is composed of two electrons, two protons, and two neutrons — and pumped in a thousand additional neutrons, along with the binding energy to keep them in place. Now we would have a very heavy atom, one easy to contain. Next we remove an electron, leaving us with a very heavy ion carrying a positive charge. These massive ions can now be pumped and compressed using an electromagnetic field. Such a field can also be used to reinforce their containment.

"Of course this doesn't matter too much," Peter said, "because our small container of neutrons would only make the gravity car heavier, and we are trying to make it lighter. The Elustreons spent many years learning the answer to this problem, an answer dependent on antimatter.

"You know that for every bit of physical matter materialized from energy, there is a mirror image created somewhere, composed of antimatter. Thus there must be an entire universe of antimatter: flaming antimatter suns, antimatter planets, perhaps antimatter people. Of course there would be antiprotons having a negative charge, antielectrons having a positive charge, and antineutrons, each of which would generate a tiny amount of antigravity. We are not likely to see very much antimatter, because when it comes in contact with matter, both are converted to pure energy and disappear in a violent explosion. This is why any successful attempt to open a gravity pack causes it to self-destruct, in an explosion which can be more violent than that of a hydrogen bomb.

"It follows that if one has a leakproof container filled with antineutrons, it would generate antigravity, and the earth's gravity would attempt to throw it off into space. If it were attached to a vehicle of lesser mass, it would lift that vehicle into the air. Of course, the nonporous container must also be non-reactive with either matter or antimatter or the whole thing would blow up.

"I have been given no clues as to how this problem was solved. Perhaps the containing membrane is composed of a substance completely free of neutrons. Perhaps it is protected from physical contact by a powerful electromagnetic field. I do not know, but somehow the Elustreons have solved all of these problems. To me it is the outstanding example of their technology, but if you ask Max about it tomorrow, he will tell you it is old stuff — that you should see what they are doing now."

Peter went on to explain that the Elustreons had made another notable discovery. They had found a way to partially shield an object from gravitational forces. The shield, or deflector, is interposed between the negative gravity pack of a gravity car and the earth.

"Consider the case of a small four-passenger gravity car with an earth-gravity curb weight of 1700 pounds. By applying more or less shielding, the antigravity effect of its gravity pack can be varied from a maximum of 3000 pounds to a minimum of 1500 pounds. All of this 1500 pound differential can be applied to lifting or lowering the gravity vehicle and its payload, or the pilot can use a portion of it to obtain horizontal movement in any direction, by changing the angle of deflection of the disk-shaped gravity shield. Now I will take your questions, but there isn't much more substance I can add."

Hedi found it interesting that Isobel Perize came alive during this discussion. Clearly she was greatly interested in the presentation and deeply concerned about its implications.

48. Curtain Calls
August 28, Z 96

As darkness fell on Wednesday night, helping hands were assisting Hedi up the spray-drenched ladder and along the walkway to the tunnel's entrance, where she was met by Noe Singh.

"Your sister wanted to be here with us," Noe Singh said, "but her job of chief communicator can best be handled from the surveillance liner."

Hedi nodded. "Quite right. What's the situation?"

"The Red Prince has assembled some 150 leaders of his organization. He has been briefing them on what he knows about the situation, while they wait for Isobel and Juan to arrive. The pictures and sounds from the Great Cavern are being relayed to us here. If we go to our stations, we can pick up the proceedings."

"Are Isobel and Juan here yet?"

"They are coming in separate gravity cars, but should arrive at about the same time, some twenty minutes from now."

Hedi took her seat in front of the viewscreen. The Red Prince was answering a question. "I believe the committee will recommend declassification of all information, and the World Council will be persuaded to go along. The president announced this afternoon that he favored declassification, and we know that Hedi Johnson and her adopted son, Peter, are pushing for that decision," he was saying.

She could see grins on the faces of some of his followers, but not on his. An impatient gesture of his made clear his attitude.

"A few weeks ago we would have been elated. Now we learn of complications. Tonight we must decide what to believe.

"Were the gravity vehicles really loaned by these space creatures called Elustreons? If so, have these Elustreons demanded return of the vehicles? What would they do if we armed all the vehicles we could get our hands on and used them to destroy the rest?

"We know from experience the vehicles are booby-trapped against tampering, but is it true they can be destroyed by remote control? The word is, the gravity pack has to be recharged after every six to twelve months. Is this true? If so, what are our chances of learning the secret of recharging?

"Finally, it may be the whole act is a trick of some sort cooked up by Hedi Johnson and her crowd to deceive us, this being Ramond's belief."

A messenger approached and handed the Red Prince a note. He glanced at it and said, "Isobel and Juan will be here in ten minutes. Maybe now we will learn the answers to our questions."

Hedi had noted the smug look on Ramond's face while his father was talking. She thought she knew why.

"Isobel is entering the cliff tunnel and Juan Sebastian is right behind her." It was Martha reporting from the surveillance liner.

"Botany contingent reports surface entrance securely blocked with guards inside. Guards are not yet aware of what has happened. Fishing crew is prepared to lower net on orders from Chief Fish. All personnel on yellow alert."

Hedi turned her attention back to the screen. The Red Prince sat on the dais, Ramond sitting beside him. The vacant seat on his left was probably for Isobel. Seats for the rest of the Prince's official family were arranged in a semicircle in front of the dais.

A side door opened and Juan entered. Isobel followed, and took her seat on the dais.

The Red Prince stood up, and immediately there was silence in the room.

"My daughter will report to us on what has happened at the capital."

Isobel rose and began to report on the committee's sessions of the past three days. She knows Peter's speech by heart, Hedi thought. Isobel did not offer an opinion. Opinions had not yet been asked for. Juan was called on, and he stated that Isobel had given an accurate account of the proceedings.

"Now I want opinions," the Red Prince said. "You first, Isobel."

"I have some knowledge of the sciences," she said. "I believe we will never be able to construct a gravity car in our lifetime, and neither can the World Government. I conclude they must have been loaned by beings from another world. That granted, it becomes reasonable to believe that return has been requested."

The Red Prince frowned, thinking. "These beings apparently do not like bloodshed, however. Do you think they might take no action if we seized some of the gravity cars in order to knock off the World Government?"

"I think the odds are, they would," she said slowly. "Even if they took no action, but just went away, what do we do when the vehicles need recharging?"

The Red Prince nodded, as if the same thought had occurred to him.

"I am also inclined to believe the Elustreons can destroy the gravity cars by remote control," Isobel said. "I think we should sit tight and see what happens."

Ramond jumped to his feet. "Your daughter is an idiot and a coward," he screamed, "I have waited long enough. I say..."

The Red Prince shouted him down. "Sit quiet. You will get your turn. Juan, what do you say?"

Juan Sebastian stood tense and silent for several moments. Ramond, who was still standing, walked over and stood beside him. Hedi could see the Red Prince's eyes narrow and he folded his arms across his chest. He has a gun under that coat, she thought.

"I believe it is a very clever act to take the gravity cars out of the hands of the people," Juan said. "The recent demonstrations have frightened the government. In the end the government will keep their vehicles, arm them, and if there are protests, they will declare martial law. I do not believe in space people, and think the robot is a clever fake. I say we move in now."

"I stand with Juan," Ramond said, "and I have new evidence to support my conclusion. I would like you to hear it." He held up a tape.

Hedi switched on her microphone and said, "Red alert, I am preparing to go in."

"Red alert," she heard Martha say. "Fisherman, lower your net. Bug watchers, wake up the guards; give them a squirt of tear gas. Pipers, put two planes in the air over the Bear's Cave."

Hedi picked up a portable receiver and started up the spiral staircase. The crew manning the hydraulic jack turned on the pump.

Ramond was playing the tape of her conversation with Martha on Saturday night.

"How long have you had that tape?" the Prince asked.

"Two days. I wanted to surprise your darling Isobel."

"You are a stupid fool, Ramond. You too, Juan Sebastian. Do you think those two women picked out that particular rose and walked away with it by accident? The whole thing was an act. They set you up."

The Prince was not shouting now, and his voice was like smooth ice. Many people were standing, and Hedi saw Juan step behind one of them and carefully raise a laser pistol. "Hit it," she snapped, and the crew chief opened wide the hydraulic valve.

Above them there was the sound of breaking stone and cement. The dias tipped slightly and started to rise. At the same moment there was a flash of light, and the Prince clutched a badly burned shoulder. A second later there was another flash and the body of Juan Sebastian slumped to the floor. "Sorry I wasn't a little faster, Your Highness," Conway Rogers said. "I did not expect he would try to kill you."

Ramond wheeled on Conway, drawing his gun as he turned. "You have killed my best friend, and you will pay..." Then for the first time he saw the rising dais. Now three feet off the floor, it was still rising. Smoke was coming up from below, largely obscuring the area around the dais. Some six feet off the floor it stopped. The Prince and Isobel had abandoned the dais when it first moved. Everyone, many with drawn weapons, had backed away, waiting to see what would happen.

Hedi's voice came to them from beneath the dais. "Hedi Johnson requests an audience with His Highness. She is not armed. We suggest you do nothing rash until you fully understand the gravity of your situation."

"I will blast the first person who steps out of that smoke," Ramond screamed. "Who stands with me?"

"The first person who fires dies by my hand," the Red Prince said. "I am in charge here, not Ramond." Then facing the dais, he continued. "We are armed and have no intention of putting down our weapons. If the Grand Lady still wishes to talk, let her step forward."

Hedi emerged from the smoke. "We meet again, Red Beard," she said. "It has been a long time."

"What brings the Grand Lady to the bear's den? If you seek revenge, you had best be well prepared. If you harbor a death wish there are 150 people here who would be glad to kill you."

"I hope it is not for revenge," Hedi responded. "Revenge, like anger and hatred, turns on the person who harbors it. My purpose is to prevent you from destroying the chances of a free people to enjoy the fruits of that freedom. I come to offer you a chance to surrender in peace, and to promise you a fair trial under our laws."

"She is bluffing you, Father," Ramond cried. "She is mad. Let me put her out of her misery."

"Maybe you were too young to remember, but it cost me one third of my army to learn that this lady does not bluff," the Red Prince responded. "She does what she says she will do." Turning to Hedi, he said, "Speak, Hedi Johnson. We will hear what the Lady has to say."

"Your surface entrance is blocked. Check it out," she said.

"Captain of the Guard," the Red Prince shouted, but that officer was already there, breathless from running.

"The surface entrance is blocked and the tunnel is full of tear gas," he reported.

"Take a gravity car; go up and see what is going on," the Red Prince ordered.

"I tried that, but some sort of heavy mesh screen is hanging in front of the cliff tunnel exit. Nothing can get out," the captain reported. "With your permission, we will try to blast out whatever is blocking the surface entrance."

"Permission granted," the Red Prince said with a sigh.

"Be careful when you step outside, Captain," Hedi said. "You will find the area being patrolled by prop planes armed with flares, fragmentation bombs, and Tommy guns."

The Red Prince looked at his assembled followers. "The time has come to make a decision," he said, "But first I will listen to a few opinions. What say you, Isobel?"

"Father," she replied, "I have fought by your side all my life, and I will abide by your decision now, but I believe we are fighting for a lost cause. I take no pleasure in dying for causes already lost. I would accept the offer of a fair trial."

"Ramond," the Red Prince said, "you are still my son, and I will listen to what you have to say."

Ramond struggled to hide his raging anger. Finally he spoke. "Father," he said, "you have given your last order. I am taking charge. She got in here, so there has to be another entrance down below. I am taking our people with me and fighting our way out of that entrance. We will take the Grand Lady with us as a shield. Once outside we will throw her into the sea. That is a decision, not a suggestion. If you try to stop me I will kill you."

The Red Prince shook his head in disbelief. "Have you forgotten, my son, that in my youth my idols were the gun fighters of the old west? I am an expert with a six shooter. I can put two bullets through your heart while you are aiming that fancy laser of yours."

"There may have been a day when you could," Ramond replied,

"but now you are old and feeble. Your hand shakes from the pain in your roasted shoulder, a wound which may kill you in any event. Perhaps I do you a favor by putting you out of your misery. Stand aside, Isobel, and you too, Conway. Try to help him, and you will also die."

The Red Prince pushed back his coat revealing an ancient long barreled revolver. Ramond raised his laser. Two shots reverberated through the cavern and a laser beam burned a groove in the stone floor. Ramond Perize shuddered and crumpled slowly to the floor... two bullet holes in his heart.

The would-be Emperor stood silently, looking at the body on the floor. "So this is how it ends," he said, "a son dying by his father's hand. I have fought for a century to be number one. I have won many battles, but lost the war. The field is yours, Grand Lady. If there is a hereafter, I hope I may come to understand why you have won."

Turning to his stunned followers, the Red Prince said, "Each of you must decide his own fate. I have no intention of being taken alive. I cannot face the humiliation of a trial or the prospect of a single day in prison. I have a bottle of cyanide tablets. One will cause certain death. I will take two. Those who would join me come and stand by my side. The rest of you go with the Lady. She will keep her promise."

Conway Rogers and his mother came to the Red Prince's side. Six others joined them. As he passed out the lethal tablets, the others began filing down the spiral staircase. Isobel watched with tears streaming down her face. Finally she embraced her father and kissed him; then she joined Hedi at the top of the stairs.

"Thank you for that, my daughter," the Red Prince said. Then he turned to Hedi. "I will not try to trick you again," he promised. "Please go and let us die with dignity."

One foot upon the top step, Hedi stopped and looked back. "Since first I heard of you," she said, "I have despised you for the things you did. Now in this final hour, I almost admire you."

The Red Prince smiled sadly as the Lady disappeared from view. It was the closest thing to a real compliment he had ever received.

Reflections

49. Reflections
April, Z 99

To Hedi Carlton Johnson, the winter of Z 99 seemed more severe than usual. Her knee and leg bones were more sensitive to the cold, and she had less than her normal desire to be out of doors. Still, she enjoyed the winter months. She was comfortable in her hillside home, and the ever-present Sam Wun took care of all her needs and most of her whims.

Her greatest pleasure came from the frequent visits of her children and of young Ralph Woodbine, who nearly every week found some reason to consult with her about one or another of his history projects. She looked forward to these discussions. His talent and dedication deserved support, and she believed she was helping him in a very worthwhile effort.

But there was something more. He seemed like one of the family, and she was aware of a special rapport between them that asked for a better explanation. Martha had once mentioned reincarnation; that perhaps he had been one of the family. This thought had crossed her mind more than once, but she refused to make a serious effort to find the answer, because she could think of no one who would profit from such knowledge. Perhaps it was best not to know.

Vermont weather was full of unpleasant surprises in late April, but this was a warm sunny day. Sam had made her comfortable on the patio where she could see and hear the sounds of early spring, while her thoughts ranged among the events of the past three years.

In August, Z 97, she had persuaded Ho Sun and Carlos Fernandez that her talents were no longer required by the government, and had retired completely from public service. Shortly afterward, Isobel Perize had sent a message from prison, asking Hedi to come talk to her for a second time.

The first time had been a few weeks after Isobel's arrest, and it too had been at her request.

"I cannot bring myself to plead guilty to betraying the public trust and gross neglect of duty in my position of World Councilor," she had told Hedi directly. "I am ready to plead guilty to all charges save these."

Hedi had heard her out. "I am proud of the fact that I was able to run an honest race for the position of World Councilor and win," Isobel had said. "My father was amazed to learn I could secure victory without buying votes, bribing pollwatchers or using threats of bodily harm. He was proud of me. He delighted in telling his supporters that I had a real head on my shoulders. He used to say if they were half as smart, there would be no problem in taking charge of the government."

"So you obtained your position honestly."

"I obtained it honestly and performed its duties honestly. I took my job seriously, and tried very hard to represent the interests of my region."

"Always?"

Isobel shrugged. "Of course when my father asked a specific favor of me, that request came first, but he never asked me to do anything very bad. I doubt I ever committed a felony."

"You knew they were being committed, though."

Isobel did not dispute the fact.

"You have a defense attorney, and I hear that you refuse to talk with him," Hedi had said. "Why do you tell me these things?"

"I listened very carefully to what my father had to say about you. Even though you hate me, I feel I can trust you."

"You should tell your attorney what you have told me. Ask him to try to get the charge of gross neglect of duty dropped. On the matter of betrayal of public trust, you knew an effort to overthrow the government by illegal means was being planned and you did nothing to stop it. You even responded to your father's requests to do things that would help promote such a conspiracy. You don't seem to understand that keeping the public trust requires you to take action against anyone you know to be trying to betray the people."

Hedi watched for her reaction. "Anyone. And she who turns her back on a crime is also guilty: I don't see how you can claim innocence of this charge. If you can't bring yourself to plead guilty, you should ask your attorney about the possibility of pleading 'no contest'."

Before leaving, Hedi had added, "One thing more. You'll have trouble understanding this, I suppose, but I don't hate you. Perhaps when the trials are over and you can think about other things, we can talk about hate."

Isobel steadfastly refused to testify either for or against others who were on trial. The only ethic she had ever known was obedience and loyalty to her father. She could neither help or hurt him now, but these were his associates, and he was not there to advise her, so she settled for silence.

She was acquitted, for insufficient evidence, of the charge of gross negligence of duty. She pleaded no contest on betrayal of public trust, and pleaded guilty to the other serious charges. She was sentenced to twenty years in prison, with the possibility of parole after twelve years. It was shortly after her sentencing that Hedi retired and Isobel asked her to come for a second talk.

When Hedi arrived at the prison, she learned that Isobel had requested a work assignment in the prison library, and had become the institution's champion reader.

Isobel went directly to the point.

"My father said he hoped someday to understand why you had won. I have done much reading about a world of philosophy, ethics, and religion that I really never knew, but I still cannot answer my father's question. Can you tell me, Grand Lady? Why did you win?"

"I did not win," Hedi had replied. "Your father lost. The master of creation grants all of us the ability to create. Your father chose to create things that degraded and destroyed. His own creations turned on him. They defeated him. In some cases this return of the boomerang is swift, in others it takes a long time, but it always comes back. It is the law of action and reaction at work."

"Tell me more," Isobel said. And thus the meeting became the first of a series of meetings. They met every month or so, Hedi learning Isobel's fascinating life history, and Isobel probing Hedi's philosophy of the life eternal.

Those meetings eventually resulted in financing Carlos Fernandez' retirement, though he never knew it.

With his administration's challenge successfully met, Carlos had felt free to announce that he would not run for a second term. He had been genuinely surprised when, just one week after the end of his term, the World University had announced that an anonymous donor had granted 10,000 ounces of gold to establish a Chair of Political Philosophy, and had invited him to fill that chair.

"Grand Lady," he had said over the phone, "I detect suspicious fingerprints behind this anonymous bequest. Did you by any chance have a hand in it?"

"Carlos," she had assured him with straight face and strict accuracy, "I give you my word. There's not a penny of mine in it. Nor have I asked one soul to contribute. But I think it's a wonderful thing, and I haven't a doubt you'll do great work there for the New Earth." She saw by his face on the screen that he wasn't fully convinced, but everybody knew the Grand Lady didn't lie.

She laughed again, remembering the conversation. She had told the truth and nothing but the truth. Not, though, the whole truth.

The whole truth was that Isobel Perize had set up two charitable foundations. The first, she said, was to be in the name of Maria Woodbine.

"I know that I cannot return what my father's organization took from Maria, but perhaps she can have some pleasure in helping others, and it will make me feel better."

She had reassured Hedi about the source of the funds. "This is honest money. When my father decided to go underground, he gave each of us a stake and told us to invest it in a legal business. 'Keep your head down and your nose clean,' he said.

"My stake was 2,000 ounces of gold. I established residence in a modest community and spent half my funds on projects to help the local people. That bought me a reputation as a good citizen and a place in the local political system. The rest I invested in a forest product business and I defy anyone to show where I cheated anyone."

"Still, you made a fortune with that stake."

"I did. And I am ready to contribute most of it to this foundation, if it can be completely anonymous. It's a considerable sum — 100,000 ounces of gold. Can you help me set it up?"

"I can."

"There is one thing more. I have sold all my holdings except my home. After funding the Maria Woodbine Foundation and providing a modest income for myself, should I live to leave this prison, I will still have 10,000 ounces of gold. I would like to see it used to further the cause of the free democratic society we tried so hard to destroy."

"Again, anonymous?"

"Entirely. I do not want it said that I am trying to buy my way out of prison. Can you help me find a worthy project?"

"Indeed I can," Hedi responded, and in the next thirty minutes the World University Chair of Political Philosophy was born.

"And Carlos will never understand the connection," Hedi said to herself, smiling.

But perhaps the biggest news of the past three years had been Martha's. Martha was invited by the Elustreons to lead the most exciting expedition in the history of mankind.

After much consultation with Envoy Max Fact Banker Jr., Martha had presented a plan for colonizing the planet discovered by the Union of Five Central Planets, a world she proposed naming 'Planet Beautiful.'

She had requested time to participate in the New Earth's centennial celebration, and to complete her genealogy project, which she had designed to include a study of heredity. The Elustreons, searching for a leader for their colonization venture, considered this interest in genetics an important asset, and they readily agreed to her requested delay.

Martha proposed leaving with an advance group of about 100 persons in January of Year Z 100. Among the first group would be Sally Becker's son, Simon and Noe Singh, the tough and competent security officer. Additional space pioneers would be invited to join the venture each year until the number reached at least 3,000.

Martha considered it a big plus that Peter Johnson agreed to join her at the end of year two, if his energy and aircraft programs were in good shape. Ho Sun decided to stick by his commitments to serve as World Councilor of the New Earth for at least a ten-year term, and Hedi said very simply that she had experienced enough excitement for one lifetime.

May, Z 99

Sally came for a visit the last week in May, exchanged some family news with her mother, and promptly undertook a series of mysterious meetings with Sam. Hedi was aware of this activity and of telephone calls being made to far-away places, but she pretended not to notice. Finally they appeared together and stated they were ready to make a confession.

"Let's have it," Hedi replied. "I'm worn out with trying to guess what you two are up to."

"I'll be brief, Mother," Sally said. "Sam and I have spent three years searching for the secret of Mr. J's seven symbols, and we have failed miserably."

"We thought a study of ancient symbols and languages would give us a clue, but nothing fits," Sam added. "I wonder if they could be symbols of the future rather than the past."

"We have run out of ideas, and I desperately want to know. Do you have any suggestions?"

Hedi turned the question over in her mind, seeking a useful response. "In the past, I have found some of my best answers while walking the beach or when attending church. We don't have a beach handy, but we do have a church. This is Saturday. Why don't you visit the Chapel in the Lake tomorrow, and try prayer and meditation? Perhaps, if you take the seven symbols with you and hold the cloth tightly in your hand, you'll find your own Mr. J."

"I'll try it," Sally said soberly, "but if something like that happens it will frighten me to death."

"I will take you and wait to bring you home," Sam offered. When they left the next morning, Hedi wished them luck, but she had a feeling that luck was not involved. When they had not returned in three hours, she was certain of it.

It was a little after three o'clock when the front door opened and Sally entered with a rush. "Oh! Mother!" she cried, "I have been told the secret of the seven symbols, but I'm not allowed to tell anyone. I mean I now understand what some of the symbols mean, but don't know how to tell you." Then as Hedi wrinkled her nose in a familiar show of impatience, Sally added hastily, "There is a lot I can tell you, but..."

"Why don't you sit down and collect your thoughts while we wait for Sam to put the car away; then tell us what you can."

When Sam arrived, Sally took a deep breath and began her story. "I was attentive while the minister read various passages of scripture. During the period of silent prayer, I prayed as hard as I could to be shown the meaning of the seven symbols that I held in my hand. Before the minister left, he invited us to stay as long as we liked in silent meditation. I closed my eyes and concentrated on an image of the circle of cloth, trying to empty my mind of all other thoughts. I think I went to sleep, and when I woke up I was listening to a pleasant voice behind me.

"It was saying, 'So you are Sally, daughter of my old friend Hedi. I understand you wish to talk with someone about the seven symbols. Is this true?' I turned around and saw an elderly man with white hair, warm brown eyes, and a kindly smile sitting in the pew behind me. There was no one else in the church.

"I said who I am and said I wanted to know the meaning of the seven symbols and asked who he was. 'I am Mr. J,' he said. 'May I come and sit beside you? It makes it easier to talk.'

"I moved over to make room, and I told him, Mother, that you think he is Joseph, eleventh son of Jacob, who long ago saved the land of Egypt from a great famine. 'You are just like your mother,' the man replied. 'The first thing she asked was: Who are you? Could I be Joseph, when I existed before he was born?'

"That confused me, and he knew it. 'True,' he said, 'I lived the life of Joseph, eleventh son of Jacob, when he was on this earth, and that life is a part of me now. But when he died, I continued to live, and I ceased to be Joseph. I am all that I have experienced since my existence began.'

"I said, 'So Joseph is gone?'

"'His life is etched in time,' he said. 'It continues to speak and influence others, for better or for worse. That life is Joseph. Please think on what I have said and try to understand it. It is an understanding you must master before you can progress very far into the fourth region.'

"'I will try,' I responded. 'Now will you tell me why you put that piece of cloth in my mother's hand and explain to me the meaning of its symbols?'

"That made him smile. 'I too will try,' he said. 'One reason I helped your father put the piece of cloth in your mother's hand was to tell her I still existed and was ready to help her if I could. I wanted to assure her our meeting on that sandy beach many years ago was not a dream; it actually happened. I also hoped it would cause her to seek me out, as you have finally done.'

"That about left me speechless.

"'You see,' he said, 'it is not advisable that I intrude on your life unless you invite me.'

"I said, 'And that's the reason why ...'

"'I had also thought to warn her that another important challenge lay just ahead. As it turned out, she handled the confrontation with the Red Prince very nicely on her own. That is all to the good, and shows I am not always as smart as I think myself to be. Be that as it may, I am glad you sought me out, and I hope I can be of service to you.'

"Well, I didn't have any doubt about that! 'I know you can,' I said. 'Please go on.'

"'Very well,' he said. 'I know you brought the symbols with you, so let's use the bit of cloth in discussing the symbolism. Just lay it face up on the pew between us. Now, you must have noticed that the spaces between the symbols are uniform with the one exception of this one space, which is wide enough to accommodate an eighth symbol. We will now turn the circle of cloth until the wide space is at the top.

"'Now, in your mind, number the symbols clockwise around the circle beginning with number one and ending with number seven. If you have done this correctly you will find symbol number four at the bottom of the circle of cloth. Are you with me?

"'Woven into the cloth are tiny gold arrows. These represent matter and symbolize the potential for physical awareness, action, and purpose. If your eyes are sharp you can see them flowing clockwise from the vacant space into symbol number one, and on around the circle in diminishing numbers.'

"'These by the seventh symbol don't look like arrows,' I said.

"'No, by the time we reach symbol number seven there are no arrows. Instead there is a flow of tiny zigzag lightning bolts flowing counter-clockwise from the vacant space into symbol number seven, and around the circle in diminishing numbers, disappearing when we reach number one. These represent energy, and in the pure form, it bestows complete spiritual awareness and understanding along with unwavering purpose.

"'It is not easy to describe with words the meaning of the symbols when the proper words do not exist, but I will come as close as I can,' he said. And he spelled them out for me:

"1. EXISTENCE: The region represented by the first symbol contains all manner of inanimate physical matter, including sub-atomic particles, cosmic dust, atoms, molecules, stars, galaxies, and planets like our earth. All of the materials exist here for the creation of living physical things.

"2. AWARENESS: Living physical things exist in the region depicted by the second symbol. The significant fact is they are aware of

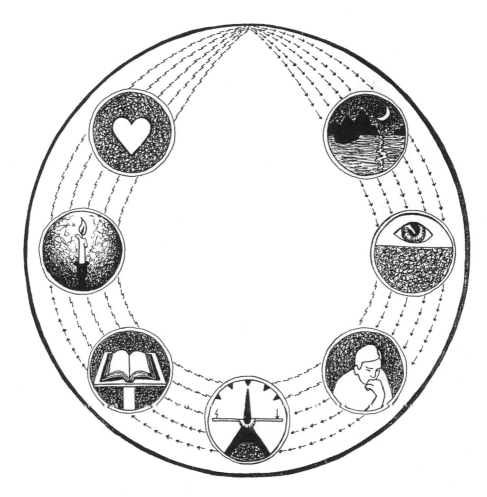

their existence, and to varying degrees, they are aware of what they are doing and how they do it.

"3. QUESTIONING: The third symbol portrays the region of reason. Here the search for the meaning of life begins, and the predominant question is Why. Here the mind ponders mysteries it can often sense but rarely understands.

"4. JUDGING: In the fourth region, the entity examines all it has learned and all it has done. It weighs its strengths and judges its weaknesses. It reviews its options, selects its next objective and decides how best to reach it. As pictured by the fourth symbol, it balances what can be gained from more of the rigorous learning experiences in Region Three against the broad opportunities that exist in Region Four, where the spirit is not limited by physical drag.

Here, if it is up to the task, it can access knowledge of all physical events and thoughts. It can observe the working of the Universal Laws, and understand the true function of time. From here, when it is ready and able, it can move on to Region Five. Region Four teaches balanced judgment and analysis of options. It requires decisions.

"5. KNOWLEDGE: The fifth symbol is a book. It portrays the region which provides the entity access to all knowledge, both physical and spiritual. Here one learns the nature of the Universal Laws that govern all creation. Here one examines the process of evolution of the spirit, and the purpose of physical matter.

"6. UNDERSTANDING: The symbol is light, and the complete answers to the "Why" questions are available. To know and understand is the ultimate wisdom, and this is the essence of Region Six

"7. LOVE: What can be left save 'the love that surpasses all understanding'? A place devoid of envy, hate, and anger, a place of pure spirit and incredible energy. It is a place where angels tread, and beyond that perhaps one may glimpse the Creator.

"He told me, 'Thus, I am picturing a vast University with its seven Colleges, where we can learn to face all the sorrows and experience all the joys of creation. Of course this is only a symbolic portrayal and a crude one at that. For example, there are a number of levels of consciousness in each of the seven regions, and many refinements within each of these levels. I would also caution that this evolution is neither a matter of chance, nor is it a fixed mechanical process ordained by a super being. Each of us can have a remarkable degree of influence over our own destiny, and the greater our understanding, the greater our control.

"'Now, Sally,' he said, 'I am prepared to offer you a tailor-made explanation of Regions One, Two, Three, and most of Four. I have not yet experienced Region Five and beyond, and will not attempt to take you further.'

"Naturally, I asked how.

"'I will use a technique I have learned here in Region Four, a technique which takes into account your total experience since you first existed, and also uses your inherent capacity to communicate by thought transfer. If I do it well, you will be able to understand concepts for which no words exist. Once you understand, you will feel an obligation to bring your awareness to others. I want to encourage you in this and at the same time urge you to use great caution in translating your understanding into words, or else you may do them more harm than good. It is best to first help them to develop an awareness that intelligence exists in nonphysical forms and that it does not die.'

"'Is it important that I be a missionary in this field?' I asked.

"'The New Earth has made great strides in reaching record heights of human development,' Mr. J said. 'You are now entering a period of great prosperity, and that means increasing amounts of free time. You have no enemies to fight except yourselves. Every success carries the seeds of failure, and in this case the seeds are idleness. You have developed most of your physical potential. Now is the time to devote your energies to developing the resources of the mind, otherwise mankind will fall back into the same old cycle of success and failure that you now have the opportunity of escaping. Do you understand?'

"I said I had the rough idea and asked him to proceed. Then for the next two hours he led me through the most fascinating experience I have ever had. I do not pretend to understand it all, but I understand enough to know it will change my life, just as it must have changed yours many years before I was born.

"That completes my story, Mother, except to say I think Mr. J would like to try his new techniques out on you."

"I'm so happy for you, Sally," Hedi said. More slowly, she said, "I will be pleased to see Mr. J again, but not now. I would rather wait a little while and meet him on his own turf."

Summer, Z 99

The summer months slipped by rapidly. Martha and Peter stopped to see Hedi frequently. They nearly always came together, and she suspected they used her as an excuse to talk excitedly with each other about the Planet Beautiful project. No matter; she was delighted to have them. "Martha was always the most competent member of the family," she told Sam Wun. "Of course she does stand high on the list of leading New Earth citizens, but no matter how noble the beat of her drum, she always seemed to be marching in the shadow of someone else. If it wasn't Hugh Scott's, it was mine. Now she is about to embark on the most exciting venture ever offered to an earth person. She is in charge, and there are no shadows that can hide the genius I know she has. I am so happy to live to see this happen."

On one of their visits, Martha and Peter arrived when Sally was there. The three of them sought Hedi out in her study. Peter was the spokesman. "We have been conniving behind your back and have agreed on a plan that we hope will have your blessing. You have told us that your will makes a provision of certain property to Aunt Martha with everything else divided equally between Sally and me. Aunt Martha will be leaving this planet in a few months, and I hope to follow in a couple of years. We have established a trust and pledged to it all of the assets we do not take with us. We have also pledged any interest we may have in your estate to this trust, and Sally has done the same."

"You are a wealthy man, Peter." Hedi said. "What will the trust do with all this money?"

"The trustees are instructed to establish a Museum of New Earth History, using this property if that should be your wish. They are also instructed to appoint Sam Wun as executive director for life or for as long as he will accept the position."

Hedi's eyes were moist. "You are wonderful people. Of course you have my blessing. How could I refuse? Have you told Sam?"

"No," Sally said, "but we will do it as soon as we can find him."

Half an hour later Sam burst into the Grand Lady's study, and in an unusual display of emotion, he threw his arms around her. "What a wonderful family this is," he said. "I wish all of you could be around for as long as I live."

Hedi smiled. "I think of you as part of the family, too," she said. "We must invite Ralph and tell him about it. He will be delighted about the Museum."

Indeed it was a wonderful family, she thought. How difficult life must be for all those who have no families.

As it turned out, there were two reasons to ask Ralph to come up for a visit. In early September, Isobel Perize gave her permission for the eventual publication of her life story. She authorized Hedi to give Sally the notes of their conversations. Ralph Woodbine could have access to these notes, and when he had used them to construct an outline of the story, Isobel promised interviews with him to fill in the details. She specified one thing; nothing was to be released while she remained in prison, except with her express permission.

Fall, Z 99

Hedi was delighted, and lost no time in inviting Sally, Peter and Ralph to visit her as soon as possible. They arrived the following Friday with plans to spend the weekend. Ralph arrived first and Sam met him at the local airstrip. Eighty percent of the gravity vehicles had already been returned to the Elustreons, and Ralph came in a snappy little four-place green and yellow single-engine prop plane. It was called a Whirlwind 104, and Ralph had bought it with the first royalties from his books.

He had done well, Hedi thought, while waiting on the patio for his arrival. He had published *A Scientist's Dream*, the story of his Grandfather Woodbine's lifetime of accomplishment; *General Scott's Wars with the Lowland Pirates*, and his *Historical Biography of Judge Mark Enslow*.

These first three major publications and several lesser ones had been well received by the academic community, and the interest by students and the general public had almost pushed them onto the best-seller list. Carlos Fernandez was also pleased, and had promised his personal support when the day came for Ralph to face the World

Council with his request for an unrestricted mandate to write the history of the New Earth.

She saw the car coming up the hill from the airport, and again felt the little thrill of anticipation over Ralph's arrival. Sam had asked permission to tell him about the Museum of History. "After all," Sam said, "we must make plans for a wing to house exhibits of the life and work of Ralph Woodbine. I might even write his historical biography myself."

Ralph was bubbling with excitement when he greeted her on the patio. "It's a great thing your sister and your children are doing," Ralph said.

"Yes it is," she replied, "but I have still more good news for you. For that, you will have to wait until Sally and Peter arrive, so run along and get ready for lunch. They'll be here this afternoon."

Hedi spent an hour giving Sally, Peter and Ralph an outline of the life of Isobel Perize. At the end Sally said, "I am pleased that she would trust me. I must be sharing some of my mother's reputation."

Ralph was delighted. "What can I do to repay you?" he asked. "You have done so much for me."

"There is one thing you can try to do," she replied. "We still know next to nothing about Major Rogers, one of our greatest heroes. It is a shame we cannot recognize him during the Centennial celebration."

Ralph held up his hand. "Say no more. Grandmother Woodbine reminds me of this situation every day. Fortunately, luck is with us. Ho Sun arranged for me to examine the Red Prince's files of information about his enemies. There was a lot of information about Major Thomas Rogers. He died a hero's death, and we will have a story, a good one, for the Centennial. After Maria Woodbine, you will be the first person to see it."

After absorbing this good news, Hedi excused herself to rest for awhile. After a short nap and a shower, she called Sam Wun and asked him to invite their guests to join her on the patio to see the sun set over the hills and the shadows fill the valley below.

When they arrived and were settled in their chairs, Hedi said, "There has never been a more fortunate woman than Hedi Carlton Johnson, and I owe a great deal of it to the four of you. I look forward to being a part of the New Earth's celebration of its one hundredth birthday, and I want to see Martha off on her great adventure. Then my life will truly be complete."

"Now, Mother," Sally said, "you can't go dashing off to the hereafter just when I've finally gotten to know you."

"I'm just so happy we did get to understand each other," Hedi replied.

"And who would look after me?" Sam said. "Without my Grand Lady to keep me pointed in the right direction, I would soon be a lost soul."

"Talk of death frightens me," Ralph said. "I can't bear to think about such a thing."

Hedi looked intently at the young man. "Are you frightened for me or for yourself?"

"For both of us, I guess," he replied. "There is so much I want to do, and I depend so much on you for support."

Hedi chose her words carefully. "I don't want any of you to think I am harboring a death wish," she said, "but I'm not running away from death, either.

"I'm glad you raised the question, Ralph, because I want to offer one more bit of advice. Old ladies like to give advice, and you have heard a lot of it from me, but if you can remember just one thing I ever said, remember this — as long as you are living and learning, hang on to life if you can. But never be afraid of dying. Death slips quickly into the past and is gone. It's a fleeting thing. But living, dear Ralph... living is forever."

THE END

J. Edwin Carter was born in Jackson, Georgia, in 1915. After earning a B.S. in Chemical Engineering from Georgia Tech, he joined the International Nickel Company as a metallurgist in 1937. During World War II, he served in the China-Burma-India theatre, advancing to the rank of Major. After the war, he rejoined INCO, eventually rising to president of its subsidiary, Huntington Alloys. He became president of INCO in Canada in 1974. From 1977 until his retirement in 1980, he served as chairman of the board and CEO.

Mr. Carter is married to the former Virginia Meredith Crickmer, has two children, and presently lives in New London, New Hampshire. *Living Is Forever* is his first novel. As he explains in his prologue, it is a book he never consciously intended to write.

About the cover...
and the seven symbols

The original of the artwork used on the cover of this edition of *Living Is Forever* is a 10-inch circle of embroidered fabric created (like the sketch in the final chapter it was designed from) by Anna Szok, a talented New Hampshire artist. To me, Anna's artistic perception has somehow enhanced the mystery and meaning of these images.

I see in these symbolic messages the broad span of possible human experiences, ranging from cold, unfeeling existence to pure spiritual love. And I believe that to grasp the full significance of this imagery would be to take a giant step in knowing the Creator's purpose in providing us with a temporary home on this unusual little planet.

Living Is Forever introduces the Seven Symbols, but provides little more than a hint of their meaning. Perhaps introducing a mystery and leaving it unsolved was unfair, but it could not be helped: The author's understanding is far from complete. I will continue to seek this understanding. I invite you, the reader, to join me in the search.

—J. Edwin Carter

HAMPTONROADS
PUBLISHING COMPANY, INC.

Books for the body • • •

Health

Beauty

Nutrition

Books for the mind • • •

Fiction

History

Psychology

Parapsychology

Current Events

Books for the spirit • • •

Spiritual

Inspirational

"New Age"

HAMPTON ROADS
PUBLISHING COMPANY, INC.

Would you like to be notified as we publish new books in your area of interest? Would you like a copy of our latest catalog? Fill in this page (or copy it, if you would prefer to leave this book uncut), and send to:

Hampton Roads Publishing Co., Inc
891 Norfolk Square
Norfolk, VA 23502

[__] Please send latest catalog

[__] Please add me to the following mailing list(s):

    [__] Books for the body

    [__] Books for the mind

    [__] Books for the spirit

NAME_____

ADDRESS_____

CITY_____ STATE___ ZIP_____